£33.25

Sociological Theories in Progress

To Theory and Bernice

Sociological Theories in Progress

New Formulations

Joseph Berger
Morris Zelditch, Jr.
Bo Anderson
editors

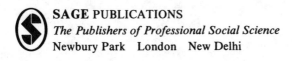

SAGE PUBLICATIONS
The Publishers of Professional Social Science
Newbury Park London New Delhi

For information address:

SAGE Publications, Inc.
2111 West Hillcrest Drive
Newbury Park, California 91320

SAGE Publications Ltd.
28 Banner Street
London EC1Y 8QE
England

SAGE Publications India Pvt. Ltd.
M-32 Market
Greater Kailash I
New Delhi 110 048 India

Printed in the United States of America

Library of Congress Cataloging-in-Publication Data

Berger, Joseph, 1924-   ed.
  Sociological theories in progress.

  Includes bibliographies and index.
  1. Sociology. I. Zelditch, Morris, Jr., joint ed.
II. Anderson, Bo, joint ed. III. Title.
HM51.B43   301'.01   66-4287
ISBN 0-8039-3525-0

FIRST PRINTING, 1989

Contents

Preface

More than two decades ago, we published the first in a promised series of *Sociological Theories in Progress* designed for use in training advanced undergraduates and beginning graduate students in theory. The theories in Volume 1 were diverse, having in common only the characteristics that define a theory in the textbook sense of the word: They were all systems of interrelated concepts and propositions that were abstract, general, and had empirical import. Beyond that, like the theories in the present volume, they were all theories "in progress." They were mostly beginnings, initial formulations, early stages in the ongoing process of test, refinement, articulation, extension, and therefore reformulation of a theory.

They were published with two ideas in mind. The first was simply that training in theory is facilitated by having models to follow. Volume 1 was a straightforward counterpart of then popular volumes such as Lazarsfeld and Rosenberg's *Language of Social Research* (1955), providing models of how to do empirical research, except that the models showed how to construct abstract, general, logically systematic, empirically oriented theory. The second was that training in theory is facilitated as much by contemporary models, especially models of work still in progress, as by classics. An interest in theory is not just an antiquarian interest in the exegesis of masters, and especially not just commentary on orthodoxies that have acquired an aura so sacred that the issue becomes what they really meant rather than what is still alive. Read alone, they encourage both the wrong attitude and the wrong starting point for further growth of sociological theory. The more sacred the text, the more passive the student, however brilliant either master or student. Even without canonizing them, the masters are not where cumulative growth of knowledge begins. The contemporary state of the art is the foundation upon which cumulative growth of theory is built. Theory did not stop with the masters, it is an ongoing concern of living sociologists.

Volume 2, now more than a decade old, was intended to serve the same purposes. In addition to providing more models, it also served to demonstrate just how much theoretical activity there was in sociology at a time when many people were wondering where all the Durkheims, Marxes, and Webers had gone. Actually, there was then as now a good deal of metatheoretical debate. What many people thought was missing was more "middle range" theory, theory oriented to empirical knowledge of specific domains as opposed to overarching frameworks for all sociology. But there was, in fact, then as now, a good deal of middle-range theory as well as metatheory going on, and we thought it useful to bring some of it together. It was not our purpose, then or now, to reject metatheoretical debate. No theory can be constructed that does not presuppose some metatheory, and in fact the introductions to both Volume 2 and the present volume are devoted to metatheoretical issues. But no research can be conducted if metatheory is all there is. On the other hand, middle-range theory is often unfinished business. We thought it useful to bring together models of theory then in the process of construction precisely to underline the fact that theory is an ongoing process, not a finished project.

Volume 3, this volume, has the same purposes as the previous two volumes. It has been a long time in coming. It is precisely for that reason that we think it will be useful. Sociological theory, theory in the sense of systematically interrelated concepts and propositions that are abstract, general, and have empirical import, grew rapidly between 1972 and 1989. There are more, and newer, models to use in learning the skills it requires to construct sociological theory. These models not only help students to understand what is required in constructing theory, they also keep alive the fact that theory is an ongoing process, cumulatively built on the current state of the art, which is continually being tested, refined, articulated, extended, and therefore reformulated. Some of the theories in this volume extend or reformulate theories published in Volumes 1 or 2; some extend or reformulate other theories appearing in other places; some are wholly new theories. It is to this sense of theory as an ongoing process that the present volume, like the series itself, is dedicated.

Joseph Berger
Morris Zelditch, Jr.
Bo Anderson

References

Berger, J., M. Zelditch, Jr., and B. Anderson, eds. 1966. *Sociological Theories in Progress*, Vol. 1. Boston: Houghton Mifflin.
— — -, eds. 1972. *Sociological Theories in Progress*, Vol. 2. Boston: Houghton Mifflin.
Lazarsfeld, P. and M. Rosenberg. 1955. *Language of Social Research*. Glencoe, IL: Free Press.

PART I

INTRODUCTION

Theoretical Structures and the Micro/Macro Problem

JOSEPH BERGER

DANA P. EYRE

MORRIS ZELDITCH, Jr.

The two main parts into which the present volume is divided bear a misleading resemblance to the common distinction between micro- and macrosociology — a resemblance so misleading that it calls for some comment. The resemblance is misleading because the volume is a collection of theories. Theories are abstract and general. Because they are abstract and general, they have multiple interpretations. And many, though not all, multiply interpretable theories are capable of applications to both micro- and macrosociology. True, not all the theories in the present volume are pure abstract structures. Many, in fact, are given particular, concrete interpretations. Thus Stryker's work on identity (Chapter 2) is applied to individuals and their relations, Hannan's on organizational ecology (Chapter 14) is applied to organizations and their environments. By contrast, Willer, Markovsky, and Patton's chapter on networks of power (Chapter 12) is a purely abstract, general theory. It applies to "actors" and their relations. It is in some sense an "interactor" theory, but the actors might be individuals, formalized positions in an organization, organizations as a whole, or even nation-states. Insofar as a theory (interactor or not) is abstract and general, it is neither micro- nor macrosociology. It is only the interpretations of a theory that are micro or macro. The division of the present volume into parts is not a division into micro and macro, because there are abstract theories in both parts. And even where the theories have particular micro or macro interpretations, they have in most cases an underlying theoretical structure admitting interpretations at other "levels."

Multiple interpretability is a property of all abstract theories. It is in a sense what *abstract* and *general* mean. However, we do not claim that all theories are therefore capable of application to both micro- and macro-

11

phenomena. Hannan's population ecology of organizations is multiply interpretable theory with, for example, application also to ethnic conflict (Hannan 1979). But, because of its underlying structure, it is unlikely to have any microapplication. It has no actors. It is a mistake, however, to overgeneralize this kind of example. Though some abstract theories are not capable of application to both micro- and macrophenomena, there is at least one very large class of theories, interactor theories, that is.

Not that there are no differences between micro- and macroapplications. However one defines micro/macro — whether as scale, level, or institutionalization, or kind of actor — the differences between micro- and macroapplication are profound. But they are not differences between qualitatively different kinds of theory. The differences are analytic; they are caused by variables in or interpretations of a theory. Neither gives rise to concretely different kinds of theory, one of which is "micro," the other "macro." Scale, level, and institutionalization are all variables; individuals, formalized positions, organizations, and nation-states are all different interpretations of the units of a theory. The differences to which they give rise are important, but they are differences within, not between, theories.

The micro/macro problem has recently attracted a good deal of attention (see Alexander et al. 1987; Coleman 1986; Collins 1981; Fine and Kleinman 1983; Knorr-Cetina and Cicourel 1981; Ritzer 1985). Understood as "levels," the effort to solve the problem has led to a proliferation of distinctions, adding "meso" (Maines 1979) and "mega" (Jones et al. 1988) to micro and macro. The proliferation of levels reveals a good deal about what is wrong in this debate. It continually waffles between treating the issue as analytic (for example, Alexander et al. 1987), which promises some sort of solution, and treating "levels" as if they were ontological realities (Maines 1979; Jones et al. 1988), which promises only a dead end. The issues become clearer, we believe, if one examines more closely the structure of multiply interpreted interactor theories, which is one of the tasks we undertake in the present introduction.

Interactor theories describe interaction in systems of actors that occur within situations that are at least partly, though usually not wholly, governed by pregiven social frameworks. Though they are "methodologically situationalist" (Knorr-Cetina and Cicourel 1981), they are often taken to be "methodologically individualist" by holists. For this reason, holists object even to macroapplications of such theories as being "micro" because, though they might not be interpersonal, they are still interactor; though the actors might not be individuals, they still have agency; and though the action is situated in structures, the actors still act. From this viewpoint, the application of, say, Emerson's (1962, 1972a, 1972b) power-dependence theory to interorganizational relations is "reduction." But, except as ritual, it is difficult to misuse the concept of reduction in this way. (On reduction, for example, see Nagel 1952; Webster 1973.) It is an attitude that only gets in the way of the more practical purpose of understanding scale, level, and structure as analytic aspects of theories.

This argument holds no matter what meaning one gives to "micro/macro" in the technical, as distinct from metatheoretical, sense, whether small/large, actor/system, action/structure, or individual actor/group actor. But one of the difficulties of the problem is the tendency to treat all these meanings as if they were correlated, when in fact they can be independent. In the present chapter we use the terms in their simplest meaning, scale. This makes it particularly easy to see the analytic, as opposed to concrete, nature of the micro/macro distinction. But we could equally well have taken level, institutionalization, or nature of the actor as a starting point for the same argument.

The present chapter is divided into three parts that correspond to three basic theses of this argument. The first part develops further the claim that the micro/macro distinction is purely analytic, a variable in or interpretation of a theory rather than a difference between theories. The second part develops further the claim that theories, because they are abstract and general, are in themselves neither micro nor macro, it is only their applications that may be micro or macro. To do this, it briefly studies two applications, one micro and the other macro, that have a common underlying theoretical structure. The third part further develops the claim that there is a very large class of theories, interactor theories, capable of application to both micro- and macrosociological phenomena. It analyzes the elements, processes, and features of this class of theories, a class to which many, though not all, of the chapters in the present volume belong.

Micro, Meso, Macro, Mega

The simplest meaning of *micro* versus *macro* is *small* versus *large*. It is not clear how anyone could ever have entertained the idea that scale gives rise to qualitatively different kinds of theory. Scale has no natural break at which micro becomes readily distinguished from macro, and differences in scale are as important at the small as at any other part of the scale. Socially, the difference between 2 and 3 actors is possibly the most important break in the continuity of the natural numbers and certainly more significant than the break between, say, 10 and 11, or 50 and 51, or 100 and 101 actors, where one might more naturally look for a distinction between micro and macro. The differences are again large at the larger end of the scale, where the difference between, say, a town of 5,000 people and a city of 500,000 people is very large, even though both are presumably macro. Scale may be lumpy, but it is still a continuum.

At first sight, levels seem to imply something both more discontinuous and more concretely "real." But what are the levels in the analysis of conjugal power structure? If Dick and Jane are married, both employed (by different employers), and live in a neighborhood of a city in the eastern part of the United States, then individuals, family, neighborhood, city, region, and nation may all play a role in the analysis of the division of powers between Dick and Jane. But firm and industry probably are not among the relevant levels. Instead, they are likely to appear in the analysis as attributes of the two actors. On the other hand, what are the levels in the analysis of social mobility? Now firm and industry are important levels of analysis but neighborhood is probably not. The levels, in other words, are abstractions that shift with the purpose of the observer. In any case, there is no natural break in them that clearly distinguishes micro from macro. It is this analytic, as opposed to concrete, nature of levels that has given rise to their proliferation into micro, macro, then meso (Maines 1979), and now mega (Jones et al. 1988). In some sense they are all real, but it is the phenomenal world that is concrete, not the "levels" abstracted by the observer. In particular, neither the individuals nor any of the higher levels are *more* real than any other of the observer's abstractions. Collins's (1981) argument that microrelations are the foundations of macrosociology because encounters are what the observer actually observes and all the rest is constructed by the observer is not a tenable position, because the micro world is no less observer-constructed than the macro world.

The problem of structure/action is subtler, especially because it is more difficult to separate technical from metatheoretical issues. Some theoretical strategies go so far as to insist that all behavior simply emanates from pregiven structure (as Meyer does in Meyer et al. 1987). Others insist that no behavior at all is pregiven: Because structure is open-textured, incomplete, cannot guarantee its own application, all behavior is action, has agency (Garfinkel 1964). Neither position is tenable: If one adopts the view that there is no pregiven structure, one cannot even analyze the "background expectancies" that figure so largely in Garfinkel's analysis. If one adopts the view that there is only pregiven structure, it becomes difficult if not impossible to understand change. But if one adopts the position that structure too is a variable, that its institutionalization varies from situation to situation, but most situations combine structure with action, it becomes difficult to identify structure with macrosociology and action with microsociology.

Thus the arguments that micro and macro are analytic distinctions, not concrete realities, does not depend on the meaning one gives to the terms. However, part of the micro/macro problem arises from treating all three as a single dichotomy. It is often assumed that scale, level, and structure are somehow intercorrelated, giving *micro* the meaning of small, unstructured systems of action while *macro* means large, structured systems without action. But it is just as obvious that they can be uncorrelated as it is that they can be analytic.

The number of levels sometimes increases as the size of a system increases, but even the smallest system has at least two levels, actor and system. It is possible to equate micro with actor and macro with system, if consistently applied. One then has a view that every theory has both a micro and a macro aspect, and solves the micro/macro problem by relating actor to system. But this has nothing to do with scale. It is certainly not what distinguishes interpersonal from international conflict or conjugal power from world-system dependency relations.

Nor is scale necessarily correlated with structure. Many sociologists focus increasingly on structure as size of system increases, but even the smallest system has structure and even the largest has action. The latter point is sometimes obscured by equating "structure" not with pregiven social framework, but with supraindividual "forces." The outcomes of action are often unintended; even when recognized they are often beyond the control of any individual; and this is especially noticed by sociologists in large-scale systems. But this is not a matter of increasing amounts of structure. "Macro" outcomes are still outcomes of actions. "Structure" is given to action by pregiven social frameworks. Just as with levels, one could construct a consistent theory of micro- and macrorelations around the distinction between structure and action, but again the problem would be to relate structure to action within a theory. It would not give rise to different theories.

Correlating scale with structure has been less misleading than correlating it with levels, because discussions of levels seldom rid themselves of the presupposition that levels are not simply analytic, they are ontologically real. If levels are reified, one is left with only three options: Treat theory at each level as independent, reduce one theory to the other, or interrelate them. All of these have been tried, repeatedly: independence by Durkheim ([1897] 1951) and Parsons (Parsons and Shils 1951), among others; reduction to microsociology by Homans (1964), Collins (1981), Denzin (1987), Fine and Kleinman (1983), and Knorr-Cetina (1981) and to macrosociology by Althusser (1971) and Meyer et al. (1987); as well as numerous syntheses, for example by Alexander et al. (1987), Coleman (1986), Giddens (1979), and Ritzer (1985). But none has laid the problem to rest. They have not laid the problem to rest because, like the mind/body problem, the categories in terms of which we have come to think about the problem force us into asking fruitless questions about it. If levels are independent, they give rise to two separate kinds of theory, one micro and the other macro. But neither scale nor levels give rise to qualitatively different kinds of theory. If they are not independent, possibly one is reducible to the other. But no one has been able to accomplish the reduction (Webster 1973). If the levels are neither independent nor reducible, the only solution is synthesis. But even synthesis often still conceives of levels as concrete "parts" to be related.[1]

Our conclusion up to this point is that scale, level, and structure are variables in, not differences between, theories. Do the same arguments hold for the difference between individual and corporate actors? Individual and corporate actors are not variables in a theory; they are interpretations of a theory.

Power in Families and Organizations

But *this* does not matter to the argument at all. The more general claim
is that theories are not micro/macro, they are abstract and general. Because they are abstract and general, they are capable of multiple interpretation. Some, though not all, abstract theories are capable not only of
multiple situational interpretation, but also to collective as well as individual actor interpretations.

Of the many examples of this kind of multiple interpretation, the one
we will look at here is the application of the exchange theory of power to
conjugal power structures and interorganizational relations. The "resource
theory" of conjugal power is a theory of the power-dependence relations
between two actors, a husband and a wife. The "resource-dependency
theory" of interorganizational relations is a theory of the power-dependence relations among a sizable community of organizations. The two
differ from each other in a number of concrete details, some of which
derive from differences in scale. Nevertheless, they have a common
underlying theoretical structure. This theoretical structure has been abstractly formulated in various ways (Thibaut and Kelley 1959; Emerson
1962, 1972a, 1972b; Blau 1964), but, especially in the organizations
literature, it has been Emerson's theory of power-dependence relations
that has been most often applied.

EMERSON'S THEORY OF
POWER-DEPENDENCE RELATIONS
AND RELATED THEORETICAL RESEARCH

Emerson's (1962) theory is formulated in terms of two actors, A and B,
whose social relations entail ties of mutual dependence. It is capable of
application, as Emerson notes, to relations between persons and persons,
persons and groups, or groups and groups, providing the actors satisfy
conditions of internal consistency and are capable of action as single
entities, of "choice" among alternatives. "Power" is a property of a
relation between A and B (i.e., not of either A or B as individual actors)
defined as the amount of resistance on the part of one actor, say B, that
can be overcome by another, say A. Thus it is potential rather than actual
power that the theory describes. Power is founded on dependence, where
"dependence" is a matter of the control by one actor of resources on which
another depends for achieving his or her goals. (A "resource" is anything
instrumental to attainment of a goal.) Dependence varies with two factors,
motivational investment in goals and the availability of alternatives. It is
directly proportional to motivational investment, but inversely proportional to availability of alternative resources outside the AB relation.
Power is a function of the net balance between B's dependence on A and
A's on B. If dependence is asymmetric, power is "unbalanced." Emerson

assumes that unbalanced relations are unstable and tend toward balance. They encourage the use of power by the more powerful actor, which in turn sets in motion processes by the less powerful to restore balance. There are four kinds of "balancing" operations: B may (1) reduce motivational investment in goals mediated by A (withdraw); (2) gain alternative sources of resources other than A (extend networks); (3) increase A's motivational investment in goals mediated by B (status emergence); or (4) deny to A alternative sources of resources mediated by B (coalition formation). Emerson's theory does not specify conditions under which one rather than another occurs; he says this will depend on conditions particular to concrete cases.

Thus the logical structure of the theory consists of two definitions, power and balance, and three assumptions — that power is a function of dependence; that dependence is an increasing function of the value of resources mediated by the other and a decreasing function of the availability of alternatives; and that unbalanced power is unstable, tending toward balance.

In a major restatement of the theory, reformulated in purely behavioral terms, Emerson (1972a) articulates its structure more explicitly, leading to both refinement and extensions. The two most notable refinements introduce uncertainty into the analysis of value and distinguish negative from positive relations between relations. (Two exchange relations are negatively related if exchange in one decreases the value of exchange in the other. They are positively related if exchange in one increases the value of exchange in the other.) The latter refinement prepares the way for the most notable extension of the theory, to more complex networks of relations (Emerson 1972b; further developed by Cook 1977). Both the earlier and later formulations of the theory have given rise to a substantial body of theoretical research, confirming the balance assumption (Emerson 1964) and especially the implication that structural position determines the "use" of power, which in behavioral terms means asymmetries in the outcomes of exchange (Burgess and Nielson 1974; Michaels and Wiggins 1976; Stolte and Emerson 1976). While the effects of position have been repeatedly confirmed, a gap between potential and actual power has been found (Cook and Emerson 1978, 1984), especially when exchange is only implicitly bargained (Molm 1981b, 1985). This has led to further theoretical elaboration of the process of "use" of power, left implicit in Emerson, by Molm (1981a, 1981b) and to theory and research on normative constraints on the use of power (Cook and Emerson 1978, 1984). Meanwhile, the extension of the theory to complex networks was empirically tested by Cook et al. (1983), who introduced the idea of a network's dependence on a position ("vulnerability") as a determinant of power, and the theory was further extended to control over negative as well as positive outcomes by Molm (1987).

THE RESOURCE THEORY OF CONJUGAL POWER
AND RELATED APPLIED RESEARCH

Wolfe's (1959) theory of power and authority in the family is, like Emerson's, a theory of actors A and B (who Wolfe also notes may be persons, organizations, or groups of any kind) who are mutually interdependent and engaged in exchanges of goods and services. Wolfe's theory precedes Emerson's by several years, both in fact growing from the even earlier "field" theory of Lewin (1951, pp. 335-36), which had already been used to formulate the concept of "power" by Festinger (1953). Although Wolfe's definition of power is more explicitly field-theoretic, it is essentially, like Emerson's, a resistance concept and, like Emerson's, it defines potential rather than actual power. Finally, like Emerson's, the central factor in power is dependence on resources, defined as any characteristic or any possession of one actor instrumental to the goals of and transferable to another. Like Emerson's concept of a resource, Wolfe's is highly general. Anything at all might be a resource — status as well as guns, love as well as money, skills as well as possessions.

Unlike Emerson's theory, Wolfe's does not take into account the alternatives available to the actors, and there is no balance assumption, hence no balancing operations. The theory is applied to families by assuming that the actors are a husband and a wife and that resources include both what each does for the collective goals of the family and what each does for the needs of the other. Thus resources include occupation, income, education, child-rearing skills, domestic skills, and skills in financial management. Following field-theoretic logic, it is assumed that who makes what decisions varies from "region" to "region" of the family's space, but it is assumed that financial decisions are bound to be important to the family, and hence the more powerful actor is more likely to make final decisions about them. As in Emerson, it is the net balance of power that determines who has the most power, that is, the husband's resources minus the wife's resources. There will be some pregiven structure of authority, derived from cultural tradition, but it will change if it is not congruent with power/resources.

This "resource" theory, though in many ways similar to Emerson's, is brought even closer to "exchange" theory by Heer (1963). Heer points out certain anomalies that resource theory cannot explain; for example, that the wife's power decreases as the number of children increases. Heer clarifies these anomalies by taking alternatives outside the family into account. What varies as wife's power varies are her alternatives, both in terms of employment prospects and prospects for remarriage after divorce.

However, the Wolfe-Heer application of power-dependence ideas to conjugal power still differs from the more abstract theory of power-dependence in two significant ways. On the one hand, the application is less than the theory; it makes no use of the balance idea. On the other, it is more than the theory; it integrates into it a theory of (pregiven) authority.

It is in fact the effect of pregiven authority that has been the most controversial issue in subsequent research grounded in the "resource" theory of conjugal power. Cross-national research at first seemed to suggest severe cultural constraints on the effects of resources on power (Rodman 1967, 1972). However, these constraints seem themselves to depend on the extent to which women contribute to the process of production (Bossen 1975; Rogers 1975). (For reviews of this theory and related applied research, at various stages of its development, see particularly Lee 1977, pp. 231-42; McDonald 1980; Szinovacz 1987.)

THE RESOURCE-DEPENDENCY THEORY OF INTERORGANIZATIONAL RELATIONS AND RELATED APPLIED RESEARCH

Emerson's theory of power-dependence relations (1962) was first applied to organizations by Thompson (1967). Even though Emerson had already abstracted the theory from interpersonal relations, it was not an obvious idea to apply a theory that at the time concerned the dyad AB to organizational interrelations. But Thompson's "open-systems" framework led him to think of the organization as an actor in relations of mutual dependence with other organizations, which in turn led him to recognize and seize on the usefulness of Emerson's theory for formulating more explicit hypotheses about the nature and consequences of this dependence. But Thompson also thought of organizations as managing their environments, as acting on them as well as being determined by them. This made Emerson's theory, because of its balance hypothesis, a particularly suitable one for formulating organization-environment exchanges as Thompson understood them.

Although the language of the application changes, referring only to organizations and their relations, Thompson's use of Emerson corresponds closely, proposition by proposition, with Emerson's 1962 work. Dependence is directly proportional to the "organization's need for resources or performances" but inversely proportional to the ability of other elements to provide them (Thompson 1967, p. 30). Power is the obverse of dependence. And Thompson makes especially prominent use of Emerson's balancing operations, which become the ways an organization manages its environment.

On the other hand, two balancing operations, withdrawal and status dynamics, disappear from the analysis, while several ideas are added. Thompson has buffering mechanisms that play no role in Emerson, and uncertainty becomes the driving force of the theory earlier in Thompson (1967) than in Emerson (1972a). But most important, Thompson follows Cyret and March (1963) in viewing organizations as coalitions rather than unitary actors.

In order to apply Emerson's theory, an organization must satisfy the theory's criteria of actorness, but within the literature on organizations there is some doubt that organizations are unitary actors. That they are coalitions, instead, implies inconsistency in preferences even if they are capable at any given instant of action as a single actor. This problem, potentially fatal for use of Emerson's theory, is solved by doubly applying it: It explains not only interorganizational relations but also the power structure of coalitions within the organization, which depends on control over resources that are critical, but scarce, in managing uncertainty.

Subsequent research on the resource-dependency theory of organizations has developed along basically three lines. One branch of it has been concerned with mechanisms through which organizations manage their environments, such as mergers, acquisitions, or boards of directors (see Pfeffer 1972a, 1972b; Pfeffer and Nowak 1976; Usdiken 1983). The second has been concerned with how resources are allocated among organizations that form some kind of system of interorganizational relations (see Pfeffer and Leong 1977; Provan 1982; Provan et al. 1980). The third has been concerned with the allocation of resources to subunits within an organization (see Hills and Mahoney 1978; Pfeffer and Moore 1980; Pfeffer et al. 1976; Salancik and Pfeffer 1974). Reformulation of Thompson's theory by Pfeffer and Salancik (1978) substantially refines the concept of interdependence and explains the gap that especially the second branch of this research has found between potential and actual power by formulating conditions under which potential power is enacted. (For reviews of this research, see Aldrich 1979; Aldrich and Pfeffer 1976; Pfeffer 1981.)

CONCLUSION

If we compare the resource theory of conjugal power to the resource-dependency theory of organizations, there are certainly substantial differences. The actors are persons in the first case, and groups in the second. There are only two actors in the first, many in the second case. And the two applications differ not only in how they operationalize concepts but also in how they model the concrete phenomena with which they are concerned: The resource-dependency theory of organizations uses balancing operations, the resource theory of conjugal power does not. And each combines power-dependence with other theories, though in the case of the resource theory of conjugal power it is a theory of family authority while in the case of the resource-dependency theory of organizations it is theories of coalitions and of uncertain environments. But none of these differences can disguise the fact that the two applications have an underlying theoretical structure in common, that of the exchange theory of power.

Thus, like the difference made by size, level, and structure, the difference between person and group is analytic: It is a difference in interpretations of one theory, not two qualitatively different kinds of theory. This conclusion is not confined to the particular theory we have used to illustrate the argument; it can be generalized to all interactor theories.

Exchange theory is only one kind of interactor theory. It is reasonable to ask what, then, limits the scope of the argument? In the next section we characterize in a more general way the kinds of theories to which the argument applies.

The Structure of Interactor Theories

Interactor theories are theories that describe the mechanisms or processes by which actors act in relation to other actors in situations of action. Here we will describe the underlying logic of such theories: Not all the theories in the present volume have all the elements, processes, and features we describe. A number, for example, do not fully describe how outcomes of interaction are institutionalized or the events that activate the processes they describe, though the logic of interactor theories requires it. Nevertheless, what we will describe is the structure of a full-fledged interactor theory, one that fully exploits the underlying logic of such theories.

We will describe them in terms of their elements, processes, and features. The elements of an interactor theory are systems of actors in situations characterized by their relations and the nature of the situation. The processes, which are generated by and addressed to some problematic event or condition, are both determined by and determine "states" of these systems of relations. The features that distinguish interactor theories have to do with the balance they strike between actor and situation, agency and external causation, structure and action.

ELEMENTS

While the "actor" seems the logical starting point for interactor theories, it is not the actor but the "actor-in-situation" that is their basic unit of analysis. A "situation" here is a specific set of conditions that can generate, define, and determine the course of a process.

Situations

Because interactor theories are process theories, they require some state or event activating a process, which is part of the situation that governs the process. Processes can be activated by almost any kind of problematic event or condition. In Emerson's power-dependence theory, it is the balance of power that activates both the use of power and balance-restoring operations. In Berger, Fisek, and Norman's "The Evolution of Status Expectations" (Chapter 5) it is a goal or a task to perform; in Ridgeway's "Understanding Legitimation in Informal Status Orders" (Chapter 6) it is differentiation by external status orders; in Sørensen's "Processes of Allocation to Open and Closed Positions in Social Structure" (Chapter 10), it is vacancies; in Jasso's "The Theory of the Distributive-Justice Force in Human Affairs" (Chapter 13) it is an external frame of reference that activates reward expectations, the difference between actual and expected rewards that activates responses to inequity.

Given such an event or condition, a situation is "defined" and its course determined by three types of elements: (1) the immediate conditions of action, (2) the larger social framework of the process, and (3) products of past interaction of the actors in the situation.

Conditions of action. Situations first of all consist of the immediate conditions of action. These include the nature of the goal, or of the disturbance, that activates the process; the ecology of the actors; and/or the amount of information available to them for defining the situation. In Foschi's "Status Characteristics, Standards, and Attributions" (Chapter 3), Foddy and Smithson's "Fuzzy Sets and Double Standards" (Chapter 4), and Cohen and Silver's "Group Structure and Information Exchange" (Chapter 7), the goal is a decision. An important feature of the situation in each of these theories is whether the decision is individual or collective. If the decisions are individual, it will also matter how centralized or decentralized they are, the crucial variable differentiating open and closed labor markets in Sørensen's vacancy competition model (Chapter 10). The actors may be few or many, their relations direct or indirect, resources may be more or less transferable, all variables that play central roles in Fararo and Skvoretz's "A Biased Net Theory of Social Structures and the Problem of Integration" (Chapter 9) and Willer, Markovsky, and Patton's "Power Structures" (Chapter 12). A collection of conditions of this kind constitute the immediate conditions of action, though which conditions matter varies from theory to theory.

The social framework of the process. In any situation in an interactor theory there is some larger social framework, some pregiven structure deriving from a larger social system. Again, there is wide variation from theory to theory in the particular mix of elements constituting this framework. It can include anything from purely cultural elements (myths, symbols, rituals, values, beliefs, rules) to purely structural elements (networks of ties, power-dependence relations) or any mix of cultural and structural elements. In Foschi's, Foddy and Smithson's, and Cohen and Silver's chapters, the status characteristics that define the situation are categories in the shared culture of the actors. In Fararo and Skvoretz's and Willer et al.'s chapters, it is networks of ties, and in Sørensen's it is hierarchies of positions. In Stryker's chapter and in Samuel and Zelditch's "Expectations, Shared Awareness, and Power" (Chapter 11), it is a mix of the two — networks and role expectations in Stryker's theory, and power-dependence relations and prior assumptions about use of power and probabilities of compliance in Samuel and Zelditch's.

Products of past interaction. In addition to a larger social framework, there is typically also some more particular, local knowledge that is the product of the past interaction of the particular actors in the situation. In Berger et al.'s chapter, expectation states formed in previous interaction are transferred to and form part of the initial situation in a subsequent task interaction. In Fararo and Skvoretz's chapter, weak ties derive from the larger social framework but some kinds of strong ties, such as friendship, derive from the past interaction of particular actors. In Samuel and Zelditch's chapter, expectations about use of and compliance with power derive in part from cultural tradition (and thus a larger social framework), but also in part from past interaction of the particular actors in a power-dependence relation. In Jasso's chapter, expectations derive from the larger social framework, but justice processes derive from differences between expectations and the actual distribution of rewards, which is local.

Actors

The actors in such situations are conceived quite generally as any unit having the capacity to control some of the variation in its own actions. The fundamental property of an actor is agency. Actors make choices, decisions, evaluations; they "orient" themselves to situations and process information about them; they anticipate, expect, have policies. The particular capacities of the actor again vary from theory to theory. It is only the general notion of agency that they have in common. In Stryker's "identity theory" (Chapter 2), actors make "commitments" (that, in turn, derive from the structure of opportunities and contingencies created by age, gender, class, and other social arrangements). In Foschi's and Foddy and Smithson's chapters, they infer abilities and make decisions. In Willer et al.'s, they bid for goods. In Sørensen's chapter, actors do not simply move, they choose to move, into and out of positions.

Agency is a property that groups may have as well as individuals. All that is required is that the group be corporate, in the legal sense of the term. Typically, this means that the group has some means by which collective decisions are made and actions as a collective are taken, as armies invade nations; nations tax citizens; universities choose faculty and students; hospitals admit and release patients; unions make bargains; firms select product lines, set prices, and employ labor; and states make laws, enter into treaties, and raise armies. Network theories have been especially explicit about this: Thus Fararo and Skvoretz, in Chapter 9, explicitly point out that their "biased net theory" applies to mergers among organizations and trade relations among nations as well as marriages between persons. Willer et al.'s "networks of power" explicitly apply to groups as well as to persons.

Agency does not necessarily imply intention or awareness. Again, there is wide variation from theory to theory in how aware actors are of the processes that engage them, particularly information-processing processes, or in how intended the outcomes of interactive processes are. Many, like Sørensen's "processes of allocation" (Chapter 10), are hidden-hand theories in which aggregate outcomes are intended by no one, in which, in fact, in "open" structures, the process compels actors even if their intention is to escape the outcome. In all of the "expectation state" theories in the volume (such as those presented in Chapters 3, 4, and 5), very complex inputs of initial status information are "processed" by the actors but the actors are not assumed to be fully or even partially aware of the process and, if asked to describe it, cannot tell an interviewer much about it. But such hidden-hand and unconscious-processing theories are nevertheless interactor theories in the sense that the orientations of the actors are a fundamental aspect of the underlying process.

Relations

Nor are actors necessarily aware of the pattern of relations that form them into systems. But, by definition, all interactor theories are made up of multiple actors, the actors form systems, and the systems are describable by the relations among the actors. The minimum required is that the actors are behaviorally interdependent, that two or more actors each affects the others, whether aware of the fact or not, as in Fararo and Skvoretz's "biased nets" or Willer et al.'s "networks of power." Furthermore, it is sufficient that this interdependence among actors be indirect; that is, what is required for a "system" is that every actor be at least indirectly connected to every other. But the interactor concept of a "system" does not require that each actor be directly connected to every other actor; it requires only that any one actor be directly connected to at least one other. Thus Ridgeway's chapter deals with a "system" in which all relations are direct, but interactor theories are not in general confined to pairwise, direct relations, and theories like Fararo and Skvoretz's, Sørensen's, and Willer et al.'s permit indirect relations and, therefore, action at a distance.

PROCESSES

A full-fledged interactor theory describes mechanisms or processes by which the elements of the theory come to be related to each other. This requires that they explain how activating conditions, the social framework, and products of past interaction are transformed into definitions of particular actors in particular situations; it requires that they explain the nature, conditions, and consequences of particular processes of action; and it requires that they explain how the outcomes of such processes are transformed into elements of the history and social framework of subsequent interaction.

All this is typically organized around some kind of "state" of the system of actors in a given situation. States, in part determined by pregiven structure and in part by action in the present situation, are situationally specific, stable, relational structures. In theories like Foschi's (Chapter 3), Foddy and Smithson's (Chapter 4), or Cohen and Silver's (Chapter 7), the states are patterns of status relations. In Stryker's "identity theory" (Chapter 2), they are salience hierarchies. In Fararo and Skvoretz's "biased nets" (Chapter 9) the states are constituted out of ways of differentiating actors, out of the heterogeneity of their relations, and functions of them. In Jasso's "distributive justice" (Chapter 13), the states are distributions of actual and expected rewards.

These states in general formulate in a precise fashion the "definition of the situation." Such definitions, though sometimes taken as givens, more typically require specific theoretical explanation because activation of a process is typically selective in the sense that a given social process uses some but not all of the available inputs into the situation. Thus particular tasks make particular aspects of the social framework and particular aspects of past interaction relevant in theories like Foschi's, Foddy and Smithson's, or Cohen and Silver's. Particular external relations make particular legitimating formulae relevant in Ridgeway's theory. Whether the system is open or closed determines the role of characteristics such as gender, race, and educational credentials in Sørensen's "processes of allocation."

The behavior described by the processes of interactor theories are in the first instance governed by these states/relations. At the same time, interactor theories typically describe two-way processes. That is, states/ relations not only determine behavior, the behavior they determine in turn determines the states/relations of the processes. Thus in Samuel and Zelditch's theory, expectations about power shape both the use of and compliance with power, but use and compliance in turn feed back into the process by which expectations are created and maintained. In Fararo and Skvoretz's analysis of mobility, mobility both affects and is affected by intergroup relations. This often leads, as in expectation state theories such as those presented in Chapters 3, 4, 5, and 6, to explanations of stability (e.g., stability of expectation states) in terms of self-fulfilling prophecies: The state of the system of actors determines behaviors, such as influence, power, or allocations of rewards, which in turn determine the states governing the system, making them effectively self-reinforcing.

In general, the social processes described by an interactor theory can be said to have some kind of outcome, such as coalition formation, division of labor, or elaboration of rules. Once a process has some outcome, an important question for an interactor theory is whether, and under what conditions, the outcome is transformed into an input into subsequent interaction. Berger et al.'s chapter explicitly addresses to this question. Especially important is the transformation of outcomes into elements of the social framework, that is, their institutionalization. Fararo and Skvoretz (1984), for example, have dealt at length with this process, though not in their chapter in this volume. Berger and Luckmann's well-known *Social Construction of Reality* (1967), another interactor theory, also deals with it. It is dealt with from an exchange point of view in Stolte's "The Formation of Justice Norms" (1987). But in general, this process is neglected in the chapters in the present volume. We mention it here not because it is frequent in the present volume but because the logic of a full-fledged interactor theory seems to us to require it.

Finally, the fact that what interactor theories describe are processes, and therefore imply some event or condition activating them, also implies that the duration of the process depends on whether the activating event or condition continues or not. For example, an outcome that accomplishes a goal (ends in a decision or performance of a task) or ends a disturbance (e.g., redresses an inequity) also deactivates a process. Exogenous factors may also change the conditions of the process, altering its course. Thus Ridgeway and Berger et al. take into account the effect that external evaluation of performance has in altering status orders. The whole concept of the duration of a process, in fact, depends on its activating events and conditions and may range from very short to extended time periods.

However, deactivation in interactor theories typically ends only manifest, observable features of a process. The states that govern the process are typically assumed to have a latent existence, in the sense that reactivation of the same process for the same actors activates initial conditions that depend in part on past history. Thus in a theory like the resource theory of family power structure, a family engaged in a decision-making task may dedifferentiate in, say, an expressive phase, but differentiate again in the same way when the decision-making task recurs. Almost no interactor theory that we know about, and certainly none of the chapters in the present volume, assumes that a process begins *de novo* every time it is reactivated.

FEATURES

In explaining processes of action, interactor theories assume explicitly or implicitly that no behavior is fully explained by (1) the biological or psychological dispositions of individual actors; (2) the external, environmental, structural, or cultural elements of the situation taken by themselves; or, on the other hand, (3) by the process of action itself. Emphasis here is on the word *fully*: Only in special cases do any of these factors fully account for, in and of themselves, how systems of actors behave. This assumption reflects three distinctive features of interactor theories: first, the role in them of situations; second, the role of pregiven structure; and third, the role of action.

The "actor-in-situation," not the actor, is the basic unit of interactor theories. They are relational, situational theories — by contrast, for example, with dispositional theories such as national-character or culture-of-poverty theories. In an interactor theory the actor may well have *any* state describable in the theory, no matter what the actor's state in any other situation: Typically, there is no assumption of transsituational constancy in the actor's behavior. This is especially true of theories like Fararo and Skvoretz's (Chapter 9), Sørensen's (Chapter 10), or Willer et al.'s (Chapter 12), in which all actors are assumed to have uniform actor-level dispositions, motives, or interests so that it is the situation, especially the larger social framework, that accounts for any variation in actor behavior. (This is true of many other theories that think of themselves as "structural"; they are "structural" because they deny that they have any special assumptions about actors, although what they mean by this is that they do not employ individual differences in explaining behavior.)

Theories like Foschi's (Chapter 3), Foddy and Smithson's (Chapter 4), Berger et al.'s (Chapter 5), or Cohen and Silver's (Chapter 7) — all expectation state theories of status-influence relations — have a similar actor variability because expectation states are relations that depend on the characteristics of the other as well as the self. Even Stryker's theory of identity (Chapter 2), the whole purpose of which is to explain actor constancies, assumes "singularity" (i.e., constancy) is a variable that is explained by variations in situational factors such as the stability and overlap of networks of relations. Actor and system, too, can vary from situation to situation. In multilevel theories like Willer et al.'s (Chapter 12), the internal power structure of an organization can be described by relations among departments, while the power structure of interorganizational relations can be described by relations among organizations. In the former the organization is the system; in the latter it is the actor. The situational relativity of actor-states thus distinguishes interactor theories not only from dispositional theories but also from any use of concrete actors, like small groups, organizations, and nation-states, as the "levels" of sociological analysis. No concrete actor is in the same situation all the time. The analytic elements that make up the situation are present only under certain conditions. The actor-in-situation is therefore at once narrower and broader than any concrete actor; narrower because it does not describe a whole actor, broader because it is made up of elements in the situation as well as in the actor. Hence the common practice of dividing sociology up into levels defined by concrete kinds of actors makes no sense from an interactor point of view.

Pregiven structure is an essential feature of the situation in an interactor theory. However varied the elements that constitute the social framework, all the theories in the present volume, and interactor theories more generally, presuppose some structure. Extreme variants of symbolic interactionism, in which the features of a social order are negotiated at every encounter (see Strauss et al. 1963; Denzin 1987) are in this sense not interactor theories, though they have most other features of such theories.

On the other hand, while interactor theories all presuppose some pregiven structure, they also presuppose the agency of the actor, and therefore that "action" also has a role in sociological explanation. This is usually accomplished by treating structure, except in special cases, as incomplete. The values, beliefs, rules, practices, and procedures that constitute a social framework do not cover every event and condition, are in any case not sufficiently specific to define fully every particular situation, and even if they were they cannot guarantee their own application to particular cases. Consequently, there are frequently conflicts of interpretation to resolve in particular situations or features of structure to elaborate. Theories in which there is no action are no more interactor theories than theories with no structure. Thus, unlike the other theories in this volume, Turner's "macrostructural dynamics" (Chapter 8) and Hannan's "organizational ecology" (Chapter 14) are not interactor theories. They explain phenomena in terms of external conditions; the mechanism at work is selection; they presuppose neither actorness nor action. Theories such as those presented by Althusser (1971) or Meyer et al. (1987), in which behavior emanates from pregiven structure, are also not interactor theories. Behavior sometimes may emanate from pregiven structure even in interactor theories: There are many cases in which patterns become so routinized that behavior follows only a well-cleared path. But in interactor theories this occurs only in particular cases, not in general.

Possibly it is of agency that some macrosociologists are thinking when they say that interactor explanations of macrophenomena are a "reduction to social psychology." Such explanations are not reduction in the technical sense (Nagel 1952). Nor is agency a matter of scale, level, kind of actor, or, except at the extreme, even of the extent of institutionalization. The micro/macro problem in this sense is a dispute over determinism, a metatheoretical rather than a technical question. Nothing in the present chapter advances argument either pro or con with respect to determinism. We have described the common features of interactor theories; such theories do take a position with respect to agency/determinism, but we have not tried to justify this position. However, if in fact the issue is determinism, it would be useful to recognize what the issue is; to separate it from the technical, and more easily solved, question of how to model effects of scale, level, institutionalization, and kind of actor; and to focus attention explicitly on the metatheoretical issues, issues such as determinism, holism, and situationalism, instead of coding them "micro versus macro."

Summary and Conclusion

Theories are neither micro nor macro; they are abstract and general. It is only their particular interpretations that are micro or macro. Scale, level, institutionalization, and nature of the actor all make a difference, but they are variables in or interpretations of a theory, not differences among theories.

Some theories are capable of application to both micro- and macrosociology, some are not. "Interactor" theories are capable of application to both. Such theories describe processes of action of systems of actors-in-situations. They characterize systems of actors by the states of their relations, and situations by the immediate conditions of action, past history, and the larger social framework. The states of the system of relations and the definition of the situation together determine, and are determined by, the process of action. The main features that differentiate the strategy of such theories from other strategies of theory construction are the agency of the actor, their situationalism, and their combination of structure and action: They are neither all structure nor all action.

It is possible that the qualitative differences between theories that have been attributed to differences between "micro- and macrophenomena" are really metatheoretical differences among methodological holism, individualism, and situationalism, or between agency and determinism. But if holism and agency are what the micro/macro problem is really about, it is explicitly on the metatheoretical questions of holism and agency that we ought to focus the issues. As far as scale, level, institutionalization, and nature of the actor are concerned, the problems to solve are practical questions of how to model the effects of these factors in any particular theory.

Note

1. We do not mean to object to synthesis either of levels or in principal. With respect to either/or formulations of questions like actor/system or structure/action, synthesis is the only useful solution. With respect to structure "versus" action, for example, it seems equally fruitless to argue that there is no pregiven structure, that *all* interaction is negotiated (see Denzin 1987; Strauss et al. 1963), and that there is no action, that all behavior does nothing but act out pregiven structure (see Meyer et al. 1987).

References

Aldrich, H. E. 1979. *Organizations and Environments.* Englewood Cliffs, NJ: Prentice-Hall.

Aldrich, H. E. and J. Pfeffer. 1976. "Environments of Organizations." *Annual Review of Sociology* 2:79-105.

Alexander, J., B. Giesen, R. Münch, and N. Smelser. 1987. *The Micro-Macro Link.* Berkeley: University of California Press.

Althusser, L. 1971. "Ideology and Ideological State Apparatuses." In *Lenin and Philosophy and Other Essays*, edited by L. Althusser. New York: Monthly Review Press.

Berger, J., M. Zelditch, Jr., and B. Anderson, eds. 1966. *Sociological Theories in Progress*, Vol. 1. Boston: Houghton Mifflin.

— —, eds. 1972. *Sociological Theories in Progress*, Vol. 2. Boston: Houghton Mifflin.

Berger, P. and T. Luckmann. 1967. *The Social Construction of Reality.* Garden City, NY: Anchor.

Blau, P. 1964. *Exchange and Power in Social Life.* New York: John Wiley.

Bossen, L. 1975. "Women in Modernizing Societies." *American Ethnologist* 3:578-601.

Burgess, R. L. and J. M. Nielson. 1974. "An Experimental Analysis of Some Structural Determinants of Equitable and Inequitable Exchange Relations." *American Sociological Review* 39:427-43.

Coleman, James S. 1986. "Social Theory, Social Research, and a Theory of Action." *American Journal of Sociology* 91:1309-35.

Collins, Randall. 1981. "On the Microfoundations of Macrosociology." *American Journal of Sociology* 86:984-1014.

Cook, K. S. 1977. "Exchange and Power in Networks of Interorganizational Relations." *Sociological Quarterly* 18:62-82.

Cook, K. S. and R. M. Emerson. 1978. "Power, Equity, and Commitment in Exchange Networks." *American Sociological Review* 43:721-30.

— —. 1984. "Exchange Networks and Analysis of Complex Organizations." *Research in the Sociology of Organizations* 3:1-30.

Cook, K. S., R. M. Emerson, M. R. Gillmore, and T. Yamagishi. 1983. "The Distribution of Power in Exchange Networks: Theory and Experimental Results." *American Journal of Sociology* 89:275-305.

Cyret, R. M. and J. G. March. 1963. *A Behavioral Theory of the Firm.* Englewood Cliffs, NJ: Prentice-Hall.

Denzin, Norman K. 1987. "The Death of Sociology in the 1980's: Comment on Collins." *American Journal of Sociology* 93:175-80.

Durkheim, E. [1897] 1951. *Suicide.* Glencoe, IL: Free Press.

Emerson, R. M. 1962. "Power-Dependence Relations." *American Sociological Review* 27:31-40.

— —. 1964. "Power-Dependence Relations: Two Experiments." *Sociometry* 27:282-98.

— —. 1972a. "Exchange Theory, Part I: A Psychological Basis for Social Exchange." Pp. 38-57 in *Sociological Theories in Progress*, Vol. 2, edited by J. Berger, M. Zelditch, Jr., and B. Anderson. Boston: Houghton Mifflin.

— —. 1972b. "Exchange Theory, Part II: Exchange Relations, Exchange Networks, and Groups as Exchanging Systems." Pp. 58-87 in *Sociological Theories in Progress*, Vol. 2, edited by J. Berger, M. Zelditch, Jr., and B. Anderson. Boston: Houghton Mifflin.

Fararo, T. and J. Skvoretz. 1984. "Institutions as Production Systems." *Journal of Mathematical Sociology* 10:117-82.

Festinger, L. 1953. "An Analysis of Compliant Behavior." Pp. 232-56 in *Group Relations at the Crossroads*, edited by M. Sherif and M. O. Wilson. New York: Harper.

Fine, Gary Alan and Sherryl Kleinman. 1983. "Network and Meaning: An Interactional Approach to Structure." *Symbolic Interaction* 6:97-110.

Garfinkel, H. 1964. "Studies of the Routine Grounds of Everyday Activities." *Social Problems* 11:225-50.

Giddens, A. 1979. *Central Problems in Social Theory: Action, Structure, and Contradiction in Social Analysis.* Berkeley: University of California Press.

Hannan, M. 1979. "The Dynamics of Ethnic Boundaries in Modern States." Pp. 253-75 in *National Development and the World System*, edited by J. Meyer and M. Hannan. Chicago: University of Chicago Press.

Heer, D. 1963. "The Measurement and Basis of Family Power: An Overview." *Journal of Marriage and the Family* 25:133-39.

Hills, Frederick S. and Thomas A. Mahoney. 1978. "University Budgets and Organizational Decision Making." *Administrative Sciences Quarterly* 23:454-65.

Homans, G. 1964. "Bringing Men Back In." *American Sociological Review* 29:809-18.

Jones, Brian J., B. J. Gallagher, and J. A. McFalls, Jr. 1988. *Social Problems: Issues, Opinions, and Solutions.* New York: McGraw-Hill.

Knorr-Cetina, K. and A. Cicourel, eds. 1981. *Advances in Social Theory and Methodology: Towards an Integration of Micro- and Macro-Sociology.* London: Routledge & Kegan Paul.

Lee, G. R. 1977. *Family Structure and Interaction.* Philadelphia: J. B. Lippincott.

Lewin, K. 1951. *Field Theory in Social Science.* New York: Harper.

Maines, David R. 1979. "Mesostructure and Social Process." *Contemporary Sociology* 8:524-27.

McDonald, G. 1980. "Family Power: Assessment of a Decade of Theory and Research, 1970-1979." *Journal of Marriage and the Family* 40:841-54.

Meyer, J. W., F. O. Ramirez, and J. Boli. 1987. "Ontology and Rationalization in the Western Cultural Account." Pp. 12-37 in *Institutional Structure: Constituting State, Society, and the Individual*, edited by J. Boli and G. Thomas. Newbury Park, CA: Sage.

Michaels, J. W. and J. A. Wiggins. 1976. "Effects of Mutual Dependency and Dependency Asymmetry on Social Exchange." *Sociometry* 39:368-76.

Molm, L. 1981a. "Power Use in the Dyad: The Effects of Structure, Knowledge, and Interaction History." *Social Psychology Quarterly* 44:42-48.

— —. 1981b. "The Conversion of Power Imbalance to Power Use." *Social Psychology Quarterly* 44:151-63.

— —. 1985. "Relative Effects of Individual Dependencies: Further Tests of the Relation Between Power Imbalance and Power Use." *Social Forces* 63:810-37.

— —. 1987. "Extending Power-Dependence Theory: Power Processes and Negative Outcomes." In *Advances in Group Processes*, Vol. 4, edited by E. J. Lawler and B. Markovsky. Greenwich, CT: JAI.

Nagel, E. 1952. "On the Statement 'The Whole Is More Than the Sum of Its Parts.' " *Philosophical Studies* 3:17-26.

Parsons, T. and E. Shils. 1951. *Toward a General Theory of Action.* Cambridge, MA: Harvard University Press.

Pfeffer, J. 1972a. "Merger as a Response to Organizational Interdependence." *Administrative Sciences Quarterly* 17:382-94.

— —. 1972b. "Size and Composition of Corporate Boards of Directors." *Administrative Sciences Quarterly* 17:218-28.

— —. 1981. *Power in Organizations.* Marshfield, MA: Pitman.

Pfeffer, J. and J. Leong. 1977. "Resource Allocations in United Funds." *Social Forces* 55:775-90.

Pfeffer, J. and W. Moore. 1980. "Power in University Budgeting: A Replication and Extension." *Administrative Sciences Quarterly* 25:637-53.

Pfeffer, J. and P. Nowak. 1976. "Joint Ventures and Interorganizational Interdependence." *Administrative Sciences Quarterly* 21:398-418.

Pfeffer, J. and G. Salancik. 1978. *The External Control of Organizations: A Resource Dependence Perspective.* New York: Harper & Row.

Pfeffer, Jeffrey, Gerald R. Salancik, and Huseyin Leblebici. 1976. "The Effect of Uncertainty on the Use of Social Influence in Organizational Decision Making." *Administrative Sciences Quarterly* 21:227-45.

Provan, K. G. 1982. "Interorganizational Linkages and Influence over Decision Making." *Academy of Management Journal* 25:443-51.

Provan, K. G., J. Beyer, and C. Kruytbosch. 1980. "Environmental Linkages and Power in Resource Dependence Relations." *Administrative Sciences Quarterly* 25:200-25.

Ritzer, G. 1985. "The Rise of Micro-Sociological Theory." *Sociological Theory* 3:88-98.

Rodman, H. 1967. "Marital Power in France, Greece, Yugoslavia, and the United States: A Cross-National Discussion." *Journal of Marriage and the Family* 29:320-25.

— —. 1972. "Marital Power and the Theory of Resources in Cultural Context." *Journal of Comparative Family Studies* 3:50-69.

Rogers, S. C. 1975. "Female Forms of Power and the Myth of Male Dominance: A Model of Female/Male Interaction in Peasant Society." *American Ethnologist* 2:727-56.

Salancik, G. and J. Pfeffer. 1974. "The Bases and Uses of Power in Organizational Decision Making: The Case of a University." *Administrative Sciences Quarterly* 19:453-73.

Stolte, J. 1987. "The Formation of Justice Norms." *American Sociological Review* 52:774-84.

Stolte, J. and R. M. Emerson. 1976. "Structural Inequality: Position and Power in Network Structures." Pp. 117-38 in *Behavior Theory in Sociology*, edited by R. Hamblin and J. Kunkel. New Brunswick, NJ: Transaction.

Strauss, A., L. Schatzman, D. Ehrlich, R. Butcher, and M. Sabshin. 1963. "The Hospital and Its Negotiated Order." Pp. 147-69 in *The Hospital in Modern Society*, edited by E. Freidson. New York: Free Press.

Szinovacz, M. E. 1987. "Family Power." Pp. 651-94 in *Handbook of Marriage and the Family*, edited by M. B. Sussman and S. K. Steinmetz. New York: Plenum.

Thibaut, J. and H. Kelley. 1959. *The Social Psychology of Groups.* New York: John Wiley.

Thompson, J. 1967. *Organizations in Action.* New York: McGraw-Hill.

Usdiken, Behlul. 1983. "Interorganizational Linkages Among Similar Organizations in Turkey." *Organizational Studies* 4:151-64.

Webster, M. 1973. "Psychological Reductionism, Methodological Individualism, and Large-Scale Problems." *American Sociological Review* 38:258-73.

Wolfe, D. M. 1959. "Power and Authority in the Family." Pp. 99-117 in *Studies in Social Power,* edited by D. Cartwright. Ann Arbor, MI: Institute for Social Research.

PART II

IDENTITY, STATUS, AND SOCIAL INTERACTION

2

Further Developments in Identity Theory: Singularity Versus Multiplicity of Self

SHELDON STRYKER

The phrase incorporated into the title of this volume, "theories in progress," is, at the very least, double-edged. It can be taken to imply that particular structures of conceptions, assumptions, and propositions are only incompletely formulated and only partially articulated, and are thus in more or less need of improvement on these scores. It can also be taken to imply that such structures are being moved or can be moved toward more complete and satisfactory formulation and articulation.

As description, the first of these implications of "theories in progress" fits identity theory well; as aspiration, the second implication asserts the motivation and, one hopes, the accomplishment of this essay. Less abstractly, I wish to move identity theory beyond its current state as a reasonable explanation of social processes and social behaviors.

The vehicle through which implementation of this aspiration proceeds is the examination of a conceptual issue contained in the literature of social psychology that is concerned with "self." In its most general terms, that issue is posed by language appearing in the title given this essay: the singularity versus the multiplicity of self. That issue poses a conceptual problem that is relevant to social psychological theory's capacity to account for both such variability over time and across situations as well as such stability as may exist in social behavior. Identity theory has proposed a tentative response to this issue. There is reason to believe that the answer currently contained in identity theory is insufficient to the task—not "wrong," but incomplete. If that is so, one route to the further development of identity theory is a consideration of the issue of the singularity versus the multiplicity of self.

Author's Note: An initial version of this chapter, stopping short of the attempt to develop the theory involved beyond its state as of that time, was presented at the Symposium on Identity as an Organized Multiplicity, at the annual meetings of the American Psychological Association, Los Angeles, August 24, 1985. Work on this chapter was facilitated by an NIMH grant, 5 T32 MH14588.

This consideration gets under way most circuitously, initially taking up matters only indirectly related to the specific issue of how self is to be conceptualized or to the development of identity theory. These matters — they have to do with how "personality" is understood from the standpoint of sociology and what may be implied by such an understanding; they have also to do with why and how self is of interest to social psychologists who approach their subject matter as sociologists (and why it should be of interest to sociologists in general) — are relevant in part because presenting them may avoid misunderstandings. More important, they are relevant as context for the ensuing discussion of alternative ways of conceiving of self and the theoretical and empirical issues at stake in those alternative conceptualizations; without them, one could well be hard put to comprehend why that discussion goes in the directions it does, how existent identity theory formulations relate to these alternatives, why further development of identity theory in these terms might be useful, or the grounds on which an elaborated identity theory can be appraised.

The context presented, the conceptual issue implied in the language of singularity versus multiplicity of self is explored. In reality, this language poses an issue that perhaps most if not all of contemporary social psychology presumes to be resolved. That resolution is challenged, and an argument made with respect to the requirements of a "proper" resolution.

Next, various approximations of a "proper" resolution are briefly examined. Only then is identity theory broached, and then only in the brief compass necessary to indicating how it, as currently formulated, attends to the issue of the singularity versus the multiplicity of self. The adequacy of this attention is evaluated; it will surprise absolutely no one who knows anything of the source of identity theory to be told that the theory is held to be fundamentally sound and worthy of further attention. It will also surprise no one who has read the preceding pages to now read that movement beyond the current formulation of identity theory is indicated. The last section of this essay suggests useful directions in that movement.

Context: Personality and Self
from the Standpoint of a
Sociologically Motivated Social Psychology

Identity theory is a social psychological theory; that is, its immediate object of explanation is the behavior of the person. Identity theory, however, emerges out of a sociological context — its metatheoretical tradition is in symbolic interactionism, a long-standing theoretical stance within sociology — and it is ultimately concerned with those most fundamental of sociological issues, the issues of social order and of change. Insofar as what identity theory has to say is successful in addressing matters relevant to these fundamental issues of sociology, the theory becomes relevant to sociology and to sociologists generally.

It is the argument contained in the previous paragraph that permits or legitimates the further argument that sociologists must pay at least some attention to matters discussed in subsequent paragraphs that have to do with "personality," with "self," with "identity," matters that sometimes escape their attention or that they sometimes dismiss as not germane to their interests qua sociologists. In point of fact, social psychological theory is, almost by definition, important to sociological theory, no matter how "structural" the latter's formulation. Every sociological theory incorporates a social psychology — that is, assertions, however implicit, about social persons, their makeup, their motivations, their contributions to group-level phenomena. Thus the only pertinent question from the standpoint of sociology with regard to social psychological theory is how adequate and how useful is the particular social psychology it utilizes.

From a sociological standpoint, "personality" is understood as a reflection of social roles and both a creation of and a creator of social interaction. This assertion offers a representation of professional concern: It says that the sociologist is interested in the person insofar as that person represents, reproduces, plays back into, or alters the social structures within which she or he is produced and within which she or he develops characteristics and patterns of interactive behaviors that are reasonably general to those occupying similar structural positions and playing (or creating) essentially similar roles. It also says that such a concern is worthwhile, that is, that something of value can be learned about both the person and the social order by conceptualizing personality in this way. To put the matter in an alternative and exclusionary way, sociologists qua sociologists avoid the clinical attitude that stresses the undeniable uniqueness and individuality, the idiosyncrasies and the ideographics, of every person.

This proclamation of professional interest and faith is useful to avoid possible misunderstandings, both on the part of sociologists who may not appreciate the value to their discipline of a social psychology, however formulated, and on the part of others, who may not appreciate the value of a sociology. Possible misunderstandings revolve around what is and what is not being claimed in the assertion that sociologists avoid a clinical attitude.

To proceed initially through disclaimers: No claim is made that social roles are all there is to what can usefully be meant by "personality." Nor is it claimed that the person simply mirrors organized social structures, meaning by that term both the systems of social relationships in which persons interact with others as occupants of social positions and the larger social boundaries of age, sex, class, and so on that constrain the possibilities of organized systems of social relationships to occur and to continue. Certainly, it is not claimed that nomothetic study is inherently better, more moral, or even more "scientific" than its polar alternative (although the opposite of these is not admitted either).

Ideally, both the generality and the uniqueness of human beings in whom social scientists, collectively, are interested would be studied; indeed, there is a reasonable argument to be made that the general cannot be known without knowing what is unique, nor can the unique be known without knowing what is general. Since, however, everything cannot be attended at once, and since what is given prior attention may well squeeze out more or less permanently what is only "initially" left out as an expedient, the present claim must be that there is considerable utility in an approach to the person that incorporates the sociological view of personality enunciated above. If it is intended that work permits generalized assertions insofar as they are warranted through that work, categorical referents are necessary, and one approach to such categorical referents is through the concept of role.

Understanding personality as a reflection of social roles leads in the sociological literature, inevitably or not, to a consideration of self in these same terms. The self, in the classic definition provided by George Herbert Mead (1934), is that which is an object to itself. That is, the self is visualized as constituted in and through self-referential processes. In keeping with the foregoing discussion, these self-referential processes are seen to be conducted importantly although certainly not exclusively by reference to social roles: The content of the self contained in the reflexive processes defining self tends, for the sociologist, to be phrased in terms of cognitive categories referencing positions occupied in social structures and the expectations for behaviors accompanying those positions. These position-linked expectations supply the meanings that, in the form of self-concepts, sociologists tend to see as important sources and organizers of social behavior.

This last assertion makes explicit yet another point of considerable importance to fully understanding the development of the present argument. For the sociologist, the self is of little if any interest in its own right. As differentiated from the clinical or the personality psychologist, for whom the self may well be the ultimate "dependent variable" of concern, the sociologist is interested in self on the assumption that self is of critical import in mediating the impact of social structures on the conduct of social interaction and in mediating the reciprocal impact of social interaction on social structures. Self is seen as proximate "cause" of social interaction, as motive (exemplified in the argument that persons seek out opportunities to enact particular selves or seek out interactions that will serve to confirm particular selves), as selective agent affecting the choice of roles to be played out in situations in which options are available, as organizer of interactive behaviors. Variations in self become important from the standpoint of a sociology insofar as they enable the prediction and explanation of the processes by which social order reproduces itself or is changed. Conceptions of self in social psychology motivated primarily by the needs of cognitive psychology to account for the information-processing or for the motivational biasing impacts of self, while in no sense "wrong," typically fall short when measured against this standard.

If self is seen as proximate cause of social interaction, its source is seen as society. Insisting on the creative potential of self in shaping society through its impact on interaction, sociologists interested in self by and large adopt Mead's dictum that self reflects and is the product of society. Thus, as will be elaborated in the following section, it cannot surprise that as sociological images of society shift, so do sociological images of the self.

Partially explicit, partially implicit in the preceding discussion is the recognition of a dual thrust in sociological interest in self. That dual thrust is represented by two long-standing traditions of sociological thought, typically perceived as contradictory. On the one hand, there is the theoretical tradition stemming from Durkheim and represented in contemporary versions of functionalism as well as Marxism that emphasizes the coercive power of society over the individual and views the relationship of society and individual as one in which society shapes the individual so as to reproduce the society. On the other hand, there is the theoretical tradition of symbolic interactionism, stressing the power of the individual to construct him- or herself, construct social interaction, and construct society, creatively introducing novelty along the way. It is no small attraction of current work on self that it may offer a way to resolve the apparent contradiction in these two traditions of sociological theory; recent work tracing the mechanisms by which self is constructed and social relationships are reconstructed by persons experiencing life course and life course environmental change provides the warrant for this hope (see Serpe and Stryker, 1987).

What has been said above supplies the context for what follows. What follows is a discussion of the general question: How can self be conceptualized so that it can serve optimally attempts to explain theoretically the interactional behavior that is the essential domain of a social psychology?

Singular Self Versus
Multiple Selves: The Issue

The answer to this question is pursued, as has been already suggested, by reposing an issue that the contemporary social psychological literature seems to have resolved to its satisfaction: the issue of the comparative utility of a view of self as singular (or unitary, or undifferentiated, or global) and a view that presumes that persons have not a self but rather a multiplicity of selves.

Is there indeed an "issue" in social psychology with regard to the comparative utility of these alternative ways of conceiving of self? Or, as the earlier assertion that the literature seems to have arrived at a resolution might be taken to imply, and as the rather quaint and outmoded ring to the term *singular* self might be taken to affirm, has the matter been settled? A strong argument can perhaps be made to the effect that there is no issue. There does not seem to be anybody in today's social psychology, sociologist or psychologist (and whatever may be true in the different worlds of clinical psychology and of philosophy), who believes that it makes sense to think of persons as having *a* self that underlies the full range of their interactive behaviors. Surely, there are some who, limiting their conceptualization to the affective realm of self-esteem, discuss esteem on the level of a global self (Rosenberg 1979). However, and especially when self-esteem is utilized not as the object of explanation but in the attempt to explain patterns of ongoing behavior, the likelihood is that discussion will proceed in terms of various role-specific self-esteems. Occasionally, textbooks use the language of the singular self or its equivalent, but they do so rhetorically in order to introduce the distinction between the singular self and a multiplicity of selves and to dismiss the former in favor of the latter. It seems to be clear that, at this point of time in social psychology, a multiplicity view of self is a taken-for-granted truth.

It is not clear that a truly singular view of self was ever seriously entertained in social psychology; after all, William James's (1890, pp. 291-294) specification of the empirical self as having three classes of constituents—the material, the social, and the spiritual—and his further specification of the social self through the assertion that persons have as many selves as there are others who respond to them (or, at the very least, as many as there are classes of others who respond to them) dates to well before the turn of the century, before the emergence of social psychology as an identifiable theoretical and research domain.

However, theorists interested in therapeutic issues, as well as personality theorists—Fromm (1947), Rogers (1951), Allport (1937), and Lecky (1945) are examples—noted that persons regard themselves as having a continuing identity and argued some form of consistency as the hallmark of the self. Too, Mead (1934, p. 144) used the language of the "complete self" and saw that complete self as having a unity that reflected, in keeping with his own dictum, the unity of the social process. Mead's philosophic commitment to the idea that all humanity was evolving toward a single society sharing a single universe of discourse has long been noted (Stryker 1956); such philosophic predilections undergird a conception of self as singular (since, again, self reflects society). Further, much sociology, from the nineteenth century through the work of Talcott Parsons (e.g., in Parsons 1951) up to roughly a quarter century ago, held a view of society as highly organized and systemic, as, in many ways, a unitary system; and, once more in keeping with Mead's dictum, the self was discussed in the same terms. It is not inappropriate to point out that throughout this time interval—that is, up to about 25 years ago—that while the self was frequently invoked in sociological discourse, it rarely entered directly into empirical research; thus there was little impetus from sociology to appraise, or to reappraise, the utility of this view of self. In psychology as well, and again with the possible exception of work on self-esteem, little research was premised on such a view.

As Gordon and Gergen (1968, p. 6) observe, self is often written about in the singular in the literature on the topic. In part, this reflects linguistic convenience. In part, and insofar as self did enter empirical research, it reflects research convenience; it is simply easier to proceed empirically on the assumption of a singular self, for then only a highly general measure of self-concept is required and not multiple measures of multiple self-concepts, or only one measure of global self-esteem, and not measures of multiple esteems.

Nevertheless, a multiplicity of selves conceptualization currently reigns. In 1970, Gergen could write in a manner that summarizes well matters as they appear to stand: "The assumption of a single, or global, concept of self seems misleading. Rather than speaking of *the* self or self-concept, it is much more fruitful to speak of multiple conceptions" (p. 20). That summary statement reflects, as Gergen notes, the fact that persons asked to describe themselves tend to do so in highly differentiated ways; and it reflects, as Gordon and Gergen (1968) observe, the perception that persons' behavior is often inconsistent and often highly variable from situation to situation. Both everyday observation and the research literature document the validity of that perception.

A multiplicity of selves conceptualization is also in accord with a variety of other conceptualizations and arguments appearing in the literature of social science over the past decades — from the other-directedness theme developed by Reisman and his collaborators (1950) that argued the chameleonlike character of modern man conforming to variable external demands as these arise in highly specialized environments, to the Goffmanesque (Goffman 1956; Schlenker 1980) view of self-presentations as highly variable, a consequence both of the deliberate use of those presentations to manipulate others and of the variability of situational requirements. Further, it is entirely consistent with the sociological view of self as previously enunciated.

That is, one distinguishing characteristic of contemporary sociological thought about society relative to earlier treatments is the recognition that the effective social units within which persons' lives are in fact lived out are relatively small-scale networks of social relationships rather than large-scale, total societies. Alternatively put, contemporary sociology views the modern, industrial societies for which the United States serves as exemplar as more adequately conceptualized as congeries of multiple, partially overlapping, partially independent networks of relationships and multiple institutions rather than as single, unitary, relatively undifferentiated wholes.

A second distinguishing characteristic of modern sociology is the understanding that any given person enters only into a selected subset of the congeries of networks constituting society, enters many such, and that these networks tend in important degree to be specialized and to consist of at least partially different sets of others. Given that self reflects society, it follows from this vision of contemporary society that self is best conceptualized in equivalent differentiated terms, as consisting of partially overlapping, partially independent multiple selves. It is precisely this argument, using a somewhat different language to describe multiple selves, that has been used in defense of what has been termed a structural symbolic interactionism and in the elaboration of identity theory (Stryker 1968, 1980; Stryker and Statham 1985). Thus there are indeed many sources for what has been termed the taken-for-granted truth of a multiplicity view of self.

Why should this "truth" be challenged, if indeed it should be? There is surely no reason to argue that a multiplicity of selves conception is in error and ought to be replaced by its polar opposite. However, there are two major problems in a multiplicity of self view. A first is that such a view lends itself to an extreme form of situationalism that renders the concept of self superfluous in accounts of social behavior. That is, self — in the sense that it has been discussed above — is a personality variable — again, in the sense that "personality" has been discussed above. The theoretical utility of personality variables in accounts of social behavior lies precisely in the need to incorporate transsituational elements in social psychological theories. A multiplicity of selves conceptualization at least hints at the possibility that persons have or develop different selves in every different situation of interaction in which they become involved. It becomes difficult to see just what is added theoretically to elements of situations invoked in explanations of social behavior by introducing selves that are unique to those situations. That behavior can and sometimes does vary dramatically across situations is an empirically valid assertion. In part, it was precisely to recognize such situational variability that a multiplicity of selves conception was developed. However, it is an equivalently valid empirical observation that there can be and sometimes is behavior that is essentially similar across quite varied situations. Some modification of a multiplicity of selves view in the direction of a singular self view may be useful to deal with that essential similarity.

The second problem bears at least a family resemblance to the first. If self is conceptualized, in keeping with William James's (1890) or Charles Horton Cooley's (1902) formulations, as any experience to which the personal pronouns *I, me,* or *mine* can be attached, or if it is conceptualized as in Rosenberg's (1979) recent work as the totality of the individual's thoughts and feelings having reference to him- or herself as an object, it becomes a wondrously differentiated and complex congeries of a vast variety of elements — differentiated processes like self-consciousness, self-awareness, self-presentation; differentiated characteristics like self-control, self-confidence, self-esteem; differentiated content like academic self-conception, spousal self-concept, age-graded self-concepts; differentiated traits like liberal, generous, compulsive; differentiated temporal and normative referents like real self, extant self, ideal self, future self, desired self, possible self. Having disaggregated the totality of possible referents of the term *self,* we are led to create measures that reflect the disaggregated conceptualizations. Doing so, particular contents of self-conceptions are studied without essential reference to other contents (e.g., family-related self-concepts are examined without reference to work-related self-concepts), particular processes without reference to other processes (e.g., self-awareness without reference to self-presentation), particular temporal referents without regard to others (e.g., possible selves without reference to extant selves). This is done, as the illustrations implicitly note, within the same categories, and does not speak of similar neglect across categories.

This is hardly a satisfactory state of affairs, for a number of reasons that can be mentioned only briefly. One, already suggested, is that for at least some and for at least some of the time, there is consistency and stability of behavior across time and across situations; and this consistency and stability warrants as much attention and theoretical explanation as does inconsistency and variability. A conception of self that incorporates in a reasonable way both the idea of multiplicity of selves and the idea of a singular or unitary self could help solve the puzzle inherent in these opposing observations of social behavior.

Second, there is phenomenological validity to the sense of continuity of self, to the perception of self as the "same" over time and situations, just as there is phenomenological validity to the perception that one is a different person at various times and places. On the assumption, previously asserted, that self has causal force, both reflexive products must make a difference; the theoretical problem is to ascertain insofar as it is possible to do so the differential whens and wheres and conditions of each phenomenologically valid perception of self having its impact.

Third, persons finding themselves in situations of action act as "whole" persons, not as a congeries of separate selves. Persons can and do put themselves together. The social science problem is how to represent, conceptually and theoretically, that putting together.

Fourth, contemporary societies, while highly differentiated, are also more or less organized: The differentiated parts of society demonstrably relate to one another in systemic ways. Using the repeatedly enunciated principle that self reflects society, this implies that the self must also be more or less organized, and the multiple selves related to one another.

One other reason is not entirely irrelevant. The image of the human that is part of the contemporary literature — in extreme form, the chameleon changing colors in response to minor changes in environmental forces; the "other directed" conducting his or her life without principle; the manipulative operator presenting whatever self suits the immediate ends of social interaction — is something less than completely attractive. A view of the self, therefore of the person, that accords the human being more principle and dignity, should it prove useful theoretically, would not be an unwelcome bonus.

This discussion of why the conventional multiplicity of selves view should be challenged began by noting that the challenge did not extend to the claim that the view was in error and in need of replacement by its polar opposite. The preceding paragraphs were intended to suggest the shortcomings of either a multiplicity or a singular view of self, taken by itself. It is not sufficient, however, simply to observe that both views of self are required to accommodate the facts of human social behavior. What is problematic — and a considerable theoretical challenge — is how to incorporate both views of self into a common conceptual frame and a common theory of how the self works to affect interaction. In short, having — neces-

sarily and usefully — allowed Humpty Dumpty to fall and to break into if
not an infinity, then at least a very large number of separate parts, what is
needed is a reasonable way to put Humpty Dumpty together again if social
psychology is to have the conceptual means essential to account for both
behavioral constancy and variation, consistency and inconsistency, within
a single theory. Parsimony and theoretical elegance, that is, demand some
alternative to the resort to different theories to explain why some people
some of the time behave in ways that sometimes exhibit variability and
sometimes exhibit relative constancy. There is, then, good reason to
believe that a conceptualization of self that captures at the same time the
multiplicity of selves idea and the idea of self as singular and unitary can
best meet theoretical, methodological, and empirical issues in social
psychology.

Alternative Conceptualizations
of Self with Respect to the
Multiplicity Singularity Issue

Are there such conceptualizations available? There are. Any approach
that sees self as structured, as some kind of system that relates several (or
a great many) parts, accomplishes in some degree the twin charge of
recognizing the multiplicity of selves and the singularity of self. There is,
for example, the concept of self-schema in the manner of Hazel Markus
(1977). Markus views self-schema as generalizations of theories about
self derived from past experience in particular domains, thus a kind of
organization of self particulars. Her formulation is not entirely different
from that of Seymour Epstein (1980), although the latter proceeds on a
different level of abstraction. For Epstein, humans behave like scientists
who develop and test hypotheses,[1] except they do so at an unconscious
level. Doing so, they develop self-concepts that are in reality self-theories
in the form of hierarchical arrangements of major and minor postulates.
One's self-theory along with one's worldview make up one's theory of
reality or total conceptual scheme, which has three functions: to assimi-
late experience, to maintain a desirable balance of pleasure and pain, and
to optimize self-esteem. Again not entirely dissimilar is the attempt of
Seymour Rosenberg (e.g., in Gara and Rosenberg 1979) to view self in
terms of multiple identity elements in the form of personality traits organized hierarchically.

What these conceptualizations have in common, not surprisingly if one
is aware that all of the cited persons are psychologists, is that they serve
the needs of a cognitive psychology (and, especially in the case of
Epstein, of a clinical psychology as well), doing so quite reasonably. That
is, if one's essential questions have to do with the processing and distor-
tion of information, self qua organized theory presents a useful conceptualization, perhaps better with respect to the singularity aspect of self,

since the multiplicity of self tends to be lost as persons' theories of self move up the ladder of abstraction. These conceptualizations do not do as well by the standard of serving the needs of social psychology oriented to the explanation of interactive behavior, for the very good reason that they do not incorporate the social constraints affecting behavior as distinct from cognitive representations and affective response to self.

Insofar as sociologists have approached the apparent need to incorporate both the multiplicity of selves and singularity of self into their conceptualizations,[2] they have done so in a different fashion from the psychologists cited. In keeping with the context-setting discussion of personality from the standpoint of a sociologically oriented social psychology, multiplicity of selves tends to be translated into a set of identities linked to a diversity of social roles; and the singularity of self tends to be seen not in terms of a principle of generalization but rather in terms of an organization of those identity elements into a hierarchy defined by some in terms of importance, by others in terms of salience (a distinction that is elaborated below). In either case, the elements of self retain their distinctiveness even within the overall organization of self, and so retain their distinctive potential with respect to the direction of interactive behavior that seems to be lost when the unity or singularity of self is seen in terms of increasingly abstract levels of generalization.

As the foregoing suggests, the organizational principles of importance and of salience are different, although they have frequently been confused and/or used as though they were interchangeable (along with still other terms, e.g., prominence and centrality). Importance is the organizational principle invoked by McCall and Simmons (1966), using the language of a prominence hierarchy that defines for them the person's preferential ordering of elements within an ideal self. This principle is invoked by a variety of others—such as Ralph Turner (1978) and Morris Rosenberg (1979)—in one way or another. Hoelter (1985a, 1985b) combines that principle with another based on the commonality of semantic meaning among role identities and behavioral possibilities, drawing heavily on suggestions offered by Burke and Reitzes (1981). Commonality of meaning has been introduced rudimentarily into identity theory as well (e.g., Stryker 1986), although identity theory has thus far placed much greater emphasis on salience as the way in which a multiplicity of identities (internalized role designations) constituting the self are organized and in that sense become "singular." The concept of identity salience implies that negatively evaluated identities may serve to motivate and to organize interactive behaviors in the same general manner as positively evaluated identities; this is the major respect in which the concept of salience as it appears in identity theory differs from the concept of importance, or prominence, or centrality, in other theoretical perspectives. A more precise definition of salience will be offered shortly, and the organizational principle involved in the idea of commonality of meaning will importantly enter the subsequent discussion as well.

It is time to turn directly to identity theory, and to how its attack on the issue of the multiplicity versus the singularity of self stands at present.

Identity Theory: Its Current State

Language used elsewhere (Stryker 1986) will be used to describe identity theory and the theoretical context from which it developed, to sketch its core ideas and its key concepts, and so on. The central proposition of identity theory argues that commitment affects identity salience, which in turn affects role performance. Identity theory emerges from a more general structural symbolic interactionist framework (Stryker 1980), which makes the further argument that the social psychological processes covered by that central identity theory proposition take place in and are critically affected by larger social structural arrangements (for example, class structure, community organization) that are assumed to operate essentially through commitment. Consequently, an expanded version of the central proposition of identity theory is that "large-scale" social structures affect commitment affects identity salience affects role performance.

This formulation represents a restatement of the traditional symbolic interactionist framework, which asserts that self is the product of society and the prime determinant of social behavior, a restatement that is intended to permit reasonably rigorous empirical test. It conceptualizes self as made up of identities, or internalized role designations. It specifies that the important aspect of society in relation to self is the interactional networks in which persons are embedded, which networks are themselves premised on the identities of the persons who constitute them. It further specifies that the important dimension of self in relation to social behavior is the way in which individual identities constituting the self are organized hierarchically by the probability of their invocation in or across social situations.

Thus identity theory, beginning with the symbolic interactionist dictum that self is an emergent from society and that self organizes social behavior, conceptualizes self as a structure of identities organized in a hierarchy of salience. It defines identities as internalized sets of role expectations, with the person having as many identities as she or he plays roles in distinct sets of social relationships. The salience hierarchy is conceived as an ordering of these identities by their differentiated probabilities of coming into play within or across different situations. Recognizing that persons enter many more or less distinct sets of social relationships, and defining commitment as the costs to the person in the form of relationships forgone should she or he no longer have a given identity and play a role based on that identity in a social network, the theory predicts that the distribution of identities in the salience hierarchy will reflect the varying levels of commitment to the roles underlying the identities. Commitments, in turn, are seen to depend importantly on the "larger" structure of society, social organizational principles (for example, age, class, sex) that either facilitate or impede the entry of persons into and the exits of persons from social relationships. To phrase the matter alternatively, the larger institutional, organizational, and stratification features of society enter the theory by influencing the formation, maintenance, and dissolution of social networks. Finally, the theory predicts that choices among behaviors reflecting alternative roles, when such choice is realistically possible, will reflect the differential location in the identity salience hierarchy of identities related to those alternatives.

To make matters explicit, this conceptualization incorporates the idea of a multiplicity of selves through the postulate that self comprises as many identities as positions occupied and roles played by the person in organized networks of social relationships. It incorporates the idea of the singularity of self via the postulate that these identities are organized in a salience hierarchy.

Identity Theory: Further Development

The wisdom of devoting time and energy to the further development of a theory depends on a prior judgment that the theory has some demonstrable merit. Identity theory has been subject to some, not extensive, empirical examination (see, for example, Stryker and Serpe 1982; Serpe 1984, 1987; Serpe and Stryker, 1987; Hoelter 1983, 1985a; Callero 1985). A conclusion warranted by such research as has now been completed is that the theory appears to have value as an explanation of various kinds of role-related choices people make; another warranted conclusion is that its performance is open to improvement. Neither conclusion can be demonstrated adequately here, although particular findings of research will be alluded to along the way. However, there is one fundamental empirical issue that relates to the first conclusion, and there is one matter of theoretical strategy that relates to the second conclusion, that deserve brief attention before proceeding.

A necessary first consideration in evaluating identity theory is the demonstration that there is reasonable stability over time in the salience ordering of identities. If there were no such stability, it would make little sense to believe that identity salience has anything to say about either over-time or over-situation consistency in behavior. On the other hand, the theory asserts the dependence of identity salience on commitments, the latter understood as the product(s) of interpersonal relationships: if the person's social relationships remain stable, the structure of identity salience should remain reasonably stable.[3] However, if the person's social relationships change, change in that structure should follow.

The requisite stability of as well as the requisite change in the structure of identity salience is demonstrated by Serpe (1984, 1987; see also Serpe

and Stryker, 1987) in research focusing on various roles of students
leaving home to attend a residential college and tracing over a roughly
three-month period the structure of identity salience, the impact of prior
changes in commitments on that structure, as well as the impact of
changes in identity salience on subsequent commitments. Important for
the judgment that, as well as evidencing the essential soundness of identity theory, this body of evidence indicates the need for further theoretical
development are the findings that stability over time is variable for
varying identities, and that the strength of the reciprocal relations between
commitment and identity salience is also variable for varying identities.

This evaluation of empirical evidence relating to identity theory links
to a matter of theoretical strategy. Identity theory has developed on
"minimalist" principles. That is, the theoretical strategy followed in its
initial development (see Stryker 1980) was to attempt to explain as much
as possible with as few concepts as possible,[4] recognizing that the strategy
entailed a variety of risks and looking to further development of concepts
and theory as the need for that development and, ideally, the direction as
well became apparent through research product.

Prefigured in the preceding paragraphs are arenas of promise for the
further development of identity theory. One concerns specification of the
ways in which the structure of multiple identities interacts with central
elements in the structure of situations to affect interactional processes and
outcomes. A second, only obliquely hinted at in the last set of paragraphs
but suggested in another context earlier in the chapter, has to do with the
potential of community of meaning as a way of understanding how a
variety of ostensibly separate identities may join in a more or less unified
structure.

This last promising arena for further development of identity theory
issues out of the symbolic interactionist underpinnings of the theory and
receives emphasis through findings from a survey[5] that permitted examination of the relationships among commitment, identity salience, and
role performances (in the form of time spent in various roles as well as
time that would be spent in these roles were persons able to allocate their
time freely). The sample was a general community sample of males and
females above age 21, selected to maximize the likelihood that subjects
played work, religious, spousal, and parental roles. Data from this research were used to try to model the ordered structure of multiple identities implied by the concept of identity salience. An analysis using a
measure of identity salience based on a factor analysis of the rank-ordered
responses of subjects to questions about which of the identities associated
with the four noted roles they would introduce into various situations
proved interesting but problematic, given the ipsative nature of the way
the salience of the separate identities was measured and given the difficulty of interpreting the conceptual meaning of the resulting numbers. Consequently, a LISREL analysis was undertaken in which age and income
were the exogenous variables (representing large-scale social structure),
commitments to each of the indicated roles were the endogenous vari-

ables, and the salience of the identities related to these roles the dependent variables. The exogenous variables were allowed to affect each of the commitment variables, each of the commitment variables was allowed to affect directly only its corresponding salience variable (e.g., parental commitment was modeled as directly affecting only parental salience), and the error terms of the salience variables were allowed to correlate with one another. Reciprocal effects among the commitment variables were allowed.

The analysis indicates that commitment to each of the four roles significantly affects its respective salience term, with the coefficients between work commitment and salience for men being relatively small in comparison with the other coefficients for men and in comparison with the coefficient between work commitment and salience for women. Parental commitment affects commitment to spouse and religious commitment, but not the other way around, and through these indirectly affects spousal salience and religious salience. In brief, there appears to be a complex of related commitments affecting the structuring of salience of identities constituting the self, in the present case a complex that is tied to family life. Work appears to be largely outside that complex, for both males and females. Further, coefficients linking commitment to salience are especially strong for religion, especially weak for work, stronger for working women than for working men, and stronger for males qua parents than for females. Models in which commitment and salience were linked to time spent in role as well as time one would choose to spend in role could that time be freely allocated indicate that the latter is "better" explained (in the sense of variance accounted for) by the theory than is the former.

Having anticipated possible lines of further development of identity theory, and having at least suggested in broad terms the character of empirical findings to which such development need be responsive, a reminder of the underlying question toward which the conceptual issue of singularity versus multiplicity of self points will serve to orient the remaining discussion. In the present context, the fundamental question becomes, How can identity theory be developed so as to throw greater light on both consistency and variability of social behavior across time and across situations?

As noted, the community-based research outlined above suggests one important line of possible development. In particular, consider now the finding that a complex of role commitments operates to organize the salience level of a given identity (in the case at hand, parental, religious, and spousal commitments join to enhance the salience of family-related identities).

Returning first to ideas underlying the early formulation of identity theory, central to its parent symbolic interactionism and thus to identity theory itself is the importance of socially derived meanings. If various identities carry differential implications for organizing behavior, it must be because the meanings that define those identities differ; this assertion merely reiterates a significant part of the rationale for visualizing self as made up of multiple identities. Utilizing the same logic in considering the potential utility of a global, unitary, or singular concept of self — at the same time retaining the multiple identities vision — it can be argued that such utility lies in the possibility that among the multiple identities that constitute the self, there is a subset that shares considerable overlap in meaning. With overlap in meaning, each of the individual identities in the set in effect reinforces the consequences of the others, both in the sense of enhancing the salience of the related identities and in the sense of enhancing the tendencies of the person to enact the behavioral implications of each of the related identities.

The cited findings in the community survey make sense on the assumption that in this largely blue- and white-collar married sample, most of whom have children, religious roles, spousal roles, and parental roles share a common core of family-based meanings that reflect family life, and that work is outside that core. With respect to this finding, the character of this sample must be kept in mind: It is typically among professionals that work suffuses a variety of aspects of life, and it typically has a more isolated and detached meaning among the kinds of persons who make up the sample in this research. Commonality of meaning, it seems more than reasonable to argue, can provide the basis for consistency in behavior across situations by enlarging the number of situations in which one or another of the identities having common meaning can be invoked.

An essentially similar idea is contained in the concept of master status as this concept has been introduced into identity theory (Stryker 1986). The master status concept argues that particular roles and, by extension, particular identities suffuse others; that, for example, the woman for whom "woman" is indeed a master status plays her other roles — spouse, professional, whatever — in ways that reflect the meaning contained in the master status. Alternatively put, the meaning contained in a master status serves to define a larger series of roles (and, again by extension, identities). Thus behavior carried out in each of the individual members of the larger series of roles represents a performance in terms of the master status and derives consistency from that "fact."

However expressed, it is logically possible even if empirically unlikely (at least in a society such as our own at the present time) that all identities carry the same behavioral implications — that is, that multiple identities operate as though only a single identity existed to order the full range of the person's behavior. At the other extreme, it is again logically possible even if empirically unlikely (perhaps being approximated only in cases of extreme pathology) that no pair of a person's identities carry the same behavioral implications. With respect to the vast arena between the two logical extremes, there is room for both the multiplicity and singularity of selves to have their effects.

The attempt to model a single structure of identity salience in the community study suggests how the research possibilities foreshadowed in this discussion might be attacked in measurement terms. Suppose that instead of attempting to factor analyze salience scores of various identities, one attempted to factor analyze the meaning structures of those identities, defined perhaps in terms of a semantic differential instrumentation, or perhaps in terms of more direct measures of what various identities implied by way of behaviors serving to exemplify them (What does it mean to be a doctor — what do such persons do, think, say, and so on? What does it mean to behave like a student? Like an adolescent? Like a son?).[6] The results of such an analysis could serve to define a set of behavioral elements related to one another that were unique to a particular role/identity. It could also serve to define a set of identities that load together on a common factor by virtue of sharing a common meaning. Relating the two configurations to the concern of identity theory for providing theoretically based explanations of behavioral consistency and variation across time and situations, persons characterized by an identity structure whose individual identities have meanings bearing little relationship to one other should, other things equal, exhibit inconsistency over time and situation; persons with an identity structure whose individual identities overlap considerably in meaning with one another should, other things equal, exhibit considerable behavioral constancy.

This matter of possible commonality of meanings among identities bears more than an analogical similarity to a concept invoked in earlier identity theory discussions of commitment. The concept is that of "structural overlap" (Stryker 1980, p. 61), and the point of the concept was to suggest that if one related to the same set or heavily overlapping sets of persons in a number of different roles, one's commitment to the roles involved would be reinforced. This earlier concern of identity theory can now be linked to the present concern through the observation that structural overlap as a characteristic of networks of social relationships will contribute significantly to the development of common meanings attached to the set of roles and identities involved, by the principle that Mead enunciated so well, namely, the emergence of common meanings in and through social interaction. In brief, it can reasonably be hypothesized that the greater the structural overlap exhibited in persons' distinct sets of role relationships, the greater the commonality of meaning among the identities attached to the roles, the more likely consistency in behavior over time and over situations. Conversely, the less structural overlap, the less commonality of meaning among identities, the less likely such consistency.

The other line of possible further development can be broached through noting various implications of the concept of identity salience. The concept implies that elements in a situation will cue role performances of highly salient identities more often and more rapidly than they will cue performances reflecting identities of low salience, that salience will affect the likelihood of given situations being seen as opportunities to introduce identities, and so on. What these implications of the concept of identity salience assert in general is that identities will interact with the structure of situations in the process by which role performances are introduced.

To this point, identity theory has recognized this principle only through specifying structural conditions permitting behavioral choice as a scope condition of the theory.[7] While acceptable tactically, and while understandable as reflecting a decision to focus initially on self rather than situation, clearly any formulation pretending to account for consistency and/or variability in role performances must incorporate situational variables that enter into organizing those performances.

One approach to the interplay of identity and situation is again to look to commonality of meaning, this time between identity and situation rather than among identities. Situations, that is, can themselves be characterized as having different meanings and as differentially calling for various behaviors; consider the differences in behavior appropriate to two poker games, one among buddies at the home of one of them, the other in a Las Vegas casino. It is appropriate for some identities to be expressed behaviorally in some situations and not in others; in the example at hand, "friend" as an identity corresponds with the meaning of one situation and not the other. Clearly, when the meanings of salient identities are in accord with the meanings attached to situations, greater consistency in behavior can be expected.[8] The obverse holds for situations whose meanings are themselves inconsistent with highly salient identities, or with one another.

Thus far, the discussion of situations has proceeded only with reference to their meanings as carried in the symbolic systems of particular actors entering them. Situations, however, have an "objective" structure, in part given by the meanings attached to them by the larger set of participants in them, in part by the social and cultural contexts, representing the heritage from prior generations of actors, in which they arise. This "objective" structure is operative with respect to the behavioral possibilities they contain, and is at least partially and often largely independent of the definitions brought to them by any given actor. What is being asserted is the sociological truism that, for example, social class is a reality that "exists" whether or not the participants in any given encounter define the situation in class terms. What is being asserted is also an implication of earlier assertions regarding the role of social structure in constraining who it is who come together, under what circumstances, for what purposes, and with what resources. In brief, "objective" characteristics of situations as well as the meaning ascribed to them by participants can be expected to interact with identities in producing behavior.

Suggesting this, however, leaves open the question, Just what situational variables are important theoretically from the standpoint of the consistency/variability issue? Sociology, that is, has not been particularly successful in cataloging "essential" dimensions of situations, and indeed can fairly be said to have not really moved much beyond the science-defeating banality of asserting that all situations differ from one another.[9] A general, "all-purpose" catalog may not be possible, and, even if possible, is not likely to prove useful. What is required is a specification of those dimensions of situations that are particularly or even peculiarly relevant with respect to the issue at hand.

Taking as a point of departure various research findings cited above suggests how this requirement might be met. That commitment and identity salience more accurately predicted preferred distribution of time allocated to roles than actual distribution seems to bespeak the existence of "real" constraints with respect to the latter: Most of these employed persons who became part of the general community sample are likely to work 40 hours a week, no more and no less, as a matter of job requirement rather than desire, with little if any option to enlarge or reduce time devoted to work. The same "fact" would appear to underlie the relative inability of identity theory to account for time spent working compared to time devoted to spouse, to children, or to religion. Women are culturally less constrained to work than are men,[10] that is, for more women than men work is an option rather than a requirement, and the identity theory variables of commitment and identity salience more adequately predict the time women spend working than the time men spend working.

All of these findings point to constraints that may exist within situations with respect to the behavioral expression of given identities. In some instances, opportunities for such behavioral expressions literally may not exist or may be severely restricted; one cannot be a swimmer in the absence of a pool or other suitable body of water. In other instances, cultural or institutional arrangements may raise the costs of exercising options that may in some degree be present. In still others, power differentials among actors within the situation can have the same impact. And in yet others, attachments among persons may be such that to choose one option threatens to disrupt some of the relationships involved.[11]

What, in general terms, is being suggested with respect to the dimensions of situations of particular relevance to the issue of consistency/variability in behavior is that structures of opportunities and costs contained in situations must be considered when one theorizes about how the structure of identities may affect role behavior over time or across situations. Such a consideration must involve estimates of power arrangements, interpersonal conflicts, institutional forces, and cultural norms, as these may be represented in situations providing the contexts in which consistency or lack thereof in role behaviors is examined. Interestingly, such a consideration points precisely to the kinds of variables a symbolic interactionist perspective has been said to neglect (see, e.g., Gouldner 1970; Huber 1973).

Obviously, situations must contain the objective conditions that would permit any expression at all of some identity. Apart from that extreme, it is reasonable to believe that the higher the salience of an identity, the greater the probability of a behavioral expression of that identity in the face of any given level of probable costs entailed in acting out that identity.

Conversely, situations containing high levels of constraints on the behavioral expression of an identity will require higher levels of identity salience for appropriate behavioral expressions to occur. Challenges to the constraints in such situations can surely occur, but just as surely will occur only comparatively rarely.

Conclusion

The burden of the argument offered in this chapter is that a conceptualization of self that combines in a theoretically coherent way both the multiplicity of selves and the singularity of self emphases that have appeared in the literature on the self can better serve the purposes of social psychological explanation than can either alone. This implies that the current heavy reliance of treatments of self in the contemporary literature on only the multiplicity of selves is inadequate. Insofar as the theoretical interest is in the explanation of two equally apparent facts of human behavior — that for some persons some of the time their behavior is consistent across time and across situation, while for some persons some of the time their behavior exhibits considerable inconsistency across either time or situation — a conceptualization of self that incorporates both multiplicity and singularity seems especially likely to prove useful.

Identity theory, in its earliest formulation, offered a way of accomplishing the necessary conceptualization through its vision of self as a structure of differentiated identities organized in a hierarchy of salience. It has become clear, however, that identity theory in its simplest form, linking commitment to identity salience to role performances, requires further development if it is to meet its potential as a social psychological theory, both in general and as an explanation of behavioral consistency and/or variability.

Other attempts at that development have sought to strengthen the theory's sociological underpinnings, in particular the ways in which large-scale social structure enters the social psychological processes of more immediate concern to the theory (Stryker 1980; Stryker and Statham 1985), and to introduce affect more systematically into what has been and continues to be foremost a cognitive theory (Stryker 1986). The present effort has looked to the linkages among identities in the form of common meaning; it has also looked to the ways in which the elements of situations may interact with identities to organize role behaviors. With regard to the latter, both the objective character of situations and the "fit" of the meanings attached to situations by participants in them and the identities carried into those situations by participants seem to be implicated in the processes producing over time or over situational consistency or variation in role behavior. Recognizing the ways in which identities, in particular identity salience, and the constraining/facilitating structure of situations interact could be fruitful for dealing with the particular problem with which this chapter has been concerned: consistency or variability in role performances. It may also prove useful for understanding the larger issue of social order and social change that has traditionally been the central problem of sociological theory.

Notes

1. I do not know whether Epstein draws on Mead (1934) for this view of humans as scientists developing and testing hypotheses, but Mead's theories of the relation of mind, self, and society build on this view.

2. I do not mean to imply that sociologists have generally been self-conscious in arguing the need for a conceptualization of self that incorporates both multiplicity and singularity. As far as I know, they have not; that is, I know of no discussion in the literature paralleling the one offered here.

3. This is not entirely so; some change in salience of various identities can be expected as a consequence of life-course processes that may not entail preceding changes in interpersonal relationships. See Wells and Stryker (1986).

4. This strategy appears to be counter to the current mood of the social sciences, which seem to proceed increasingly on the assumption that models incorporating "all possible" relevant variables be built and analyzed.

5. The survey, directed by the author, was conducted in 1979 under the auspices of the Indianapolis Area Project, Department of Sociology, Indiana University, Bloomington. The analyses reported here have not been published previously. The findings also reinforce the belief expressed above that the first two arenas for possible further development of identity theory are worth exploring.

6. Ideally, one would want to tap behaviors directly. Given the variability of behaviors potentially attached to a large set of roles, practical requirements alone may dictate a strategy of seeking a small set of "meaning" dimensions along which any behaviors could be arrayed. The semantic differential system recommends itself, whether it be in terms of the evaluation, potency, activity triumvirate of dimensions or some expanded set of dimensions, not least because of the prodigious work of Heise (1979) in building "dictionaries" of semantic differential ratings of role labels as well as behaviors. The work of Burke and his colleagues (Burke and Tully 1977; Burke and Reitzes 1980; Burke and Mutran 1979) in mapping the meaning of identities onto a semantic space defined by the EPA dimensions suggests how measurement of commonality of meanings could proceed.

7. But see Serpe (1984, 1987) for beginnings of change in this respect.

8. Similarly, correspondence of meaning and situations themselves elevates the likelihood that an actor entering those situations will behave consistently.

9. My judgment is that things have not changed in this respect in the 20-plus years since I first had occasion to offer a similar observation (see Stryker 1968).

10. This does not deny that particular women might well be under far greater constraint to work (in paid employment) than some or all men; it asserts only that it is culturally more acceptable for women in general not to undertake paid employment than it is for men in general.

11. Situations may facilitate as well as constrain the behavioral expression of particular identities. In general, what is said of constraints could be said, with reverse sign, of facilitators.

References

Allport, Gordon W. 1937. *Personality: A Psychological Interpretation.* New York: Holt.

Burke, Peter J. and Elizabeth Mutran. 1979. "Feeling 'Useless': A Common Component of Young and Old Adults' Identities." *Journal of Research on Aging* 1:187-211.

Burke, Peter J. and Donald Reitzes. 1980. "College Student Identity: Measurement and Implications." *Pacific Sociological Review* 23:46-66.

— — —. 1981. "The Link Between Identity and Role Performance." *Social Psychology Quarterly* 44:83-92.

Burke, Peter J. and July Tully. 1977. "The Measurement of Role-Identity." *Social Forces* 55:881-97.

Callero, Peter L. 1985. "Role-Identity Salience." *Social Psychology Quarterly* 48:203-14.

Cooley, Charles H. 1902. *Human Nature and Social Order*. New York: Scribner's.

Epstein, Seymour. 1980. "The Self-Concept: A Review and the Proposal of an Integrated Theory of Personality." In *Personality: Basic Aspects and Current Research*, edited by E. Staub. Englewood Cliffs, NJ: Prentice-Hall.

Fromm, Erich. 1947. *Man for Himself*. New York: Rinehart.

Gara, Michael A. and Seymour Rosenberg. 1979. "The Identification of Persons as Supersets and Subsets in Free-Response Personality Descriptions." *Journal of Personality and Social Psychology* 17:2161-70.

Gergen, Kenneth J. 1970. *The Concept of Self*. New York: Holt, Rinehart & Winston.

Goffman, Erving. 1956. *The Presentation of Self in Everyday Life*. Edinburgh: University of Edinburgh.

Gordon, Chad and Kenneth J. Gergen. 1968. *The Self in Social Interaction*. New York: John Wiley.

Gouldner, Alvin W. 1970. *The Coming Crisis in Western Sociology*. New York: Basic Books.

Heise, David. 1979. *Understanding Events: Affect and the Construction of Social Action*. New York: Cambridge University Press.

Hoelter, Jon W. 1983. "The Effects of Role-Evaluation and Commitment on Identity Salience." *Social Psychology Quarterly* 46:140-47.

— — —. 1985a. "The Structure of Self-Conception: Conceptualization and Measurement." *Journal of Personality and Social Psychology* 49:1392-1407.

— — —. 1985b. "A Structural Theory of Personal Consistency." *Social Psychology Quarterly* 48:118-29.

Huber, Joan. 1973. "Symbolic Interaction as a Pragmatic Perspective: The Bias of Emergent Theory." *American Sociological Review* 38:278-84.

James, William. 1890. *Principles of Psychology*, Vol. 2. New York: Holt.

Lecky, P. 1945. *Self Consistency: A Theory of Personality*. New York: Island.

Markus, Hazel. 1977. "Self-Schemes and Processing Information about the Self." *Journal of Personality and Social Psychology* 35:63-78.

McCall, George J. and J. T. Simmons. 1966. *Identities and Interaction*. New York: Free Press.

Mead, George H. 1934. *Mind, Self and Society*. Chicago: University of Chicago Press.

Parsons, Talcott. 1951. *The Social System*. Glencoe, IL: Free Press.

Reisman, David, Nathan Glazer, and Raoul Denney. 1950. *The Lonely Crowd*. New Haven, CT: Yale University Press.

Rogers, Carl R. 1951. *Client-Centered Therapy: Its Current Practice, Implications, and Theory*. Boston: Houghton Mifflin.

Rosenberg, Morris. 1979. *Conceiving the Self*. New York: Basic Books.

Schlenker, Barry R. 1980. *Impression Management: The Self-Concept, Social Identity and Interpersonal Relations*. Monterey, CA: Brooks/Cole.

Serpe, Richard T. 1984. "Identity Salience and Commitment: Measurement and Longitudinal Analysis." Unpublished Ph.D. dissertation, Indiana University.

— — —. 1987. "Stability and Change in Self: A Structural Symbolic Interactionism Explanation." *Social Psychology Quarterly* 50:44-55.

Serpe, Richard T. and Sheldon Stryker. 1987. "The Construction of Self and the Reconstruction of Social Relationships." In *Advances in Group Processes*, edited by Edward J. Lawler and Barry Markovsky. Greenwich, CT: JAI.

Stryker, Sheldon. 1956. "Relationships of Married Offspring and Parent: A Test of Mead's Theory." *American Journal of Sociology* 63:308-19.

— — —. 1968. "Identity Salience and Role Performance: The Relevance of Symbolic Interaction Theory for Family Research." *Journal of Marriage and the Family* 30:558-64.

— — —. 1980. *Symbolic Interactionism: A Social Structural Version.* Menlo Park, CA: Benjamin/Cummings.

— — —. 1986. "Identity Theory: Developments and Extensions." In *Self and Identity: Psychosocial Perspectives,* edited by Terry Honess and Krysia Yardley. London: John Wiley.

Stryker, Sheldon and Richard T. Serpe. 1982. "Commitment, Identity Salience, and Role Behavior." In *Personality, Roles and Social Behavior,* edited by William Ickes and Eric Knowles. New York: Springer-Verlag.

Stryker, Sheldon and Anne Statham. 1985. "Symbolic Interaction and Role Theory." In *Handbook of Social Psychology,* 3rd ed., edited by Gardner Lindzey and Elliot Aronson. New York: Random House.

Turner, Ralph H. 1978. "The Role and the Person." *American Journal of Sociology* 84:1-23.

Wells, L. Edward and Sheldon Stryker. 1986. "Stability and Change in Self over the Life Course." In *Life Span Development and Behavior,* edited by David L. Featherman and Richard M. Lerner. New York: Academic Press.

3

Status Characteristics, Standards, and Attributions

MARTHA FOSCHI

Over the last two decades, a large number of studies have investigated gender differences in the attribution of success and failure. Stemming from attribution theory (for reviews and formulations, see Kelley and Michela 1980; Harvey and Weary 1984; Olson and Ross 1985), the hypotheses of central interest have focused on the assignment of a given outcome to different causes, depending on the sex of the performer.[1] Thus, for example, several studies have found that success by a man tends to be seen as due to ability, whereas the same performance by a woman tends to be attributed to good luck. The opposite pattern of attributions has been found in the case of failure.

More recently, various studies have reported a similar asymmetry in attributions regarding ethnicity, race, and social class. This, in turn, has led several attribution theorists to propose hypotheses reformulated in more general terms to refer to social categories (Crittenden 1983; Deschamps 1983; Deaux 1984).

The hypotheses may also be made more general in another respect. Although attribution work has focused on the various causal factors (such as ability, luck, effort, and task difficulty) assigned to the performances, it is worth noting that the hypotheses about success and failure have the following in common: Outcomes by certain performers (e.g., the success of men and the failure of women) are seen as an ability (or lack of ability) issue, whereas other performances (e.g., the success of women and the failure of men) are attributed to nonability factors. Since the result of such attributions is the maintenance of the status quo when competence is valued and social category membership is used to infer competence, the area is of central importance to the understanding of how stereotypes and prejudices persist.

Several authors have attempted to summarize and evaluate the literature on social categories, outcomes, and attributions. Since most of the empirical work has been on gender differences, reviews have concentrated in this area (see, for example, Sohn 1982; Foschi and Plecash 1983; Hansen and O'Leary 1985; Whitley et al. 1986; for a review of studies on ethnicity and race, see Takagi 1988). For the most part, the support found in these reviews has been moderate rather than strong. However, it should be noted that many of the studies do not do full justice to the attribution ideas. As a result, the quality of the research included in these assessments varies widely, both in terms of the designs used and the extent to which relevant variables have been incorporated. Such a variety of interpretations of the attribution ideas suggests that the hypotheses need considerable reformulation.

Some areas of status characteristic theory are concerned with a similar issue as these attribution studies, namely, the relative effects of performance and social category information on assignment of task ability. Status characteristic theory is part of expectation states theory, the research program on status-organizing processes in small, task-oriented groups (for formulation and reviews, see Berger et al. 1977, 1980, 1985). The theory has been extensively tested, and results show strong empirical support (for assessments, see Dion 1985; Wiley 1986).

Status characteristic theory investigates how status differences determine performance expectations and how these, in turn, affect the power and prestige order of the group (defined as the unequal distribution of opportunities to perform, evaluation of outputs, and influence rates among group members). "Status characteristics," or valued attributes implying competence, are defined as varying from specific to diffuse, depending on the range of their applicability. Thus, for example, mechanical ability is relatively specific, whereas sex and ethnicity are usually diffuse, or perceived as relevant to a large number of different task situations. The concepts of "diffuse status characteristic" and "social category" as utilized in attribution theory are therefore closely related notions.

Status characteristic and attribution theories share an interest in situations in which two types of information are available: social category membership of the performer, and performance outcome. The main objective of this chapter is to present a theory elaborating status characteristic theory to include some of the attribution ideas. This is done through the concept of "standards," or rules for the inference of ability and lack of ability. Standards are introduced as an intervening variable, or the mechanism regulating whether or not a performance is attributed to ability (or to lack of ability). Standards, in turn, are seen as a function of diffuse status characteristics. For example, it is proposed that when two successful performers differ along one such characteristic (e.g., one person is male and the other female, or one has a college degree and the other does not), a double standard is applied to their performances: The success of the low-status person is assessed through a stricter standard than the success of the high-status person, and therefore the performance by the former has a smaller chance of being attributed to ability. The chapter also includes a section with suggestions for extensions of the proposed theory.

The Theory

This theory elaborates on status characteristic theory by incorporating ideas from other branches of the expectation states program, in particular work on standards, on the relationship between evaluations and expectation states, and on source of expectations. Only those theoretical elements that are necessary for the argument are presented here. For a more detailed account and a formal statement of status characteristic theory, see Berger et al. (1977). For work on standards, see Foschi and Foschi (1979), Foschi et al. (1985), and Foschi and Foddy (1988). Work on source of expectations is presented in Savage and Webster (1971), Webster and Sobieszek (1974), and Foddy (1988); for research on evaluations and expectation states, see Berger et al. (1969), Moore (1969), and Foschi (1971). A recent discussion of the various branches of the expectation states program and more complete references may be found in Berger et al. (1985).

The present theory is formulated from the point of view of a person p (self), who performs a task with one other person o (other), and forms expectations about the two of them. Let us first introduce two basic definitions from status characteristic theory.

- *Definition 1:* A characteristic C is a *specific status characteristic* if and only if

    (1) the states of C are differentially evaluated and
    (2) to each state x of C there corresponds a distinct performance expectation state having the same evaluation as the state C(x), and being relevant to a specified task outcome state T(x).

For example, the ability to play chess is a specific status characteristic if p considers it better to be a good chess player than to be a poor one. Further, if the task at hand is a chess game, p will hold expectations for success at the task for the superior chess player and expectations for failure for the other.

The extent to which ability is required for T may vary, but nevertheless in all cases ability is assumed to be a major component of C. That is, success at the task does not depend exclusively on nonability factors such as chance or effort. Thus, although such factors may play a part in the above example, chess-playing ability is of crucial importance to winning a chess game.

- *Definition 2:* A characteristic D is a *diffuse status characteristic* if and only if

    (1) the states of D are differentially evaluated,
    (2) to each state x of D there corresponds a distinct set of specific status characteristics associated with D(x), and
    (3) to each state x of D there corresponds a distinct *general* expectation state Γ (x) having the same evaluation as the state D(x).

For example, sex is a diffuse status characteristic for p if it is more highly valued to be male than to be female, if p assumes males to be more mechanical, or better at chess, or more logical, than females, and if p assumes males to be more intellectually competent *overall* than females.

States of specific and diffuse status characteristics are represented by a symbol for the characteristic, followed by an algebraic sign within parentheses. Thus C(+) and D(+) represent, respectively, the positively evaluated state of a specific and a diffuse status characteristic. Outcome states are similarly indicated, with T(+) used for *anticipated* success and T(–) for *anticipated* failure, and T*(+) for *actual* success and T*(–) for *actual* failure.

Let us next assume a *task situation* S having the following properties at the beginning of the interaction, or time t_1:

(a) There are two performers, p and o.
(b) There is a single characteristic C required for task performance.
(c) p and o *differ* with respect to a single D.
(d) p treats D as a diffuse status characteristic, and C as a specific status characteristic neither explicitly associated with D nor explicitly dissociated from it. No other information about the two performers' states of C is available to p.
(e) p is motivated to form correct expectations regarding p's and o's states of C.
(f) There are no previously set and agreed-upon standards for the inference of C(+) from T*(+), or of C(–) from T*(–).

Status characteristic theory specifies that in such a situation states of D will become first salient and then relevant to similarly evaluated states of C and T. Relevance links will be established through the general expectation states Γ associated with states of D, a process known as "burden of proof" (see Berger et al. 1977, pp. 106-13, for a detailed discussion). For example, if sex is the diffuse status characteristic and C is a specific but sex-neutral status characteristic, D will become relevant to C through such a process. Thus:

• *Proposition 1:* In task situation S at t_1, p will assign states of C and T to p and o in a manner consistent with their states of D.

If, for example, p possesses D(+) and o possesses D(–),[2] this assignment may be represented in graphic form as shown in Figure 3.1.[3]

p   – – – – D(+) – – – – Γ(+) – – – – C(+) – – – – T(+)

o   – – – – D(–) – – – – Γ(–) – – – – C(–) – – – – T(–)

Figure 3.1. Example of Situation S at t_1 (from Proposition 1)

Proposition 1 specifies p's expectations regarding the likely outcome for each person in a task *to be* performed. Given that there are no standards for the inference of either ability or lack of ability, it is proposed that differences along the diffuse status characteristic will also result in p activating standards with which to assess performances once they occur. Before such a relationship is stated, however, a few ideas regarding standards are introduced and discussed below (for a more complete presentation of the definitions, the reader is referred to Foschi and Foddy 1988).

- *Definition 3:* A *standard for ability* SA is a rule specifying requirements for the inference of $C(+)$ from one or more successful task outcomes $T^*(+)$.

Such requirements (or evidence of competence) may be stated along several dimensions. They may involve, for example, the degree of difficulty of the task to be performed, the degree of success in terms of percentage of the task to be completed correctly, or the number of times that the task has to be repeated successfully. The question of how much ability is to be inferred (e.g., whether an outstanding or a moderate level) is of course another factor to be considered. For simplicity, the level of ability inherent in state $C(+)$ is assumed to have been defined beforehand, and to be kept constant by p throughout the interaction with o.

Notice also that the definition of an outcome as a success is not necessarily equivalent to the standard used to infer ability from it. For example, a successful outcome could be defined as *either* at least 60% *or* at least 75% of the task correctly completed. Let us assume that the latter has been agreed upon as the definition of $T^*(+)$. Such an outcome, in turn, may or may not meet the standard for ability. The standard could be a performance at least 75% correct (i.e., the same as the definition of success), but it could also be a performance at least 80% correct, or a score of at least 80% in a specified number of repeated performances.[4] These three standards vary in how demanding their requirements are. Thus:

- *Definition 4:* Let us assume that two persons, p_1 and p_2, differ in their *standards for ability*, and that p_1's standard includes more demanding requirements than p_2's. If the two persons use their respective standards to infer the same level of ability $C(+)$, then p_1's standard is said to be *strict* (SA[s]) and p_2's *lenient* (SA[l]).

The next two definitions are mirror images of Definitions 3 and 4.

- *Definition 5:* A *standard for lack of ability* $\overline{SA}$ is a rule specifying requirements for the inference of $C(-)$ from one or more unsuccessful task outcomes $T^*(-)$.

Requirements for lack of ability (or evidence of incompetence) are described as "more or less forgiving." Thus:

- *Definition 6:* Let us assume that two persons, p_1 and p_2, differ in their *standards for lack of ability*, and that p_1's standard includes more forgiving requirements than p_2's. If the two persons use their respective standards to infer the same level of lack of ability $C(-)$, then p_1's standard is said to be *lenient* (SA[l]) and p_2's *strict* (SA[s]).

In other words, a standard $\overline{SA}$ that forgives more is lenient because it requires (allows for) more evidence of incompetence before assigning $C(-)$. For example, requiring a performance of 70% or more incorrect answers before assigning lack of ability is a more lenient standard than the one concluding incompetence from 60% or more incorrect answers.

In sum, a strict standard for ability demands more evidence of competence than a lenient one, and a lenient standard for a lack of ability allows more evidence of incompetence than a strict one.

The following proposition associates states of the diffuse status characteristic to standards. It is proposed that, regarding lack of ability, the assignment of standards is done in such a way that the benefit of the doubt is given to the $D(+)$ performer but not to the other. Conversely, evidence of ability by the $D(-)$ performer is not as readily accepted as the same evidence from the other person.

- *Proposition 2:* In task situation S at t_1, p will activate different standards for *ability* for p and o, depending on their states of D: a lenient standard SA(l) for the $D(+)$ performer and a strict standard SA(s) for the $D(-)$ performer. Similarly, p will activate different standards for *lack of ability*: a lenient standard SA(l) for the $D(+)$ performer and a strict standard SA(s) for the $D(-)$ performer.

Thus if p possesses $D(+)$ and o possesses $D(-)$, Propositions 1 and 2 can be jointly represented as shown in Figure 3.2.

$$p \; - - - - \; D(+) \; - - - - \; \Gamma(+) \; - - - - \; C(+) \; - - - - \; \begin{bmatrix} T(+) \\ SA(l), \overline{SA}(l) \end{bmatrix}$$

$$o \; - - - - \; D(-) \; - - - - \; \Gamma(-) \; - - - - \; C(-) \; - - - - \; \begin{bmatrix} T(-) \\ SA(s), \overline{SA}(s) \end{bmatrix}$$

Figure 3.2. Example of Situation S at t_1 (from Propositions 1 and 2)

To summarize, at t_1 p will make an initial assignment of levels of C on the basis of D, anticipate that the next performance will be successful for one person and unsuccessful for the other, and have ready a set of requirements for the assessment of the performances that actually occur. These standards will be used in the next stage, t_2, to decide whether to maintain or to change the initial assignment of levels of C. Note that p is *not* assumed (at either t_1 or t_2) to go through these steps in a conscious manner. In particular, p is not seen as explicitly formulating standards or as computing probabilities. Rather, the theory is a model to be used to predict p's behavior. To that end, it is convenient to think of p *as if* this person performed the operations specified in the theory.

Let us now assume that the following elements are introduced to S at time t_2:

> (g) p and o perform the task individually and the outcome by each person is evaluated as either T*(+) or T*(−) by a third party or source. These evaluations are communicated to p, who assumes them to be objective.

An evaluation is "objective" if it is perceived to have been obtained through a fair or nonbiased judgment. For simplicity, p and the source are assumed to have the same definitions of successful and unsuccessful performances.

Let us first consider that the two persons have been *equally successful*. Each outcome T*(+) will be assessed through the standard for ability that had been activated for that performer, and a decision regarding C(+) will be made. Let us assume that p has to decide between only two alternatives: *either* to assign ability (i.e., to conclude C(+)) or not to assign it (i.e., to conclude $\overline{C}(+)$). The latter possibility includes assigning C(−) *as well as* attributing T*(+) to nonability factors (such as good luck or effort) *and* suspending judgment. The following relationship is predicted:

- *Proposition 3:* Since a performance T*(+) is more likely to meet an SA(l) than an SA(s), the probability of being assigned C(+) after T*(+) is larger for the D(+) than for the D(−) performer.

This can be presented in graphic form as shown in Figure 3.3, where a, 1 − a, b, and 1 − b indicate probabilities. Prediction: a > b.[5]

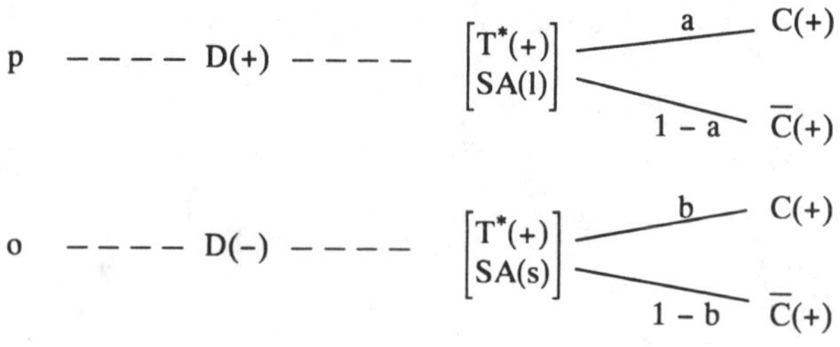

Figure 3.3. Example of Situation S at t_2 (from Proposition 3)

Next let us consider that the two persons have been *equally unsuccessful*. In this case, assigning $\overline{C}(−)$ includes assigning C(+) *as well as* attributing T*(−) to nonability factors (such as bad luck or lack of effort) *and* suspending judgment. Reasoning along the same lines as in the previous case, the following is proposed:

- *Proposition 4:* Since a performance T*(−) is more likely to meet an $\overline{SA}(s)$ than an SA(l), the probability of being assigned C(−) after T*(−) is larger for the D(−) than for the D(+) performer.

This can be presented in graphic form as shown in Figure 3.4, where c, 1 − c, d, 1 − d indicate probabilities. Prediction: d > c.

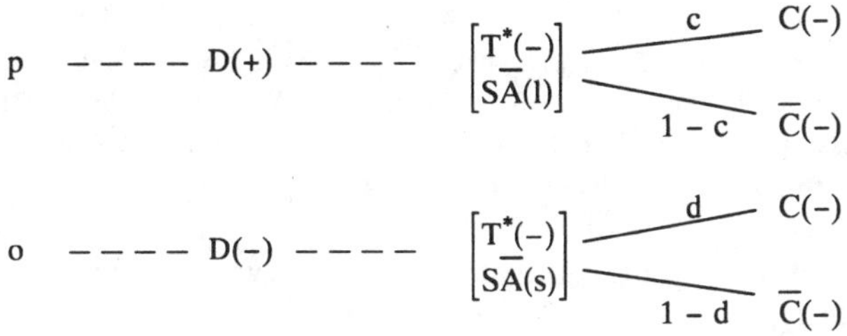

$$
\begin{array}{l}
p \;\; ----\; D(+) \;\; ----\; \begin{bmatrix} T^*_-(-) \\ SA(l) \end{bmatrix} \underset{1-c}{\overset{c}{<}} \begin{array}{l} C(-) \\ \overline{C}(-) \end{array} \\[3em]
o \;\; ----\; D(-) \;\; ----\; \begin{bmatrix} T^*_-(-) \\ \overline{SA}(s) \end{bmatrix} \underset{1-d}{\overset{d}{<}} \begin{array}{l} C(-) \\ \overline{C}(-) \end{array}
\end{array}
$$

Figure 3.4. Example of Situation S at t_2 (from Proposition 4)

In the other two cases the performers obtain different outcomes, and these are either consistent or inconsistent with states of D, as indicated in Figures 3.5 and 3.6. In order to make predictions about assigned levels of C, these cases require comparisons across standards. Let us consider the *consistent* case first. For simplicity, let us assume that the two are comparable in their requirements, that is, that SA(l) requires as little evidence of competence as $\overline{SA}$(s) allows for incompetence. For example, the former may require only 55% or more correct answers and the latter may allow for no more than 55% incorrect answers. In that case:

• *Proposition 5:* Since a performance T*(+) is as likely to meet an SA(l) as a performance T*(−) is to meet an $\overline{SA}$(s), the probability of the D(+) performer being assigned C(+) after T*(+) is equal to the probability of the D(−) performer being assigned C(−) after T*(−).

This can be presented in graphic form as shown in Figure 3.5, where a, 1 − a, d, 1 − d indicate probabilities. Prediction: a = d.[6]

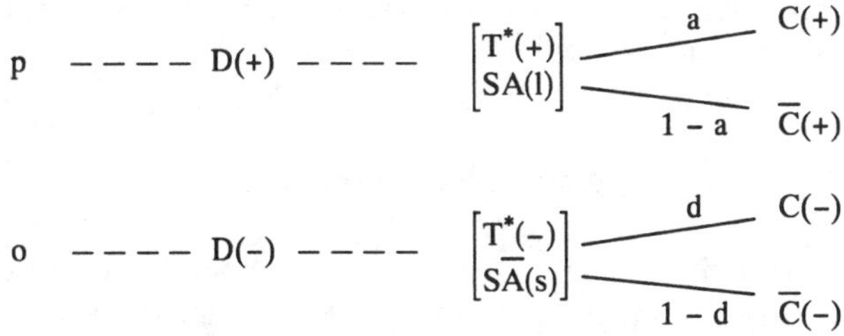

$$
\begin{array}{l}
p \;\; ----\; D(+) \;\; ----\; \begin{bmatrix} T^*(+) \\ SA(l) \end{bmatrix} \underset{1-a}{\overset{a}{<}} \begin{array}{l} C(+) \\ \overline{C}(+) \end{array} \\[3em]
o \;\; ----\; D(-) \;\; ----\; \begin{bmatrix} T^*_-(-) \\ \overline{SA}(s) \end{bmatrix} \underset{1-d}{\overset{d}{<}} \begin{array}{l} C(-) \\ \overline{C}(-) \end{array}
\end{array}
$$

Figure 3.5. Example of Situation S at t_2 (from Proposition 5)

Finally, let us consider the case where levels of T* are *inconsistent* with levels of D, and let us make the following assumption (similar to the one made above) regarding the activated standards: SA(s) is as demanding of evidence of competence as $\overline{SA}(l)$ is forgiving of evidence of incompetence. For example, the former may require 80% or more correct answers whereas the latter allows up to 80% incorrect answers. Thus:

- *Proposition 6:* Since a performance T*(+) is as likely to meet an SA(s) as performance T*(−) is to meet an SA(l), the probability of the D(+) performer being assigned C(−) after T*(−) is equal to the probability of the D(−) performer being assigned C(+) after T*(+).

This can be presented graphically as shown in Figure 3.6, where b, 1 − b, c, 1 − c indicate probabilities. Prediction: b = c.

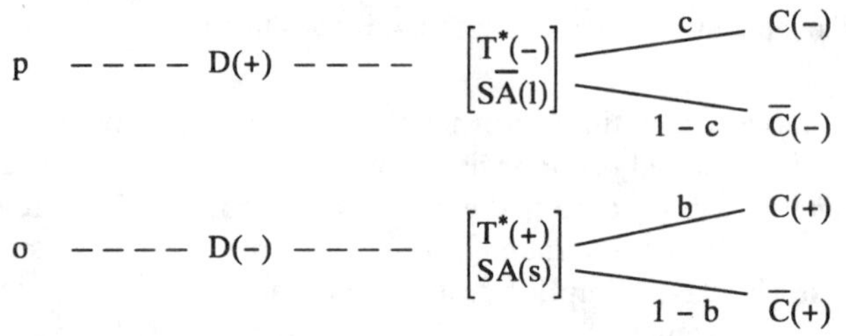

$$
p \;\; ----\; D(+) \;----\; \begin{bmatrix} T^*(-) \\ \overline{SA}(l) \end{bmatrix} \xrightarrow[\;1-c\;]{\;c\;} \begin{array}{l} C(-) \\ \overline{C}(-) \end{array}
$$

$$
o \;\; ----\; D(-) \;----\; \begin{bmatrix} T^*(+) \\ SA(s) \end{bmatrix} \xrightarrow[\;1-b\;]{\;b\;} \begin{array}{l} C(+) \\ \overline{C}(+) \end{array}
$$

Figure 3.6. Example of Situation S at t_2 (from Proposition 6)

The prediction from Propositions 3-6 combined is a = d > b = c. That is, when a performance is consistent with D(x), the likelihood that either C(+) or C(−) will be assigned is larger than when a performance is inconsistent with D(x). Standards are the mechanism through which a performance is deemed either sufficient or insufficient evidence for such an assignment.

_ Finally, note that in none of the above are the probabilities for $\overline{C}$(+) or $\overline{C}$(−) assumed to be zero. For example, even with a lenient standard it is possible that C(+) will not be assigned to D(+) after only one T*(+): The performance may not even meet a lenient, single-performance standard, or the standard may involve more than one performance.

Suggestions for Extensions

The previous section contains the core ideas for a theory on diffuse status characteristics, standards, and assignment of task ability. This core may be extended in several directions, some of which are apparent from an examination of the simplifying assumptions. For example, the diffuse status characteristic D has been conceptualized as having two states, D(+) and D(−). However, if this characteristic were to be thought of as having more than two states (e.g., if it consisted of three ethnic groups or of four socioeconomic classes), the theory could be easily extended to predict various levels of strictness in the corresponding standards for ability and for lack of ability.

This section identifies and examines four possible extensions of theoretical interest. As the text indicates, the first two are relatively straightforward, while the other two need more discussion.

(1) As formulated, the theory specifies that p performs the task with a partner o, and forms expectations about both of them. However, these two roles held by p may be separated, that is, p may form expectations without being a performer. In that case, p would receive evaluations from the source regarding the performances of two persons (o_1 and o_2) differing with respect to a D. This extension is not restricted to the present formulation, but can also be applied to other parts of the expectation states program (as proposed in Foschi and Foschi 1979). But the extension is of special interest here since it would facilitate the interpretation of results from the attribution literature, most of which includes designs where subjects are attributors but not performers (see Foschi and Plecash 1983; Takagi 1988). (The propositions do not need rewriting to accommodate this extension.)

(2) This theory proposes that, under certain conditions, a double standard is activated by the states of a diffuse status characteristic. But such a standard may also result from other characteristics, such as a second specific status characteristic C' having no explicit association with (or dissociation from) C. Let us assume a task situation S such as the one described earlier, but with D replaced by C'.[7] Status characteristic theory predicts that C' will become relevant to C through a burden of proof process (Berger et al. 1977, pp. 109-11). Thus, if the performers are known to have different levels of artistic ability, the task at hand involves color discrimination, *and* these two abilities have been neither explicitly associated nor dissociated, then the person ranked high in the former will be expected to do better at the latter. If extended to include such situations, the present theory would predict that the C'(+) person will also be treated with more lenient standards in both success and failure. (For the propositions resulting from this extension, simply replace D with C' in Propositions 1-6.)

(3) As presented, this theory applies to a situation in which C, at first neither explicitly associated with nor explicitly dissociated from D, later becomes relevant to it through the burden of proof process. The example used was that of a sex-neutral task performance characteristic that becomes associated with the states "male" and "female." States of C, however, may have been previously associated with states of D, in either a *consistent* or an *inconsistent* manner. (In line with the second extension, above, the following discussion also applies to C' and C.)

Let us assume that S now involves such a *consistent* association. Since it is common to believe that men are more logical than women, sex could serve as the diffuse characteristic, and logical ability as the specific characteristic. This would be represented as shown in Figure 3.7.

p   ─ ─ ─ ─   D(+)   ─ ─ ─ ─   C(+)   ─ ─ ─ ─   T(+)

o   ─ ─ ─ ─   D(−)   ─ ─ ─ ─   C(−)   ─ ─ ─ ─   T(−)

Figure 3.7. Example of Situation S at t_1 (states at D and C previously associated in a consistent manner)

Status characteristic theory specifies levels in the strength of the assignment of opposite states of C (i.e., the expectation advantage of one performer over the other). In Figures 3.1 and 3.7, this advantage will be an inverse function of the length of the path connecting each performer to states of C. Since path length is shorter in Figure 3.7 than in Figure 3.1, p's advantage over o is greater in the former than in the latter. This extension proposes that the extent of the advantage is also reflected in the strictness of the standards applied. Thus:

- *Proposition 7:* In task situations S at t_1, the stronger the assignment of opposite states of C, the more lenient the standards SA and S̄A activated for the person assigned C(+), and the stricter the standards SA and S̄A activated for the person assigned C(−).

Note that Proposition 2 then becomes a special case of Proposition 7. The *inconsistent* case can also be subsumed under the latter. Thus let us consider a situation S in which states of D and C have been previously associated so that D(+) is relevant to C(−) and D(−) is relevant to C(+). Sex may again serve as the example of a diffuse characteristic; intuitiveness could be used as the specific characteristic if p considers it to be both valuable and feminine. This is shown in graphic form in Figure 3.8.

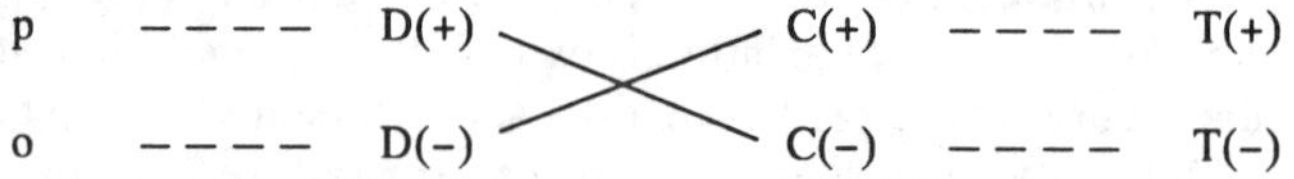

p   ─ ─ ─ ─   D(+) ╲   ╱ C(+)   ─ ─ ─ ─   T(+)
                         ╲   ╱
                          ╳
                         ╱   ╲
o   ─ ─ ─ ─   D(−) ╱   ╲ C(−)   ─ ─ ─ ─   T(−)

Figure 3.8. Example of Situation S at t_1 (states at D and C previously associated in an inconsistent manner)

Since both Figures 3.7 and 3.8 involve a direct association, the assignment of states of C is equally strong in the two cases. Accordingly, Proposition 7 would predict that the same standard for ability would be used in both. Thus the standard applied to infer logical ability in the man would be as lenient as the one used to infer intuitive ability in the woman. Conversely, the standard for lack of ability for the man performing a logical task would be as lenient as that applied to the woman performing an intuitive task.

(4) The strength of the initial assignment of states of C may not only depend on the length of the path connecting D and C. The situation may include other characteristics (both specific and diffuse), besides D, that

have become salient to p. These characteristics may vary in number, the length of the path between each of them and C may differ, and there may be paths connecting p (and o) to C(+) as well as to C(−). For example, p may be aware that he is a male graduate student with a low level of artistic ability while o is a female undergraduate with superior artistic skills. If the task involves color discrimination, and none of gender, academic rank, and artistic ability have been explicitly dissociated from the task, status characteristic theory predicts that all that information will first become salient to p and then relevant to C, and that p will combine it to form an aggregate expectation state. Combining will be done according to the principle of organized subsets: Inconsistent information will first be organized into consistently evaluated, separate subsets, and then these will be combined. It is also assumed that, within each subset, each increment of status information will have a diminishing effect. Thus, in the previous example, states of sex and academic rank will be combined for each of the performers. Academic rank would have less effect in conjunction with sex than such rank would have if it were the only information available about p and o. Next, p will combine "male graduate" with "low artistic ability," and "female undergraduate" with "high artistic ability." The aggregate expectation states resulting from the operation of this principle will reflect variations in the strength of the assignment of states of C. For example, "male graduate with high artistic skills" would result in a greater expectation advantage than "male graduate," which in turn would render a greater advantage than either "male" or "graduate." Proposition 7 can be used to predict differences in standards in these cases as well.

Summary and Conclusions

This chapter presents a theory linking aspects of status characteristic and attribution theories. The scope of the formulation is defined by those task situations in which two types of information are available: social category membership of the performer, and performance outcome. The theory introduces standards as the variable through which outcome information is filtered: Success by a low-status person is assessed with a stricter standard than the same performance by a high-status person, and therefore that success is less likely to result in the assignment of task ability. A similar process occurs in the case of failure, resulting in the high-status performer being less likely to be assigned lack of ability than the low-status performer. The theory focuses on the extent to which ability, or C(+), is inferred after success and lack of ability, or C(−), is inferred after failure. All other possible inferences, including attribution to various nonability factors, are subsumed under $\overline{C}(+)$ or $\overline{C}(−)$, respectively.

Thus the formulation captures the key contribution of the attribution ideas, namely, the asymmetry, based on the social category of the performer, with which evidence is judged to be sufficient for an inference of ability (or lack of ability). The formulation also refines and goes beyond these ideas, by placing them in the context of the expectation states program. Thus the asymmetry in attributions is seen as due not to intrinsic traits of the performers, but to their statuses relative to each other. Two other refinements include the addition of conditions: The propositions apply only to tasks involving a valued ability, and the initial difference between the performers must be an activated status characteristic for the attributor.

The chapter also includes suggestions for extensions to situations involving other performers as well as additional characteristics. The theory, however, remains limited to the assessment of a single performance. It would, of course, be important to ask what happens if a *series* of performances were involved. The answer is not simple, as the possibility of changes in standards would have to be included. Let us, for example, consider that the situation presented in Figure 3.3 were repeated over time. The case of the D(–) person who has been assigned C(+) after a single T*(+) is of special interest. One would expect that this person would be treated with a more lenient standard if repeated demonstrations of competence were provided. But then it could also be the case that such evidence has no effect on the standard used, or even that this performer is treated with a stricter standard (perhaps one requiring competence in related abilities), as a mechanism allowing for the maintenance of the status quo in spite of the evidence. It is not difficult to think of different situations exemplifying all three cases. These possibilities, and the conditions under which they occur for each combination of outcome and status characteristic of performer, will be explored in a process model to be presented in a separate paper.

Notes

1. As generally used in the social psychological literature, the term *sex* refers here to biological differences, whereas *gender* is used for cultural aspects associated with these differences. Thus beliefs about the relative competence of men and women are social products and therefore a gender issue, whereas what activates these beliefs is usually nothing more than the perception of sex differences among the performers. In those cases where only evidence of the latter may be assumed, the term *sex* is used.

2. This case is used as an illustration throughout the chapter. For the case of p possessing D(–) and o possessing D(+), simply exchange p and o in the figures. The propositions are formulated to cover both cases.

3. Lines in the figures indicate relations (of either possession or relevance) between elements of the situation as well as the sequencing of these relations. Generally speaking, a relevance relation involves an inference, whereas possession describes a linkage between actual events. For example, in Figure 3.1 the line between p and D(+) indicates that p *possesses* the positively evaluated state of a diffuse status characteristic, and the line between Γ (+) and C(+) indicates that the general expectation state has become *relevant* to one's ability to perform the task. Similarly, in Figure 3.2 C(+) is *relevant* to T(+), SA(l), and SA(l). In Figures 3.3-3.6, the lines joining states of D with states of T* and SA (or SA)

indicate the performer's *possession* of an actual outcome and an activated standard. If the reader finds it useful to think in probabilistic terms about the relations discussed here, the *relevance* relations in Figures 3.1 and 3.2 may be interpreted as "high probability that the elements will be thus linked to each other." Since each *possession* involves an actual occurrence, this relation may be interpreted as having a probability of one. As discussed in the text, the bifurcated lines from T* and SA (or SA) in Figures 3.3-3.6 indicate the probabilities with which these elements become *relevant* to complementary states of C.

4. To simplify the presentation, examples in this chapter use only one dimension of standards, namely, percentages of the task correctly (or incorrectly) completed.

5. For simplicity, standards have been dichotomized as either strict or lenient. A refinement specifying levels of strictness would enable predictions about a and 1 – a, and b and 1 – b. For example, if SA(s) is very strict, 1 – b would be predicted to be larger than b. A similar comment applies to Proposition 4.

6. The next step would be to relax the assumption of comparable standards, and thus allow variations in the relationship between a and d (and between c and b). The same as in the situations described in note 5, this could be done once levels of strictness are specified for each type of standard. Let us assume that SA(l) is more lenient than SA(s) is strict — for example, that the former requires only 55% correct responses whereas the latter allows 65% incorrect responses. The prediction in that case would be that a is larger than d.

7. Note that the expression "task situation S" is used in this chapter to include the situation described earlier as well as several variants (such as this one).

References

Berger, J., T. L. Conner, and W. L. McKeown. 1969. "Evaluations and the Formation and Maintenance of Performance Expectations." *Human Relations* 22:481-502.

Berger, J., M. H. Fisek, R. Z. Norman, and M. Zelditch, Jr. 1977. *Status Characteristics and Social Interaction: An Expectation-States Approach.* New York: Elsevier.

Berger, J., S. J. Rosenholtz, and M. Zelditch, Jr. 1980. "Status Organizing Processes." Pp. 479-508 in *Annual Review of Sociology*, Vol. 6, edited by A. Inkeles, N. J. Smelser, and R. H. Turner. Palo Alto, CA: Annual Reviews.

Berger, J., D. G. Wagner, and M. Zelditch, Jr. 1985. "Introduction — Expectation States Theory: Review and Assessment." Pp. 1-72 in *Status, Rewards and Influence: How Expectations Organize Behavior*, edited by J. Berger and M. Zelditch, Jr. San Francisco: Jossey-Bass.

Crittenden, K. S. 1983. "Sociological Aspects of Attribution." Pp. 425-46 in *Annual Review of Sociology*, Vol. 9, edited by R. H. Turner and J. F. Short, Jr. Palo Alto, CA: Annual Reviews.

Deaux, K. 1984. "From Individual Differences to Social Categories: Analysis of a Decade's Research on Gender." *American Psychologist* 39:105-16.

Deschamps, J. C. 1983. "Social Attribution." Pp. 223-40 in *Attribution Theory and Research: Conceptual, Developmental and Social Dimensions*, edited by J. Jaspars, F. D. Fincham, and M. Hewstone. London: Academic Press.

Dion, K. L. 1985. "Sex, Gender, and Groups: Selected Issues." Pp. 293-347 in *Women, Gender, and Social Psychology*, edited by V. E. O'Leary, R. K. Unger, and B. S. Wallston. Hillsdale, NJ: Lawrence Erlbaum.

Foddy, M. 1988. "Paths of Relevance and Evaluative Competence." Pp. 232-47, 501 in *Status Generalization: New Theory and Research*, edited by M. Webster, Jr., and M. Foschi. Stanford, CA: Stanford University Press.

Foschi, M. 1971. "Contradiction and Change of Performance Expectations." *Canadian Review of Anthropology and Sociology* 8:205-22.

Foschi, M. and M. Foddy. 1988. "Standards, Performances, and the Formation of Self-Other Expectations." Pp. 248-60, 501-3 in *Status Generalization: New Theory and Research*, edited by M. Webster, Jr., and M. Foschi. Stanford, CA: Stanford University Press.

Foschi, M. and R. Foschi. 1979. "A Bayesian Model for Performance Expectations: Extension and Simulation." *Social Psychology Quarterly* 42:232-41.

Foschi, M. and J. S. Plecash. 1983. "Sex Differences in the Attribution of Success and Failure: An Expectation-States Explanation." Paper presented at the annual meeting of the Canadian Sociology and Anthropology Association, Vancouver, BC.

Foschi, M., G. K. Warriner, and S. D. Hart. 1985. "Standards, Expectations, and Interpersonal Influence." *Social Psychology Quarterly* 48:108-17.

Hansen, R. D. and V. E. O'Leary. 1985. "Sex-Determined Attributions." Pp. 67-99 in *Women, Gender, and Social Psychology*, edited by V. E. O'Leary, R. K. Unger, and B. S. Wallston. Hillsdale, NJ: Lawrence Erlbaum.

Harvey, J. H. and G. Weary. 1984. "Current Issues in Attribution Theory and Research." Pp. 427-59 in *Annual Review of Psychology*, Vol. 35, edited by M. R. Rosenzweig and L. W. Porter. Palo Alto, CA: Annual Reviews.

Kelley, H. H. and J. L. Michela. 1980. "Attribution Theory and Research." Pp. 457-501 in *Annual Review of Psychology*, Vol. 31, edited by M. R. Rosenzweig and L. W. Porter. Palo Alto, CA: Annual Reviews.

Moore, J. C., Jr. 1969. "Social Status and Social Influence: Process Considerations." *Sociometry* 32:145-58.

Olson, J. M. and M. Ross. 1985. "Attribution Research: Past Contributions, Current Trends, and Future Prospects." Pp. 281-311 in *Attribution: Basic Issues and Applications*, edited by J. H. Harvey and G. Weary. Orlando, FL: Academic Press.

Savage, I. R. and M. Webster, Jr. 1971. "Source of Evaluations Reformulated and Analyzed." *Proceedings of the Sixth Berkeley Symposium on Mathematical Statistics and Probability* 4:137-41.

Sohn, D. 1982. "Sex Differences in Achievement Self-Attributions: An Effect-Size Analysis." *Sex Roles* 8:345-57.

Takagi, J. 1988 "Ethnicity, Expectations, and Attributions: A Theoretical Review." Unpublished M.A. thesis, Department of Anthropology and Sociology, University of British Columbia.

Webster, M., Jr., and B. Sobieszek. 1974. *Sources of Self-Evaluation: A Formal Theory of Significant Others and Social Influence*. New York: John Wiley.

Whitley, B. E., M. C. McHugh, and I. H. Frieze. 1986. "Assessing the Theoretical Models for Sex Differences in Causal Attributions of Success and Failure." Pp. 102-35 in *The Psychology of Gender: Advances Through Meta-Analysis*, edited by J. S. Hyde and M. C. Linn. Baltimore: Johns Hopkins University Press.

Wiley, M. G. 1986. "How Expectation States Organize Theory Construction." *Contemporary Sociology* 15:338-41.

4

Fuzzy Sets and Double Standards: Modeling the Process of Ability Inference

MARGARET FODDY

MICHAEL SMITHSON

Expectation states theory has been used with increasing frequency to account for the emergence of status hierarchies in informal groups (Berger et al. 1977, 1980; Berger and Zelditch 1985; Meeker 1981). The theory provides a systematic account of how characteristics of participants — both "diffuse" status characteristics and more specific abilities — are used as a basis for inferring competence at a valued group task. People who are believed to have higher task ability, on the basis of these characteristics, are then accorded more informal status. They initiate more, exert greater influence over group decisions, and receive more attention and more positive evaluations of their performances.

Psychologists have become interested in this approach because it provides a link between social structural sources of expectations for competence and interpersonal influence (Lockheed and Hall 1976; Deaux 1984, 1985; Eagly and Steffen 1984; Lenney 1977). In particular, the determination of status emergence by performance expectations based on the characteristics of group participants has received attention from psychologists interested in the differential participation of males and females in group interaction (Instone et al. 1983; Eagly 1983). Expectation states and status characteristics theories (Berger et al. 1977; Berger 1988; Webster and Foschi 1988) are useful here because they provide a systematic account of how the social category of gender can be activated as a relevant variable in interaction, how gender can determine status emergence in mixed-sex groups, and how such effects may be counteracted (Meeker and Weitzel-O'Neill 1977; Wagner et al. 1986; Pugh and Wahrman 1983). Recent developments in the theory of reward expectations provide the basis for a similarly systematic explanation of gender differences in pay and promotion in the workplace (Berger and Zelditch 1985).

A central part of the expectation states program concerns the inference of underlying competence on the basis of evaluated performances, as well as from diffuse and specific status characteristics. The process by which ability attribution is affected by status characteristics, and how they subsequently enter into the status organizing process has been relatively unexplored (but see Foschi, Chapter 3, this volume; and Foschi and Plecash 1983). This is a facet of the theory that merits development, since it refers to the more general question of how actors infer ability and worth.

In this chapter, we will review a theoretical framework for conceptualizing the process of ability inference. We will then show how various features of this process can be modeled using fuzzy set theory. While fuzzy sets may be unfamiliar to many readers, it does not take much effort to become familiar with the basic concepts. We hope to demonstrate that fuzzy set theory is particularly well suited to modeling some of the more intractable aspects of ability inference (e.g., the assignment of different levels or grades of ability, different degrees of certainty about whether an actor possesses ability, and differential requirements for ascertaining ability in actors who possess different characteristics). We demonstrate the suitability of fuzzy sets through examples of discrimination on the basis of gender in the workplace. We also show how a number of findings in the status characteristics program can be given a plausible explanation in terms of our framework, and we make a number of suggestions for empirical research. We conclude the chapter with a brief discussion of the implications of our framework for understanding equality of opportunity.

Standards for Ability

Foschi and Foddy (1988) propose a conceptualization of "standards for ability evaluation," which claims that identical performances may not produce inferences to identical levels of ability, because stricter standards of evidence may be applied to some categories of performer. "Standards for ability evaluation" specify how well or poorly a person has to perform in order for an ability to be attributed to or denied her or him. In most expectation states theory research, the standards for assessing performance have been provided by the researcher. It is possible to allow these standards to become a variable, whereby variability in the standards themselves becomes another part of the process through which individuals are assigned ability and differential status in groups. The exploration of standards and their effects in status ascription bears on a wide variety of real-world processes, from formal evaluations in education or employment to informal status formation in groups.

We view standards as rules providing performance requirements for the inference of either ability or lack of ability. The standard defines the minimum amount of evidence required to decide whether or not a person has the ability to be inferred.[1] Depending on the standard used, the same level of success may be either interpreted as a major accomplishment and a clear sign of ability or dismissed as unimportant and hence an insufficient indication of ability. In the case where a low level of performance leads to an inference of *lack* of ability, the standard defines how badly people must perform before it can be concluded that they do not have the ability.

Attribution of ability is distinct from performance evaluation.[2] While a performance may be judged to be a success, it may not meet the standard for inferring ability. If the performance fails to meet the standard, the person may (1) attribute the successful performance to nonability factors, (2) attribute the performance to a lower level of ability, or (3) reserve or suspend judgment. When an individual performs at a level surpassing the standard, then he or she can confidently conclude that the individual has ability, that is, form strong expectations. If the standard is not met, then this performance outcome cannot be used as clear evidence of ability; weaker performance expectations are formed, or judgement is suspended. Confident attributions of ability lead to stronger expectations, and these in turn produce more strongly differentiated groups (Foschi et al. 1985).

In the following formulation, the focal actor, or performer, will be referred to as p, and the coactor will be referred to as o. In the case in which the focal person is an evaluator, this person will be referred to as p and the evaluated actors as o_1 and o_2. It is our view that expectation states (or status characteristics) theory, though formulated for the case of two coactors, applies equally well to the case in which an evaluator must decide which of two actors has greater ability or what level of ability a single performer possesses (see, for example, Crundall and Foddy 1981; Webster and Sobieszek, 1974).

STRICT AND LENIENT STANDARDS

A standard defines how a given level of performance will be assessed as evidence for the existence of an underlying ability (or lack thereof). A *strict* standard is one that requires stronger evidence of ability (or lack thereof) compared to a *lenient* standard. In a task repeated over several trials, a strict standard might be for p to get 17 out of 20 correct, while the lenient standard might be for o to get 12 out of 20. As a result, while p and o might produce different levels of performance (e.g., 18/20 and 13/20), both performances would yield a confident inference of ability. Similarly, if the standard for lack of ability were strict (e.g., any more than 5/20 incorrect is evidence of lack of ability) rather than lenient (e.g., 8/20), a performer who scored 7/20 errors would be judged incompetent by the strict standard, but would not attract this label if judged by the lenient one.

In their conceptualization of standards, Foschi and Foddy (1988) propose five dimensions on which standards for ability can be defined. These dimensions reflect the notion that a stricter standard is being applied if a person is required (1) to succeed at more difficult tasks, or (2) to obtain a higher proportion of correct answers, over (3) more repetitions of a task, and to show competence at (4) other tasks requiring the same or (5) related abilities. The examples outlined above have concentrated on the simplest case: What proportion of correct answers on a single task is adequate evidence for ability or lack thereof? Dimensions 1-3 can all be seen as "single-dimension" cases, where the standard is a cutoff or qualifying threshold applied to the performance(s). In addition, when information is available about performance on several tasks (dimensions 4 and 5), or if there is information about a number of the five dimensions, it will be aggregated. Foschi and Foddy suggest that in these "multidimensional" cases, the stricter standard will be one involving more of the strict or fewer of the lenient standards on the contributing dimensions, which would presumably be aggregated according to some sort of linear combination rule.

Since inferences about ability are frequently made on the basis of performance at more than one task, the manner in which this information is combined is worthy of closer consideration. In addition to specifying the minimum performance requirements for each task, standards also specify rules for aggregating information about performances on all of the tasks. These rules or functions may vary, and so they may also be stricter or more lenient. We will return to this important issue. It is a central aim of our chapter to show that strictness and leniency of standards can take many forms, and that the various meanings of the phrase "requires more evidence of ability," when specified adequately, reveal underlying processes by which evaluations of performances may serve to preserve the status order.

DOUBLE STANDARDS

Double standards (Foschi and Foddy 1988) may be defined in terms of the differential application of strict or lenient standards to people who possess different states of a status characteristic. Diffuse status characteristics, either alone or in combination with specific status characteristics, generate predictions for performance against which the performance is judged expected or not. An unexpected performance elicits a stricter standard, because the judge requires stronger evidence that this performance was due to an ability. Stricter standards will, on average, make it more likely that any given performer cannot meet the standard, and prevent a clear inference from successful performance to ability. Thus if a strict standard is applied systematically to performers who possess the low state of a diffuse status characteristic, there is yet another means by which consistency between external status and status within the group can be maintained.

It should be apparent in what follows that we do not assume that double standards are applied consciously or deliberately; this is one reason they are often difficult to detect.

EMPIRICAL STUDIES OF STANDARDS

Since the standards formulation is relatively new, there have been few empirical studies to test it. Foschi has conducted a number of studies to test whether performances that surpass a standard (set by the experimenter) would lead to stronger/more confident inferences of ability, or lack of ability, as reflected in the performers' susceptibility to influence from another who is clearly/not clearly superior or inferior in ability (see, e.g., Foschi et al. 1985; Foschi and Freeman 1987). Results of these studies provide support for the hypotheses tested. Further, it appears that standards for lack of ability may not be a simple mirror image of standards for ability.

An unpublished study of double standards also provides evidence for the viability of the standards formulation. Graham (1989) used a group influence paradigm (Moore 1968; Berger et al. 1977) to investigate the effects of gender on influence in a simple group decision task. The experiment had two phases. First, the experimenter arranged for subjects to succeed or fail on a pattern recognition task, which was presented to them on a computer terminal. Then each subject was paired with a same- or opposite-sex partner who had scored better (15/20) or worse (7/20) than the subject during the individual phase of the experiment. In the group phase, each subject gave an initial answer to the pattern recognition problem on each trial, then learned the initial answer of the partner, before making a final choice. The partner was simulated by a computer program, which systematically disagreed with the naive subject's choice on the majority of trials. Subjects who had scored better than their partners during the individual phase were expected to reject influence (stay with their own choices in the case of disagreement), while lower-scoring subjects were expected to change their answers if they found they disagreed with higher-scoring partners. It was predicted that females would set higher standards for ability, and that this would lead them to defer more to male partners than would male subjects, holding scores in the first phase constant.

Graham found that females did defer more to their male partners, especially when the task was described as "male" or "neutral" rather than "female." In addition, when subjects were asked to state the score they would need to obtain over 20 trials before they could definitely conclude they had ability, female subjects set higher standards for themselves than did males, requiring on average between 16 to 18 out of 20 to conclude they had ability, while males required between 14 to 16 out of 20. This tendency was more pronounced in mixed-sex dyads, except when the task was perceived to be one in which females normally excelled. In the latter case, females who performed better than male partners rejected influence almost as much as did successful males with partners of either sex. In this "female" task, females still set higher standards than did males, but males also set higher standards for ability than did males in the other conditions. In other words, if the task was one in which females were supposed to do better, males said they would need more evidence to conclude they had ability. Even so, males continued to reject influence at a higher rate than did females, both in same- and opposite-sex dyads. These results support the theoretical argument that more evidence of ability is required if a successful performance is unexpected.

Earlier research concerning the effects of gender on expectations and subsequent influence can be interpreted as providing indirect evidence that double standards were operating. Pugh and Wahrman (1983), for example, found that even when a woman's performance was equal to a man's, it was not sufficient to make the male and female accept influence to equal degrees. As these authors comment, "Being as good as a man is not enough to enable a woman to succeed" (p. 760). Indeed, females had to perform *better* than males before the decision outcomes indicated that the females were being considered to be *equal* to the males.[3]

A recent study by Wagner et al. (1986) also shows that females in mixed-sex dyads defer to males more than males do to females, given equivalent levels of success or failure. While Wagner et al. focused on the tendency for subjects to be more affected by performance feedback that was surprising (high scores for a female, low scores for a male), an analysis of variance applied to their data shows that by far the strongest effects were due to the success/failure feedback, and to sex of subject. The significant sex difference could be interpreted to mean that females were applying a stricter standard to their success and the males a stricter standard to their failure. These results are striking, since performance outcomes for a given feedback condition were identical for both sexes (16/25 for high and 9/25 for low ability), and the experimenter provided a set of "national standards" indicating what level of ability was reflected by the subjects' scores. Since Wagner et al. did not assess the subjects' own standards, this interpretation of their results would need to be tested in future research.

A number of studies done from different theoretical perspectives also provide indirect evidence for the operation of double standards. For example, Etaugh and Kasley (1981) found that both male and female subjects devalued the competence of a female job applicant relative to a male when asked to judge a job application and journal article that were identical for the male and female applicants. Gerdes and Garber (1983) found that female applicants for an engineering job were discriminated against when applying for a technical managerial job, even when they had a high level of competence. These authors argued that since there is little specific information about women engineers, judges resort to the overall stereotype that women are less competent than men to predict the potential of applicants for the job; the result is that equal qualifications are downgraded as evidence for competence, a finding that is consistent with the operation of double standards. (For further examples, see Eichler 1977; Yarkin et al. 1982.) These studies equated the performances of males and females; where the female performs *better than* the male, she may be seen as only equally competent. Research that examines females who perform better tends to concentrate on the locus of causal attribution: A superior performance by a female may be attributed to nonability factors, especially effort (O'Leary and Hansen 1982; Hansen and O'Leary 1985; Heilman and Guzzo 1978). The net effect of such attributions is that the female's superior performance does not lead to inferences of superior ability, but rather to a "discounting" of the evidence or a withholding of judgment.

Foschi has shown the fertility of the conceptualization of standards by showing how it can be used to explain these and other findings from the research literature concerning the attribution of ability (see Foschi and Plecash 1983; Foschi, Chapter 3, this volume). Expectations for performance based on the diffuse status characteristic of gender are used to define a successful or unsuccessful performance as expected or not; stricter standards are used to judge unexpected performances, and those that fail to meet this stronger evidential requirement are then attributed to nonability factors such as effort, task ease, and luck. Foschi's account is consistent with analyses offered by social psychologists who have studied differences in attribution from a "gender bias" perspective (Hansen and O'Leary 1985; Nieva and Gutek 1980; Eagly 1983; Frieze et al. 1982; McArthur 1985; McArthur and Obrant 1986; Riger and Galligan 1980).[4] By integrating them with a status characteristics formulation, predictions from this theory concerning the conditions under which such biases will be invoked can be specified and tested.

The Order-Preserving Principle

As indicated at the outset of the section on double standards, our basic proposition is that standards are order preserving. In the case of success, strictness of standards is inversely related to the evaluation of the state of a status characteristic — the higher the status value, the more lenient the standard. In other words, people with the high state of a status characteristic will not be required to show as convincing evidence of ability as will those with the lower state of the status characteristic. We will refer to this proposition as the *order-preserving principle.*

In the case of lack of ability, strictness of standards varies directly with status value. The higher the status, the stricter the standard for incompetence — a high-status person must perform very badly indeed to be judged to have no ability, while a low-status person will be deemed incompetent even though the evidence of incompetence might not be convincing if she or he possessed the high state of the status characteristic. For both success and failure, the greater the difference in status between p and o, the greater the difference in the strictness of standards applied to them.

In status-heterogeneous groups, the operation of different standards should be evident from the early stages of interaction. In status-homogeneous groups, however, double standards are likely to emerge as the power and prestige order develops.

The claim that standards are order preserving is a simple principle. However, it can take a number of different forms, depending on whether one is dealing with simple or complex performance information, and whether one is dealing with a single status characteristic or aggregating information about a number of diffuse and specific status characteristics. This complexity means that strictness/leniency of standards may also take a number of different forms. A difficulty with the research on biased evaluation of ability, which assumes double standards, is its failure to incorporate this multiplicity, which in turn prevents researchers from being able to distinguish among (or even recognize) various kinds of double standards.

In order to explicate the various meanings of strictness, we require a framework for representing standards, performance evaluations, inferences of ability, and ways of combining those evaluations and inferences. This framework must be capable of representing gradations of ability, since the assignment of the same level of performance to different levels of ability is one of the predicted outcomes of the operation of double standards. It would also be desirable to be able to represent qualitative as well as quantitative judgments of ability. The graph-theoretic framework used in expectation states theory is too limiting, because it restricts representation of ability to two states (+ and –).[5] The next section introduces a framework (fuzzy set theory) that possesses these capabilities.

A Fuzzy Set Framework
for Strictness and Leniency

Readers may immediately wonder why we are proposing to use an exotic framework such as fuzzy set theory rather than a more conventional approach. Perhaps the most obvious way to represent gradations in ability would be simply to replace the + and – notation with ordinary rating scales (e.g., from "low" to "high" ability). But this step is not sufficient to represent various kinds of strictness and leniency, since it provides no accompanying formalism for handling aggregation or qualitative judgments.

A more sophisticated strategy would be to invoke subjective probability as the framework for representing gradations in ability and performance judgments. After all, the concept of an expectation state seems compatible with subjective probability, and probability theory certainly provides normative guidelines for matters such as the aggregation of judgments. Moreover, there is a powerful axiomization of subjective probability (Cox 1946) that links it with quantified degrees of belief. This linkage entails translating statements such as "I believe X has high ability" into the proposition "My subjective probability that X has ability is high [or some appropriate number]."

Unfortunately, it is our considered opinion that probability theory alone is inadequate for capturing the bulk of judgments about graded concepts such as ability. While some such judgments may well involve making intuitive bets about whether X could accomplish some task, there are at least two requirements for probability to be an adequate representation of the uncertainty inherent in those judgments. First, the task itself must be a discrete entity that either is or is not accomplished. Second, the nature of the judge's uncertainty about whether X can perform the task must be probabilistic.

In a wide variety of cases, those requirements are not fulfilled. The statement "I believe X has high ability" may mean that the judge is absolutely certain that X possesses said ability to a considerable degree, in which case the ability is not discrete and the nature of the uncertainty (if any) in that statement is not probabilistic. This observation accords with statements by psycholinguists that many natural language quantifiers are not amenable to being represented probabilistically (see Newstead 1988) and by philosophers that there are other kinds of uncertainty expressed in language than probability (e.g., Black 1937; Alston 1964).

In this chapter we propose to adopt the framework of fuzzy set theory for representing judgments of gradations in ability primarily because fuzzy set theory was designed to handle categories that are graded and blurry. A set is fuzzy if its elements may belong to it in degree rather than only either completely or not at all. Degrees of membership usually are assigned values in the 0,1 interval, with 0 denoting complete nonmembership and 1 complete membership (although other scales may be used, including weakly ordered verbal labels).

Degree of ability is easily and directly translated into a fuzzy set, in at least two ways. First, the statement "Doris has high mathematical ability" may refer to a judgment about the extent to which Doris closely approximates the relevant features of mathematically able people (that is, her degree of belonging to a referent set). Likewise, task performance may also be evaluated fuzzily in this sense, so that one may speak of degrees of success or failure. Second, the same statement may refer to judgment of Doris's potential to perform mathematically difficult feats.

Neither of these meanings is directly captured by probability (as has been argued by Gaines 1975 and Zadeh 1980). Fuzziness is not the same as probability. The first kind of fuzziness introduced above corresponds to the notion of "degree vagueness" articulated by Alston (1964; see also Smithson 1987, chap. 1, for an outline of the distinctions among vagueness, fuzziness, probability, ambiguity, and generality). The second kind characterizes degree of ability in terms of a "possibility distribution" (see Zadeh 1978 for a formal theory of possibility based on fuzzy sets) over various tasks that require different levels of ability. This latter concept is compatible with the notion that ability is a potentiality and not a likelihood with respect to performance. Clearly, then, possibility is not probability either, since it merely places an upper bound on probability (whatever is impossible must be improbable, but the converse need not hold).

While not wishing to claim that fuzzy set theory is the only suitable framework for extending expectation states theory, we will argue that it has some advantages over the subjective probability framework for representing judgments that involve graded categories. One advantage that has already been pointed out is the ease of translation from natural language into a formal system. Fuzziness handles the essence of category gradations better than probability when the nature of the gradations does not refer to bets or expectation. Second, fuzzy sets have been incorporated into psychological theories of natural categories and prototypes for some years now (e.g., Rosch 1973, 1978; Niedenthal and Cantor 1984; Burgess et al. 1983; Oden and Lopes 1982). There is a substantial body of research that indicates that fuzziness has psychological reality and that fuzzy set membership scales can be elicited from "naive" subjects.

Third, fuzzy sets may overlap one another, which is not permitted in any probabilistic event space. This means that while probabilities must sum to 1 across all events, fuzzy set membership values need not. In addition to being a more realistic characterization of natural categorical judgments, this feature of fuzzy set theory imposes fewer restrictions on judges than does probability theory. Moreover, because fuzzy sets overlap, they may intersect, which implies that fuzzy set theory must have an account of fuzzy set aggregation. The rules governing fuzzy set intersection and union provide useful building blocks for analyzing strictness in multiattribute standards.

The basic formal vocabulary of fuzzy set theory is simple. Letting m_{ij} denote the membership of the ith element in the jth set, the membership of that element in the complement of the jth set is $1 - m_{ij}$, just as in probability theory (assuming that the m_{ij} lies in the 0,1 interval). The usual definition for the membership of the ith element in the intersection of the jth and k^{th} fuzzy sets is $\min(m_{ij}, m_{ik})$, and the corresponding definition for the union of two fuzzy sets is $\max(m_{ij}, m_{ik})$. These are not the only possible definitions, but they will suffice for our purposes (see Smithson 1987 for a review of alternative definitions and their applications). Thus someone whose degrees of membership in the sets "good at mathematics" and "good at English" are 0.6 and 0.8, respectively, will have a membership of 0.6 in the intersection ("good at mathematics and English") and a membership of 0.8 in the union ("good at mathematics or English").[6]

As outlined earlier, we wish to reorganize the five "dimensions" of standards outlined by Foschi and Foddy (1988), and distinguish between single-dimension and multiple-dimension cases. By *single-dimension*, we refer to standards defined on only one of the first three of Foschi and Foddy's five dimensions (number correct in a series of trials, number of repetitions of the series, and degree of difficulty of the task). A fuzzy set

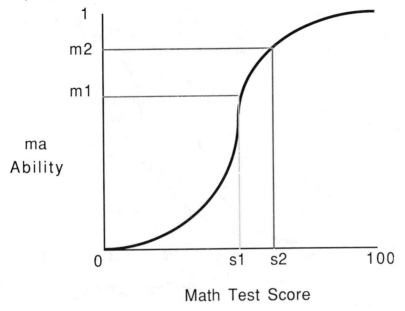

Figure 4.1.

framework provides a means to represent these single-dimension standards. It also lets us identify other types of single-dimension standards not dealt with in Foschi and Foddy's conceptualization. More important, fuzzy set intersections can be used to model a number of meanings of double standards in the multidimensional case, that is, instances in which the standard specifies more than one task or ability. A double standard in this case refers to the application of different combination rules, depending on the status characteristics of the performers. We will deal with these cases in turn.

Fuzzy Sets and Double Standards

THE SINGLE-DIMENSION CASE

Both the inference of ability from performance and the expectation of performance levels based on assumed ability may be modeled by a one-to-one mapping between a performance scale and a degree of ability scale. Consider the example of a mapping between mathematical ability, m_a, and scores, s, on a mathematical test. In the case where the category membership of the performer is irrelevant, there is only one curve, and the ability membership can be determined by the performance level of the actor (see Figure 4.1). A stricter standard would require a higher score, as when a higher graduate record score (S_2) is required before a student is considered to have adequate ability (m_2) to gain entrance to a "good" graduate school.

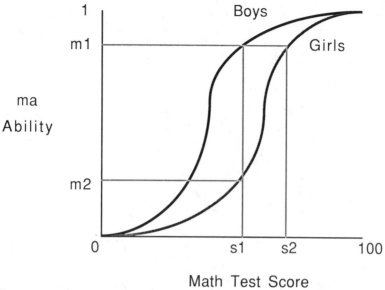

Figure 4.2.

A double standard as outlined in Foschi and Foddy (1988) would be reflected in different cutoff points for different categories of people. For example, females might have to perform at level s_2 to be considered to have ability, whereas males would only have to perform at level s_1. It is unlikely that a diffuse status characteristic would evoke such a blatant double standard where scores are being compared directly (but see Walden and Walkerdine 1981). Instead, it is likely to affect the entire mapping from performance to ability in a way that is characterized in Figure 4.2. For instance, if the diffuse status characteristic is gender, then judges will have lower performance expectations for females so that higher test scores (e.g., s_2 for females versus s_1 for males) are required of them for inference of the same ability level (m_1) as males. This expectation is shown in the different gradients of the curves mapping the relationship between scores and ability levels (these curves should be taken to be notional, insofar as they would have to be derived empirically in order to model a real case). Conversely, if a female gets a score of s_1 then she is judged to have less ability (m_2) than a male with an identical score.[7]

Figure 4.2 shows that these two phenomena are linked by the depressive effect that being female has on the performance — ability mapping. Relative to the male curve, the female curve has been pushed further up the test score axis. In fuzzy set terms, a person's state on the diffuse status characteristic of gender activates a concentrator or dilator on the ability membership scale with respect to the test performance scale. In Zadeh's (1972) original conceptual formulation of concentrators and dilators as models of verbal hedges, Figure 4.2 translates into the natural language observation that while males must do "well" to infer "high" ability,

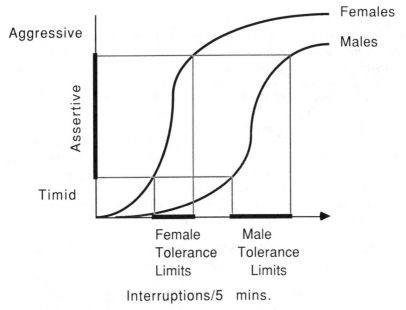

Figure 4.3.

females must do "very" well to infer the same level of "high" ability. *Very* in this framework is a concentrator.[8]

The model in Figure 4.2 allows us to represent a particular kind of double standard for the single-dimensional case. If an employer requires mathematical ability level m_1 for a candidate to be hired and if that employer believes men to be more mathematically able than women, then clearly men must score only s_1 on the diagnostic test while females must score s_2 to convince the employer that they possess ability at the level of m_1. Furthermore, this model is sufficiently robust to represent the case where the performance and ability scales are only ordinal. Thus a female applicant might be asked a harder question (s_2) during a job interview simply because the employer requires her to show more evidence of ability m_1 than a male (who gets asked s_1). Given that difficult questions are failed more frequently than easy ones, an equally able female may not pass the standard for ability applied to her, while the male successfully passes his.

Another major variant on the single-dimensional double standard occurs where the same behavior or performance leads to *qualitatively* different classifications stemming from a diffuse status characteristic. A classic example in gender differences is the labeling of women as "aggressive" for behavior that would be labeled "assertive" in men. Again, where these labels involve graded categories, fuzzy set concepts provide an effective model.

Figure 4.3 shows two hypothetical membership gradients, one for males and one for females, for "timid," "appropriately assertive," and "aggressive," as a function of the number of interruptions per five minutes. There are two distinct kinds of double standard that could operate here for men and women. One is the simple concentrator-dilator effect discussed earlier, so that in this case, a level of interruption that gets the female labeled "aggressive" might get the male labeled merely "assertive." In this case, the male curve is displaced further along the interruptions axis, allowing a higher rate of interruptions to attract the label "assertive," rather than "aggressive."

More difficult to detect is a double standard that sets narrower tolerance ranges for women's interruption rates in order for them to be judged assertive. This is represented by the difference in shape — the male's curve has a lower slope than the female's curve, as well as being located further along the interruptions axis (see Figure 4.3). As a result, males can exhibit a wider range of values on interruptions per five minutes and still be seen as assertive.

We have characterized the qualitative difference above as reflecting an underlying continuum, so that categories such as timid, assertive, and aggressive are points along some dimension that incorporates behaviors such as speaking loudly and confidently, interrupting, and taking the initiative. It would also be possible to model assignment of members with different status characteristics to qualitatively distinct categories even though their behavior is the same. For example, the same set of behaviors on the job may qualify a male for membership in the sets "supervisor," and "authoritative," and a female for membership in the sets "coordinator" and "facilitator" (Eichler 1980; Hartmann 1985; Burton et al. 1987). To the extent that these sets are differentially evaluated, membership in one produces different expectations for general competence and rewards than does the other. This will be reflected in the power and prestige order, including the assignment to jobs that vary in prestige and remuneration (see Malkiel and Malkiel 1973; Treiman and Hartmann 1981; Wiley and Eskilson 1983; Ruble et al. 1984; Hartmann 1985; Stead 1985; Pettigrew and Martin 1987; Bielby and Bielby 1988).

It should be noted that the existence of different membership functions for different categories of people does not necessarily constitute a double standard, at least not in a discriminatory sense. Since women are in general shorter than men, it is not surprising that the membership gradient for membership in the set "tall" starts at an earlier point, and may even have a different shape. Similarly, a "masterful" marathon time may be different for a woman than for a man. However, different gradients are frequently applied to domains in which there is no a priori justification for difference (as in the distinction between assertion and aggression).

We started with a simple definition of single-dimensional double standards. The representation of the various meanings that double standards can take, by means of fuzzy set concepts, suggests the fertility of this approach. We now proceed to the more complex question of multidimensional standards.

THE MULTIPLE-DIMENSION CASE

Once we admit more than one relevant status characteristic to the operation of standards, the problem of aggregation arises. How do double standards operate to preserve the status order when performers complete a number of tasks or have demonstrated varying levels of competence across a number of tasks? The most obvious approach would be the conventional weighted linear combination, and indeed that might suffice to model certain kinds of standards. However, other aggregations are possible and some are suggested by both commonsensical arguments and research findings.

The aggregators occurring most often in natural language expressions are *and* and *or*. Neither of these is modeled by a linear combination, but appropriate fuzzy set versions of the Boolean logical operators for *and* and *or* have been defined above in terms of fuzzy set intersection and union, respectively. Their importance for modeling double standards stems from the fact that *and* is a stricter aggregator than addition, which in turn is stricter than *or*. Discrimination, therefore, may not occur in the criteria pertaining to any individual status characteristic, but can still enter by means of variation in how these characteristics are aggregated.

At this point, we need to distinguish two different ways in which we believe multiple standards may be involved in the combination of status and performance information. In the first, the existence of an expectation advantage triggers a double standard in the evaluation of p's and o's performance over a number of tasks. In the second, the aggregation of diffuse and specific status characteristics incorporates a double standard. That is, the aggregation rule itself is different for different categories of people. Once the available status information has been thus differently combined, one actor may emerge with an expectation advantage, and may subsequently have more lenient standards for ability applied to subsequent performances, while the lower-status person may be subject to stricter ones, as defined above.

DOUBLE STANDARDS IN
THE COMBINATION OF PERFORMANCE INFORMATION

As in the single-dimension case, if a diffuse status characteristic such as gender or race is activated, then the associated expectations for performance are used to judge if a set of performances across a number of tasks is expected or surprising. A more lenient standard may be used if a high-status person produces a good performance, and a stricter standard may be used if the same person performs poorly. Thus one might be happy to conclude that a high-status person had ability after she or he had shown success on one or two tasks requiring related abilities, but hesitate to decide that she or he lacked ability until negative evidence on a wider range of tasks had been acquired. This is like saying one would infer ability if the performer had succeeded at T_1 or T_2 or T_3, but would not infer lack of ability unless he or she had failed at T_1 and T_2 and T_3.[9] The reverse applies for the low-status performer.

A particularly discriminatory use of double standards in the multiple-dimension case occurs when the characteristic that is deemed necessary for task competence to be inferred is one that members of one group cannot possess or are most unlikely to possess. If an uninterrupted career path is a necessary characteristic for appointment to a tenured position, for example, the requirement may be very difficult for a married woman with children to meet. More extreme examples can be found in the literature on job discrimination, where women have been denied employment because they do not possess a skill or job experience that has previously been denied them because of their sex (for example, see Doeringer and Piore 1971; Smith 1979; Olson and Becker 1983). A (possibly apocryphal) example of this is the case of the female astronaut. For some time, women were denied positions in the space program because, to qualify as an astronaut, one required jet fighter pilot training. However, only men were allowed to acquire jet fighter pilot training.

To test predictions about the application of this type of double standard, one could employ a multiple-task situation in which subjects were differentiated on a single diffuse status characteristic and performed a number of related tasks (see, for example, Norman et al. 1988). Given differing patterns of success and failure across tasks, P(s) should reflect willingness to give the high-status person "the benefit of the doubt."

Elizabeth Cohen's intervention studies can be interpreted as showing an aggregation "double standard" of this kind (see, e.g., Cohen 1982; Cohen and Roper 1972). Subjects with low external status (ethnic or racial) who were trained to demonstrate competence on two tasks (T_1 and T_2) related to a group's activities usually attained equality but not superiority of influence in the group interaction. Such task competence would have made subjects with high external status clearly dominant in the group task. In this case, competence at T_1 and T_2, a stricter standard is required of the low-status actors, and even then it may not be enough.

The examples given above of this type of double standard assume that information about performance on a fixed set of tasks is available about each actor, and a stricter standard is one that requires success on a larger number of tasks (more ands than ors). It is also possible that there is a pool of performance information available, and then the number of tasks about which performance information is required can become the variable that reflects the operation of double standards. One would need to employ experimental paradigms in which subjects' biases and decision rules are inferred from the order and amount of performance information required by the subject (about self and/or other) prior to making a decision about competence. The important point to stress here is that for this sort of multidimensional standard, the size and the composition of the set of tasks on which one requires evidence before inferring ability can vary, and these can be aggregated in stricter or more lenient fashion.

To this point we have restricted our attention to the case in which there is a single activated status characteristic that triggers a double standard. The analysis can be easily extended to expectation advantages that result from more than one status characteristic. The greater the net expectation advantage, the higher the expected performance, and the more lenient the standard for ability applied to the higher-status actor. While it is plausible to suggest that the expectation advantage would be arrived at by aggregation of status information according to the combining principles outlined in status characteristics theory (e.g., Norman et al. 1988), we would like to argue that this process of aggregation may itself incorporate double standards.

DOUBLE STANDARDS IN
THE COMBINATION OF STATUS INFORMATION

It is not always the case that ability is inferred on the basis of immediate performance information. In the same way that expectations for future performance may be based on diffuse, specific, and performance characteristics, a performer's underlying ability may be estimated or predicted on the basis of such status information. The manner in which this information is combined or aggregated may vary. If aggregation rules or functions vary systematically with the state of the actors' diffuse status characteristics, this is a form of double or multiple standard. As in case a, this means that larger or different sets of evidence will be required to infer ability in the lower-status person. It differs from case a in that not all the information need be about performances; further, the use of case b double standards does not exclude the subsequent application of case a double standards to performances, as demonstrated in studies of "tokens" and "solos" (see Pettigrew and Martin 1987).

We have in mind a case where an evaluator has to decide if p possesses sufficient ability to be assigned to a job, to be given a promotion, to be trusted to carry out a task, and so on. The evaluator has available information about a number of specific and diffuse characteristics, and about previous performances. We will illustrate the operation of variable standards in the combination of status information with studies conducted to test features of expectation states theory.

Meeker and Weitzel-O'Neill (1977), in reviewing evidence about leadership in mixed-sex groups, note that females act as if they have lower expectations for self. Further, they argue that in informal groups, females need to be cooperatively oriented before they can make high task contributions and have these accepted. Males, on the other hand, need not be cooperatively oriented. Indeed, Meeker and Weitzel-O'Neill suggest that there is some evidence that males might need only be cooperative *or* competent, while females have to be cooperative *and* competent. Ridgeway (1982) conducted an experiment in which both male and female confederates were introduced into groups of naive subjects. The confederates were competent at the group task (i.e., specific competence was held constant) and varied in their motivation (self or group oriented). In mixed-sex groups, it did not significantly reduce the influence of a male to be self rather than group oriented, while the competent female also had to be group oriented to exert influence and be perceived as a leader. Ridgeway concludes that "the size of the effect of motivation (on a member's influence) is dependent on the member's external status characteristics" (p. 76).

It is possible to conceptualize these effects in terms of the differential aggregation of status information. For these purposes, we will consider "motivation" or "orientation" to be a status characteristic, in that there are at least two states (self and group orientation) that are differentially evaluated. Let m_t denote task competence and m_c denote cooperative orientation, where both are scaled on the 0,1 interval. Let us denote the aggregated judgment of an individual on these two characteristics by m_a. For the low-status person, our model of the Meeker and Weitzel-O'Neill hypothesis is $m_a = f(\min[m_t, m_c])$, while for the high-status person, $m_a = f(\max[m_t, m_c])$, where f is an appropriately chosen monotonic increasing function (e.g., linear in the case where m_t and m_c are interval-level scales). Thus if $m_t = 0.8$ and $m_c = 0.2$, $m_a = 0.2$ for the low-status individual, but $m_a = 0.8$ for the high-status person.

Our second example is somewhat more speculative. Zelditch et al. (1980) conducted an experiment to test whether subjects would aggregate inconsistent diffuse and specific status characteristics by "combining" (using all the information) or by "balancing" (ignoring one or the other of the status characteristics). Female subjects from a junior college were made to believe they were interacting with a status inferior (a high school freshman) or a status superior (a Stanford graduate student). The experimenters compared the P(s) rates for conditions in which only external status was known (high/low), only task competence was known (high/low), or task competence was inconsistent with external status. They argued that if balancing was operating, this inconsistency would be resolved by attending to task competence levels only. If combining was used, then low-status/high-ability subjects would "downgrade" their competence as reflected in P(s), compared to the high-ability-only condition, and high-status/low-ability subjects would "upgrade" their competence. The results were inconclusive, as the low-external-status subjects seemed to combine, and the high-external-status subjects seemed to be balancing. Zelditch et al. explain their inconsistent results as due to unsuccessful experimental manipulation, arguing that subjects in the high-external-status condition might not have perceived themselves to be different to their relatively lower-status partners, in which case they were differentiated only on task ability. When a second experiment was run, with male Stanford undergraduates as the high-status/low-ability performers, there was evidence for combining; that is, these subjects "upgraded" their low performance relative to a low-ability-only condition.

While Zelditch et al. (1980) may be correct in arguing that status information is normally combined, it seems more plausible to argue that the aggregation rule is a variable. For this experiment, if we consider the possibility that sex was activated as a status characteristic (the authors note that female junior college students might assume a Stanford graduate student is a male), then males and females might combine the two pieces of status information (ability and educational status) in different ways. We would expect the combination to be stricter when the females were using positive information, and more lenient in the case of negative information; the reverse would hold for males, although not all conditions were run for males. The results support this interpretation. Females in the high-status/low-ability condition acted as if they were applying a lenient standard for lack of ability: Their low performance was sufficient evidence that they lacked ability; they thus appear to be balancing. Males in this condition, however, acted as if low performance were not so convincing, and their P(s) reflects this. Low-external-status females who (unexpectedly) succeeded at the task appeared to be combining information about their educational status and their task ability, the stricter standard for possession of ability.

As this experiment was not designed to test an explanation in terms of variable standards, it can only be suggestive. Other studies of aggregation have produced differing results (e.g., Norman et al. 1988; Freese and Cohen 1973), although the bulk of evidence seems to favor a combining principle (see Wagner et al. 1986). It is difficult to compare across studies, because some use *only* specific or task characteristics (Norman et al. 1988) and others use diffuse and specific status characteristics of varying strength, so that even if combining occurs, the effects of some status characteristics may be too weak to detect.

Rather than try to resolve which aggregation principle may be the "true" one in status organizing processes, we believe it is more fruitful to work out the conditions under which different aggregation principles are likely to operate. We have been suggesting that one determinant is whether the aggregation of information is realizing a double standard.[10] That is, the aggregation rule will be stricter for lower-status performers. The double standard would presumably operate in conjunction with the activation principles of status characteristics theory (e.g., Humphreys and Berger 1981). A status characteristic will enter into the status situation if there is a path of relevance from it to the task at hand, or if the actors possess different states of it. Further, there may be "master statuses," such as gender, race, and age, that are always activated, as well as organizational contexts that ensure activation of certain status characteristics even when actors are not differentiated on them (see Ridgeway 1988 for a discussion of the activation of gender in organizations). A status characteristic will enter into the status situation if there is a path of relevance from it to the task at hand, or if the actors possess different states of it. Further, there may be "master statuses," such as gender, race, and age, that are always activated, as well as organizational contexts that ensure activation of certain status characteristics even when actors are not differentiated on them (see Ridgeway 1988 for a discussion of the activation of gender in organizations). A remaining task in the development of the conceptualization of double standards is the determination of which of several status characteristics will set off a differential aggregation process (Hembroff and Myers 1984).

Types of Relevance

The use of different aggregators implies different types of relevance for the contributing status characteristics that are combined to infer ability. This issue is ignored in current status characteristics theory: Either a characteristic is relevant or it is not. In case of *and*, where $m_a = \min(m_t, m_c)$, a high score on either m_c or m_t is necessary but not sufficient to obtain a high m_a. The implicit assumption here is that a person who is using the min (*and*) aggregator does not feel confident in predicting m_a from either m_t or m_c alone. When $m_a = \max(m_t, m_c)$, that is for *or*, a high score on either of them is sufficient but not necessary to yield a high m_a.

Sufficiency is arguably a stronger relevancy relationship than mere necessity. The case where high m_t is necessary but not sufficient for high m_a is logically equivalent to the proposition "If high m_a, then high m_t," (but not the converse). On the other hand, the case where high m_t is sufficient but not necessary for high m_t is equivalent to the statement "If high m_t, then high m_a." Applying this analysis to the example from Meeker and Weitzel-O'Neill, we can say that adequate performance is sufficient for males, but only necessary but not sufficient for females.[11] Concepts of necessity and sufficiency have wide potential in representing extra "gates" through which members of one group must pass, and for modeling allowances or "leg-ups" allowed for one group but not another.

These gates and allowances are not always explicit. There is a class of well-known double standards that are not currently handled by status characteristics theory, namely, those involving a "hidden" or "rider" status characteristic. Consider the following examples:

(1) The standard for evaluating ability m_a on the basis of task competence m_t is identical for two groups (G1 and G2), and yet not all high-m_t individuals in G2 are accorded appropriately high evaluations on m_a.

(2) The standard for m_a based on m_t is identical for G1 and G2 and yet some low-m_t individuals in G1 are accorded inappropriately high evaluations on m_a.

In the first example, G2 is apparently being disadvantaged despite the apparent lack of a public double standard, while in the second, G1 is being advantaged. In both examples m_t is the relevant status characteristic, so how can the discrepancy be explained?

The simplest plausible explanation is that the relevancy strength of m_t differs when applied to G1 versus G2. Specifically, in example 1, m_t is both necessary and sufficient for members of G1 to be evaluated favorably, but it is necessary only for members of G2, since not all of them who perform well receive favorable evaluations. Women who score as highly as men on publicly fixed standards for employment (e.g., public service examinations) but then find they are being selected on the basis of physical attractiveness as well have fallen afoul of this kind of double standard. Likewise, in example 2, m_t is both necessary and sufficient for members of G2 to be evaluated favorably, but merely sufficient for members of G1. Some low-performing members of G1 are getting high evaluations, either from the diffuse status characteristics associated with G1 itself or from some other overlapping characteristic. The "old boy" phenomenon and any kind of nepotism are examples of this double standard. Were a double standard on the criterion for m_t itself operating, then of course *all* members of the disadvantaged group would be evaluated less favorably for any given value of m_t. Since this is not so for either example 1 or 2, no one-to-one function of m_t (e.g., differential weighting, exponentials, or additive constants) can account for these cases.

Our discussion of multiple-dimension cases so far suggests the following propositions, which correspond to the order-preservation principle on which double standards are based:

(1) For high-status groups, high performance on a relevant task will be sufficient but may not be necessary to infer high ability.

(2) For low-status groups, high performance on a relevant task will be necessary but may not be sufficient to infer high ability.

Finally, we must consider multiple-aggregator as well as multidimensional status characteristic models. Unlike the usual weighted linear models, combinations involving fuzzy logical *and* and *or* operators permit us to consider the effect that differential groupings of characteristics can have on standards. For instance, is an individual expected to do well on an engineering problem insofar as she or he has high logical ability or has high mechanical ability and great persistence, or insofar as she or he has high logical or mechanical ability and great persistence? In the first combination persistence is not a necessary requirement for an expectation of high performance, but in the second it is. Denoting logical ability, mechanical ability, and persistence by m_1, m_2, and m_3, respectively, the first combination is modeled by $\max(m_1, \min[m_2, m_3])$ and the second by $\min(\max[m_1, m_2], m_3)$. Taking into account the question of grouping (or bracketing) permits us to model double standards in which subgroups of characteristics are given differential relevancy statuses, or even where different subgroups of characteristics are used for evaluations for one group compared to another.

Equal Opportunity and Double Standards

Put simplistically, equality of opportunity is the absence of double standards. If two performers, one with a high and one with a low state of a diffuse status characteristic, emit identical performances, they would be judged, with equal certainty, to have the same level of ability. In the multidimensional case, the same standard would be used for both actors to infer ability on each dimension, and status information would be combined using the same aggregators. More generally, if it could be assumed that only status characteristics and task characteristics that are in fact directly related to task performance would be used to predict performance (in a job, at an educational institution, or in any task-oriented group), then equally "qualified" actors would be assigned equal levels of ability, giving no grounds for job, wage, or promotion discrimination. Less directly related diffuse status characteristics would not enter into the inference of ability, the prediction of performance, or the assignment of "value" (Mahoney 1983). Put this way, equal opportunity would demand not only that the same standard be used to judge performances and qualifications, but that the differentiation of task groups on the basis of imported external statuses should not occur, unless these imported status characteristics had direct task relevance. The determination of such relevance is not a simple one, because some characteristics are predictive of performance for historical reasons. We do not wish to underplay the complexity of this issue, but space here does not allow us to provide a more thorough discussion.

Researchers concerned with the application of expectation states theory to interventions in settings in which discrimination has occurred (Cohen 1982; Lockheed and Hall 1976) recognize the importance of eliminating diffuse status characteristics from the inference of task competence. Their intervention programs are designed to prevent or destroy paths of relevance between characteristics such as race or sex and expectations for task performance. Interventions that give high performance characteristics to the low-status person through manipulated success utilize the assumption that specific and performance characteristics have a greater influence on aggregated expectations than do diffuse characteristics (Lewittes and Bem 1983). One of the features of these interventions is that it is very difficult to eliminate the effects of a diffuse status characteristic; if the low-status person shows superiority on a performance characteristic, the result tends to be status equality in group interaction, not reversal of the power and prestige ordering. Our analysis of double standards suggests a further reason that this might be so — the successes of the low-status performers may be judged against a stricter standard for ability, leading to weaker effects on the interaction hierarchy. The usual intervention offered is to make standards for the inference of ability explicit and unambiguous. While this eliminates one form of bias, we have suggested that other forms of double standards might still operate, in the selection and aggregation of other specific and diffuse status information. Further, as Bielby and Bielby (1988) note, even if a single standard is specified clearly, the *evidence* about the abilities of minorities — for example, school performance, references, work experience — may be regarded as less credible, that is, as lower-quality evidence, so that more of it is needed to enable them to meet the same standard.

By conceptualizing a number of different forms that double standards can take, we provide ideas about where to look for them and how to detect their operation. However, while we can specify what in principle would eliminate double standards, the conditions are difficult to engineer, and even when this can be done, the multitude of forms that double standards can take ensures their durability. Our optimistic assumption is that the explication of these forms makes double standards more identifiable; however, other processes must be engaged before identification can lead to elimination. Much of affirmative action policy rests on the assumption that people do not actively wish to discriminate among employees on the basis of nonrelevant characteristics (but see Mahoney 1983; Shepela and Viviano 1984; Pettigrew and Martin 1987).

Conclusions

In this chapter, we have presented a framework for the representation of double standards in the inference of ability. Our strategy has been to provide a plausibility argument for the framework. The evaluation of the approach will depend on its capacity to generate empirical predictions that stand up to test, and to provide integrated explanations of a range of findings. We have made a number of suggestions for future research and for theory development, particularly with respect to modeling different types of relevance relations. Finally, we have suggested that this framework can provide a basis for extending status characteristics theory to questions of equal opportunity policy and diagnosis.

Notes

1. We assume that it is possible to evaluate performances as successful or unsuccessful, but nevertheless to reach a variety of conclusions about the *level* of ability, or lack of ability, reflected in these performance outcomes.

2. From its earliest formulations, expectation states theory has included biased evaluations of outputs as a mechanism through which the power and prestige order of a group may emerge and be maintained. There is a substantial research literature documenting the effects of status characteristics on the perception of performances (e.g., Etaugh and Kasley 1981; Pettigrew and Martin 1987). We see this process to be different from the application of varying standards.

3. There are other studies that give indirect evidence of double standards (e.g., Ridgeway 1982; Meeker and Weitzel-O'Neill 1977), but since we regard them as involving a somewhat different process, they will be reviewed at a later stage.

4. Pettigrew and Martin (1987) review an analogous literature concerned with "the ultimate attribution error" in the evaluation of black employees. Success in a job by a black produces surprise and is less likely to be taken as evidence of ability; failure confirms prior stereotype-based beliefs and, since poor performance was expected, is taken as evidence of (low) ability.

5. In expectation states theory, the emphasis is on the relative ability of p and o, and so the +, – representation has been adequate for most purposes, although it does not allow a convenient representation of large, compared to small, expectation advantages or a comparison of the relative strength of prediction from two characteristics linked to a task by paths of relevance of the same length and sign.

6. It is important to realize that the fuzzy set framework described here involves several parameter estimation problems, starting with the elicitation of membership scales and values. These problems are not beyond the scope of standard psychometric theory (see, e.g., Smithson 1984 and some selections from Zetenyi 1988, for review material), nor are they fundamental to the utility of the framework for expectation states theory. However, some of the parameters themselves may prove theoretically interesting. One example is the strictness of the aggregator, which may vary from a strict *and* to a lenient *or* (see Smithson 1987 for a least squares approach to modeling aggregators with a parameter that may take values from a pure *and* to a pure *or*).

7. While these examples may seem fanciful, Hansen and O'Leary (1985) provide empirically obtained relationships that are very similar to our manufactured examples. They show that for any given level of performance, a woman is believed to have exhibited more effort than a man; for equivalent levels of performance above average, a woman is considered to have less ability than a man.

8. There is insufficient space here to describe Zadeh's (1972) framework for representing dilators and concentrators (fuzzy hedges). For our purposes, hedges such as *very* are concentrators in the sense that they modify the fuzzy set into a more exclusive set, while dilators (e.g., *somewhat*) result in a more inclusive set.

9. Strictness might also vary within any of the tasks, T_i, but we will avoid this complication at present.

10. Other conditions may include whether subjects are combining only clearly specified, salient performance characteristics (when one might expect combining) or are free to select from a larger pool of status information, in which case they may ignore inconsistent information.

11. Meeker and Weitzel-O'Neill also discuss the impact of legitimate status, where externally endowed leadership position in a group seems to follow the same pattern as cooperative orientation.

References

Alston, W. P. 1964. *Philosophy of Language*. Englewood Cliffs, NJ: Prentice-Hall.

Berger, J. 1988. "Directions in Expectation States Research." In *Status Generalization: New Theory and Research*, edited by M. Webster, Jr., and M. Foschi. Stanford, CA: Stanford University Press.

Berger, J., M. H. Fisek, R. Z. Norman, and M. Zelditch. 1977. *Status Characteristics and Social Interaction: An Expectation States Approach*. New York: Elsevier.

Berger, J., S. J. Rosenholtz, and M. Zelditch, Jr. 1980. "Status Organizing Processes." *Annual Review of Sociology* 6:479-508.

Berger, J. and M. Zelditch, Jr. 1985. *Status, Rewards, and Influence: How Expectations Organize Behavior*. San Francisco: Jossey-Bass.

Bielby, D. D. and W. T. Bielby. 1988. "She Works Hard for the Money: Household Responsibilities and the Allocation of Work Effort." *American Journal of Sociology* 93:1031-59.

Black, M. 1937. "Vagueness: An Exercise in Logical Analysis." *Philosophy of Science* 4:427-55.

Burgess, D., W. Kempton, and R. E. MacLaury. 1983. "Tarahumara Color Modifiers: Category Structure Presaging Evolutionary Change." *American Ethnologist* 10:133-49.

Burton, C., R. Hag, and G. Thompson. 1987. *Women's Worth: Pay Equity and Job Evaluation in Australia*. Canberra: Australian Government Publishing Service.

Cohen, Elizabeth G. 1982. "Expectation States and Interracial Interaction School Settings." *Annual Review of Sociology* 8:209-35.

Cohen, Elizabeth G. and Susan Roper. 1972. "Modification of Interracial Interaction Disability: An Application of Status Characteristics Theory." *American Sociological Review* 37:643-65.

Cox, R. T. 1946. "Probability, Frequency, and Reasonable Expectation." *American Journal of Physics* 14:1-13.

Crundall, I. and M. Foddy. 1981. "Vicarious Exposure to a Task as a Basis of Evaluative Competence." *Social Psychology Quarterly* 44:331-38.

Deaux, K. 1984. "From Individual Differences to Social Categories: Analysis of a Decade's Research on Gender." *American Psychologist* 39:105-16.

— — —. 1985. "Sex and Gender." *Annual Review of Psychology* 36:49-81.

Doeringer, P. B. and M. Piore. 1971. *Internal Labor Markets and Manpower Analysis.* Lexington, MA: D. C. Heath.

Eagly, A. 1983. "Gender and Social Influence." *American Psychologist* 38:971-81.

Eagly, A. and V. J. Steffen. 1984. "Gender Stereotypes Stem from the Distribution of Women and Men into Social Roles." *Journal of Personality and Social Psychology* 46:735-54.

Eichler, M. 1977. "The Double Standard as an Indicator of Sex-Status Differentials." *Atlantis* 3:1-30.

— — —. 1980. *The Double Standard.* New York: St. Martin's.

Eskilson, A. and M. G. Wiley. 1976. "Sex Composition and Leadership in Small Groups." *Sociometry* 39:83-96.

Etaugh, C. and H. C. Kasley. 1981. "Evaluating Competence: Effects of Sex, Marital Status, and Parental Status." *Psychology of Women Quarterly* 6:196-203.

Foschi, M. and M. Foddy. 1988. "Standards, Performances, and the Formation of Self-Other Expectations." Pp. 248-60 in *Status Generalization: New Theory and Research*, edited by M. Webster, Jr., and M. Foschi. Stanford, CA: Stanford University Press.

Foschi, M. and S. Freeman. 1987. "Inferior Performance, Standards, and Influence in Same-Sex Dyads." Paper presented at the annual meetings of the American Sociological Association, Chicago.

Foschi, M. and J. S. Plecash. 1983. "Sex Differences in the Attribution of Success and Failure: An Expectation States Explanation." Paper presented at the annual meeting of the Canadian Sociology and Anthropology Association, Vancouver.

Foschi, M., G. K. Warriner, and S. D. Hart. 1985. "Standards, Expectations, and Interpersonal Influence." *Social Psychology Quarterly* 48:108-17.

Freese, L. and B. P. Cohen. 1973. "Eliminating Status Generalization." *Sociometry* 36:177-93.

Frieze, I. H., B. E. Whitley, B. H. Hanusa, and M. C. McHugh. 1982. "Assessing the Theoretical Models for Sex Differences in Causal Attributions for Success and Failure." *Sex Roles* 8:333-43.

Gaines, B. R. 1975. "Stochastic and Fuzzy Logics." *Electronic Letters* 11:188-89.

Gerdes, E. G. and D. M. Garber. 1983. "Sex Bias in Hiring: Effects of Job Demands and Applicant Competence." *Sex Roles* 9:307-19.

Graham, H. 1989. "Double Standards and the Achievement of Women and Men: An Expectations States Approach." Unpublished Ph.D. dissertation, La Trobe University, Bundoora, Victoria, Australia.

Hansen, R. D. and V. E. O'Leary. 1985. "Sex-Determined Attributions." Pp. 67-99 in *Women, Gender, and Social Psychology*, edited by V. E. O'Leary, R. H. Unger, and B. S. Wallston. Hillsdale, NJ: Lawrence Erlbaum.

Hartmann, H. I., ed. 1985. *Comparable Worth: New Directions for Research.* Washington, DC: National Academy Press.

Heilman, M. E. and R. A. Guzzo. 1978. "The Perceived Cause of Work Success as a Mediator of Sex Discrimination in Organizations." *Organizational Behaviour and Human Performance* 21:346-57.

Hembroff, L. A. and D. E. Myers. 1984. "Status Characteristics: Degrees of Task Relevance and Decision Processes." *Social Psychology Quarterly* 47:337-46.

Humphreys P. and J. Berger. 1981. "Theoretical Consequences of the Status Characteristics Formulation." *American Journal of Sociology* 86:953-83.

Instone, D., B. Major, and B. B. Bunker. 1983. "Gender, Self-Confidence, and Social Influence Strategies: An Organizational Simulation." *Journal of Personality and Social Psychology* 44:322-33.

Lenney, E. 1977. "Women's Self-Confidence in Achievement Settings." *Psychological Bulletin* 84:1-13.

Lewittes, H. J. and S. L. Bem. 1983. "Training Women to Be More Assertive in Mixed-Sex Task-Oriented Discussions." *Sex Roles* 9:581-96.

Lockheed, M. E. and K. P. Hall. 1976. "Conceptualizing Sex as a Status Characteristic: Applications to Leadership Training Strategies." *Journal of Social Issues* 32:111-24.

Mahoney, T. A. 1983. "Approaches to the Definition of Comparable Worth." *Academy of Management Review* 8:14-22.

Malkiel, B. G. and J. A. Malkiel. 1973. "Male-Female Pay Differentials in Professional Employment." *American Economic Review* 63:693-705.

McArthur, L. Z. 1985. "Social Judgment Biases in Comparable Worth Analysis." Pp. 53-70 in *Comparable Worth: New Directions for Research*, edited by H. I. Hartmann. Washington, DC: National Academy Press.

McArthur, L. Z. and S. W. Obrant. 1986. "Sex Biases in Comparable Worth Analyses." *Journal of Applied Social Psychology* 16:757-70.

Meeker, B. F. 1981. "Expectation States and Interpersonal Behavior." Pp. 290-319 in *Social Psychology: Sociological Perspectives*, edited by M. Rosenberg and R. Turner. New York: Basic Books.

Meeker, B. F. and P. A. Weitzel-O'Neill. 1977. "Sex Roles and Interpersonal Behavior in Task-Oriented Groups." *American Sociological Review* 42:91-105.

Moore, J. C. 1968. "Status and Influence in Small Group Interaction." *Sociometry* 31:47-63.

Newstead, S. E. 1988. "Quantifiers as Fuzzy Concepts." In *Fuzzy Sets in Psychology*, edited by T. Zetenyi. Amsterdam: North Holland.

Nguyen, H. T. and I. R. Goodman. 1985. *Uncertainty Models for Knowledge-Based Systems* Amsterdam: North Holland.

Niedenthal, P. and N. Cantor. 1984. "Making Use of Social Prototypes: From Fuzzy Concepts to Firm Decisions." *Fuzzy Sets and Systems* 7:5-27.

Nieva, V. and B. Gutek. 1980. "Sex Effects on Evaluation." *Academy of Management Review* 5:267-76.

Norman, R. Z., R. F. Smith, and J. Berger. 1988. "The Processing of Inconsistent Status Information." Pp. 169-87 in *Status Generalization: New Theory and Research*, edited by M. Webster, Jr., and M. Foschi. Stanford, CA: Stanford University Press.

Oden, G. C. and L. T. Lopes. 1982. "On the Internal Structure of Fuzzy Subjective Categories." In *Fuzzy Set and Possibility Theory: Recent Developments*, edited by R. R. Yager. New York: Pergamon.

O'Leary, V. E. and R. H. Hansen. 1982. "Trying Hurts Women, Helps Men: The Meaning of Effort." Pp. 100-23 in *Women in the Work Force*, edited by H. J. Bernardin. New York: Praeger.

Olson, C. A. and B. E. Becker. 1983. "Sex Discrimination in the Promotion Process." *Industrial and Labor Relations Review* 36:624-31.

Pettigrew, T. F. and J. Martin. 1987. "Shaping the Organizational Context for Black American Inclusion." *Journal of Social Issues* 43:41-78.

Pugh, M. D. and R. Wahrman. 1983. "Neutralizing Sexism in Mixed-Sex Groups: Do Women Have to Be Better Than Men?" *American Journal of Sociology* 88:746-62.

Ridgeway, C. L. 1982. "Status in Groups: The Importance of Motivation." *American Sociological Review* 47:76-88.

– – –. 1988. "Gender Differences in Task Groups: A Status and Legitimacy Account. In *Status Generalization: New Theory and Research*, edited by M. Webster, Jr., and M. Foschi. Stanford, CA: Stanford University Press.

Riger, S. and P. Galligan. 1980. "Women in Management: An Exploration of Competing Paradigms." *American Psychologist* 35:902-19.

Rosch, E. 1973. "Natural Categories." *Cognitive Psychology* 4:328-50.

— — —. 1978. "Principles of Categorization." In *Cognition and Categorization*, edited by E. Rosch and B. B. Lloyd. Hillsdale, NJ: Lawrence Erlbaum.

Ruble, T. L., R. Cohen, and D. N. Ruble. 1984. "Sex Stereotypes: Occupational Barriers for Women." *American Behavioral Scientist* 27:339-56.

Shepela, S. T. and A. T. Viviano. 1984. "Some Psychological Factors Affecting Job Segregation and Wages." In *Comparable Worth and Wage Discrimination: Technical Possibilities and Political Realities*, edited by H. Remick. Philadelphia: Temple University Press.

Smith, R. E., ed. 1979. *The Subtle Revolution: Women at Work*. Washington, DC: Urban Institute.

Smithson, M. 1984. "Multivariate analysis using 'and' and 'or.'" *Journal of Mathematical Social Sciences* 7:231-251.

Smithson, M. 1987. *Fuzzy Set Analysis for Behavioral and Social Sciences*. New York: Springer-Verlag.

Smithson, M. and K. Knibb. 1986. "New Measures of Association for Numerical Variables." *Journal of Mathematical Social Sciences* 11:161-182.

Stead, B. A. 1985. *Women in Management*, 2nd ed. Englewood Cliffs, NJ: Prentice-Hall.

Treiman, D. J. and H. I. Hartmann, eds. 1981. *Women, Work and Wages: Equal Pay for Jobs of Equal Value*. Washington, DC: National Academy Press.

Wagner, D. G., R. S. Ford, and T. W. Ford. 1986. "Can Gender Inequalities Be Reduced?" *American Sociological Review* 51:47-61.

Wahrman, R. and M. D. Pugh. 1974. "Sex, Nonconformity and Influence." *Sociometry* 37:137-47.

Walden, R. and V. Walkerdine. 1981. *Girls and Mathematics: The Early Years* (Bedford Way Papers 8). London: Heinemann.

Webster, M., Jr. and M. Foschi, eds. 1988. *Status Generalization: New Theory and Research*. Stanford, CA: Stanford University Press

Webster, M., Jr. and B. Sobieszek. 1974. *Sources of Self-Evaluation: A Formal Theory of Significant Others and Social Influence*. New York: John Wiley.

Wiley, M. G. and A. Eskilson. 1983. "Scaling the Corporate Ladder: Sex Differences in Expectations for Performance Power and Mobility." *Social Psychology Quarterly* 46:351-59.

Yarkin, K. L., J. P. Town, and B. S. Wallston. 1982. "Blacks and Women Must Try Harder: Stimulus Person's Race and Sex Attributions of Causality." *Personality and Social Psychology Bulletin* 8:21-24.

Zadeh, L. A. 1972. "A Fuzzy Set Theoretical Interpretation of Hedges." *Journal of Cybernetics* 2:4-34.

— — —. 1978. "Fuzzy Sets as a Basis for a Theory of Possibility." *Fuzzy Sets and Systems* 1:3-28.

— — —. 1980. "Fuzzy Sets Versus Probability." *Proceedings of IEEE* 68:421.

Zelditch, M., Jr., P. Lauderdale, and S. Stublarec. 1980. "How Are Inconsistencies Between Status and Ability Resolved?" *Social Forces* 58:1025-43.

Zetenyi, T., ed. 1988. *Fuzzy Sets in Psychology*. Amsterdam: North Holland.

5

The Evolution of Status Expectations:
A Theoretical Extension

JOSEPH BERGER

M. HAMIT FISEK

ROBERT Z. NORMAN

By now it is well known that when individuals interact in problem-solving situations the external characteristics they possess determine important aspects of their interaction. Individuals who are high on external status characteristics, in comparison to those who are low, are more likely to have chances to perform, to initiate problem-solving performances, and to have their performances positively evaluated, and are less likely to be influenced when there are disagreements. The distributions of these behaviors in a group tend to be highly correlated and collectively represent the observable power and prestige order in the group. It is also the case that this relationship between external status and position in the power and prestige order in the group holds whether or not the external status is initially relevant to the group task (Caudill 1958; Croog 1956; Hurwitz et al. 1960; Mishler and Tropp 1956; Strodtbeck et al. 1957; Strodtbeck and Mann 1956; Torrance 1954; Zander and Cohen 1955; Ziller and Exline 1958).

The theory of status characteristics was originally developed to explain this status generalization process (Berger et al. 1966, 1972). The theory describes how and under what conditions status characteristics order the interaction in the group. The original formulation has been extended in several stages to deal with single or multiple characteristics; to deal with two or more interactants and the effect of "referent others" — actors who are not involved in the immediate interaction but who provide status information that is used in that interaction; and to deal with the relation of reward expectations to performance expectations in status situations (Berger and Fisek 1974; Berger et al. 1977, 1985). In addition, the most recent version of the theory embodies a formal model that enables us to describe a wide range of status situations and to derive general theoretical assertions about status processes (Berger et al. 1977). A body of research now exists that is relevant to the principles and derivations of these theories (see, for example, Moore 1968; Webster and Driskell 1978; Berger et al. 1980; Berger and Zelditch 1985; Webster and Foschi 1988).

There also exists an extensive body of applied research based on the status characteristics formulations. As part of this research, it has been shown that, under certain conditions, it is possible to intervene in the operation of status processes so as to mitigate some of the undesirable effects of different status characteristics. For examples of such research on gender, see Lockheed and Hall (1976) and Pugh and Wahrman (1983); on race, see Cohen and Roper (1972), Lohman (1972), and Webster and Driskell (1978); on physical attractiveness, see Webster and Driskell (1983); on reading ability and generalized academic reputation, see Tammivaara (1982) and Rosenholtz (1985).

Although the scope of the basic theory has been extended through successive formulations, it is still the case that the theory describes the operation of status processes in situations where the actors are working on a single valued and collective task. As such, it does not deal with what happens when actors are confronted with a sequence of tasks. In this chapter we want to describe how expectations and power and prestige behaviors evolve in settings in which actors are interacting on a *sequence* of valued collective tasks. The extension of the status theory to such settings will enable us to deal with other important theoretical issues. Two of these are particularly worth mentioning.

First, there is the issue of the effect on the status process of external evaluations of task success or task failure. There are status situations, of course, where such evaluations occur, and when they do occur they can have dramatic effects on the status process. An extension of the theory to a situation involving a sequence of tasks enables us to describe the effect that the assignment to actors of task success or task failure at the *completion of one task* has on their expectations and behavior in subsequent tasks.

Second is the issue of the effectiveness of status interventions. A major theoretical issue is to determine the extent to which such interventions can persist beyond the situations in which they are introduced. The type of extension we intend here should enable us to address this issue, and, in fact, the issue of assessing the effectiveness of status interventions has been an important motivation in developing this extension.

The scope of our extended theory will cover a situation that can involve a sequence of tasks that extend through time. In the next section, we describe our general conception of such a situation.

The Image of an Expanding Situation

Central to the concept of a situation S in status characteristics theory is the idea of a *valued and collective task*. To begin with, this is a task in which there are outcome states that can be defined as "success" and "failure." Further, we assume that an actor working on such a task believes that there exists a performance characteristic (or a set of correlated characteristics) that is instrumental to the task in that if the individual possesses the high state of the characteristic (is highly competent), he or she can expect to succeed at the task, while if the individual possesses the low state of the characteristic (is incompetent), he or she can expect to fail. Also, we assume that part of the actor's definition of the situation in working on the task is the understanding that it is both necessary and legitimate to take the behavior of others into account in solving the task.

We now conceptualize the situation S as one in which there can be a sequence of such valued collective tasks and one in which the abilities that are instrumental to each of these tasks can be distinct and different from each other. The only restriction we place on the tasks in the situation is that they are not culturally "dissociated" from each other (a term we shall shortly define).

The image we have of this situation can be described as follows. Actors interact on a sequence of valued and collective tasks. When they complete work on one task, they may move on to work on a second task, so that this context may be conceived of as a "situational shell" that expands through time as it encompasses new tasks. As actors interact on a given task, they form expectations for each other, and they engage in behaviors that are functions of these expectations. As they move from task to task, the expectations and behaviors on the first task affect those that emerge on the subsequent task. A history of past expectations and behaviors is developed in the situational shell.

Viewing the situation from the standpoint of a given focal actor, this actor may find himself interacting on tasks with the same other or a different other, and, as a consequence of his interacting with different others, new types of performance and status information may become salient to him.

Aside from the information that enters the actor's situation as a result of the particular others with whom he interacts, there are other kinds of information that can have dramatic effects on his behavior. Perhaps the most significant types of such information are the evaluations of task success and task failure that can be assigned to the actors by an external evaluating source at the completion of a given task. Finally, just as there may be periods in the evolution of the situation when the process is open to new status, performance, and evaluational information from its environment, so there may also be periods when the process is closed to its environment at the same time that expectations and behavior continue to evolve in the expanding situation. With this image of the action process in mind, we can formulate the types of questions that are of concern to us.

First, we are concerned with the overall effect that status structures that emerge on one task have on those that emerge on a subsequent task. Under what general conditions will the expectations and behavior of one task affect those of a subsequent task? In addition, what are the general factors that determine the magnitude of the effect that past status structures have on current ones?

Second, we are concerned with the evolution of expectations and power and prestige behaviors when, from the standpoint of a focal actor, the situation is open to new actors and new information. In particular, we are interested in the effects of the attribution or assignment to the actor of task success or task failure. Given that such assignments are consistent with the power and prestige order in one task setting, how will that affect the status differentiation in the subsequent setting? Also, what is the effect on the current status structure if such assignments are inconsistent with the power and prestige order of the previous structure?

Third, we are concerned with the process when, from the standpoint of the focal actor, the situation is closed to the environment, and yet the actor's expectations and behaviors continue to evolve. Under these conditions do the actor's expectations and power and prestige behaviors stabilize? If they do, what factors affect the values of the actor's stabilized status relations?

Our final set of concerns deals with the long-term effect of status interventions. What happens to the effect of such interventions as the actor moves to new task settings and confronts new others? Do such interventions have long-term effects? If so, under what conditions do these occur?

In the next section we describe the basic elements of status characteristics theory and introduce an auxiliary assumption that enables us to apply the theory to a situation involving sequence of tasks. Following this, we shall consider substantive consequences of the theory, including general theoretical assertions. We then examine empirical research that is relevant to this extension, and conclude with a summary of our work.

Status Characteristics Theory[1]

The theory of status characteristics describes the evolution of a status organizing process in a task situation. A *status organizing process* is one in which evaluations and beliefs about the characteristics of actors become bases of observable inequalities in face-to-face interaction.

A crucial concept in describing such a process is that of *status characteristic*. A status characteristic is any characteristic around which expectations and beliefs about actors come to be organized. We distinguish two types of status characteristics, specific and diffuse. Key to this distinction is the difference between specific and general expectations. Expectations are *specific* if they refer to an individual's expectations to perform in a clearly defined and specified situation. They are said to be *general* if they are not restricted to any specified situation. Thus "mathematical ability" carries specific and "intelligence" carries general expectations. We say that a characteristic is a *specific status characteristic* if it involves two or more states that are differentially evaluated; and associated with each state is a distinct specific expectation state. For example, reading ability may function as a specific status characteristic. We distinguish different levels of the characteristic that are differentially evaluated, and we associate with it beliefs about how individuals possessing the different states will perform specified tasks. We say that a characteristic is a *diffuse status characteristic* if it involves two or more states that are differentially valued; and associated with each state are distinct sets of specific expectation states, each itself evaluated; and associated with each state is a similarly evaluated general expectation state. Gender, race, occupation, educational attainment, ethnic distinctions, and physical attractiveness each may be a diffuse status characteristic. Whether any of these are a diffuse status characteristic for a given group at a given time is a factual question, not a theoretical question.

In this formulation we apply the theory to situations that satisfy certain conditions. Actors in the situation may be interactants or referents. The interaction process involves only two actors interacting with each other at any one period of time. These are the *interactants*. In the course of the interaction, which actors are the interactants may change. A *referent* is an actor who is a noninteractant during a given period (this may be a former interactant) whose status information is used by the interactant pair. There must be at least one valued collective task in the situation toward which interactants are oriented. However, under the extension that we are formulating, a situation can consist of a sequence of such tasks where these tasks are not dissociated from each other.

The core of status characteristics theory contains five assumptions. The first describes two conditions under which status information becomes *salient* to the actors. One of these is where the status characteristics are defined as relevant to the task, as would be the case, for example, in the sex typing of tasks as "masculine" and "feminine." The second is the situation where the status characteristic is a basis of discrimination in the group, as would be the case, for example, in a mixed-gender or biracial group.[2] We assume in this extension that the salience process also operates whenever actors interact on new tasks, and whenever they interact with new actors, where such interaction introduces new status information into the process.

The second major assumption argues that, if a particular status element is not dissociated from the task, then the interactants will act as if it is relevant. According to this *burden of proof* process, status characteristics and status advantages will be applied to every new task and every new situation as a matter of normal interaction unless their inapplicability is demonstrated or justified. This burden of proof process is one of the two principal mechanisms by which status information that has become salient in the past connects the past to current task structures.

The third assumption states that if new actors enter during the interaction on a given task, then the restructuring of a situation will proceed in *sequence*. The structure for the focal actor will further develop through the operation of the salience and burden of proof processes whenever he or she encounters a new interactant or starts a new task, while, at the same time, his or her previously completed structures remain as long as the actor is in the given task situation.

The fourth assumption claims that the actor combines all information that has become salient and relevant to the immediate task. While, in all likelihood, the process by which this occurs is outside the individual's awareness, we can construct a model to describe it.[3] In terms of this model, all status information leading to positive performance expectations is combined to determine a value, e^+. All negative information similarly combines to form e^-. In these combining processes there is an attenuation effect. That is, there is a decrease in the increment of expectation values with the addition of each like-signed piece of information. The aggregated expectations for an actor are given by summing e^+ and e^-. The actor's expectation advantage (or disadvantage) relative to an other is equal to the aggregated expectation for self less that formed for the other.

The fifth assumption states that an actor's position relative to an other on the observable power and prestige order of the group is a direct continuous function of his or her expectation (dis)advantage relative to this other in the group.

To extend the scope of the theory to situations involving a sequence of group tasks, we introduce an auxiliary assumption that describes how outcomes on successive tasks come to be related to each other:

- *Auxiliary assumption (relevance of tasks):* Given any two successive group tasks in situation S that are not dissociated from or inversely related to each other. When, upon completion of the first task, the actor engages in the second, then relevance relations will be established in a consistent manner between the outcome states (success and failure) of these tasks.

Two tasks are *dissociated*, if, by cultural convention, the abilities involved in each of these tasks are so defined that it is not possible to predict the level of one ability from information about the second. Two tasks are *inversely related* to each other if, on the basis of cultural definitions or beliefs specific to the actors in the situation, high ability on one task is associated with low ability on the second and low ability on one is associated with high ability on the other. Thus, for example, if one task is defined as "masculine" — that is, men have (or are expected to have) high and women low ability on the task — and the second is defined as "feminine" — that is, women have (or are expected to have) high and men low ability on it — then the two tasks are inversely related in the sense of this concept as it is used here.

This auxiliary assumption describes the second principal mechanism by which past status structures are connected to current tasks, namely, through relevance relations established between task outcomes. It says, given two tasks that are not dissociated or inversely related, then if an actor engages on a second task after completing the first task, he or she will behave as though an individual who has done well on the first will expect to do well on the second, and an individual who has done poorly on the first task will expect to do poorly on the second. In other words, the actor behaves as if the outcomes of these tasks (success and failure) are related to each other in a consistent manner.

Consequences of the Formulation

With the addition of the assumption of the relevance of tasks to the core theory, we can deal with the specific problems that are of concern to us. Not only can we describe the particular dynamics that occur in an extremely larger number of specific status situations, but we can also derive from the theory general assertions that describe the evolution of expectations and power and prestige relations. In this section, we present some of these theorems, which we group into four sets.

In the first set, we document the basic features of the process by which expectations formed on one task affect those on a second. In the second, we deal with the issue of changes in expectations and power and prestige behavior and, in particular, with the effects of the assignment to the actors of evaluations of task success or task failure. In the third, we deal with the issue of stability: How and under what conditions will expectations become stable and create behavioral constancies across different tasks? And in the fourth set, we consider an issue of particular importance to theory applications — the long-term effects of status interventions.

Before turning to our theorems, it is necessary to introduce some new ideas that will be useful in describing these general assertions.

This theory is formulated from the point of view of a focal actor, p, who in any task setting interacts with another actor who can be the same other, or a similar other, or a different other from the one p interacted with in the previous task setting. o_2 is *similar* to o_1 from the standpoint of p, if o_2 possesses the same performance and status characteristics that o_1's were salient in interaction with p. o_2 is *different* from o_1, from the standpoint of p, if o_2 possesses at least one performance or status characteristic that becomes salient in the interaction with p that was not salient in p's interaction with o_1, or does not possess a salient characteristic possessed by o_1.

Status elements possessed by the actors are connected by "paths of relevance" to task outcome states.[4] These paths may differ in length, and the general idea is that the longer or shorter the path, the weaker or stronger, respectively, its contribution to the actors' performance expectations. We assume that there are characteristic numbers associated with paths of different lengths, and we think of these numbers as representing the *degree (strength) of relevance* of a path. While not committing ourselves to a single substantive interpretation of these numbers, we can say that they represent the strength of the actors' expectancy that a certain outcome will be attained, given the information embodied in a particular path.

We have already discussed what we mean when we speak of the focal actor interacting on tasks that are not dissociated from or inversely related to each other. We shall also speak of the actor interacting on a sequence of independent tasks. A *sequence of independent tasks* consists of a sequence of tasks in which (1) no two tasks in the sequence are dissociated from or inversely related to each other and (2) there are no "special" relevance bonds connecting actors to any task in the sequence. By "special" relevance bonds, we mean relations other than those created by the burden of proof and the relevance of task processes, for example, the task is gender typed, or the actors possess states of the task characteristic.

EXPECTATIONS AND STATUS RELATIONS ACROSS TASKS

The most general conclusion we can draw from our theory is that, under the conditions to which this extension applies, the expectations and behavior of actors on one task in the evolving situation will affect their expectations and behavior on a subsequent task. Before presenting the theorem that states this general effect, it may be useful to describe this phenomenon with respect to a specific example.

Imagine that two actors, p, a male, and o, a female, interact on a succession of tasks in the following possible situations. p and o work on a task that is gender neutral, that is, there are no cultural beliefs that define gender categories as relevant to the outcome states of the task. In such a situation, given that gender is the only basis of discrimination, it will become salient and relevant, and the actors will form expectations and engage in behaviors in which p will hold a higher status position than o. We shall refer to this situation as our "comparison" case.

Now let's imagine two different scenarios. In the first, p and o work on an initial task that is sex typed as a "masculine" task and then work on the gender-neutral task (under the same conditions as in our comparison case). In the second scenario, they work on an initial task that is sex typed as a "feminine" task and then on the gender-neutral task (again under the same conditions as in our comparison case).

If p and o first work on the masculine-typed task, p's expectation advantage and power and prestige advantage over o will be relatively large. When they then interact on the gender-neutral task, p's expectations and power and prestige advantage over o will be greater than in the comparison case because of their experience on the first task.

If p and o first work on the feminine-typed task, o, the female, is predicted to have a relatively large expectation advantage over p, and to become the status superior to the male. When they then work on the gender-neutral task, p's expectation advantage and power and prestige advantage over o will be less than that found in the comparison case. This is because of their experience on the first task, where o, the female, held a higher power and prestige position than p, the male.

In general, we shall describe the effect that expectations and behaviors that develop on the immediate past task have on the current task. In fact, the structure of the current task consists of two types of components. The first of these are the status and task characteristics involved in the current task considered in isolation, or without elements transferred from the past task. The second component of the current task is the set of elements of the past task structure that is transferred to create the current structure. The *effect* of the past task structure on the current task structure is then defined as the difference in expectations and behaviors that occurs in the current structure from what would occur in that structure considered in isolation.

More generally, we can say that, for any given task in the situational sequence on which the actors interact, their relative expectations and relative status positions will be affected by the past history of their interaction as well as the conditions of their immediate task. This very general idea is given in Theorem 1:

- *Theorem 1 (effect of past expectations):* Given that p and o (or any other o) interact on two successive tasks that are not dissociated. Then the expectations formed on the first task will affect the power and prestige differentiation on the second.

Theorem 1 tells us that expectations developed in past tasks have an effect on expectations in a current task. But what is the magnitude of the effect? What factors affect the magnitude? The answer to this question involves understanding the nature of the elements that are transferred from one task to another and the way these elements interact with elements inherent in the current task.

This section, therefore, consists of two parts. In the first we examine the transferred elements and how certain basic status factors affect their magnitudes. In the second part we investigate how these transferred elements interact with status elements already in the current task to determine the power and prestige positions of the actors so we can assess the effect of the past experience on the current task.

The Transfer of Status Expectations

Elements from the past structure become transferred to the current structure in two ways. One is through the type of actor created by experiences in the situation, and the other is through the connections between tasks.

As the focal actor interacts with different others on different tasks and receives different evaluations of task success or task failure, performance and status characteristics become associated with the actor as salient elements. The actor is thus constructed as a particular configuration of salient elements out of experience in the interaction process. Then, by the burden of proof process, the performance and status characteristics in this configuration become relevant to the current task setting, and this way become transferred elements to that setting.

The other way elements of a past structure become transferred elements to the current structure is through the relevance of tasks process. Status and performance characteristics become relevant in past task settings and are the bases of the actor's expectations and behavior in those settings. The pattern of expectations in the past task setting is then connected, by the relevance of tasks process, to the structure of the current task setting and becomes transferred elements to it.

One of the major kinds of effects carried over from one task to a second involves the transmission of status advantages and disadvantages. It is natural, therefore, to ask what features of the status structure within which the actors interact on a given task affect the magnitude of these expectation advantages that are transferred. There are three features of the status structure that are important in this matter: the degree of consistency of discriminating status characteristics, the number of such characteristics, and the degree of relevance of these characteristics to the outcome states of the task.

Status structures differ in their degree of status consistency. In consistent structures all the status characteristics possessed by each of the actors provide the same kind of information as to how the actor is connected to the task outcome. In such a structure, status advantages are congruent and reinforce each other. On the other hand, where the status characteristics possessed by the actors provide them with conflicting information relating them to their task — that is, where some parts of the status information lead them to expect success and other parts lead them to expect failure — the structure is inconsistent.

We can assess structures in terms of their degree of status consistency and the impact of this factor on the expectations that are transferred. In general, for a given status structure in which the actors possess states of a specific number of discriminating characteristics, each with a fixed degree of task relevance, the more consistent that structure within one task setting the greater the status advantages or disadvantages transferred from that setting into a succeeding one.

If we now restrict ourselves to task situations with consistent discriminating status characteristics, we can easily see how the number of such characteristics and their degree of relevance affect the transfer of expectations. Basically, the idea is that, for a particular consistent structure with a fixed number of such characteristics, each with a given degree of relevance, if we increase the number of such characteristics in that structure by adding characteristics consistent with those already present, we increase the magnitudes of the advantages and disadvantages that are transferred. Similarly, for a particular consistent structure with a fixed number of status characteristics, each with a given degree of relevance, if we increase the degree of relevance of any one of these characteristics while keeping their number and consistent state, we again increase the magnitude of the transferred advantages and disadvantages. Increasing the number of characteristics and their degree of relevance increases the number of status distinctions that are operating in a consistent manner and increases the strength of those status distinctions in connecting actors to the task outcome states.

To determine task expectations for the actors in the current task, we make use of all the status information available, including the transferred elements and any new status information that may be introduced in the current task. We first look at the simple case in which, in the current task, no new status information appears. Then the entire set of relevant status information for the task consists of transferred elements. Thus if two actors engage in a sequence of tasks for which no new status elements are introduced, we can, by looking at the successive structures of transferred elements, explore how the relative status positions of the actors develop over time.

Consider two actors, p, a man and o, a woman, working on a gender-neutral task as in our comparison case. Here, p has an expectation advantage over o, as we have seen. Suppose they then work on a gender-neutral second task in which no new status information is introduced. Then in the second task the entire status structure consists of transferred elements. These come from the first task through the relevance of tasks links and the burden of proof process operating on the discriminating gender characteristic. On this second task, also, p will have an expectation advantage over o, and the magnitude of this advantage will be greater than in the first task as a result of the transferred elements.

In general, when the current structure *does* contain new status information, if we wish to determine the expectation positions of the actors the process is more complicated, and it involves the interactions of the transferred elements with the new information. We will return to this matter shortly. What is important for us now is that the amount of information transferred from the past structure is the same regardless of whatever new information may be introduced on the current task.

Summarizing these discussions, we observe that increasing the consistency of a set of characteristics assigned to actors, adding in a consistent manner to a set of consistent distinguishing characteristics for the actors, or increasing the degree of relevance of a characteristic increases the magnitude of the status advantages and disadvantages transferred from one task to the next.

The Effect of Transferred Expectations

Although the amount of status information transferred from past tasks to the current task is independent of the current task, as we have pointed out, the effect that this information has on status differentiation in the current task depends on the new status information that is introduced.

Indeed, to determine the power and prestige order in the current task we make use of all the positive status information in the current task, including that transferred from the past as well as any new positive information. These are combined, subject to attenuation. At the same time, all negative status information, both past and new, is similarly combined. Only then are the two components combined together.

For any current status structure, our theory allows us to determine the power and prestige positions of the actors in the current structure in isolation, without taking the past into account. It also allows us to determine the power and prestige positions of the actors in the current structure when we include the status elements transferred from the past. It therefore allows us to determine the effect of the past on a current structure.

Our theory enables us to analyze completely the effect of transfer in an extremely large number of specific status situations. However, making general assertions about these effects is difficult. When either the past or the new status information is itself inconsistent — that is, consists of both positive and negative elements — the way in which attenuation comes into play is often quite complex. However, when the status characteristics information for the actors involved in the past task is consistent and the information for the current task considered in isolation is also consistent, the analysis of the situation is straightforward and the results interesting.

Consider a situation where two actors are engaged in a current task after working on a past task. Suppose that in the past task structure all characteristics consistently discriminate the actors. Suppose further that the status information introduced in the current task also consistently discriminates the actors. Then the status information transferred from the past to the current task is the same whether the new information is consistent or inconsistent with the past. However, the effect is quite different in these two conditions. In the consistent case the two components of like sign, one from the past and one from the information just introduced, are attenuated when they are combined to produce the power and prestige order in the current task. On the other hand, in the inconsistent case no such attenuation takes place. Thus the effect of the past is greater when the past is inconsistent with the current task than when it is consistent. This result is stated in general form in Theorem 2:

- *Theorem 2 (inconsistent and consistent status transitions):* Given that p and o (or any other o) interact on two successive tasks that are not dissociated or inversely related. Assume that status elements on the past task consistently discriminate p and his partner, and that those on the current task in isolation also consistently discriminate p and his partner. Then the effect of past task expectations on the power and prestige differentiation of the current task will be greater if the status elements on the current task in isolation are inconsistent with the status elements on the past task rather than if they are consistent.

CHANGES IN EXPECTATIONS
AND BEHAVIOR OVER TIME

As the actors interact with the same other or a similar other or a different other over time, both changes and stability in expectations may characterize different phases in this evolving process. In the theorems in this section, we consider some of the conditions that are involved in producing changes in expectations and power and prestige relations.

As actors move through the situation, they may be confronted with new tasks, with different others, and with new information, all of which can produce major changes in their expectations and behavior vis-à-vis the other. Imagine, for example, that a male, after interacting with another male on one task, finds himself interacting with a female on a subsequent task. Gender, which was not a basis of discrimination on the first task, is now such a basis and becomes salient to the actors. Once salient and task relevant (assuming nothing interferes with the burden of proof process), it becomes a component of the actor's expectations and produces a change in his behavior as he moves into a new situation.

As a second example of change, imagine that, on a subsequent task, the interacting male and female are confronted with a task that is culturally defined as a feminine task. Were there no prior history to their interaction, we predict that the male would be at an expectation disadvantage to the female and would be a status inferior to her. But there is a history of prior interaction, and we know that this will modify their expectations and power and prestige relations on the feminine task. Nevertheless, the introduction of a new task that is culturally defined as being connected with gender differences will produce changes in expectations and behavior. In general, then, the introduction of new others and new tasks can produce major changes in the actor's behavior, and this can occur at any stage in the process.

The same is true for the introduction of new information about the actors already in the situation—for example, that one actor or the other possesses special talents and abilities (or disabilities) that are relevant to the task. Perhaps one of the most important sources of such new information occurs in situations where the problem-solving performances of the actors are evaluated by some external source or authority in terms of task success or task failure. Such external evaluations may be either a regular or an occasional feature of the interaction process. When they occur, we assume that they take place at the end of one task setting and before the beginning of a second and that these assessments of success or failure are evaluations of the actors' overall performances in a given task setting.

Evaluation by an external source of the actors' performance outputs will have profound effects on their expectations and their subsequent behavior because such information involves a direct assignment to the actors of the different task outcome states of the just-completed task. These assignments in turn will become directly relevant in a consistent manner (by the relevance of tasks process) to the outcome states of the next task they will confront.

Specifically, what is the effect of such evaluations on the expectations of the actors involved? In general, it can be shown that if p holds an expectation advantage over o on the past task (and therefore a higher position on the power and prestige order on that task), then if the assignment of task success or task failure by an external evaluator is consistent with that order, the magnitude of p's expectation advantage and power and prestige advantage over o will be increased as they move to the next task. If these assignments are inconsistent with that order, then p's expectation advantage and power and prestige superiority over o will decrease and may actually be reversed on the new task. Furthermore, it is the case that the magnitude of change in expectation advantage and power and prestige relations is greater when such evaluations are inconsistent than when they are consistent.

We can also consider the cases where the evaluations of p and o are the same. Again assume that p has expectation advantage and power and prestige superiority over o. If the evaluations of p and o are the same — both are assigned either task success or task failure — then p's expectation advantage over o is decreased on the subsequent task.

Thus, in general, consistent differential evaluations accentuate power and prestige differences, similar evaluations reduce them, and inconsistent differential evaluations either reduce them or reverse them as the actors move to the subsequent task. These ideas on the effect of the assignment of success and failure by an external evaluator are stated in Theorem 3:

- *Theorem 3 (assignment of success or failure):* Given that p and o interact on two successive tasks that are not dissociated or inversely related. Assume that p holds an expectation advantage over o on the past task. Further assume that p's and o's performances on the past task are evaluated in terms of task success or failure; then:

  (1) If the evaluations differ and are assigned to p and o consistent with the power and prestige order, then the magnitude of p's expectation advantage over o will be increased on the current task. If the assignments are inconsistent with the power and prestige order, then the magnitude of p's expectation advantage over o will be decreased (and may be reversed) on the current task.
  (2) If the evaluations differ, then the magnitude of change in p's expectation advantage over o will be greater when they are assigned inconsistent with the power and prestige order, rather than consistent with that order.
  (3) If these evaluations are alike (both positive or both negative), and if all the salient status characteristics discriminate p and o, then the magnitude of p's expectation advantage over o will be decreased on the current task.

STABILITY OF EXPECTATIONS OVER TIME

Just as there may be periods in which expectations are changing as the situation evolves, so there may be periods in which the expectations of the actor and other become more stable and the pattern of their power and prestige behaviors becomes rigid. This will occur in those periods when the actors interact under *closed* conditions, that is, when no new information (such as external evaluations) are being introduced, when the other with whom the actor interacts is the same or similar other, and when the sequence of tasks being performed is independent. It is also the case that, under these conditions, the values of the actors' stabilized expectation advantages and stabilized power and prestige differences will be independent of the way their status characteristics were initially connected to their tasks. However, as we shall see, these values do depend on the pattern of salient characteristics that discriminate the actors.

These ideas on stability are formulated in Theorem 4, which tells us that, under closed conditions, the expectation differences and the power and prestige relations will stabilize, and the stable values are independent of the way status characteristics are initially related to tasks.

• *Theorem 4 (stability of status positions):* Given that p and o (or similar o) interact on a sequence of independent tasks. Assume that p and o are discriminated by one or more characteristics, and from some task on no new status elements become salient in the situation. Then p's power and prestige position relative to o will tend to become stable. Furthermore, this stable position will be independent of the way the characteristics are initially task connected.

While the initial degree of relevance of the status and performance characteristics possessed by the actors does not affect the value of the stabilized expectation and power and prestige differences that are approached when the process is operating under closed conditions, the number of discriminating characteristics possessed by the actors and the degree of inconsistency of these characteristics do affect these values.

In the case of the effect of a number of characteristics, the general argument is the familiar one applied to this situation, that the greater the number of consistent status characteristics discriminating the actors, given that the process is evolving under closed conditions, the more highly differentiated will be the stabilized power and prestige order that develops. Furthermore, an attenuation effect also operates in the case of these stable values. While it is true that with each discriminating characteristic there is an increase in the magnitude of inequality between stabilized expectations and power and prestige positions, it is also true that as the number of characteristics increases the incremental effect on these stabilized values due to adding an additional characteristic decreases. These ideas relating the number of status characteristics to the magnitude of inequality in stabilized power and prestige positions are presented in Theorem 5:

- *Theorem 5 (magnitude of stable status positions):* Given that p and o (or similar o) interact on a sequence of independent tasks. Assume that p and o are discriminated by a set of consistent characteristics, and from some task on no new status elements become salient. Then the greater the number of these characteristics the more extreme (higher or lower) the stable power and prestige position of p relative to o. But as the number of characteristics increases, the incremental effect of each additional characteristic gets smaller.

Theorem 5 assumes that the status characteristics discriminating the actors are consistent. However, if the characteristics are inconsistent, their degree of inconsistency will affect the value of stabilized expectation and power and prestige differences. The general argument is also a familiar one now applied to this situation that says that, if the discriminating status characteristics are inconsistent, and if the process is evolving under closed conditions, then the greater the inconsistency of these characteristics, the greater the equality in the stabilized power and prestige order. Or, put another way, the more nearly equal the number of positive and negative states of characteristics discriminating the actors, the greater will be the equality of their stabilized status positions. These ideas are stated in Theorem 6:

- *Theorem 6 (inconsistency and status equality):* Given that p and o (or similar o) interact on a sequence of independent tasks. Assume that p and o are discriminated by a set of inconsistent characteristics, and from some task on no new status elements become salient. Then the more nearly equal the numbers of positive and negative states of characteristics possessed by the actors, the more nearly equal the stable power and prestige positions of p and o.

Before we finish this discussion of stabilizing processes, it is important to emphasize again that these processes occur during those periods in which the interaction process is evolving in a relatively isolated state from the environment. These are the conditions when the process is closed to new inputs. On any task in the evolution of the interaction, the process may leave this closed state — new relevant information may be introduced, actors with new discriminating performance or status characteristics may enter the situation, or the actors may confront new tasks that have special relations to a performance or status characteristic they possess, such as when the characteristic is culturally defined as relevant to the task. These are conditions when the process is open to new inputs. When the process moves into an open state, the actors' expectations and power and prestige relations may undergo change. Such changes may even be profound, as we have seen would be the case, for example, when evaluations of task success and task failure by an external source are assigned inconsistently with a power and prestige order that has evolved. If, after such a period of change in expectations and behavior, the interaction process further develops under closed conditions, the stabilizing processes described here will once more come into play. It is in this sense that change and stability can describe different phases in the evolution of status processes.

THE EFFECT OF STATUS INTERVENTIONS

One of the important applications of status characteristics theory has been in research on overcoming the effects, in open interaction situations, of diffuse status distinctions based on gender, race, and ethnic differences. A typical (and successful) study of this type involves teaching black students valued task skills and having them in turn instruct white students in the same skills. Black students who undergo this type of task competence training later interact with white students on a much more equal level than other black students who do not go through similar task competence training (see Cohen and Roper 1972).

The idea involved in such research is to assign to actors high and low competence states that are *inconsistent* with the states of the diffuse status characteristic they possess, for instance, highly competent females versus incompetent males. Such interventions rest on the basic argument that the greater the degree of status inconsistency, the greater the equality in the power and prestige order that emerges in a task situation. For other examples of research investigating this type of intervention, see Pugh and Wahrman (1983), Markovsky et al. (1984), and Webster and Driskell (1978, 1983). For a general discussion and review of status intervention research, see Cohen (1982).

Status interventions typically involve specific actors in specific task settings. The question that is raised by this research is how lasting is the effect of such interventions. On the basis of this formulation, we expect that the effect of such interventions, from the standpoint of the focal actor, will transfer from an initial task to a second and different task and from an initial other to a second but similar other. However, it can also be shown, on the basis of this formulation, that there should be an erosion of this status intervention effect in moving to the new task and to a new but similar other. If there is such an erosion, what, if anything can we say about the long-term and stable effects of such interventions? If we restrict ourselves to when the action process is closed, we can describe the long-term effects of such interventions under these conditions.

Imagine that p and o are discriminated on a diffuse status characteristic the effect of which we are interested in mitigating. Also, imagine that a set of specific performance characteristics are introduced, each of which discriminates p and o and each of which is assigned, in a task situation, inconsistently with the states of the diffuse status characteristics the actors possess. Now assume that, following the introduction of this intervention, the actors interact on a sequence of tasks under closed conditions. Under these conditions, the long-term effect of the inconsistent information is to reduce the magnitude of that inequality in p and o's status relations that would be produced by the diffuse status characteristics if they were operating alone.

It is important to keep in mind *when* this effect occurs — no evaluations or new information are being introduced to the situation and the actor is always interacting with the same or a similar other and is working on a sequence of tasks that is independent. These are clearly very special circumstances. However, there are situations that, from the standpoint of the given focal actor, may approximate these action conditions. As a consequence, this stability result informs us of both the possibilities and the limitations of the persistence of status interventions. It therefore is of both theoretical and applied significance. This result on the possible long-term effects of status interventions in a closed interaction situation is given in Theorem 7:

- *Theorem 7 (effects of interventions):* Given that p and o (or similar o) interact on a sequence of independent tasks. Assume that p and o are discriminated by a diffuse status characteristic and one or more specific characteristics that are inconsistent with the diffuse status characteristic, and from some task on no new status elements become salient. Then p's power and prestige position relative to o will tend to stabilize at a value between what would result from the diffuse status characteristic alone and what would result from the inconsistent characteristics alone.

Relevant Intervention Research

We shall not attempt, at this stage, to consider the different bodies of empirical research that may be in some way related to this extension. Instead, we restrict ourselves to status intervention research that is *directly* relevant to our formulation. As we have previously said, one of the principal motivations in developing this extension is to describe and assess the ways in which status interventions in one task setting affect expectations and behaviors in a subsequent setting. In fact, the research literature on status interventions that bears on our formulation is highly informative.

In a series of studies concerned with the status effects of gender in a small group interaction, Lockheed and Hall (1976) sought to determine the extent to which male domination of the power and prestige order in mixed-gender groups could be altered by permitting females to develop what they call task-specific expectations for competence. Females were provided the opportunity to develop such expectations by first interacting in gender-homogeneous groups and then interacting in mixed-gender groups. It was found that females who had this prior experience were more likely to occupy higher positions in the power and prestige order in mixed-gender groups than those who had not had such prior experience. They also found that when the members of these mixed-gender groups interacted on a different task the following day there was consistency in their behavior across tasks. Those who were highly or less active on the first task tended to be, respectively, highly or less active on the second task. However, Lockheed and Hall also noted what they call a slight tendency for the experienced females to hold more low ranks in the power and prestige order on the new task. These results are fully consistent with our formulation. If we interpret this situation as one in which females develop specific competencies in gender-homogeneous groups, the study suggests that this experience of the females affected the power and prestige order when they were in gender-heterogeneous groups, and there was some attenuation of this effect when the group subsequently addressed a new and different task.

Pugh and Wahrman (1983), in a series of experiments, provide further information on the effects of status interventions. They first demonstrate that gender operates as a status characteristic to organize the behavior of men and women by showing that when they worked together on a valued collective task, women were more likely to yield to men than men were to women when they disagreed. However, differences in deferring behavior on the part of men and women disappeared when they were in groups where men worked with men and women worked with women. Pugh and Wahrman then intervened in mixed-gender groups, providing the female with the information that she was highly competent and that her specific male partner was not competent on an ability that was relevant to the task ability. (The male was provided corresponding information about himself and his specific female partner.) This reduced the effect of gender difference on deference behaviors. Finally, in the fourth set of studies these authors showed that the effect of their status intervention continued to operate without diminution when the female interacted with another male (or when the male interacted with another female) on the same task. While these results are consistent with our theory in that they show that the effect of the intervention is transferred from the specific other to a similar other (a second actor who occupies the same status category as the first), we note this transfer occurs on the *same* task, and that Pugh and Wahrman did not find any evidence for the attenuation of this transfer effect.

A study by Markovsky et al. (1984) builds directly on the work of Pugh and Wahrman. In two of the conditions of the experiment, subjects were led to believe that they were discriminated from their partners on level of educational attainment. In a third condition the relatively low-educated subject was provided with information that he possessed the high state of an ability while his partner possessed the low state of that ability directly relevant to success on the task. In the fourth condition complementary information (to that in condition three) was provided to the subject who possessed a relatively high level of educational attainment. In all conditions, subjects first worked on one task and, upon completion of that task, worked on a different second task with a different other who was similar in educational attainment to the first partner. Markovsky et al. found that the intervention mitigated the effect of the attainment characteristic on the first task. But more significant from our standpoint is the finding that the effect of this intervention carried over in determining the subject's behavior on the second task and with respect to his new status partner. At the same time, Markovsky et al. found that the effect of the intervention on the second task was reduced. The results of this study are consistent with the extension, including providing information on the erosion of the status intervention.

The final experiment we consider is another two-task, two-part study by Prescott (1986), which carries previous research one step further by investigating the effects of prior expectations and behavior on a new task that involves a new partner who in turn possesses a new discriminating status characteristic. In all conditions on the first task, the subject, a male college freshman, was led to believe that he was working with a female college freshman. In the experimental condition, the first task was gender typed as one in which women generally do better than men. In the control condition, the first task was not gender typed. Upon completion of the first task, all subjects worked on a second task that was not gender typed with a new female partner who was also identified as a high school dropout. Prescott found that males in the experimental condition had a higher rate of deferring, when they disagreed with their partner, than those in the control condition. But of even greater interest is his finding that the rate of deferring for both these conditions decreases on the second task at the same time that the rate for the experimental subjects is still higher than the control subjects. We interpret these results as showing that the discriminating status characteristic of educational attainment has become salient on the second task, resulting in a decrease in deferring responses for all subjects. However, the status position of the male on the sex-typed task continues to affect his behavior on the neutral task, so that his status position is lower than that of the male who first interacted on the gender-neutral task.

Prescott's research is also consistent with our extension. He has shown how the particular pattern of expectations and behaviors that emerge in a task setting affects expectations and behaviors in a particular manner on a second task with a new partner. He has also shown that the introduction of new information—a new discriminating status characteristic that is possessed by the new partner—will produce predictable changes in the individual's expectations and behavior.

Summary

In this chapter we have formulated a theory that describes how expectations and power and prestige behaviors evolve in situations where actors are interacting on a series of valued and collective tasks. Our formulation is an extension of the status characteristics theory. As such, this extension involves the introduction of an auxiliary assumption that describes how the structure of one task setting is connected with that of a subsequent task setting. The extension also involves making modifications of some of the core assumptions of the theory so that they are applicable to situations that can involve a sequence of tasks.

The theory we have developed enables us to describe the dynamics of particular expectation states processes as these occur in an extremely large number of specific status situations. In addition, we can formulate general theoretical assertions about these dynamics. Aside from describing the overall features of the process by which past task structures affect current ones, these assertions deal with the conditions and processes by which expectations and behaviors undergo change. Of particular importance in this context of change is the fact that these assertions enable us to describe how assignments to the actors of task success or failure at the completion of one task affects their expectations and power and prestige behaviors on a subsequent task.

In addition to questions of change, these assertions deal with the conditions and processes by which expectations and power and prestige behaviors stabilize. Whether there is change or stability in the interaction process depends on whether or not the process is open to new inputs — new status information that becomes salient, new evaluations of task success or failure that are assigned, and new actors who introduce new status and performance characteristics. In this sense, change and stability in expectations and behavior can characterize different phases in the evolution of a status organizing process.

While the findings from status intervention research that are directly relevant to this formulation are fully consistent with it, this research is limited. It is clear that we require a program of empirical as well as theoretical research to assess the utility of this extension. This is the task that is now before us.

Appendix

This appendix presents a formal statement of the assumptions of the theory of status characteristics and expectation states, a brief discussion of the combining function, and an illustrative example of a graph structure. The formal proofs for the theorems presented in the main body of the chapter are also included.

THE FORMULATION

The first four assumptions of the theory describe how a graph theoretic representation of a status situation is constructed.

- *Assumption 1 (salience):*

   (1) Given existing paths connecting an interactant to outcome states, the status elements and relations in these paths become salient in the task situation; and
   (2) Given status elements that provide a basis for discrimination between interactants, the states of these elements become salient in the task situation.

- *Assumption 2 (burden of proof):* Given that a salient status element possessed by an actor is not connected to the task component or is connected only by an extended task path, then:

   (1) If the status element is the state of a diffuse characteristic, the associated generalized expectation state will be activated, and it will become relevant to a similarly evaluated state of the instrumental characteristic.
   (2) If the status element is the state of a specific characteristic, its relevant task outcome state will be activated. This task outcome state will become relevant to a similarly evaluated state of abstract task ability, and the latter will become relevant to a similarly evaluated outcome state of the group task.

- *Auxiliary Assumption 1 (relevance of tasks):* Given any two successive group tasks in situation S that are not dissociated, if upon completion of the first task the actor engages in the second, then relevance relations will be established in a consistent manner between the outcome states of these tasks.

- *Assumption 3 (sequence of completion):* A given structure will be developed through the salience and burden of proof processes for the interacting actors for a given task. If a noninteracting actor should later become an interactant, or a new actor or new information is introduced to the situation, or a new task started, then the structure will become further developed through the operation of the salience and burden of proof structure completion processes. For any actor, those parts of his or her structure completed in relation to a former interactant remain while the actor is in the situation.

Figure 5.A1 gives a completed structure that represents two actors discriminated by a diffuse status characteristic interacting on a task after having completed a previous task, where the diffuse status characteristic is not relevant to either task.

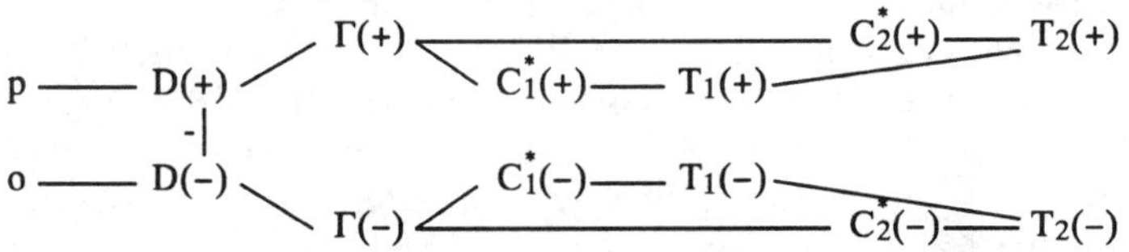

Figure 5.A1. A Completed Structure for Two Actors Discriminated by a Diffuse Status Characteristic on a Two-Task Sequence

Given a completed structure, the remainder of the formulation is concerned with analyzing the structure to obtain self-other expectations for
the actors in the situation. The analysis of graph structures proceeds by
tracing the paths that connect each actor to the task outcome states. The
length of a path is the number of lines that makes up the path, and the sign
of a path is the product of the signs of the lines in the path and the sign of
the outcome state the path connects to. In the completed structure of
Figure 5.A1, p is connected to T_2 by four positive paths of lengths 4, 5, 5,
6, and o is connected by four negative paths of the same lengths.

The "strength" of a path is given by a function f(i), where i is the length
of the path. The function is assumed to be continuous and monotonically
decreasing, yielding values in (0,1). To find the aggregated expectations
for an actor, the paths joining the actor to the task outcome states are first
combined in like-signed subsets according to the rule

$$f(i \cup j) = f(i) + f(j) - f(i) \times f(j)$$

and given the sign of the paths in the subset. Then the two values are
algebraically summed to obtain the aggregated expectation value. Any
actual computation of these values depends on knowing the values of the
function f(i). These values are normally estimated from data as empirical
parameters; however, numerical values are not necessary for current purposes. The formulation can generate general statements about the transfer
of expectations from task to task without having to specify a specific form
for the function f(i).

The mechanism for the combining of paths has two general features
that should be noted. The first, called the "attenuation principle," states
that when like-signed paths combine, their strengths are attenuated in the
sense that the combined result is less than the sum of their individual
strengths. This can be seen clearly in the simple form of the combining
rule for two paths as the product of the two strengths is subtracted from
their sum: The result, while greater in strength than either, is less than the
algebraic sum of the two. Thus when paths of like sign combine, the
contribution of each is diminished, and this effect is magnified as the
strengths involved increase. The second is the "inconsistency principle,"
which states that inconsistent additional paths have more effect on the
result than consistent additional paths of equal strength would. This is
because, while like-signed paths are attenuated in combining, paths of
unlike sign are algebraically summed. Consider an actor who possesses
two positive paths and one negative path of the same lengths. The two
positive paths will combine first, with the result being less than their
algebraic sum. Then the strength of the negative path will be subtracted
from the combined value for the positive paths, resulting in a value that is
less than the strength of one of the paths. The attenuation and inconsistency effects have important implications for how expectations are formed
and change as actors move from one task to the next.

The following two assumptions summarize the combining rule and relate expectations to power and prestige orders.

* *Assumption 4 (formation of aggregated expectation states):* If an actor x is connected to the outcome states by sets of positive and negative paths, these paths will first be combined within like-signed subsets to yield a positive-path value e^+ and negative-path value e^- in the following fashion. Given strengths $f(i), \ldots, f(n)$ and $f(i'), \ldots, f(n')$ of paths within the positive-path subset and negative-path subset, respectively, then:

$$e^+_x = 1 - [1 - f(i)] \ldots [1 - f(n)]$$
$$e^-_x = -(1 - [1 - f(i')] \ldots [1 - f(n')])$$

The aggregated expectation state is then given by

$$e_x = e^+_x + e^-_x$$

* *Assumption 5 (basic expectation assumption):* Given that p has formed aggregated expectation states for self and other, p's power and prestige position relative to o will be a direct continuous function of p's expectation advantage over o.

Given these assumptions, it is possible to derive theorems about how expectations change as actors perform a sequence of tasks. A number of basic theorems and their proofs are given in the next section.

THE DERIVATIONS

It will facilitate the presentation of proofs of theorems to define a few terms and notational conventions. Tasks $T_1, T_2, \ldots, T_n$ are tasks that have been performed in the past, and T_{n+1} is the current task. T'_{n+1} stands for the current task "in isolation," that is, as if there were no history of past tasks. Given a graph structure, it is helpful to differentiate among three different types of paths:

(1) *C-paths:* Current task paths are those paths that would be in T'_{n+1}, that is, the current task taken in isolation.
(2) *T-paths:* Task-relevance paths are those paths that connect the actors to the current task through the relevance lines connecting the outcome states of T_n and T_{n+1}.
(3) *B-paths:* Burden of proof paths are those paths that connect states of characteristics that became salient in earlier tasks with the current task outcome states through the action of the burden of proof process.

The term *effect of a path* (or a set of paths) refers to the difference in expectations with and without this path (or set of paths). Similarly, the effect of a past (status) structure is the difference in expectations with and without this past structure.

The theorems are fully stated in the text, and their proofs are given below.

Proof of Theorem 1: The proof follows at once from the relevance of tasks assumption. According to this assumption, the two sets of task outcome states will be connected by relevance lines. Therefore, any path connecting an actor to an outcome state on the first task will give rise to a path of length one greater connecting the actor to an outcome state on the second task. Since these paths will enter into the formation of aggregated expectation states, it follows that expectations formed on the first task affect the status differentiation on the second task.

Proof of Theorem 2: Since p and o are consistently discriminated on past tasks, for each actor B-paths and T-paths will have the same sign. For each actor all C-paths will also have the same sign. Since the B-, T-, and C-paths all combine to form the expectations on the current task, if for each actor the C-paths have the same sign as the B- and T-paths—that is, if the new and old status information is consistent—the strengths of the paths will be attenuated in the combining process. If, however, the new and old status information is inconsistent, then C-paths will have different signs from the B- and T-paths, and combining them will not lead to attenuation. This completes the proof.

Proof of Theorem 3: The first conclusion follows at once. Consistent evaluations will lead to a new positive path for p and a new negative path for o, thus increasing e_p^+ and e_o^- without changing e_p^- and e_o^+, so p's expectation advantage will increase. Inconsistent evaluations lead to a new negative path for p and a new positive path for o, thus increasing e_p^- and e_o^+ without changing e_p^+ and e_o^-, and so p's expectation advantage relative to o will decrease.

The second conclusion requires some preliminary considerations. Since f(i) is a decreasing function, it is possible to say that k paths (where k is not necessarily an integer but is greater than 1) of length m + 1 are equivalent to a path of length m. The theory assumes, as a simplifying assumption, that k is constant. Thus any path is equivalent to a given number of paths of some greater length. In particular, in any given structure all paths may be represented as sets of paths of length equal to the longest path in the structure. Assume the longest path in a structure is of length j, and that its strength is x. Let a and b denote the equivalent number of j-length positive and negative paths for p respectively, let c and d denote the similar quantities for o. Then,

$$e_p = [1 - (1 - x)^a] - [1 - (1 - x)^b] = (1 - x)^b - (1 - x)^a$$

To simplify the expression, let y = 1 − x:

$$e_p = y^b - y^a$$

And similarly,

$$e_o = y^d - y^c$$

Therefore,

$$(y^b - y^a) - (y^d - y^c) > 0$$

since the expression on the left is the expectation advantage of p over o, and it is assumed to be positive. The assignment of a task outcome state on the first task connects an actor to the outcome states of the new task by a path of length 2 and a path of length 3, assuming that evaluations are differential, that is, both task outcome states are assigned. Suppose that the strength of these two paths is equal to t paths of length j. Consistent evaluation then means adding t to a and d. Similarly, inconsistent evaluation means adding t to b and c. Thus the increase in p's expectation advantage given consistent evaluation is

$$[(y^b - y^{a + t}) - (y^{d + t} - y^c)] - [(y^b - y^a) - (y^d - y^c)] =$$
$$y^a - y^{a + t} + y^d - y^{d + t}$$

and the decrease in p's expectation advantage given inconsistent evaluation is

$$[(y^b - y^a) - (y^d - y^c)] - [(y^{b + t} - y^a) - (y^d - y^{c + t})] = y^b - y^{b + t} + y^c - y^{c + t}$$

Subtracting the first expression from the second and rearranging terms, we obtain

$$(y^b + y^c - y^a - y^d)(1 - y^t)$$

The first factor is positive, as was demonstrated earlier, and the second factor is also positive since y is less than 1, therefore the entire expression is positive, as was to be demonstrated. The third conclusion is reached assuming that all salient characteristics are discriminating, therefore the expression for p's expectation advantage is simplified to

$$(y^b - y^a) - (y^a - y^b) > 0$$

where $a > b$. Assigning success to both actors adds t to the exponents of the second and fourth terms, and assigning failure to both actors adds t to the exponents of the first and third terms. In both cases the result is the same, that is, p's expectation advantage is

$$(y^b - y^{a + t}) - (y^a - y^{b + t})$$

Subtracting the postevaluation value from the preevaluation value and rearranging, we have

$$(y^b - y^a)(1 - y^t)$$

Since $0 < y < 1$ and $b < a$, both factors are positive, that is, the expectation difference after evaluations is less than before. This completes the proof.

Proof of Theorem 4: Since it is assumed that after some task, say T_j, where $j < n$, in the sequence of tasks no new status information becomes salient, there are no C-paths in the structure at $T_{n + 1}$, and we need be only concerned with B-paths and T-paths. Considering B-paths first, every salient characteristic state will become connected to the current task through the burden of proof process. Each salient characteristic will give rise to one path of length 4, and if its dimensional state is also salient, to a path of length 5 as well. Thus there will be a certain number of paths of length 4 and a certain number of paths of length 5 in the set of B-paths. However, the same structure will be formed for all subsequent tasks. That is, on each task after $T_{n + 1}$ there will be an identical set of B-paths.

Each T-path, by definition, contains an outcome state of T_n, and it may contain any number of outcome states from the earlier tasks. Assume that the first task outcome state a T-path contains is T_i. It is necessary to distinguish the two cases where T_i is after T_j and where T_i is identical to or before T_j. Consider the T-paths that contain a first task outcome state coming after T_j first: Examine T-paths that contain outcome states for T_n only; each of these paths is generated by a B-path at T_n (B-paths at T_n are identical to B-paths at $T_{n + 1}$ by the previous argument) being lengthened by one line, the line joining the two task outcome states. Obviously, T-paths containing an outcome state from $T_{n - 1}$ are generated by B-paths at $T_{n - 1}$ being lengthened by two lines, and this argument can be extended as far back as T_j. Therefore, for every B-path of length 4 at $T_{n + 1}$, there is a T-path of length 5, a T-path of length 6, and so forth, as far back as it goes. Similarly, for every B-path of length 5 there are T-paths of lengths 6, 7, 8 . . . . The combined strength of a set of paths "generated" by a length 4 B-path at $T_{n + 1}$ is given by

$$1 - [1 - f(4)][1 - f(5)][1 - f(6)][1 - f(7)][1 - f(8)] \ldots$$

Because a path of a given length is equivalent to k paths of one greater length, the following relation holds.

$$1 - f(i + 1) = [1 - f(i)]^{1/k}$$

Therefore, the above expression can be rewritten as follows:

$$1 - [1 - f(4)]^{1 + 1/k + 1/k^2 + 1/k^3 + \ldots}$$

The series in the exponent will converge for values of $k > 1$, and the entire expression will converge to a value between 0 and 1. Exactly the same argument can be made for B-paths of length 5. Thus it is the case that both B-paths and this type of T-paths will have an effect that approaches a limiting value as the sequence of tasks proceeds. Considering T-paths that include task outcome states from task T_j or tasks before, the first point to be noted is that there is a finite and constant number of such paths, since after task T_j is completed there is no way any new paths including an outcome state from a task before T_j can come into existence. Each of these paths has to be longer than $(n - j)$, therefore as n increases they will get longer, and as n tends to infinity their effect will tend to zero. This completes the proof for both the stability of expectations and the independence from initial connections.

Proof of Theorem 5: Consider the case where p possesses the positive states of the characteristics. His expectation advantage will simply be twice his self-expectations, since this is a symmetric situation where o's expectations are the negative of p's expectations, so that looking at p's self-expectations is sufficient for determining his power and prestige position. Theorem 4 states that the effect of tasks before the last status characteristic became salient can be ignored, and that for each characteristic p will have a set of paths of lengths 4, 5, 6, 7, 8, . . . due to the state he possesses and a set of paths of lengths 5, 6, 7, 8, 9, . . . which go through the dimensional pair of the state he possesses. Further, Theorem 4 asserts that each set will converge to a value between 0 and 1. These two values will further be combined to obtain a value — call it α. Then p's expectations given that he possesses r characteristics is given by

$$e = 1 - (1 - \alpha)^r$$

Obviously, e increases as r increases. That the incremental effect of each additional characteristic will be less follows from the attenuation principle, since as the magnitude of the strengths being combined increases so does the amount of attenuation, and this completes the proof.

Proof of Theorem 6: As in the previous theorem the structure is symmetric, that is, since all characteristics are discriminating characteristics, for every path connecting p to the task there is a path of the same length but opposite sign connecting o to the task. Therefore, the power and prestige difference between the actors, that is, p's expectation advantage, is equal to twice his self-expectations. If p possesses r positive states and s negative states of status characteristics, letting α stand for the effect of one characteristic as in the previous theorems, his self-expectations will be

$$e_p = [1 - (1 - \alpha)^r] - [1 - (1 - \alpha)^s]$$

that is,

$$e_p = (1 - \alpha)^s - (1 - \alpha)^r$$

This number obviously decreases as the difference between r and s decreases, and is actually equal to 0 when r is equal to s. This completes the proof.

Proof of Theorem 7: The statement of this theorem is in terms of a single diffuse status characteristic because the substantively interesting cases are concerned with trying to counteract the effects of single diffuse status characteristics such as race and sex. However, the proof is actually more general and is valid for a set of consistent diffuse status characteristics. The structure is a symmetric structure and consideration of p's self-expectations is sufficient. Assume that p possesses the positive states of r diffuse status characteristics and s negative states of specific status characteristics. Then by the previous theorem, p's self-expectations will be

$$e_p = (1 - \alpha)^s - (1 - \alpha)^r$$

If there had been only diffuse status characteristics in the situation, then p's self-expectations would have been

$$e_p' = 1 - (1 - \alpha)^r$$

And if there had been only specific characteristics in the situation, then p's self-expectations would have been

$$e_p'' = (1 - \alpha)^s - 1$$

The first value is between the other two, as was to be shown. The same argument holds for when p possesses the negative states of the diffuse status characteristics, the only difference being that the signs of all terms are changed. Therefore the proof is completed.

Notes

1. In this section we present an informal description of the status characteristics theory and its extension. A formal description of the theory and this extension is presented in the Appendix.

2. Note that the theory makes no claim that information that is not initially task relevant or that *equates* individuals on status characteristics becomes salient, although such information may be well known and highly visible to the members of the group. For research evidence that is consistent with this idea that equating information does not become salient, see Webster (1977) and Martin and Sell (1985), among others.

3. Because the combining process is not a conscious process to the actor, the tests for this process have had to be *indirect*. These tests involve deriving behavioral consequences of the process under different status conditions and then testing for these consequences (see Norman et al. 1988).

4. The construction of these paths is described in Berger et al. (1977) or Berger et al. (1985). (Part 2 of the rule for effective paths is extended here: If a graph contains a line

joining two points, neither of which is an actor nor an outcome state, then any path containing a subpath of length 2 or more joining these same two points is not effective.)

References

Berger, Joseph, Bernard P. Cohen, and Morris Zelditch, Jr. 1966. "Status Characteristics and Expectation States." Pp. 29-46 in *Sociological Theories in Progress*, Vol. 1, edited by Joseph Berger, Morris Zelditch, Jr., and Bo Anderson. Boston: Houghton Mifflin.
— — -. 1972. "Status Characteristics and Social Interaction." *American Sociological Review* 37:241-55.
Berger, Joseph, Thomas L. Conner, and M. Hamit Fisek, eds. 1974. *Expectation States Theory: A Theoretical Research Program*. Cambridge, MA: Winthrop.
Berger, Joseph, and M. Hamit Fisek. 1974. "A Generalization of the Theory of Status Characteristics and Expectation States." Pp. 163-205 in *Expectation States Theory: A Theoretical Research Program*, edited by Joseph Berger, Thomas L. Conner, and M. Hamit Fisek. Cambridge, MA: Winthrop.
Berger, Joseph, M. Hamit Fisek, Robert Z. Norman, and David G. Wagner. 1985. "Formation of Reward Expectations in Status Situations." Pp. 215-61 in *Status, Rewards, and Influence: How Expectations Organize Behavior*, edited by Joseph Berger and Morris Zelditch, Jr. San Francisco: Jossey-Bass.
Berger, Joseph, M. Hamit Fisek, Robert Z. Norman, and Morris Zelditch, Jr. 1977. *Status Characteristics and Social Interaction: An Expectation States Approach*. New York: Elsevier.
Berger, Joseph, Susan J. Rosenholtz, and Morris Zelditch, Jr. 1980. "Status Organizing Processes." *Annual Review of Sociology* 6:479-508.
Berger, Joseph and Morris Zelditch, Jr. eds. 1985. *Status, Rewards, and Influence: How Expectations Organize Behavior*. San Francisco: Jossey-Bass.
Caudill, William. 1958. *The Psychiatric Hospital as a Small Society*. Cambridge, MA: Harvard University Press.
Cohen, Elizabeth G. 1982. "Expectation States and Interracial Interaction School Settings." *Annual Review of Sociology* 8:209-35.
Cohen, Elizabeth G. and Susan Roper. 1972. "Modification of Interracial Interaction Disability: An Application of Status Characteristics Theory." *American Sociological Review* 37:643-65.
Croog, S. H. 1956. "Patient Government: Some Aspects of Participation and Social Background on Two Psychiatric Wards." *Psychiatry* 19:203-07.
Hurwitz, Jacob I., Alvin F. Zander, and Bernard Hymovitch. 1960. "Some Effects of Power on the Relations Among Group Members." Pp. 448-56 in *Group Dynamics*, edited by Dorwin Cartwright and Alvin Zander. New York: Harper & Row.
Lockheed, Marlaine E. and Katherine P. Hall. 1976. "Conceptualizing Sex as a Status Characteristic: Applications to Leadership Training Strategies." *Journal of Social Issues* 32:111-24.
Lohman, Mark R. 1972. "Changing a Racial Status Ordering: Implications for Desegregation." *Journal of Education and Urban Society* 4:383-402.
Markovsky, B., L. Smith, and J. Berger. 1984. "Do Status Interventions Persist?" *American Sociological Review* 49:373-82.
Martin, M. W. and J. Sell. 1985. "The Effect of Equating Characteristics and the Generalization Process." *Social Psychology Quarterly* 48:178-82.
Mishler, Elliot G. and Asher Tropp. 1956. "Status and Interaction in a Psychiatric Hospital." *Human Relations* 9:187-205.

Moore, James C., Jr. 1968. "Status and Influence in Small Group Interactions." *Sociometry* 31:47-63.

Norman, Robert Z., Roy Smith, and Joseph Berger. 1988. "The Processing of Inconsistent Status Information." Pp. 169-87 in *Status Generalization: New Theory and Research* edited by Murray Webster, Jr., and Martha Foschi. Stanford, CA: Stanford University Press.

Prescott, W. S. 1986. "Expectation States Theory: When Do Interventions Persist?" Unpublished manuscript, Dartmouth College.

Pugh, Meredith D. and Ralph Wahrman. 1983. "Neutralizing Sexism in Mixed-Sex Groups: Do Women Have to Be Better Than Men?" *American Journal of Sociology* 88:746-62.

Rosenholtz, Susan J. 1985. "Modifying Status Expectations in the Traditional Classroom." In *Status, Rewards, and Influence: How Expectations Organize Behavior*, edited by Joseph Berger and Morris Zelditch, Jr. San Francisco: Jossey-Bass.

Strodtbeck, Fred L., Rita M. James, and Charles Hawkins. 1957. "Social Status in Jury Deliberations." *American Sociological Review* 22:713-19.

Strodtbeck, Fred L. and Richard D. Mann. 1956. "Sex Role Differentiation in Jury Deliberation." *Sociometry* 19:3-11.

Tammivaara, Julie T. 1982. "The Effects of Task Structure on Beliefs About Competence and Participation in Small Groups." *Sociology of Education* 55:212-22.

Torrance, E. Paul. 1954. "Some Consequences of Power Differences on Decision Making in Permanent and Temporary Three-Man Groups." *Research Studies* 22:130-40.

Webster, Murray A., Jr. 1977. "Equating Characteristics and Social Interaction: Two Experiments." *Sociometry* 40(1):41-50.

Webster, Murray A., Jr. and James E. Driskell, Jr. 1978. "Status Generalization: A Review and Some New Data." *American Sociological Review* 43:220-36.

— —. 1983. "Beauty as Status." *American Journal of Sociology* 89:140-65.

Webster, Murray A., Jr. and Martha Foschi, eds. 1988. *Status Generalization: New Theory and Research*. Stanford, CA: Stanford University Press.

Zander, Alvin and Albert R. Cohen. 1955. "Attributed Social Power and Group Acceptance: A Classroom Experimental Demonstration." *Journal of Abnormal and Social Psychology* 51:490-92.

Ziller, Robert C. and Ralph V. Exline. 1958. "Some Consequences of Age Heterogeneity in Decision-Making Groups." *Sociometry* 21:198-201.

6

Understanding Legitimation in Informal Status Orders

CECILIA L. RIDGEWAY

There is an extensive tradition of theoretical as well as empirical inquiry into the legitimation of large-scale social institutions and formally structured organizations (e.g., Weber 1968; Berger and Luckmann 1966; Blau 1964; Dornbusch and Scott 1975; Habermas 1975, 1979; Zelditch and Walker 1984; Della Fave 1980, 1986). There is also empirical evidence that legitimation has an important impact on the operation of informal status orders in face-to-face task groups (Burke 1967, 1968, 1971; Verba 1961; Eskilson and Wiley 1976; Fennell et al. 1978; Meeker and Weitzel-O'Neill 1977; Ridgeway 1982). However, little theoretical analysis of the process in such groups has been available. Recently, Ridgeway and Berger (1986, 1987) proposed an expectation states theory of some conditions under which legitimation might occur in informal task groups. To address further the need for theory in this area, this chapter seeks to expand Ridgeway and Berger's theory and to develop further the understanding of the legitimation process it offers.

To do this, the chapter examines the relationship between Ridgeway and Berger's theory and the analyses of legitimation contained in some approaches to the problem within larger institutions with formal status orders. Specifically, I draw upon Zelditch and Walker's (1984) analysis of legitimacy in formal orders, which brings together much previous research and theory. To a lesser extent, I consider as well Berger and Luckmann's (1966) and Habermas's (1975, 1979) views on the nature of legitimation, which emphasize the importance of cultural ideas and the social construction of reality. These examinations will guide a closer analysis of the central assumptions of Ridgeway and Berger's theory, leading to further development of its view of the object of legitimation in an informal status order, the nature of the process by which legitimation actually occurs in such groups, and the relationship of this process to members' explicit justifications of their status order. Employing this more developed view of legitimation in informal status orders, I will extend the theory to cover additional conditions under which legitimation may occur.

The Nature of Legitimation

LEGITIMATION AS NORM FORMATION

Legitimacy has been variously defined, but in its most general sense it refers to a belief that certain patterns of actions within a social unit are governed by norms upheld by the members of the unit (Walker et al. 1986; Della Fave 1986; Dornbusch and Scott 1975; Collins 1975; Habermas 1975, 1979; Weber 1968). In particular, the study of legitimacy has focused, as I do here, on those patterns of action by which power is exercised in a social unit, generally designated as the status or authority structure. Zelditch and Walker (1984; Walker et al. 1986) argue that, at least within the formally stratified organizations they address, status structures are composed of actors, positions, and behaviors, each of which can be a separate object of legitimacy.

When power is exercised according to group norms (i.e., legitimately), it is exercised with the collective consent of the governed. As a result, legitimacy gives an actor the ability to mobilize group support for his or her norm-governed actions (Zelditch and Walker 1984; McCarthy and Zald 1977). This in turn makes legitimate actors more able to induce compliance in others, even when some of these others do not personally prefer to comply, than are actors without legitimacy (see Zelditch and Walker 1984 for a review). Furthermore, legitimate actors have less need to resort to explicit coercion to obtain this compliance, since, faced with the normative support for a legitimate directive, most comply voluntarily (Zelditch and Walker 1984). Since legitimacy induces greater compliance with the status order by group members, it increases that order's stability.

TYPIFICATIONS AND EVALUATIONS

Norms are generally understood to involve both typifications of behavior and evaluations of right and proper behavior. Legitimacy is usually associated with the latter. However, cultural theorists argue that the evaluative qualities of legitimating norms usually develop out of the distinctive nature of the typifications they contain. Habermas (1975, pp. 95-117) distinguishes between two classes of governing norms: ones that merely stabilize relations of force and others that are called "justifiable" norms.[1] Since the former are merely regularizations of behavior in a group on the basis of a frank recognition of the relations of force, they do not lead to legitimation.[2] Justifiable norms, on the other hand, not only regularize behavior, they carry a sense of "ought" that comes from their perceived "validity" or "truth" for participants in the system governed by them. These are the norms that legitimate the system they define.

The apparent "truth" of justifiable governing norms arises from the participants' conviction (however counterfactual) that consensus on the norms could be achieved among them through reasoned argumentation (Habermas 1975). Thus it is the perceived probability of rationally obtained consensual support for a norm that makes it seem "right" and proper. According to Habermas, then, the evaluative element of a legitimating norm arises out of what appears to system participants to be the apparent rationally incontrovertible nature of its typification elements and the appearance this gives that the norm can command consensual support. In a different but somewhat convergent analysis, Berger and Luckmann (1966) propose that, to the extent that the typification aspects of governing norms make the reality of the behavioral order appear more "objective" or "solid" to the members, compliance with the order seems to members more subjectively plausible, reasonable, and right.

Habermas uses this basic point about the evaluative aspect of legitimating norms for purposes that are very different from those here. Furthermore, his view of the processes that bring about consensual validity for norms differs from mine and, indeed, he would criticize the nonnormative view of legitimation presented here. Nevertheless, I will argue, in general agreement with Berger and Luckmann and with this insight of Habermas's, that legitimation in informal task-oriented status orders results from the formation of norms defining the status order that seem to members to be correctly based upon shared "reality" and, consequently, carry a consensually supported sense of "objective" validity. An explication of Ridgeway and Berger's theory will show that this view is central to its analysis of the legitimation process in informal, task-oriented status orders.

Sources of Legitimation

How do status orders acquire such legitimating norms? That is, how do members of a social unit come to feel that their status order is defined by norms that they collectively uphold as consensually and "objectively" valid? A first, deceptively simple answer is that this will occur when a majority of members personally believe the status order to be plausible and valid, act to support it, and, in doing so, create shared governing norms defining it as such. This answer, however, leads to other questions. How do a majority of members come to personally believe the status order to be valid and, indeed, is such personal belief or approval the most important determinant of their actions to support it? Several writers have pointed out that personal approval of a pattern of action because it matches internalized standards is not always sufficient to produce behavior consistent with that pattern of action (Walker et al. 1986; Thomas et al. 1986; Zelditch and Walker 1984; French and Raven 1959). The beliefs of *other* group members will have an important effect on what any one of them will do.

In their theory of the legitimation of authority structures in formal organizations, Dornbusch and Scott (1975) distinguish between individual belief in ("propriety") and collective support for ("validity") the structure. With this distinction in mind, Zelditch and Walker (1984) reviewed the experimental evidence on legitimation in formal structures. They found that individual-level propriety is neither necessary nor often sufficient to produce most of the effects usually attributed to legitimacy. Validity, on the other hand, proves to be both necessary and sufficient to generate these effects. As a result, Zelditch and Walker conclude that legitimation is fundamentally a collective process although it is enacted through individual action.

What then are the sources of collective support for one person's status over another? Following Blau (1964), Stinchcombe (1968), and Dornbusch and Scott (1975), Zelditch and Walker (1984; Walker et al. 1986) argue that there are two such sources. One is support for a member's authority given by one's own peers in the group or organization, called "endorsement" of that authority. The second is support for a member's authority that comes from levels higher than oneself, referred to as "authorization." As Dornbusch and Scott use the term, authorization involves the transfer of resources of support to the authority from higher levels or from outside the group or organization. While evidence shows that endorsement does play a role in producing the voluntary compliance to an authority that is a sign of legitimacy (Walker et al. 1986; Raven and French 1958), Zelditch and Walker's research review indicates that authorization is the more powerful source of such legitimacy.

Others also have concluded that the most important source of an order's legitimacy is the sense that it is "authorized" or supported by something beyond itself. Berger and Luckmann (1966) argue that people create an institutional order behaviorally and then "harden" and externalize the order's reality by representing it in cultural typifications that become "institutionalized" as the order's governing norms. This is the beginning of legitimacy. However, they argue that an institutional order will not be fully legitimated until it has been further objectified by being passed on to a new generation of members who did not participate in its creation. These new members do not have access to the original practical reasons for its creation or a sense that they may change the order because they themselves have created it. For them, the reality of the institution's normative order is completely external to themselves. The very "objectivity" of its existence will incline them to take it as given and develop justifying explanations for its structure. Thus the fact that a social order is supported from outside the members' own experience with it increases its plausibility to them, and hence their inclination to treat it and explain it as justified.

If authorization from outside a status order is that order's most powerful source of legitimation, there is, of course, the question of an infinite regress. One aspect of the answer to this question is contained in Berger and Luckmann's (1966) and others' (e.g., Ridgeway and Berger 1986) contention that a completely *de novo* status order developed without a cultural past or surrounding social structure would have a low likelihood of being treated as legitimate by its members. No real group, of course, operates under such conditions. A second aspect of the answer derives from Berger and Luckmann's, Zelditch and Walker's, Della Fave's (1980, 1986) and, indeed, Habermas's recognition that the ultimate source of the apparently "outside" or "external" support for a status order lies in a larger normative cultural order that, although it lies outside the individual member, was yet created by individuals and can be maintained only by the actions of the order's members. Indeed, the extent to which a status order comes to have individual-level propriety for its members will be largely due to the extent to which the members have personally internalized this outside normative order. There is a circular relationship, then, where what is outside the status order came from and in some sense continues to come from the actions of those inside the status order even though those actions also depend on what is perceived to be outside.

There are, then, several points to be gleaned from these selected theories' general views on the nature and sources of legitimation in large-scale, formally structured social units. First, a social order acquires legitimacy when it becomes normative and when these norms that define the order are collectively upheld by its members. Second, like all norms, these defining or governing norms contain an evaluative as well as a typification aspect. However, the all-important evaluative aspect of legitimating norms seems often to arise from the members' sense that the typification aspect of the norms represents a plausible or "correct" interpretation of shared "reality." Third, for governing norms to acquire this crucial sense of "objective" plausibility, some degree of support or authorization of them appears necessary from a social unit or tradition outside of and often superordinate to the social order in question. Such outside authorization is a more important determinant of voluntary compliance with legitimating norms than is each member's personal acceptance of these norms' propriety.

Legitimation in Informal Status Orders

The above points derive from examinations of a society's institutional order (Berger and Luckmann; Weber), the state (Habermas), formal organizations (Dornbusch and Scott; Stinchcombe) or formally stratified systems (Zelditch and Walker). It remains an open question how these general insights into the nature and sources of legitimation can be applied to the legitimation of the informal status structures that characterize many small task-oriented groups. To address this question we must first examine legitimation in such groups more carefully.

There is persistent evidence that legitimacy affects task group status processes. The extent to which members treat positions in an informal status order as legitimate appears to affect the type of power use high-ranking members may successfully engage in, although it may also reduce their need to use power to gain compliance (Verba 1961; Hollander 1964; Burke 1968; Ridgeway 1982, 1984). With legitimacy, high-ranking members appear able to engage more effectively in directive or domineering behaviors. Thus researchers have argued that legitimacy is vital for atypical group leaders such as women and minorities to engage successfully in directive, leaderlike behavior (Eskilson and Wiley 1976; Fennell et al. 1978). Problems of legitimacy also affect the strategies members with low external status must use to gain influence in a task group (Meeker and Weitzel-O'Neill 1977; Ridgeway 1978, 1982). Finally, Verba (1961) has argued that the relationship between legitimacy and power use suggests that Bales and Slater's (1955) well-known finding of separate task and socioemotional leaders may have resulted from low legitimation of the groups' status orders. Burke (1967, 1971) later demonstrated that legitimacy did indeed affect the extent to which task groups developed integrated status structures in which the powerful were also liked.

These legitimation effects are similar to those found in larger and more formal structures and are important to the operation of informal status orders. Yet they have received little explicit theoretical analysis. To address this problem, Ridgeway and Berger (1986) propose an expectation states theory of legitimation in task groups with informal status orders. Drawing concepts and assumptions from expectation states theories of status organizing and reward processes, this approach to legitimation differs somewhat from those discussed so far. However, as we shall see, it is not inconsistent with the major points of those other approaches. To understand Ridgeway and Berger's theory of legitimation, we must first briefly review the expectation states approach to the nature and formation of informal status orders in task groups.

INFORMAL STATUS ORDERS

The informal status order of a task group is made up of and enacted through stable differences in certain observable behaviors called by expectation states theory power and prestige behaviors and task cue behaviors. Power and prestige behaviors consist of receiving opportunities to make task contributions, offering task contributions, receiving positive evaluations of these contributions, and having influence in group decisions (Berger et al. 1974, 1977). Task cues consist of relative levels of a variety of eye gaze, vocal, and proxemic cues that are associated with high and low status positions (e.g., a firm versus tremulous voice) and that make claims or permit inferences about how well the actor will do or is doing at the task (Ridgeway et al. 1985; Berger et al. 1986).

Expectation states theory argues that the level of these behaviors a member enacts is determined by the level (e.g., high or low) of the performance expectation held for that member by self and others in comparison to those held for others in the group (Berger et al. 1974, 1977). A performance expectation is a generalized anticipation of one's own or another's capacity to make useful contributions to the group task. When group members are task oriented and collectively oriented in that they are willing to take others' behavior and opinions into account in relation to the task, the theory argues that group members form such underlying performance expectations for themselves and one another. These become the basis for behavioral status differences among them, which in turn indicate their positions in the status order.

When task group members differ with respect to one or more external status characteristics such as sex, race, occupational position, or educational attainment (called a heterogeneous group), these differences substantially determine the performance expectations members form. Status characteristics are culturally associated with general expectations for superior (or inferior) overall ability and/or with specific expectations for ability with regard to a specified task, depending on the diffuse (e.g., sex) or specific (e.g., legal training) nature of the characteristic. When a status characteristic is salient in a group, either because it differentiates among members or is relevant to the task, the cultural expectations associated with it are activated and become the basis of the expectations the members form for their own and each others' performance at the task. If more than one status characteristic is activated, the effects of each, weighted by its relevance to the task, are combined to form aggregated expectation states. Because status characteristics determine performance expectations in heterogeneous groups, they in turn shape the power and prestige and task cue behaviors that constitute the status order.

Even when task group members are similar in status characteristics, as in homogeneous peer groups, observable status orders nevertheless develop (Bales 1950; Berger et al. 1974, 1986). Expectation states theory explains this by noting that members, in the process of discussing the task, necessarily engage in power and prestige and task cue behaviors. That is, they ask and are asked for task contributions, offer task contributions, have their ideas accepted or rejected by others, and so on. These actions will be accompanied by high (e.g., firm voice and direct gaze) or low (e.g., hesitant voice, indirect gaze) task cues that, evidence suggests, will affect how competent they appear to other members (see Berger et al. 1986 for a review). If for any reason an inequality develops in any of these behaviors, it can be shown that it will soon lead to inequalities in the rate at which members' task contributions are accepted by the group (Berger and Conner 1974). Such differences then create differential expectations for the number and quality of future contributions from a member. Acting on these shared, differentiated performance expectations, members further differentiate themselves in power and prestige and task cue behaviors and, in doing so, reinforce their differentiated performance expectations. In this fashion, power and prestige behaviors and task cues create performance expectation states that in turn determine further behavior. In brief, then, this is expectation states theory's analysis of the nature of informal status orders in face-to-face task groups and its explanations for their emergence.

A THEORY OF LEGITIMATION IN INFORMAL ORDERS

Ridgeway and Berger (1986, 1987) extend the expectation states approach to account for some of the processes by which such status orders acquire or fail to acquire a sense of legitimacy in the eyes of their members. They argue that with legitimation, informal status positions based on performance expectations acquire a normative, moral quality that changes behavior inconsistent with those positions from events that are merely surprising to events that should not happen. To explain how this occurs, they approach standing in an informal status order as a reward for whose distribution group members develop expectations. Drawing on expectation states theories of rewards and distributive justice (Cook 1975; Berger et al. 1972, 1985), they argue that, as with other rewards, people respond to the actual distribution of status in a particular group by invoking referential structures of belief from a larger collectivity about the way valued status positions are usually distributed. They further argue that these referential beliefs can provide outside support for the status order that functions as "authorization" in the sense that Zelditch and Walker (1984) find so important for legitimation. As we will see, the idea that referential beliefs may provide outside support for a status order is also consistent with Berger and Luckmann's (1966) cultural analysis of legitimation.

Referential structures are sets of socially validated beliefs held in common by actors that describe what is thought to be the usual association between a valued characteristic and levels of reward, in this case, the occupation of valued status positions (i.e., positions in a social order that are differentially respected and esteemed) (Berger et al. 1972; Ridgeway and Berger 1986). Referential structures are part of the cultural beliefs of a larger collectivity to which the actor belongs, such as an organization, a subculture, or the larger society. These collectivities are more comprehensive and enduring social units than the local task group. Task group members draw upon their cultural beliefs about the nature of social reality, including beliefs linking valued characteristics with the occupation of status positions, to support the members' ideas about "what everybody knows to be true."

Following Berger et al. (1985), the theory suggests three types of referential structures that can be activated in an informally ordered task group. Categorical beliefs link the occupation of status positions to states of status characteristics. The belief that men in our society hold more highly valued status positions than women is an example. Assuming they are held by the members, categorical beliefs are activated whenever the status characteristic is activated. Ability structures associate valued status positions with task ability. These are so-called meritocratic beliefs that people who are more talented at a collective task have higher status positions in the collective than those who are less talented. If held, they are activated when the members are in a task-oriented situation. Outcome beliefs connect status positions with actual task accomplishment. They suggest that those who succeed have higher status positions than those who do not. For outcome beliefs to be activated, members must have a means of evaluating their actual task success as distinct from their presumed abilities in the situation. Arguing that this involves additional task conditions, Ridgeway and Berger do not deal specifically with outcome structures in deriving predictions from their theory. (As we shall see, extending the theory to deal explicitly with outcome structures provides a way to incorporate within this model the effects of interaction over time in increasing the legitimation of a status order.) This account of the activation of referential beliefs assumes that interactants share generally similar referential structures and the theory is restricted to groups meeting this assumption.

The theory argues that, when activated in a specific situation, members apply referential beliefs to their local group and use them to form expectations for their own and others' status positions in that group. Although referential beliefs are beliefs about "reality" rather than moral assessments, the expectations they give rise to can come to have a normative quality and can be the basis of legitimacy in a status order. So, despite its dependence on the outside support provided by referential structures, the theory argues, legitimacy is actually created in the group itself.

According to the theory, expectations for status positions acquire a normative quality through a social construction of reality process. When members use referential beliefs to form assumptions about the distribution of status in their local group, they are also creating expectations about the type of status order they anticipate will be supported by *other* members, who, they presume, draw upon the same referential "reality" as they do. Presuming their expectations to be shared, they are likely to treat other members in accord with these expectations. This means treating each others' actual positions as if they actually had the differences in status value suggested by the members' expectations for valued status positions. Since others in the group are in fact assumed to share generally similar referential beliefs, such actions in accord with resulting status expectations are likely to elicit corresponding actions from other members. These corresponding actions effectively confirm and support the existence of the status differences implied by the behavior of the first actors, making these differences normative in the group. The theory actually assumes that if the behavioral reactions of others either support or do not contradict the actors' behavior, then they provide validation for the actors' behavior that creates a presumption of collective normative support for the status order, giving it the quality of legitimacy.

This explanation of the legitimation process in informal orders has a number of aspects worthy of comment. The theory explicitly notes the connection between the concept of authorization and referential beliefs. However, authorizing beliefs, as they are discussed by legitimation theorists, are of at least two kinds. They may be simple descriptions, or "namings," of a collective definition of reality. Berger and Luckmann (1966, p. 94) call these "incipient" legitimations of that reality because they do not yet contain moral justifications for it. Referential beliefs are simple namings of collective reality and so are authorizing beliefs of this first type.

The second kind of authorizing beliefs contain not only a description of "reality" but a moral explanation of it. They are explicit justifications of a reality. Berger and Luckmann and other cultural legitimation theorists (e.g., Habermas, 1975; Della Fave, 1986) concentrate on this second type of beliefs, although they occasionally argue that this type develops from the first. If a group created its status order on the basis of such moral authorizing beliefs, which are, in effect, ideologies, these beliefs would transfer legitimacy directly from the larger collectivity to the informal status order. Ridgeway and Berger (1986) acknowledge this possibility. However, this is not the legitimation process that is the center of their theory, since they argue it is not the most important one by which legitimation occurs in informal orders.

The theory, then, describes a legitimation process that begins with a weak form of authorization by means of shared beliefs about certain aspects of "reality" contained in what it calls referential beliefs. However, the distinctive point of the theory is that this weak authorization gives rise to a collective construction of reality within the group that resembles what Zelditch and Walker (1984) call an endorsement process. That is, the group members themselves (who are all peers in Zelditch and Walker's terms, since they do not occupy *formally* different positions in the group) create mutual normative support for (i.e., endorsement of) their *informal* order. The process described, then, is one where weak (but crucial) authorization creates endorsement, which in turn gives the status order the normative quality of legitimacy.

According to the theory, the actual likelihood that this process of legitimation will occur in a given group depends on three additional factors. First, although it is assumed that members form status expectations at the same time that they form performance expectations, the theory argues that it is only after performance expectations have created a stable observable status order that status expectations lead to a legitimation process. As we shall see, the theory can be usefully expanded by removing this specification.

Second, the theory assumes that the members' rank orders of performance expectations and expectations for status positions are congruent. It does not consider how the legitimation process would be affected if this were not true. Since, as we shall see, there are circumstances where such incongruence can occur, this, too, is an area where the theory should be extended.

Third, and most important, the theory's central legitimation assumption argues that once the above assumptions are met and the order has stabilized, then the likelihood that legitimation will occur depends on how *differentiated* the members' status expectations are. The greater one member's expectation advantage (or disadvantage) over another to possess valued status positions in the group, the more likely both are to act on these expectations and treat the status order as legitimate. The theory's formal assumption puts this argument in terms of the likelihood that the status order of one group will be treated as legitimate compared to that of another group. It states that if two groups have status orders with the same number of ranks and if, in the first group, the expectation advantage (or disadvantage) of one member over each other member to occupy valued status positions is greater than that of the member in the same rank position in the second group in relation to each other member of the second group, then members of the first group compared to those of the second group will be more likely to behave as if their order were a legitimate order.

The theory then analyzes types of groups that should produce different degrees of differentiation in their status expectations, and, consequently, differ in their likelihood of legitimation. When group members are heterogeneous in external status characteristics, and these are consistently allocated in that members high on one characteristic are high on others, then referential beliefs activated by these characteristics lead to substantially differentiated expectations for status positions. In homogeneous groups, on the other hand, ability referential beliefs are activated but differences in the members' task abilities can be only indirectly inferred from behavior rather than more directly observed as differences in status characteristics usually are. As a result, the status expectations in homogeneous groups, based on inferred ability differences, are likely to be less differentiated than those in consistent heterogeneous groups that are based on known external status differences.

Groups of a third type are likely to develop even less differentiation in their status expectations than are homogeneous groups. These are inconsistent heterogeneous groups, where two discriminating status characteristics are activated but are inconsistently allocated in that a member high on one is low on the other. Furthermore, one but not the other of these characteristics is directly relevant to the task. The example given is of a woman with legal training working on a legal-type task with a man without such legal training. Because of the greater relevance of one of the characteristics to the task, performance expectations favor the member high on that characteristic and that member achieves higher informal status. However, in terms of activated referential beliefs, one characteristics is not more directly associated with the possession of valued status positions than the other. Consequently, since each member is high on one characteristic but low on the other, status expectations held for each should be similar, yielding a very low degree of differentiation.

From the legitimation assumption and the above analysis, the theory derives three predictions (Ridgeway and Berger 1987). First, within a given period of time, legitimation of the status order will be more likely in consistent heterogeneous than in homogeneous groups and the status orders of homogeneous groups are more likely to become legitimatized than those of the type of inconsistent heterogeneous groups just described. Second, in consistent heterogeneous groups, the greater the number of discriminating status characteristics, the greater the differentiation in status expectations and, consequently, in the likelihood of legitimation. Third, in inconsistent heterogeneous groups where, unlike the example above, members possess a fixed number of equally task-relevant discriminating status characteristics, the greater the degree of inconsistency in the way these characteristic are allocated, the less the likelihood that their status orders will be legitimated.

Finally, the theory addresses some of the behavioral changes that are likely to result when an informal status order acquires legitimacy. The power and prestige behaviors and task cues that constitute the informal order take on meaning as status "markers" or "violations" in addition to their task significance as sources of performance-related information. In a legitimated order, argues the theory, members expect one another to support the order by displaying an appropriate level of power and prestige behaviors and task cues. Used in this way, such behaviors become status markers that affirm the order. However, when a member engages in a level of these behaviors out of proportion to his or her rank, they act as status violations that may be subject to sanctions from other members. In addition, legitimacy increases the likelihood that when high-ranking members direct coercive dominance behavior toward lower-ranked members they will receive compliance rather than resistance because of their greater resources of group support (Ridgeway and Berger 1986; Ridgeway 1984). These anticipated behavioral effects of legitimation are used to suggest ways that the theory's predictions might be tested.

Explicating the Theory Further

Although this theory provides an important first step in understanding legitimation in informal orders, some aspects of the model it offers remain unclear. First and most crucially, the theory's key assumption itself requires further explication to make clearer why differentiated status expectations are more likely than undifferentiated ones to lead members to treat the order as normative and, in so doing, make it normative. Second, the object of legitimation in an informal order, that is, what it is that becomes normative, should be better defined. Third, the relationship of this norm formation process to members' explicit justifications of their order, often associated with legitimacy, needs to be specified. Each of these issues can be illuminated by a consideration of its relationship to the other analyses of legitimation that have been discussed.

DIFFERENTIATED STATUS EXPECTATIONS AND LEGITIMATION

The behavioral legitimation process described by the theory contains two stages. In the first, differentiated status expectations cause one or more members to act in accord with these expectations by treating others as though their status positions actually carried the expected status value. In the second stage, the subsequent behavior of others serves to validate these initial reactions behaviorally, either by not contradicting them or by similarly supporting the expected order. This validation by others creates a presumption of collective normative support for members' status expectations and the informal order that corresponds to it, making the order normative and legitimate (Ridgeway and Berger 1986, p. 608).

Once the initial stage occurs, argues the theory, the fact that status expectations are shared creates a strong probability that the process will continue through the second stage to legitimation even if some members do not personally approve of the expected order. Thus the crucial question is how the first stage is initiated. That is, how do differentiated status expectations increase the likelihood that one or more members will go beyond merely anticipating a given order to treating that order in evaluative terms as right and proper? There are two issues involved. First, why are members more likely to act in accord with differentiated than undifferentiated status expectations? Second, why is the nature of the action induced by differentiated status expectations an evaluative reaction to the status order?

Differentiation and Certainty in Expectations

Two members' expectations (for either status positions or performance) are more differentiated the greater the advantage they imply for one member over the other (for either the occupation of a valued status position or task performance). It is possible to conceive of the size of this advantage in terms of degrees of difference in either the status value of the position associated with the member or the quality of the performance expected from him or her. However, I believe that conception is misleading because it obscures the relationship between differentiation in expectations and an actor's propensity to act on those expectations. The size of an expectation advantage can be seen instead as the *degree of certainty* in the minds of the members that a given rank order exists among them in either the status value of the position or the quality of the performance expected for them.[3] By this second approach, the greater the differentiation in two actors' mutual expectations for valued status positions, the greater the degree of certainty each has that a particular one of them will be associated with a higher-valued status position than the other.

An example may clarify the difference between these two views of an expectation advantage. According to the first, if Mary has a large expectation advantage over Mike, Mary expects the status value of her position to be greater than his by an amount proportionate to the size of her expectation advantage. According to the second view, Mary expects to rank above Mike in the status value of her position, but it is her degree of certainty that this will be the case that is proportional to the size of her expectation advantage over him.

This second view of differentiation in status expectations is more consistent with their source in referential beliefs than the first. Referential beliefs describe *who* has status and power over *whom* in the larger collectivity (e.g., men versus women, the skilled versus the unskilled) but not *how much* more status and power one type of actor has over another. Furthermore, expectations for status in the local group created by referential beliefs are more differentiated the more sets of consistent referential beliefs are activated. The effect of these accumulating, consistent beliefs should be to increase the certainty with which the actors expect the rank order status relation predicted between two actors actually to exist. It seems reasonable that the more certain expectations are, the more likely they are to be acted on, making clearer the theory's argument that members are more likely to act in accord with differentiated expectations. On the other hand, undifferentiated expectations provide uncertain and, therefore, unclear guidance and so are unlikely to be a basis for action.

Expectational Certainty, Evaluative Reactions, and Legitimation

The theory argues that members are not only more likely to act on the basis of more differentiated status expectations, but that the nature of their actions will be to treat their actual status positions as if they carried the status value implied by their expectations. This means members treat each other's status behaviors evaluatively. That is, they react with support and approval to their fellow members' status behaviors when those behaviors enact the expected order and respond with disapproval when they violate the expected order. Thus the type of action induced by differentiated status expectations is a propensity to react evaluatively to *others'* status behaviors. Group members' *own* actual propensity to engage in a given level of status-related behaviors relative to others depends on their performance expectation advantages or disadvantages in relation to those others, not their status expectations. However, since the theory assumes that the order of performance and status expectations are ordinally congruent, members, by acting on performance expectations, produce for one another a behavioral status order that corresponds to their status expectations.

Why, then, do differentiated status expectations create a propensity to react to others' status behaviors in evaluative terms? The answer derives from their source in referential beliefs. Referential beliefs are cultural beliefs about reality that are presumed to be shared by the actor's many fellow participants in the larger, more enduring social unit from which they are derived (as well as members of the actor's local group). Consequently, these are beliefs that actors presume are intersubjectively valid for a great many others. Studies of actors' constructions of social reality through social comparison processes suggest that the greater the number of an actor's fellows who accept a given definition of that reality, the more certainly and "objectively" true it appears to that actor (Festinger 1954; Suls and Miller 1977). Given the perceived breadth of intersubjective agreement about referential beliefs, their objective truth should seem quite certain to most actors.

When the basis of a belief's "objective truth" is intersubjective agreement, it has an additional quality as well: Its truth appears to be socially supported. That is, it appears to an actor that others will stand up for the belief's veracity by challenging those who question it. It is this combination of objectivity and social acceptance that allows referential beliefs to act as authorizing beliefs in the local group.

When multiple consistent referential beliefs are activated in a local group, creating highly differentiated status expectations, each provides another socially supported, "objectively" valid reason why a given status order is to be expected. In this situation, the expected status order is likely to seem to members both objectively inevitable and likely to be expected and accepted by their groupmates, who, members presume, share their referential "reality." Because they combine these two qualities, differentiated status expectations can induce some members to initiate evaluative reactions to others' status behaviors.

When expectations are derived from widely supported "truth" as are differentiated status expectations, I believe that actors tend to feel they have a "right" to expect events to corroborate them and, as a result, treat such corroborating events with approval. This assertion, although derived from social comparison theory, is consistent with Habermas's (1975) view that expectations acquire a sense of "ought" or "right" when the actors feel these expectations would be consensually accepted as rationally valid by others in the group. Because differentiated status expectations appear both objectively inevitable and socially accepted, behavior that does not correspond to them is surprising but also a little "crazy" or deviant. It appears not to be based on "realistic" or "reasonable" views and so cannot be expected to be supported by others. Consequently, rather than revising these expectations on the basis of a disconfirming event, an actor is likely to react with disapproval. In this way, differentiated status expectations incline members to treat each other's status behaviors in evaluative terms.

As Meeker and Weitzel-O'Neill (1977) have suggested, this sense of "right" and the evaluative reactions it generates may result partly from cognitive consistency needs that make people actively prefer events that confirm their expectations, particularly their certain expectations

(Festinger 1957, 1964; Wicklund and Brehm 1976). However, it is also based on the apparent manifest reasonableness of differentiated expectations and actors' felt assurance that both their fellow group members and those in the outside collectivity will support them in these expectations.

The sense of a right to confirmation of differentiated expectations and, thus, the propensity to react evaluatively, is strongest for those who do not personally disapprove of the expected order (whether or not they actively approve of it). It is these people who are most likely to trigger the legitimation process by initiating evaluative reactions to status behavior. However, even those who do disapprove of the expected order may well feel it is virtually inevitable, given the differentiation (i.e., certainty) of their status expectations and, as a result, react with shock to another member's behavioral violation of it. Such a shock reaction could be read by others as a sanction or disapproval of that violation, which, in turn, has the effect of supporting the expected order. This analysis suggests that, as long as a member holds the shared differentiated status expectations, personal disapproval of the expected order will not necessarily cause the member to challenge others' behavior supporting that order. As a result, such personal disapproval alone is not likely to stop the behavioral validation process by which the expected order becomes normative in the group, once that process has been triggered by others' initial approval reactions.

THE OBJECT OF LEGITIMATION

Zelditch and Walker (1984; Walker et al. 1986) argue that in formal status orders actors, actions, and positions are all possible objects of legitimation. In Ridgeway and Berger's theory for informal status orders, positions are the stated object of legitimation. Unlike a formal order, however, positions in an informal status structure that has not yet acquired legitimacy cannot be discussed independently of members' specific status-related behaviors or actions. These behaviors are themselves determined by judgments of each actor (i.e., his or her task capacities). Consequently, in an informal order, judgments of the legitimacy of an actor, his or her actions, and position are not independent but constitute a single system that is the object of legitimation.

Clarification of the object of legitimation in Ridgeway and Berger's theory allows a fuller explication of the way this object is altered by the acquisition of legitimacy. The theory states that legitimation adds a normative quality to informal status positions that gives status-related behaviors additional significance as status markers or violations. In effect, then, the legitimation of an informal order entails the formation of norms that prescribe particular rank relationships in actors' status behaviors toward one another based on their relative performance expectations. In so doing, legitimating norms harden actor-action regularities into normative status positions in the group.

JUSTIFYING THE STATUS ORDER

This account of the process by which informal orders become normative is compatible with Berger and Luckmann's (1966) view of legitimation as a process by which the apparent reality of an order is "hardened" and objectified. It is also compatible with Habermas's (1975) view of the development of the evaluative "should" element of legitimating norms. What, however, does this account have to say about that additional aspect of legitimation that deals with group members' actual propensity to articulate explicit justifications of their status order?

Members of a legitimate status order are more likely to feel that they "deserve" their positions and to articulate reasons for feeling that way than are the members of an order that lacks legitimacy. In task-oriented groups, positions are often justified on the basis of the performance expectations held for given members. This feeling of greater deservingness is interesting because there is in fact no difference between task-oriented orders with and without legitimacy in the extent to which their members' positions in the status order are actually based on performance expectations. In inconsistent heterogeneous groups with a predicted low likelihood of legitimation, the actual behavioral status order is created by the members' performance expectation advantages or disadvantages in relation to one another just as it is in consistent heterogeneous groups with a high probability of legitimation. Thus the members of both kinds of groups could equally well argue that their positions are deserved on the basis of apparent task competence. Why, then, are they more likely to do so when their status order has acquired legitimacy?

The answer lies with the effect of legitimating norms in objectifying the status order for the members (Berger and Luckmann 1966). Such norms make the status order more explicit and, in doing so, make more plain for the members its basis in their assessments of their own and each other's task competence. In a legitimate order, then, there is a greater likelihood that performance expectations will move from out-of-awareness anticipations to acknowledged judgments of actors' relative task abilities. As such judgments become explicit, members are more likely to use them in explaining their status order to themselves and others. This has the effect, in turn, of explicitly justifying the order.

There are several aspects of interactions in a normative status order that, over time, increase the probability that such explicit justifications will be developed and articulated. First, there are the accumulating effects of members' power and prestige and task cue behaviors that enact and affirm the normative order. Second, when members do occasionally violate their normative rank in status behaviors, their actions attract group attention to the order. Reacting to both the violation and the highlighted order, other members may be stimulated to justify or explain their disapproval of the offending behavior explicitly. As time passes, the probability grows that some such justification-stimulating violations will occur.

Finally, when over time new members join the group, older members will attempt to explain the existing order to the newcomers and in the process are likely to develop and express rationales justifying it.

Justifications of a status order increase its resistance to change and add an additional dimension to group members' reactions to status violations. Consider a group where a member ranks low in the legitimated informal order due to low external status, for instance, a female in an otherwise male decision-making group. If the woman tries to raise her status in the group by increasing her task contributions she will be committing a status violation and her efforts are likely to be met with disapproval. Her behavior seems unreasonable in relation to status expectations but it also is unjustified in relation to the low performance expectations held for her. In this situation the other members are likely to question the woman's motivation for behaving so inappropriately. Since she is presumed to be of lower task ability than the others, her efforts will not seem to them to be a sincere attempt to help with the shared task. Instead, unless she does something to counteract the impression, they are likely to judge her efforts to be a self-interested attempt to aggrandize herself at the expense of the group as a whole (Meeker and Weitzel-O'Neill 1977; Ridgeway 1978).

Evidence suggests that, having made such a judgment, group members will feel freer to ignore or resist the woman's task efforts without actually assessing their possible contribution to the task (Ridgeway 1982). As a result, it will be doubly difficult for her to prove to the others that she is in fact more competent than they thought, and therefore worthy of higher status in the group. We see, then, that a legitimate order's capacity for explicit justification allows its members to retard change in their order not just by sanctioning violators but also by "justifiably" ignoring the task content of the violations without feeling they have abandoned their own commitment to the task in doing so.

Extensions of the Theory

Thus far, in the effort to develop Ridgeway and Berger's theory further, I have concentrated on explications, refinements, and modifications that fall within the theory's original scope. These modifications, however, make it possible to extend the theory beyond its initial scope conditions to account for early legitimacy effects, the activation of outcome structures, and inconsistent orders of status and performance expectations.

EARLY LEGITIMACY EFFECTS

As currently formulated, the theory assumes that legitimation begins *after* the status order has emerged and stabilized. However, there is evidence suggesting that group members sometimes act from the initial moments of interaction as though certain levels of status-related behaviors are normatively appropriate for specific members while other levels of such behaviors are inappropriate (Katz 1970; Katz and Cohen 1962; Meeker and Weitzel-O'Neill 1977; Ridgeway 1982). That is, they treat certain behaviors as legitimate or illegitimate from their first enactment, apparently before the status order could have stabilized. How can such effects be accounted for in this theory?

These early legitimacy effects have been observed in consistent heterogeneous groups whose members differed on visible, immediately recognizable status characteristics such as sex and race. In such a situation, members can easily observe the unequal value of one another's external status characteristics before task interaction begins. Such observations activate associated general expectations and referential beliefs, causing members to form differentiated initial expectations for one member relative to another for task performance and the occupation of valued status positions. Consequently, the members of such groups are likely to begin interaction with already differentiated status and performance expectations.

Recall that differentiated status expectations give actors specifiable degrees of confidence that a given rank order of status relations will occur in the group. This confidence inclines them to react with disapproval to status behaviors from others that are not commensurate with their expected status rank, since such behavior seems "unreasonable" and a violation of the collectively accepted reality. The fact that members in such groups can form differentiated status expectations before interaction begins can, therefore, account for the observed early legitimacy effects. This in turn means that the theory can be successfully applied to the analysis of legitimacy effects from the first moment that differentiated status expectations are formed in a group.

In heterogeneous groups where differences in status characteristics are visible or otherwise known, this will be the case from the beginning of interaction. However, in homogeneous groups, differentiated status expectations develop only after members, on the basis of interaction, form differentiated assessments of one another's task ability. These assessments (or performance expectations), of course, also stabilize the behavioral status order. This means that differentiated status expectations and, consequently, the possibility of legitimacy effects emerge in homogeneous groups only after the status order has begun to stabilize. Thus early legitimacy effects are improbable in homogeneous groups.

If legitimacy effects occur in some heterogeneous groups from the first, before the status order can have emerged, what could be the object of legitimation? The answer is the expected order of given members' levels of status-related behaviors. As noted earlier, this is assumed to correspond to (i.e., be ordinally congruent with) the order of performance expectations, and this analysis of early legitimacy effects is limited to groups that meet this assumption.

Early legitimacy effects are produced by each member's own initial status expectations for the others. Since members are assumed to share referential beliefs, these are likely to be similar, and so members are likely to react similarly to a given level of status behaviors from a particular member. The conjoint disapproval of unexpected ranges of behavior this produces is likely to pressure members not to act outside the range of status behaviors expected of them. Since this expected range is also the range implied for them by shared performance expectations, they are in fact likely to stay within it. However, the knowledge that others may not only be surprised by but actually disapprove of out-of-range status behaviors may further inhibit any personal tendency to go beyond what is expected. As a consequence, the behavioral status orders of such groups should stabilize very quickly. In fact, status orders do emerge very quickly in consistent heterogeneous groups (Berger et al. 1974) and these early legitimacy effects may be part of the reason.

Having noted the conservative effects of initially differentiated status expectations on behavior, it is important also to note that initial status expectations themselves may be modified by early interaction in the group. While generally similar, members' initial expectations will not always be identical, leading to mutual adjustment in initial exchanges. Furthermore, early exchanges may bring to light additional task or status characteristic information for a member, modifying both performance and status expectations. As status and performance expectations change before stabilizing, the range of status behaviors expected from a given member in relation to others will also change, altering the boundaries beyond which disapproval reactions are evoked.

INCONGRUENT ORDERS OF EXPECTATIONS FOR STATUS AND PERFORMANCE

As currently stated, according to the legitimation assumption, the order of status positions in the group corresponds to both the order of performance expectations from which it arises and the order of status expectations. This in turn means that the orders of performance and status expectations must be ordinally congruent. Such congruence seems empirically likely for several reasons.

Status expectations, as a variety of reward expectations, will be interdependent with the performance expectations that create the actual order so that a change in one will affect the other (Cook 1975; Parcel and Cook 1977; Berger et al. 1985). In addition, both performance expectations and expectations for status positions derive primarily from the same two sources: status characteristics possessed by the actor and task behavior. Task behavior evaluated positively or negatively will always have the same directional impact on both performance and status expectations. Consequently, rank orders of performance and status expectations could be reversed only through the effects of activated status characteristics.

There are, however, at least two situations in which activated status characteristics might lead to high (or low) expectations for status and low (or high) expectations for performance for one actor vis-à-vis another. In the first situation, an activated status characteristic is positively associated with valued status positions in referential beliefs but negatively associated with the specific skill necessary to accomplish the group's task. An example might be black and white group members working on a task requiring knowledge of black culture.

In the second situation an actor possesses the high state of two or three initially nonrelevant diffuse status characteristics, but the low state of the ability characteristic required for the task. Consider, for example, a well-educated male with little budgetary expertise working on a budget with a younger, less educated female who is highly skilled with budgets. Because of the powerful impact of the ability characteristic and the weak impact of the diffuse status characteristics, the female will have a slight performance expectation advantage over the male and so will have higher actual power and influence. However, since the diffuse status characteristics and the ability characteristic are equally relevant for expectations for valued status positions, the order of status expectations will favor the male, making it incongruent with the actual status order. Since people with higher status in the larger society usually have greater power to determine the types of tasks they work on and thus can better avoid specific tasks for which they are disadvantaged, such situations with rank order reversals may occur only rarely in actual task groups. They are not, however, impossible.

The question then remains whether group members whose differentiated expectations for status positions imply one rank order would treat as legitimate an actual status order that reversed their expectations. The answer must be no. If the actual order reversed the expected order, differentiated status expectations could no longer make the actual order seem "realistic" or "reasonable," and so would be unlikely to contribute to the supportive behavior that will make the actual order normative.

An outright reversal of their expectations for status may actually cause the group members to treat their status order as *illegitimate* rather than merely prevent them from making it normative and legitimate. As currently formulated, the theory deals only with the probability that an informal order will be treated as legitimate, not that it will be treated as actually illegitimate. However, if differentiated expectations lead members to expect with great certainty a given rank order, then an actual order reversing these rank positions should be experienced as startlingly atypical and deviant or bizarre. This sense of invalidity in Habermas' (1975) terms, of a violation of what "ought" to be, given reasonably based, certain expectations, amounts to a reaction to the order as illegitimate.

Such a reaction would likely make interaction in the group uncomfortable, at least for the members in the reversed positions. Those who expect high but actually have low status may be particularly uncomfortable. Consequently, actors finding themselves in such reversed positions may be more likely than in other situations to try to avoid interaction with one another, remove themselves or the other from the group, or even disband the group altogether. All other things being equal, such actions might provide a behavioral indicator of members' sense that their relative status positions are illegitimate. This argument can be stated as a corollary to Ridgeway and Berger's (1986) legitimation assumption:

- *Legitimation corollary:* Given S_1 and S_2, which are the structures of two collectively oriented task groups of the same size such that within each there exists an order of expectations for performance and for valued status positions. Given further that within each of these groups the order of power and prestige (i.e., status positions) corresponds to those of the order of performance expectations and contains the same number of rank positions. Given finally that for any two actors, p_1 and o_1, who, respectively, occupy the same rank positions in S_1 as p_2 and o_2 do in S_2, p_i's rank position relative to o_i's rank position in their order of performance expectations is the inverse of p_i's rank position relative to o_i's rank position in their order of expectations for valued status positions. If the expectation advantage (or disadvantage) of p_1 over o_1 in S_1 for valued status positions is greater than the expectation advantage (or disadvantage) of actors p_2 over o_2 in S_2, then there is a greater likelihood that p_1 and o_1 compared to p_2 and o_2 will behave as if their power and prestige order is an illegitimate order.

Empirical tests are required to determine whether such illegitimacy effects actually occur. However, at least, groups with incongruent performance and status expectation orders should have a very low likelihood of acquiring legitimacy, even lower than that of inconsistent heterogeneous groups, because such inconsistent groups simply lack extra outside support for their orders due to undifferentiated status expectations that do not tell members with any certainty what order to expect. On the other hand, in incongruent groups outside beliefs actually suggest that the status order of the group is a deviant one.

OUTCOME STRUCTURES AND LEGITIMATION OVER TIME

Referential structures linking task outcomes to status positions are included by Ridgeway and Berger (1986) as possible sources of differentiated status expectations along with categorical and ability structures. However, they limit their formulation to task conditions in which outcome structures are not activated, leaving open the important question of how a status order's legitimacy is affected by its success or failure at the task. Similarly, by specifying that, for their predictions to hold, the period of time under consideration must be held constant, they implicitly acknowledge that interaction over time may affect an informal order's likelihood of legitimation. Yet they provide no explanation for such effects. Both these issues can be addressed by extending the theory to incorporate the activation of outcome structures over time.

Outcome structures are activated when either the individual members' or the group's collective task outcomes (e.g., final decisions, choices, or actions) are evaluated from outside the group as successful or unsuccessful. Such outside evaluation can come from a relevant outside authority, for instance, a work group's organizational supervisor. It can also come from the "bottom line" of rewards or costs accruing to the group as a result of its task outcomes. An example might be the financial results of a group's investment decisions or the ratings achieved by a scriptwriting group's television program.

The inherent ambiguity of many actual tasks dealt with by groups and the uncertainties of the feedback most groups receive from their environment mean that such clear outside evaluation cannot be expected in response to each of a group's task outcomes. However, over time, the odds increase that a group will receive some such clear feedback on its task achievements. One effect of the passage of time, then, may be the eventual and perhaps repeated activation of outcome structures.

The effect of clear outside evaluation is to link those associated with the evaluated task outcome directly to task success or failure. If the evaluated outcome is a collective product of the group, I assume that it is only the high-status members of the group who are linked to its success or failure. If what has been evaluated is one member's individual contributions compared to another's, then each member is associated with relative degrees of success or failure. The former is probably more common in actual task groups. However, in both cases, members are differentiated from one another in task achievement, activating outcome referential beliefs and powerfully affecting performance expectations.

The modification of performance expectations alters the evaluated members' positions in the status order. In addition, the activation of outcome beliefs provides a new source of differentiation in expectations for status that combines with previously activated beliefs to change the members' status expectation advantages (or disadvantages) in comparison to one another. This change may increase or decrease the degree of differentiation in the order of status expectations, with corresponding effects on group members' propensity to treat their status order as legitimate.

Over time, however, the successive effect of outcome feedback is likely to be a net increase in the differentiation of status expectations (up to a limit), and thus the likelihood of legitimation. There is evidence that high-status members often use their power to direct the group, as much as they are able, toward task objectives at which they are highly skilled and away from objectives at which they are less able (Short and Strodtbeck 1963; Verba 1961). This greatly increases the chances that task outcomes for which they are accountable will receive positive rather than negative outside evaluations. Positive feedback, in turn, increases their status and performance expectation advantages over lower-ranked members.

A second reason for increasing differentiation applies only when a stable outside environment provides the group with consistent evaluations, a luxury not afforded many task groups. Since outside evaluation powerfully affects performance expectations, if the basis for positive or negative feedback remains reasonably consistent over time it may gradually sort more skilled members into high-status positions. To the extent more skilled members achieve high status, the ratio of positive to negative outcome evaluations should grow, increasing those high-status members' status expectation advantages over lower-status members. This process of increasing differentiation will level off, however, due to the diminishing marginal impact of additional consistent feedback (Berger et al. 1977, 1985). It may also, of course, be overturned by changing environmental conditions.

If this analysis is correct, even status orders such as the inconsistent heterogeneous ones that begin with relatively undifferentiated status expectations may over time develop greater differentiation and acquire legitimacy. This suggests, in turn, that atypical group leaders such as women or blacks in mixed-sex or biracial groups who achieved their positions because of task ability characteristics should look for outside evaluations of their task outcomes in order to legitimate their status positions in the group.

The effects of the activation of outcome structures over time will be a bit different in the case of illegitimate status orders in groups with incongruent orders of expectations for status and performance. As noted, these groups are not likely to persist. However, if they do, positively evaluated task outcomes will reduce the incongruence of expectations for status and performance, decreasing the likelihood that the status order will be treated as illegitimate.

Incorporating outside feedback on task success and the activation of outcome structures into Ridgeway and Berger's theory allows it to account for the way the legitimation process is affected over time by an informal order's interactions with its environment. Given the importance of such interactions for a status order's survival, this represents a significant improvement in the theory's adequacy as a model of legitimation in informal orders.

Conclusion

This chapter has sought to increase our understanding of the legitimation process in task-oriented, informal status orders by further developing and extending Ridgeway and Berger's (1986) expectation states approach to the problem. My strategy has been to analyze the relationship between this theory and analyses of legitimation in larger-scale, formally ordered status systems. Ridgeway and Berger's theory, like most others, views legitimation in informal status orders as the process by which members come to feel that their order is governed by norms that they collectively uphold as socially valid. Members create such norms for their status order through a complex process in the social construction of shared reality in their group. Indeed, analyses of legitimation in larger-scale groups suggest that a fundamental source of the moral quality of legitimating norms is the apparent socially incontrovertible nature of the status order that they define, which, in turn, makes the order seem "reasonable" (Berger and Luckmann 1966; Zelditch and Walker 1984; Habermas 1975). Such analyses also suggest that an important source of this appearance of social incontrovertibility is a sense that the status order's defining norms are supported by or "authorized" by a social reality that is outside and in some sense superordinate to the order (Dornbusch and Scott 1975; Berger and Luckmann 1966; Zelditch and Walker 1984).

On careful examination, the view of legitimation in informal status orders offered by Ridgeway and Berger's theory proves to be in accord with this understanding of the process. The theory assumes that the members of informal status orders hold referential structures of belief from a larger, more enduring collectivity that associates abilities, status characteristics, and task outcomes with the occupation of valued status positions. Referential beliefs are, in effect, authorizing beliefs about collectively validated social reality. When these beliefs are activated by circumstances described in the theory, members use them to form expectations for status positions in the informal order. The theory's key assumption argues that the more differentiated these expectations are for the positions to be held by self and other, the more likely both are to treat their existing differences in power and prestige as if they were also legitimate.

In the explication and development of this assumption, I have argued that differentiated expectations for status positions should be seen as highly "authorized" expectations because they result from the activation of multiple consistent referential beliefs. As a result, degrees of differentiation in status expectations should be understood as degrees of certainty with which members expect a given status order to exist among them. Such degrees of certainty amount to the degrees to which members of the order feel their expectations are rationally and incontrovertibly based on intersubjectively agreed-upon "reality." Drawing on cognitive consistency theory and the effects of social support, I have argued that the greater their certainty (i.e., the more differentiated their status expectations), the more likely members are to feel that behaviors that confirm these expectations are correct and "right" and the more likely they are to sanction behaviors that contradict them. Thus if the status order does confirm differentiated status expectations (which it will if the orders of performance expectations and expectations for status are congruent), these expectations will cause one or more members to treat the status order in evaluative terms, triggering a behavioral validation process that, in effect, creates legitimating norms for the status order.

These legitimating norms in turn highlight for the members the informal status structure and its basis in performance expectations. As a result, they facilitate the development of explicit justifications for the order. This, then, argues that such explicit justifications are not usually part of the process by which legitimation is created in informal orders, but rather are themselves a result of the process.

This more developed view of the legitimation process was used to extend the theory beyond its original scope conditions. Although Ridgeway and Berger assume that a status order will have stabilized before legitimation occurs, there is some evidence that apparent legitimacy effects can occur from the first moments of interaction in groups where highly differentiated status expectations can be formed quickly from visible or known status characteristics. The first extension used the modified view of legitimation to account for such effects.

The more precise and explicit view of the legitimation process developed here highlights the importance of a congruence between the orders of performance expectations and expectations for status positions. Yet a careful consideration of the theory suggests that there are some situations where these orders will not be congruent. The second extension addressed the impact of such incongruence on the legitimation process, suggesting that such orders will treated not merely as lacking in legitimacy, but as actually illegitimate, resulting in problems for the maintenance of the status order.

Finally, Ridgeway and Berger's formulation proposes that referential beliefs associating task outcomes with status positions can provide a source of differentiated expectations for status in the group, but does not discuss the circumstances under which such beliefs will play a significant role in the legitimation process. Similarly, the theory implicitly acknowledges that with increased interaction over time the legitimation of many informal status orders is likely to increase, but provides no explanation for this phenomenon. In the third extension, I suggest that such effects of interaction over time could largely be accounted for by the increased likelihood that events in the group's interaction with its environment will activate outcome-referential beliefs. While activated outcome beliefs could either reduce or increase the differentiation of members' expectations for status positions, there are several reasons the latter is more likely. Consequently, the effect of their activation will most commonly be to increase the probability that the members will begin to treat their status order as legitimate.

These extensions increase the scope of this expectation states theory of the legitimation of informal status orders in task-oriented groups. Even in extended form, however, it is a theory of conditions that are sufficient rather than necessary for legitimation to occur in such orders. Much more work, both theoretical and empirical, must be done if we are genuinely to understand the legitimation process in informal orders. However, it is encouraging that the central process of legitimation as it is described in this theory can be understood in terms that are reasonably comparable to those used to describe the process in larger, formally stratified systems. Since the legitimation of larger systems is to some extent interdependent with the legitimation of the smaller, more informal systems within them, it makes sense that there should be commonalities in the process at both levels.

Notes

1. Habermas's (1975, 1979) purpose in examining the problem of legitimation is not merely analytical, as is mine here, but also normative in an attempt to construct a society without domination. In this effort, he goes on to make a number of further distinctions among types of legitimation that I will not draw on here, relying instead on his basic analysis of the nature of the legitimation process.

2. I will not deal here with groups whose informal authority structures are based on force alone, since they do not meet Ridgeway and Berger's scope condition of collective orientation (Ridgeway 1984).

3. This interpretation of an expectation advantage is also consistent with Foschi's (1971, 1972) elaboration of the concept of expectations and her interpretation of their "strength."

References

Bales, Robert F. 1950. *Interaction Process Analysis: A Method for the Study of Small Groups.* Cambridge, MA: Addison-Wesley.

Bales, Robert F. and Phillip Slater. 1955. "Role Differentiation in Small Decision-Making Groups." Pp. 259-306 in *The Family, Socialization and Interaction Processes*, edited by T. Parsons and P. Slater. Glencoe, IL: Free Press.

Berger, Joseph and Thomas L. Conner. 1974. "Performance Expectations and Behavior in Small Groups: A Revised Formulation." Pp. 85-110 in *Expectation States Theory: A Theoretical Research Program*, edited by Joseph Berger, Thomas L. Conner, and M. Hamit Fisek. Cambridge, MA: Winthrop.

Berger, Joseph, Thomas L. Conner, and M. Hamit Fisek, eds. 1974. *Expectation States Theory: A Theoretical Research Program.* Cambridge, MA: Winthrop.

Berger, Joseph, M. Hamit Fisek, Robert Z. Norman, and David G. Wagner. 1985. "The Formation of Reward Expectations in Status Situations." Pp. 215-61 in *Status, Rewards, and Influence: How Expectations Organize Behavior*, edited by Joseph Berger and Morris Zelditch, Jr. San Francisco: Jossey-Bass.

Berger, Joseph, M. Hamit Fisek, Robert Z. Norman, and Morris Zelditch, Jr. 1977. *Status Characteristics and Social Interaction.* New York: Elsevier.

Berger, Joseph, Murray Webster, Jr., Cecilia Ridgeway, and Susan Rosenholtz. 1986. "Status Cues, Expectations, and Behavior." Pp. 1-22 in *Advances in Group Processes*, Vol. 3, edited by E. Lawler. Greenwich, CT: JAI.

Berger, Joseph, Morris Zelditch, Jr., Bo Anderson, and Bernard P. Cohen. 1972. "Structural Aspects of Distributive Justice: A Status Value Formulation." Pp. 119-46 in *Sociological Theories in Progress*, Vol. 2, edited by Joseph Berger, Morris Zelditch, Jr., and Bo Anderson. Boston: Houghton Mifflin.

Berger, Peter L. and Thomas Luckmann. 1966. *The Social Construction of Reality.* Garden City, NY: Doubleday.

Blau, Peter. 1964. *Exchange and Power in Social Life.* New York: John Wiley.

Burke, Peter J. 1967. "The Development of Task and Social-Emotional Role Differentiation." *Sociometry* 30:379-92.

_____. 1968. "Role Differentiation and the Legitimation of Task Activity." *Sociometry* 31:404-11.

_____. 1971. "Task and Socioemotional Leadership Role Performance." *Sociometry* 34:22-40.

Collins, Randall. 1975. *Conflict Sociology: Toward an Explanatory Science.* New York: Academic Press.

Cook, Karen S. 1975. "Expectations, Evaluations, and Equity." *American Sociological Review* 40:372-88.

Della Fave, L. Richard. 1980. "The Meek Shall Not Inherit the Earth." *American Sociological Review* 45:955-71.

_____. 1986. "Toward and Explication of the Legitimation Process." *Social Forces* 65:476-500.

Dornbusch, Sanford M. and W. Richard Scott. 1975. *Evaluation and the Exercise of Authority.* San Francisco: Jossey-Bass.

Eskilson, Arlene and Mary Glenn Wiley. 1976. "Sex Composition and Leadership in Small Groups." *Sociometry* 39:183-94.

Fennell, Mary L., Patricia Barchas, Elizabeth G. Cohen, Anne M. McMahon, and Polly Hildebrand. 1978. "An Alternative Perspective on Sex Differences in Organizational Settings: The Process of Legitimation." *Sex Roles* 4:589-604.

Festinger, Leon. 1954. "Theory of Social Comparison Processes." *Human Relations* 7:117-40.

_____. 1957. *A Theory of Cognitive Dissonance.* Evanston, IL: Row, Peterson.

_____. 1964. *Conflict, Decision, and Dissonance.* Stanford, CA: Stanford University Press.

Foschi, Martha. 1971. "Contradiction and Change of Performance Expectations." *Canadian Review of Sociology and Anthropology* 8:205-22.

_____. 1972. "On the Concept of 'Expectations.' " *Acta Sociologica* 15:124-31.

French, J.R.P. and B. Raven. 1959. "The Bases of Social Power." Pp. 150-67 in *Studies in Social Power*, edited by D. Cartwright. Ann Arbor: University of Michigan Press.

Habermas, Jurgen. 1975. *Legitimation Crisis.* Boston: Beacon.

_____. 1979. *Communication and the Evolution of Society.* Boston: Beacon.

Hollander, Edwin P. 1964. *Leaders, Groups, and Influence.* New York: Oxford University Press.

Katz, Irwin S. 1970. "Experimental Studies in Negro-White Relationships." Pp. 71-117 in *Advances in Experimental Social Psychology*, Vol. 5, edited by L. Berkowitz. New York: Academic Press.

Katz, Irwin S. and Melvin Cohen. 1962. "The Effects of Training Negroes upon Cooperative Problem Solving in Biracial Teams." *Journal of Abnormal and Social Psychology* 64:319-25.

McCarthy, John D. and Mayer N. Zald. 1977. "Resource Mobilization and Social Movements: A Partial Theory." *American Journal of Sociology* 83:1212-41.

Meeker, B. F. and P. A. Weitzel-O'Neill. 1977. "Sex Roles and Interpersonal Behavior in Task Oriented Groups." *American Sociological Review* 42:92-105.

Parcel, Toby L. and Karen S. Cook. 1977. "Status Characteristics, Reward Allocation, and Equity." *Sociometry* 40:311-24.

Raven, B. and J.R.P. French. 1958. "Group Support, Legitimate Power and Social Influence." *Journal of Personality* 26:400-09.

Ridgeway, Cecilia L. 1978. "Conformity, Group-Oriented Motivation, and Status Attainment in Small Groups." *Social Psychology Quarterly* 41:175-88.

_____. 1982. "Status in Groups: The Importance of Motivation." *American Sociological Review* 47:76-88.

_____. 1984. "Dominance, Performance, and Status in Groups: A Theoretical Analysis." Pp. 59-93 in *Advances in Group Processes*, Vol. 1, edited by E. Lawler. Greenwich, CT: JAI.

Ridgeway, Cecilia L. and Joseph Berger. 1986. "Expectations, Legitimation, and Dominance Behavior in Task Groups." *American Sociological Review* 51:603-17.

— —-. 1987. "The Legitimation of Power and Prestige Orders." In *Status Generalization: New Theory and Research*, edited by M. Webster, Jr., and M. Foschi. Stanford, CA: Stanford University Press.

Ridgeway, Cecilia, Joseph Berger, and LeRoy Smith. 1985. "Nonverbal Cues and Status: An Expectation States Approach." *American Journal of Sociology* 90:955-78.

Short, James F. and Fred L. Strodtbeck. 1963. "The Response of Gang Leaders to Status Threats: An Observation on Group Processes and Delinquent Behavior." *American Journal of Sociology* 68:571-79.

Stinchcombe, Arthur. 1968. *Constructing Social Theories*. New York: Harcourt, Brace and World.

Suls, J. M. and R. L. Miller. 1977. *Social Comparison Processes: Theoretical and Empirical Perspectives*. New York: Washington Hemisphere.

Thomas, George M., Henry A. Walker, and Morris Zelditch, Jr. 1986. "Legitimacy and Collective Action." *Social Forces* 65:378-404.

Verba, Sidney. 1961. *Small Groups and Political Behavior: A Study of Leadership*. Princeton, NJ: Princeton University Press.

Walker, Henry A., George M. Thomas, and Morris Zelditch, Jr. 1986. "Legitimation, Endorsement, and Compliance." *Social Forces* 64:620-43.

Weber, Max. 1968. *Economy and Society*, edited by G. Roth and C. Wittich, translated by E. Fischoff et al. New York: Bedminster.

Wicklund, R. A. and J. W. Brehm. 1976. *Perspectives on Cognitive Dissonance*. Hillsdale, NJ: Lawrence Earlbaum.

Wuthnow, Robert, James D. Hunter, Albert Bergesen, and Edith Kurzweil. 1984. *Cultural Analysis*. Boston: Routledge & Kegan Paul.

Zelditch, Morris, Jr. and Henry A. Walker. 1984. "Legitimacy and the Stability of Authority." Pp. 1-27 in *Advances in Group Processes*, Vol. 1, edited by E. Lawler. Greenwich, CT: JAI.

7

Group Structure and Information Exchange: Introduction to a Theory

BERNARD P. COHEN

STEVEN D. SILVER

Group structure has important consequences for information exchange in interactive groups that range in size from large bureaucratic organizations to small face-to-face groups. For tasks in which members are interdependent, structural factors often have critical effects on the achievement of task objectives. In the worst cases, the structure of the group can by itself induce failure at the task and disintegration of the group. In more benign cases, where the group is able to complete the task, structural influences often result in recognizable performance decrements.

While recognition of dysfunctional effects of group structure has led to practical techniques for enhancing the amount and quality of information exchange, such as the Delphi or nominal group techniques (Dalkey and Helmer 1964; Delbecq and Van de Ven 1971, respectively) and, more recently, some proposals for computer-mediated information exchange (e.g., Hiltz et al. 1980), these efforts have not generally been theory driven. We believe that both our understanding of the consequences of group structure and our efforts to manage information exchange in groups effectively would benefit from a codification of the insights and empirical findings of the last four decades. Hence we are engaged in the development of a theoretical framework that draws on the work of Bales (e.g., 1951, 1970), Bavelas (e.g., 1950; also see Leavitt 1951), and their associates, and the formulations and empirical research of the expectation states research program. In this chapter, we will present an initial statement of our theory and a set of hypotheses drawn from this statement.

We begin by noting that social organization typically imposes restrictions or constraints on information exchange among its members.

Authors' Note: This research was supported in part by National Science Foundation grant 1R1 8617948.

Such constraints are sometimes by-products of role differentiation and specialization of function. In other cases, information exchange is constrained primarily as a means of control, that is, to maintain leadership and influence.

Bureaucracies, for example, typically have well-defined channels of communication that are limited or proscribed to members based on rank or position. Moreover, positive and negative sanctions frequently support the adherence to constraints on communication channels. Since the flow of information often serves multiple functions, it becomes important to understand the full range of outcomes of information constraints in social organizations. In doing this we immediately observe that information constraints in the service of one goal often have unintended but dysfunctional consequences for other goals. For example, the same constraints on information exchange that serve coordination and control may seriously interfere with the flow of factual information and objective evaluations and the exchange of ideas. This may occur because when information provided by a subordinate unit, group, or individual is the basis for evaluation of their performance and/or the allocation of resources, it becomes in the interest of the source to restrict or bias its content.

While the foregoing discussion of information exchange is in the context of bureaucratic organization, we believe that such contradictory outcomes of information exchange potentially occur in any hierarchical collective. Fundamental processes remain operative across differences in size and complexity. Research on small group problem solving, for example, has documented the effects of social differentiation on interaction among group members (e.g., Berger 1958). It is clear that even informal groups tend to be hierarchically organized; actual or imagined differences in task-relevant abilities and variation in other visible member characteristics typically result in a structuring of the members in a power and prestige order (Bales and Slater 1955; Berger et al. 1972).

The development of a theoretical framework as undertaken in this chapter will formulate mechanisms by which structure affects the flow of information in problem-solving activity. We initially focus on group problem solving, but consider the framework to be applicable to other forms of activity, such as conflict resolution, and across social and organizational contexts.

The framework to be presented attempts to integrate existing knowledge from several different research traditions. The next section will outline a view of structure and process in information exchange within problem-solving groups. We will first distinguish several general classes of formal problems groups typically face and specify a focal problem class for the present inquiry. We will then briefly turn to cognitive processes in problem solving and their relationships to the interpersonal exchange of information. Finally, we will take up the operation and consequences of social structure in interactive groups. These discussions will then become the basis for an initial statement of a formal theory of group structure and information exchange.

Conceptual Foundations for a Theory
of Group Structure and Information Exchange

In this section, we outline conceptual foundations that support a formal theory of group structure and information exchange in problem solving. We begin with a consideration of problem typologies and their relationship to cognitive processes in group problem solving.

CLASSIFYING PROBLEMS
IN TERMS OF THEIR STRUCTUREDNESS

Although experimental studies of group problem solving have typically generalized their findings across problem types, we believe there are important differences in problem dimensions that affect underlying cognitive processes, the type and amount of information exchanged, and the influence of group structure on solution quality. Accordingly, we begin our discussion by suggesting a typology for problem classes.

For the discussion that follows, we adopt MacCrimmon and Taylor's (1976) distinctions among well-structured, semistructured, and ill-structured problems, and algorithmic, heuristic, and "creative" responses. We would characterize well-structured problems by the accessibility of all information needed to solve the problem. Since existent knowledge bases most often provide transferable solution paradigms and routinized solution procedures, algorithmic responses are generally adequate for this problem class.

In the case of semistructured problems, enough information is available to define the "nature" of the knowledge gap partially and for some transfer of information on the connectedness of problem elements. However, limitations in the knowledge base preclude exclusively algorithmic responses. In such cases, problem solvers can optimally employ "heuristics," procedures that rather than guaranteeing a satisfactory answer only increase the odds of converging on a satisfactory solution.

Finally, in ill-structured problems there is generally no more than background information on the knowledge gap and few or no transferable solution paradigms. Since clear-cut procedures for closing problem gaps do not exist, problem solvers must generate connections and solution forms through improvised or "creative" response procedures. Issues in the definition of such procedures have a long history (Kelley and Thibaut 1969), but few controlled studies have evaluated their efficacy. There is also controversy as to the commonality and ordering of cognitive processes in the solving of ill-structured problems (Bell 1982).

Thus, while ill-structured problems are often complex and of critical importance, operational procedures to generate solutions have been elusive and irregular in their results (Yetton and Bottger 1982). It is clear that ill-structured problems are most typically taken up by groups of experts. This is in contrast to well-structured problems, which are more typically assigned to individuals supported by machine technology. Additionally, as differentiation and specialization in complex organizations increase, ill-structured problem solving increasingly involves small group interactions of individuals with diverse personal characteristics and expertise (Steiner 1972).

While we believe that the theory to be presented has some applicability to all three types of problems, we primarily address the class of ill-structured problems. We choose this because we believe that the effects of social structure on both information exchange and solution quality will be most salient in this class of problems.

COGNITIVE PROCESSES AND INFORMATION EXCHANGE IN ILL-STRUCTURED PROBLEM SOLVING

Most conceptualizations of the cognitive processes underlying problem-solving behavior suggest an interplay of convergent and divergent thinking that varies across both phases in solution generation and problem types. As used here, the term *convergent thinking* refers to operations that lead to singular "correct" solutions. This ability class is represented in intelligence and achievement measures. *Divergent thinking* refers to operations that are directed to generating a large number of disparate solutions that meet no singular criterion of "correctness." This latter class of operations has been discussed as a basis of creative thinking.

In such views, problem definition and idea evaluation depend for the most part on convergent thinking operations, while idea generation typically entails divergent thinking. Considering problem types, we would expect well-structured problems to emphasize convergent-thinking operations in the matching of problems to known procedures and their implementations. Ill-structured problems, in contrast, would be expected to depend more on divergent-thinking operations to generate solutions that meet no singular criterion of correctness.

In group problem solving, we would correspondingly expect different types of information to be exchanged during different cognitive operations. For example, we would expect the convergent-thinking operations in problem definition and idea evaluation to be typified by the exchange of facts and evaluations, whereas the divergent-thinking operations of solution generation should show relatively greater exchange of ideational information.

SOCIAL ORGANIZATION IN INTERACTIVE GROUPS

Along with formal problem-solving operations, we expect other social processes to occur in interactive groups. Among the most important of these are the emergence and maintenance of a hierarchical structure or status order. As a consequence, information exchange in an interactive group serves several functions. The first of these relates to the problem-solving task, while the second has importance to the definition and maintenance of social order; each affects the amount and type of information exchanged. To understand the flow of information in interactive groups, one must understand the components of these functions and their etiologies.

Having briefly considered information exchange in support of the cognitive operations of problem solving, we now turn to information exchange in support of the hierarchical social structure of the group. In the discussion to follow we will consider the organization and operation of group social structure and its effects on the amount and type of information exchanged in interaction.

STATUS ORGANIZING PROCESSES IN INTERACTIVE GROUPS

From the early work of Bales to current work in the expectation states research program, researchers have focused on interpersonal evaluation as one of the key mechanisms linking social structure to group interaction. Evaluation processes play a significant part in accounting for the two major types of empirical findings in these research traditions: (1) the emergence of a status order in groups whose members are initially undifferentiated with respect to salient status characteristics such as race, sex, organizational position, and task competence; and (2) the capacity of a preexisting status order that is external to the group to organize a status hierarchy in the group even when the basis of the external differentiation is totally unrelated to the group task. For expectation states theorists, the concept of an expectation state — a relational construct incorporating individuals' beliefs about their own competence vis-à-vis the others with whom they were interacting — accomplished the linkage; individuals deferred to others for whom they held higher expectations than they held for themselves, and thus individuals in interaction are treated unequally *because* they are thought to have unequal task-relevant abilities. Once high expectations are formed for a specific member, he or she is (1) encouraged to talk more, (2) more likely to be perceived as having good ideas, (3) less likely to encounter disagreement, and (4) generally allowed more influence.

Evaluation processes, however, play an important role in determining an individual's self-other expectations. Individuals in interaction communicate both very specific and very generalized, diffuse evaluations; for example, A can tell B that she agrees with B's last suggestion or she can tell B that she likes B's style. Berger and Snell (1961), in a stochastic model of the action process by which a hierarchy emerges, limited themselves to very specific "unit evaluations"; each "performance output" by an actor leads to a unit evaluation of that performance. These unit evaluations build up expectation states, which then influence later unit evaluations. In contrast, the process by which diffuse status characteristics affect group interaction and group structure involved generalized evaluations such as the global negative stereotypes associated with race (Berger et al. 1966, 1972).

That people differentially evaluate occupants of different status levels constitutes a principal underlying property of status hierarchies. Therefore, one should expect that interpersonal evaluations contribute to the emergence of a hierarchy and that hierarchies affect interpersonal evaluations. Furthermore, given the existence of a hierarchy, all evaluations of a specific action do not carry the same weight; evaluations from higher-status evaluators undoubtedly have more impact than those from lower-status evaluators (Berger et al. 1972).

Expectation states research thus informs us about the formation, stability, and operation of power-prestige hierarchies and the general role of evaluation processes. In the discussion that follows, we will use the communication of evaluations as building blocks in looking more closely at the interaction process as that process operates to solve the group problem and to construct and maintain the group structure. This use is roughly analogous to the use of the "unit evaluation" concept as a building block in the formation of expectation states.

In our view, communications of evaluations represent critical aspects of information exchange in problem solving. On one hand, such communications contribute to the emergence and/or maintenance of the status order. On the other hand, evaluations can contribute to problem-solving functions by discriminating quality and direction in ideation. Furthermore, not only actual communication but anticipated communication affects both sets of functions; concern for avoiding negative evaluations from superiors often prevents essential information exchange, as the *Challenger* disaster well illustrates. We believe that actual and anticipated communications of evaluation link social structure to the problem-solving process and to the outcome of that process. To explicate this view, in the next section we will briefly consider the connections between status organization and the cognitive and social processes underlying information exchange in group problem solving.

STRUCTURE AND PROCESS
IN GROUP PROBLEM SOLVING

We have thus far presented a typology of problems, a brief discussion of cognitive operations, and an examination of the relationship of status structures to interaction processes. We will now turn to the integration of these diverse content areas. We begin with the specific processes that link group structure to problem-solving operations. We believe that these are affective processes that emerge in group interaction, reflect the status structure of the group, and influence cognitive processes addressed to solving the group problem.

Considering affective processes first, we note that along with studies of types of cognitive operations in problem solving, a concurrent body of research has dealt with affective correlates and facilitating and inhibiting performance conditions for different cognitive operations (see Amabile 1983; Wallach and Kogan 1965). Although the research represents a range of conceptual perspectives, it essentially suggests that while evaluative information may in some cases facilitate convergent thinking, such information most often has an inhibiting effect on divergent thinking. Partly in response to such findings, many heuristic procedures for ill-structured problem solving have the inhibition of explicit evaluation as a primary end.

However, since ill-structured problem solving seems to depend on the operation of both divergent and convergent thinking in ordered sequences, outcomes seem more likely to benefit from procedures that regulate the amount and timing of the exchange of evaluative information. Such procedures require an understanding of sources of evaluative information.

STATUS EFFECTS ON INFORMATION EXCHANGE

Consistent with previous discussion, we propose that the direction and amount of evaluative information exchanged in interacting groups are functions of status organizing and maintenance processes. The research and theory cited above allow strong inferences about the consequences of status differences for the flow of information in general and evaluative information in particular. For example, we would ordinarily expect negative evaluations to be disproportionately sent by high-status persons and directed toward low-status persons and their communications. Correspondingly, the content of low-status persons' communications should predominantly be positive evaluations that are disproportionately directed toward high-status persons. As we have noted, these structural sources of the flow of evaluative information represent sender characteristics that are often independent of the substantive content of the information. The dysfunctional effect of asymmetric communication is intensified if, as is often the case, characteristics such as the age or rank rather than task-relevant abilities are the basis of status position in the social hierarchy.

Thus we may expect that the status order of interactive groups will systematically shape their communication so that initially medium- and low-status individuals send proportionately more facts and positive evaluations and correspondingly fewer ideas and negative evaluations than high-status individuals. Our discussion of cognitive operations in problem solving leads us to expect that such distortions in the transfer of ideational information have particular importance for ill-structured problems.

In ill-structured problems, hypothesis generation assumes greater importance than in semi- or well-structured problems because the connectedness of problem elements is less well defined, and solution procedures, even if known, cannot be as readily linked to poorly specified problems. Effectiveness in hypothesis generation clearly depends on unencumbered idea initiation and minimal but objective evaluation — exactly the processes that are most distorted in hierarchical groups.

We would further observe that since (1) there is typically little ability in the group to recognize initially which members are consistent sources of superior ideas, and (2) convergence on a single solution is not a major feature of the cognitive operations, social hierarchization can have significant costs to outcomes of hypothesis generation.

In contrast to hypothesis generation, we note that hypothesis evaluation typically is based on a greater exchange of facts and shared evaluations that are seen as less risky to members than the exchange of ideas. Thus social hierarchy effects on information transfer may interfere less with the exchange of hypothesis evaluations and their contribution to the quality of final solutions. In cases where member positions in the hierarchy are based on ability-relevant characteristics, hierarchical organization may in fact contribute to the outcome of hypothesis evaluation by weighting knowledgeable communications most highly and reducing the time the group takes to converge on a single solution.

For ill-structured problems, then, the asymmetric communication of evaluation that occurs in hierarchies is likely to have both inhibitory and facilitating effects. In the idea-generation phase, actual or anticipated negative evaluation may constrict the flow of ideas. But in the idea-evaluation phase, communication of evaluation may promote the strengthening or discarding of weak ideas. In the final sections to follow, we will attempt to formalize and elaborate on the mechanisms that produce these effects with a set of theoretical propositions.

A Heuristic Theory of Structure-Mediated Evaluation and Information Exchange

While our framework is in an early stage of development and is a first approximation at representing the processes involved, we believe it is a useful way to structure systematically the relationships among influential variables in information exchange and problem solving in interactive groups. Although we will present the theory in the form of a set of propositions, it is not yet sufficiently formalized to allow us to deduce consequences from these propositions in a rigorous manner. We are, however, able to extract testable hypotheses about processes of information exchange and their consequences for group problem solving from the propositions in the present form.

UNIT OF ANALYSIS AND OBJECTIVES

The basic unit of the model is the *channel*, which is defined as a one-way link from a particular source, S(i), to a particular target, T(j), through which a specific type of content may be transmitted. We should emphasize that in this view, a channel is not simply a neutral conduit like a telephone line (e.g., Bavelas 1950), but depends on the type of content that flows through it as well as its address; a useful analogy may be a set of pipes, one restricted to transmitting water, one for oil, and one for natural gas, each with specific destinations. Following this definition, there are $M(K)(K - 1)$ potential channels, where M = the number of information modes and K = the number of group members. For the present, we restrict channels to five types of information content: (1) task data (D), (2) solution proposals (I), (3) positive evaluations (P), (4) negative evaluations (N), and (5) source and third-party data (E). While the first four are self-explanatory, E channels require some amplification. E channels transmit data about the source or the source's evaluation of a particular target to group members other than the target. Thus we use E channels to represent $S(i)$'s comment about $T(j)$ as it is overheard by others.

As this definition indicates, a channel is an analytic construct that allows us to specify important elements of an actual information transfer. Channels may be available but not used and, in an actual group, many channels may be inextricably tied together so that use of one means use of all the others. In a face-to-face group, for example, source i transmitting a negative evaluation to target j, $N[S(i) \rightarrow T(j)]$, also involves transmitting third-party information to all other targets — that is, involves the use of E channels to all other targets. In particular cases, the medium of communication or the norms of the groups may close some of these channels so that they are unavailable.

The principal aims of our model are as follows: (1) to represent key factors that affect a given source's usage of a given channel; (2) to represent the consequences of usage of that channel to the source, the target, and the group; and (3) to represent the aggregate consequences of the use of all channels for the content of information exchange in the group. Although we recognize that group interaction has emergent properties beyond those that can be represented by the aggregation of dyadic relations, in this first formulation we treat the channels as having additive effects across individuals and types of information.

BASIC DEFINITIONS

We begin the exposition by defining the basic terms we will use to state our propositions: status differential, cost differential, expected cost, and expected gain.

Let the *status differential* be the difference between the status in the group of the source and the status in the group of a given target. If $S(i)$ has higher status than $T(j)$, then the status differential is positive. The status differential can be the resultant of comparing $S(i)$ and $T(j)$ on a number of status dimensions, including both task-relevant and non-task-relevant status characteristics. S(i) can have more technical competence than T(j) while T(j) has more seniority than S(i); the status differential would then be a weighted combination of the competence difference and the seniority difference.

Let the *cost differential* of using a given channel be defined as the *expected cost* of using that channel minus the *expected gain* from using it (this ordering of expected cost and expected gain in cost differential will allow subsequent propositions in cost differential to be more intuitive), where the expected cost of using a channel is the probability that the source will become a target for an N channel (negative evaluation) weighted by an estimate of the amount of loss of status or self-esteem to S resulting from receiving that negative evaluation, and the expected gain of using a channel is the probability that the source will become a target for a P channel weighted by an estimate of the amount of gain in status or self-esteem to S resulting from receiving that positive evaluation.

We consider expected costs and expected gains to be separate dimensions that may vary independently. In other words, one is not the inverse of the other; a factor can affect a source's expected cost and not effect that source's expected gain. Even when a factor affects both, the effect may be asymmetric; for example, when a factor produces a unit change in expected gain, it may produce much more than a unit change in expected cost. While we formulate these as "expected value" concepts, in this exposition we will make use only of ordinal comparisons, as, for example, if S(i) uses an N channel to T(j) where the status differential is negative, the cost is higher than if N[S(i) → T(k)] where the status differential is positive.

We have chosen to focus on individual concerns with gains and losses of status and self-esteem and their consequences for the flow of evaluative information. Such a focus is consistent with our view of the importance of these processes to the amount and quality of ideation in interactive groups. In this view, the flow of initial ideas — their amplification, clarification, transformation, and acceptance by the group — is most closely related to the direction, amount, and sequence of positive and negative evaluation (i.e., the use of N and P channels).

With these definitions, we can now turn to the propositions of the model. The driving force of the model is an individual's concern over loss of self-esteem and status in the group's social hierarchy or other groups to which members belong. Thus an individual is motivated to use a channel in order to prevent status and self-esteem losses due to the group's failure to solve its problem and/or to gain status and self-esteem. A person is constrained from using a channel because of possible negative evaluations from others that result in losses to self-esteem and status. In the present formulation, we assume that anticipated costs of group failure (and anticipated benefits of group success) are constant for all members and exogenously determined.

PROPOSITIONS

We begin with three propositions that serve as background for subsequent propositions and derivative hypotheses.

Background Assumptions

- *Proposition 1.1:* Ill-structured problem solving is facilitated when the process of generating ideas is separated from the process of evaluating ideas.
- *Proposition 1.2:* Quality in problem solving is facilitated when the evaluation of an idea is separated from the evaluation of the person who is the source of the idea.
- *Proposition 1.3:* Where solution paradigms do not exist (ill-structured problems), ideas that entail high potential cost to their source are necessary for the group to have any chance of solving the problems.

Proposition 1.1 may be seen as an inherent consequence of the sensitivity of ideation to evaluation and negative affect. This proposition has its bases in formulations from diverse theoretical perspectives in social psychology (e.g., Amabile 1983; Wallach and Kogan 1965).

In our terminology, we will suggest that throughout the life of the group, all members perceive expected costs to exceed expected gains from using I channels. Separating the use of I channels from the use of N channels would therefore decrease the expected cost to members of using the former and increase the total number of ideas.

Proposition 2.1 has a rationale similar to that for Proposition 1.1; separating the individual from the idea again lowers the probability that being a source of I channel usage will result in being the target of an N channel.

In Proposition 1.3, we observe that by definition ill-structured problems require more uncommon ideas to span or link their problem elements than do well-structured problems. Such ideas are commonly perceived as increasing the probability of being the target of an N channel communication more than they increase the probability of being the target of a P channel communication.

Channel Choice

- *Proposition 2.1:* The probability that a source will use a given channel increases as the cost differential of using that channel decreases.
- *Proposition 2.2:* Given an option among channels, a source will choose the channel(s) with the least cost differential(s).

As we have defined the terms, when a source expects more gains than costs, the cost differential will be negative and the probability of a given channel's usage will increase, since the source expects greater gains. These propositions refer to choices of both targets and types of information in the set of available channels; when channels to different targets are tied together as in face-to-face groups, a source may choose subsets rather than individual channels.

Cost Differential

The expected cost and expected gain of being a target and source of communication are both relevant to the individual's probability of using a channel. We assume that in considering whether to be a source each person takes the position of a target of various types of information and calculates the costs and gains he or she may expect as a result of using a channel. Thus we precede propositions on the source's expected costs and cost differential with a proposition on the target's expected cost:

- *Proposition 3.1:* For a person i, the expected cost of being the target of an N channel from a source S(j) increases as the status differential between i and j becomes increasingly negative (i.e., j becomes of increasingly higher status than i).

Proposition 3.1 formulates the target's perception that negative evaluations are more costly from higher-status sources. Even if the probability of using an N channel did not vary with the status of the source, the negative consequences of being a target of an N channel are greater from higher-status sources. For example, in the case of formally organized groups, it is obvious that a negative evaluation from one's superior is much more serious than one from a peer. Even in informal groups, negative evaluation from one believed to be higher in competence can be more damaging to the target's self-esteem than negative evaluation from some other.

Propositions 3.2 and 3.3 use Proposition 3.1 to state the source's perspective on expected cost.

- *Proposition 3.2:* The expected cost to person i of being a source, S(i) → T(j), in any type of channel increases as the status differential between S(i) and T(j) becomes increasingly negative.
- *Proposition 3.3:* The cost differential to person i of being a source, S(i) → T(j), in any type of channel increases as the status differential between S(i) and T(j) becomes increasingly negative.

In Propositions 3.2 and 3.3, person i is applying the results of calculations of his or her potential as a target to his or her future role as a source. Maintaining the assumption of a constant probability that usage of a given channel will result in the target's negative response, the cost of that negative response will increase with increases in the relative status of the target.

We note that these propositions posit beliefs of the source that may or may not have any relation to the actual situation. Sometimes the person's perceptions will be an adequate basis for expectations, but at other times social processes will distort the perceptions and the expectations based on them. This point is important because, as we have previously noted and will subsequently argue, status-organizing processes are often based on individual characteristics that are minimally related to problem requirements or task-relevant abilities. We should also reemphasize that these expectations are relative, not absolute — to S(i), a high-status source, there may be very little expected cost with either S(i) → T(j) or S(i) → T(k), but if the status differential between i and j is more negative (or less positive, since status differentials are symmetric) than the differential between i and k, then the expected cost of the former channel would be greater than the expected cost of the latter.

The effects of positive evaluations from high-status sources are more beneficial than positive evaluations from equal or low-status sources, but propositions about positive evaluations and status gains are not mirror images of Propositions 3.1 and 3.2. Since we focus on negative evaluations and costs, we omit propositions about positive evaluations to avoid additional complexity.

- *Proposition 3.4:* For a given T, an N channel is more likely than an I channel to have a negative cost differential and an I channel is more likely than a D channel to have a negative cost differential.
- *Proposition 3.5:* For a given T, in the absence of social constraints the cost differential of an I channel is more likely to be negative than positive where *social constraints* are mechanisms that separate evaluations of products from evaluations of persons producing those products or limits cost differentials to a given source from a set of targets.

Proposition 3.4 formalizes the previous discussion. Since individuals seek to maintain or increase status and self-esteem, N channels with themselves as targets are likely to have the most negative cost differentials. Being the source of N channel usage is most likely to result in being a subsequent target of an N channel. Since facts and data are generally neutral, being the source of a D channel usage is least likely to result in being the target of an N channel in a subsequent period.

We further believe that use of I channels in interactive groups where the source is known can be more costly (i.e., have more negative cost differentials) than is sometimes recognized. This is because, in the absence of formally adopted, dominant criteria for judgments, groups tend to resist initial, new, uncommon, or "radical" solution proposals when they are first offered. Such a behavioral assumption is supported by informal observations and related research findings (e.g., Moscovici and Nemeth 1974). Thus being the source of an I channel communication is more likely to have the short-run consequence of becoming the target of an N channel than of a P channel communication.

Simply put, since groups tend to resist initial proposals, the most likely reaction to a proposal is either an explicit or an implicit negative evaluation (the latter is most often expressed by silence or by totally ignoring the proposal). The longer-run consequences of being an I channel source are likely to be more complex and depend on such factors as the quality of the communication, the status of the source, the group's interaction "history" in terms of previous N and P channel usage of the source, and the willingness to use N channels further (with their expected costs) in support of the communication.

In Proposition 3.5, we introduce a claim about the sign of the cost differential for the source of an I channel communication. Proposition 3.6 asserts the interdependence between usage of N and I channels. In Proposition 3.7, we generalize influences from the dyad unit in previous propositions to the group unit.

- *Proposition 3.6:* For all sources, as the frequency of usage of N channels increases, the expected cost of I channels increases.

In general, social etiquette or concerns about retaliation limit the expression of explicit negative evaluations. In much group interaction, ignoring a message is the way of expressing negative evaluation. Being implicit, this expression is somewhat ambiguous and thus has lower cost. However, once sources recognize that inhibitions against explicit negative evaluations are not operative, they increase their estimates of the probability that one of their proposals will receive an explicit negative evaluation.

- *Proposition 3.7:* The cost differential of using a given channel is the sum of the cost differentials of that channel and all other channels that are tied to it.

This proposition refers to two kinds of situations, those in which targets cannot be segregated and those in which E channels are intertwined with D, I, P, and N channels. If a source must communicate to several targets simultaneously, that source must anticipate possible reactions from all targets, not only the target for whom the message was intended.

Relative to using a channel to a single target, a source can expect both more gains and more costs from a multiple-channel communication, but we again consider the effects of the increase in costs to be more significant.

Similarly, using E channels — transmitting information about self or third parties — may result in both gains and costs, but the same argument implies that costs are more influential. Using an N channel to one target is very different from using that channel while also transmitting the fact of S(i) negatively evaluating T(j) through E channels. Public negative evaluations are more damaging than private ones and hence may invite costly retaliation.

Outcomes

Having offered our propositions on channel choice, expected cost, and cost differential, we now turn to propositions on outcomes.

- *Proposition 4.1:* In groups dealing with ill-structured problems, the probability of a successful solution is an asymptotic increasing function of the usage of I channels.
- *Proposition 4.2:* In groups dealing with ill-structured problems, the probability of a successful solution is a U-shaped function of the total usage of N channels.
- *Proposition 4.3:* In groups dealing with ill-structured problems, the probability of a successful solution is increased when N channel usage is a monotone increasing function of time spent in interaction, and I channel usage is a monotone decreasing function of interaction time.

Here we restate more formally ideas that we presented earlier. We have suggested that the solution of ill-structured problems depends on both the generation of many ideas and the operation of negative evaluations to eliminate unsatisfactory or less-than-optimal proposals. Thus negative evaluation is a two-edged sword — necessary to the selection of better proposals but inhibiting the generation of these proposals.

Propositions 4.1 through 4.3 result from observations of the sequencing of cognitive operations in ill-structured problem solving. Since ideation precedes evaluation and N channel usage inhibits I channel usage, we would anticipate solution quality to be increased when N channel usage is kept at low levels in early phases of interaction but allowed to increase slowly as interaction proceeds and remain at its highest level throughout the final phases of evaluation and consensus.

Although the above propositions are preliminary, they do codify ideas about the relation of status to the transmission of solution proposals and negative evaluations and allow us to generate some initial hypotheses on interaction and outcomes in status-differentiated and status-homogeneous groups.

HYPOTHESES

These hypotheses will consider information exchange in status-differentiated and status-undifferentiated groups. While we recognize that even relatively undifferentiated groups have status hierarchies, we will for expository purposes consider a class of status-homogeneous groups in which there is no status hierarchy of consequence.

Status Factors and the
Transmission of Ideas and Solution Proposals

- *Hypothesis 1.1:* Frequency of usage of I channels will be greater in status-homogeneous groups than in status-differentiated groups.

- *Hypothesis 1.2:* In status-differentiated groups, the frequency of I channels usage will be directly related to the status levels of individual members.
- *Hypothesis 1.3:* In status-differentiated groups, frequency of I channels will be inversely related to the frequency of usage of N channels.
- *Hypothesis 1.4:* The difference between the frequency of usage of I channels in status-homogeneous and status-differentiated groups will decrease as the possibility of segregating channels increases.
- *Hypothesis 1.5:* The difference between the frequency of usage of I channels in status-homogeneous and status-differentiated groups will be minimal when sources can use I channels anonymously.

Hypothesis 1.1 maintains that equalizing the expected costs of using an I channel across group members will not only equalize the frequency of member usage of this channel, but will also increase total group usage of the I channel. This is because the expected cost of being the target of an N channel in response to being the source of an I channel decreases as status differences between members decrease.

Hypothesis 1.2 applies the frequent findings of expectation states research that individual participation varies with individual status to the generation and exchange of ideas. In the case of I channel usage, higher-status individuals face fewer expected costs for being the target of an N channel.

A general climate effect of the transmission of negative evaluations on the flow of ideas is represented in Hypothesis 1.3. Simply stated, increases in the frequency of N channel usage as observed by individual group members increase the probability term of expected cost (i.e., the probability of being an N channel target as a consequence of being an I channel source).

Hypotheses 1.4 and 1.5 introduce the technology of constrained information or limited interaction to information exchange in interactive groups. Restricting information and distinctions between public and private dyadic communication have important implications for efficiency in attaining the goals of interacting groups. Technology in the form of electronic communication (such as computer conferences and mail-drop procedures) allows channel usage to be limited or expanded flexibly.

In Hypothesis 1.4 we recognize that when an uncommon idea can be communicated to an individual rather than the entire group, the expected cost in terms of status loss from becoming the target of a negative evaluation and having it observed by other group members is decreased. The expected cost of public evaluation to low-status members is highest in status-differentiated groups. Segregating an N channel communication from members other than the dyad involved would be likely to reduce this cost and consequently increase the use of I channels to a level close to that of a status-homogeneous group.

Hypothesis 1.5 points out that in the limiting case where I channel communications are not publicly matched to their source, the probability of becoming the target of N channel communication becomes unrelated to the generation of ideas. Thus there would be little or no differences in expected costs from I channel usage in status-differentiated and status-homogeneous groups.

Status Factors and the
Transmission of Negative Evaluations

- *Hypothesis 2.1:* Frequency of usage of N channels will be greater in status-differentiated groups than in status-homogeneous groups.
- *Hypothesis 2.2:* In status-differentiated groups, the frequency of N channel usage will be directly related to the status level of individual members.
- *Hypothesis 2.3:* In status-differentiated groups, higher-status members will most often be the source and lower-status members will most often be the target of N channel communications.
- *Hypothesis 2.4:* The difference between frequency of usage of N channels in status-homogeneous and status-differentiated groups will decrease as the possibility of segregating channels increases.
- *Hypothesis 2.5:* The difference between the average frequency of usage of N channels in status-homogeneous and status-differentiated groups will be minimal when sources can use I channels anonymously.

Hypotheses 2.1 and 2.2 parallel Hypotheses 1.1 and 1.2, and claim that the transmission of negative evaluations is similar in operation to the transmission of ideas and solution proposals.

In Hypothesis 2.3, we recognize that the cost differential of N channel usage will always be more negative for low-status members than for high-status members. This implies that in an exchange of N channel communications, a lower-status member will face a greater loss of status and/or self-esteem. Therefore, lower-status members will avoid being the source of communications that result in their being the target of an N channel.

Hypotheses 2.4 and 2.5 offer conjectures on the consequences of constraining information transfers to less than full member exchanges and removing source labels. (Such computer-aided modifications of interaction have important implications for the source, amount, and type of information exchanged.)

In Hypothesis 2.4, we anticipate that reducing or eliminating E channels in status-differentiated groups will reduce the cost differential of N channel usage and increase its frequency. Similarly, in Hypothesis 2.5 we anticipate that removing source labels from I channel usage will reduce the cost differential of using this channel in status-differentiated groups and increase its usage to approximate levels observed in status-homogeneous groups.

In our final set of hypotheses, we turn directly to effects of communication structure on information exchange. We focus on the transfer of negative evaluations because of their influence on group interaction and ideation.

Communication Structure and the Transmission of Negative Evaluations

- *Hypothesis 3.1:* Frequency of usage of N channels in interactive groups will be greater when the communication structure allows private dyadic (single-channel) exchange rather than public (multiple-channel) exchange.
- *Hypothesis 3.2:* Frequency of N channel usage will be greater when the source can be anonymous than when the source's identity is known.
- *Hypothesis 3.3:* The use of an N channel will have less impact in single-channel media than in multiple-channel media.

Arguments that multiple channels involve greater expected costs than single channels and that anonymous sources have minimal expected cost for using a channel also provide the basis for Hypotheses 3.1 and 3.2. Hypothesis 3.3, however, depends on a slightly more complex argument. The reasoning about lower expected costs implies less fear of retaliation on the part of a potential source. If all sources have less fear of "retaliation," — that is, of being the target of a negative evaluation — then the behavior of all sources is less constrained. A given level of usage of N channels will constrain the usage of other channels to a much greater extent in public (multiple-channel) communication structures than in private (single-channel) communication.

Hypotheses 3.1 through 3.3 suggest the use of communication technology to create and modify communication structure as one potential means of realizing advantages of status differentiation for problem solving while mitigating its disadvantages. For example, when information exchange is restricted to dyadic communication, the expected cost of initiating an A channel communication in terms of subsequently becoming a public target of an N channel communication should decrease.

Imposing structure on member communication offers similar potential benefits to idea generation in groups with even minimal status differentiation. If I channels are used anonymously, the expected cost of initiating an N communication should decrease.

The foregoing hypotheses exemplify testable implications of the propositions we have presented. These hypotheses together with the propositions on which they are based seek to provide additional insight into the influence of structure on information exchange and problem solving in interactive groups. In the next and final section, we will briefly summarize the efforts of this work and suggest directions for subsequent theory and research.

SCOPE OF THE THEORY

We posit four conditions under which the theory is applicable and that must be taken into account in constructing tests of the model:

(1) The group must be engaged in a group task.

(2) There are no norms in the situation that proscribe or mitigate negative evaluations.

(3) Members cannot leave the group until the group achieves its goals or disbands.

(4) The only relevant external evaluations of the group or its members are those for group success or failure in accomplishing the group task.

By *group task* we mean a task that requires resources (information, knowledge, materials, and skills) that no single individual possesses so that no single individual can solve the problem or achieve the task objectives without at least some input from other group members. This definition requires that the task impose some degree of interdependence in the group.

The second condition addresses cultural norms that emphasize courtesy and politeness to such a degree that negative evaluations directed to an individual are taboo. Politeness norms operate in a wide variety of task situations; indeed, some techniques for enhancing group problem solving deliberately invoke norms against direct disagreement with, or disparagement of, another's contribution. While such norms may be conducive to group success, their operation interferes with the processes underlying the present theory. Hence we rule out such situations as testing grounds. While there are probably very few natural situations with no normative constraints on the communication of negative evaluation, in constructing experiments to test this theory we want to minimize as much as possible the operation of such norms.

The group has less power over individuals who can freely choose to leave than over members who are constrained to remain in the group. The possibility of leaving the group mitigates the impact of negative evaluations from others; furthermore, the threat that a member might quit operates to inhibit directing negative evaluations to that member, particularly where interdependence among members is high. Thus additional complex processes arise when members have the option to resign from the group. The purpose of our third condition, then, is to simplify situations in which to test the theory by reducing the effects of additional processes. To be sure, even when physically leaving the group is not an option, it is often possible for an individual to withdraw psychologically, and the frequently observed lack of participation of low-status group members may reflect, in part, such psychological withdrawal. While it may not be feasible to eliminate the possibility of psychological withdrawal entirely, we need to design research that makes such withdrawal very costly and therefore highly unlikely.

Restricting external evaluations to those directed at group success or failure also serves to simplify situations in which to investigate the theory. If a member's actions in this group will lead to positive or negative evaluations from some other group, then the individual's actions are affected differentially by concerns for other groups and the weight of the attachments to the competing groups. The intention of this scope restriction is to exclude effects of social comparison processes and reference group conflicts on the problem-solving activities of the group (Kelly and Thibaut 1969; Berger et al. 1972).

Undoubtedly, these scope constraints are too restrictive in their present form. As we develop the theory we hope to relax and perhaps eliminate one or more of them entirely.

Summary and Conclusions

We have presented the initial formulation of a theory of information exchange mediated by group structure. We believe that the theory provides a framework within which to consider the effects of structure on interaction and outcomes of group problem solving.

The basic unit of the theory is the "channel," and channels are differentiated according to source, target, and content mode of a communication. We distinguish five modes: ideas, data, positive evaluations, negative evaluations, and what we term "source and/or third-party data." Source or third-party data channels typically refer to communications where person k observes that source (i) negatively evaluates target (j). The propositions of the theory link channel usage and channel choice to the status structure of the group through propositions about the cost of receiving negative evaluations from various sources who differ in status. For ill-structured problems, the theory relates successful solution to the frequency of usage of idea and negative evaluation channels and also to the time patterns of this usage.

In the theory, usage (or anticipated usage) of N channels is the principal mechanism that drives the process, and differences in member status determine the amount and targets of such usage. While other writers have noted the importance of negative evaluations in group process (e.g., Bales 1951, 1970), the present theory systematically explicates key antecedents and major consequences of variation in the communication of negative evaluations in problem-solving groups.

Receiving negative evaluations from others can reduce an individual's status in the group or diminish his or her self-esteem. Failure to accomplish group objectives can have similar consequences. Hence avoiding such costs involves an individual in delicately balancing when to communicate and when not to, what to communicate and what to avoid communicating, to whom to initiate and to whom to respond, whether to communicate publicly or privately, whether to identify oneself or to be anonymous, and so on. In terms of the theory, an individual deals with these choices by choosing a channel, and the probability of choosing each type of channel depends in part on the status structure of the group and the individual's position in that structure.

We posit that the probability of choosing a channel varies inversely with "cost differential" (the difference between expected loss and gain in, say, status). We also assert that negative evaluations and ideas are more likely to have negative cost differentials than data or positive evaluations. Moreover, we claim that the cost differential for transmission of ideas increases as member status differences increase, for all but the highest-status group member. As a consequence of this analysis, the transmission of ideas in a group is likely to decrease as status differences increase.

The last section presented three sets of hypotheses. Although we do not rigorously derive these hypotheses, they are generally consistent with the lines of reasoning we have explicated. The first two sets relate status factors to the communication of ideas and negative evaluations, while the third set deals with the effects of the communication structure on the communication of negative evaluations. Where the communication structure allows the segregation of channels and/or the anonymity of sources, the theory assumes that it is possible to reduce the negative costs of channel usage. Thus we hypothesize that use of negative channels will increase when private and/or anonymous channels are available, and that the impact of negative evaluations will be reduced in such structures. If these hypotheses are supported, then such structures could mitigate some of the effects of status differentiation (Kiesler 1986; Kiesler et al. 1984).

The heuristic framework we have presented clearly requires elaboration, clarification, and integration. Further development of the theory, however, would benefit from a set of empirical studies that would indicate which ideas of the theory are adequate, which need modification, and which should be abandoned. With the advent of computer-mediated interaction (Hiltz and Turoff 1987), we now have the technology to create experiments where we can focus specifically on the use of negative channels, for example, and the effects of such usage. We are in the process of developing an experimental paradigm that will allow us to compare face-to-face interaction with various degrees of restricted interaction.

If the basic ideas of the theory are supported empirically, then there are scientific and practical implications that need to be explored. This framework should enable us to reconsider the problem of the sequencing of problem-solving operations and information exchange; we intend to reconstruct our propositions to deal with developments in time over the life of the group. In addition, the theory can be elaborated to provide guidelines for enhancing group performance in dealing with ill-structured problem solving. For example, one appropriate objective for developing our framework would be to answer the question, How can groups retain the benefits but minimize the negative consequences of status structures on information exchange? Further consideration of these possibilities as well as additional background for our theory are presented in Silver et al. (1988). We believe the importance of information exchange at all levels of social organization underscores the potential value of this line of inquiry.

References

Amabile, T. 1983. *The Social Psychology of Creativity*. New York: Springer-Verlag.

Bales, R. F. 1951. *Interaction Process Analysis*. Cambridge, MA: Addison-Wesley.

— — —. 1970. *Personality and Interpersonal Behavior*. New York: Holt, Rinehart & Winston.

Bales, R. F. and P. Slater. 1955. "Role Differentiation in Small Decision Making Groups." In *Family, Socialization, and Interaction Process*, edited by T. Parsons and R. F. Bales. Glencoe, IL: Free Press.

Bales, R. F. and F. Strodtbeck. 1951. "Phases in Group Problem Solving." *Journal of Abnormal and Social Psychology* 46:485-95.

Bavelas, A. 1950. "Communication Patterns in Task-Oriented Groups." *Journal of the Acoustical Society of America* 22:725-30.

Bell, Mae A. 1982. "Phases in Group Problem Solving." *Small Group Behavior* 13:475-503.

Berger, J. 1958. "Relations Between Performance, Rewards, and Action-Opportunities in Small Groups." Unpublished Ph.D. thesis, Harvard University.

Berger, J., B. P. Cohen, and M. Zelditch, Jr. 1966. "Status Characteristics and Expectation States." Pp. 19-46 in *Sociological Theories in Progress*, Vol. 1, edited by J. Berger, M. Zelditch, Jr., and B. Anderson. Boston: Houghton Mifflin.

— — —. 1972. "Status Characteristics and Social Interaction." *American Sociological Review* 37:241-55.

Berger, J., M. H. Fisek, R. Z. Norman, and M. Zelditch, Jr. 1977. *Status Characteristics and Social Interaction: An Expectation States Approach*. New York: Elsevier.

Berger, J. and J. L. Snell. 1961. *A Stochastic Theory for Self-Other Expectations* (Technical Report No. 11). Stanford, CA: Laboratory for Social Research, Stanford University.

Dalkey, N. and O. Helmer. 1964. "An Experimental Application of the Delphi Method to the Use of Experts." *Management Science* 9(2):458-66.

Delbecq, A. L. and A. Van de Ven. 1971. "A Group Process Model for Problem Identification and Program Planning." *Journal of Applied Behavioral Sciences* 7(4):466-92.

Hiltz, S. R., K. Johnson, C. Aronvith, and M. Turoff. 1980. *Face to Face vs. Computerized Conferences: A Controlled Experiment* (Vol. 1, Findings, Report No. 12). Newark: New Jersey Institute of Technology.

Hiltz, S. R. and M. Turoff. 1987. *The Network Nation: Human Communication via Computer*. Reading, MA: Addison-Wesley.

Kelley, H. H. and J. W. Thibaut. 1969. "Group Problem Solving." In *The Handbook of Social Psychology*, Vol. 4, 2nd ed., edited by G. Lindzey and E. Aronson. Cambridge, MA: Addison-Wesley.

Kiesler, S. 1986. "Thinking Ahead: The Hidden Messages in Computer Networks." *Harvard Business Review* 64(January/February):46-60.

Kiesler, S., J. Siegel, and T. W. McGuire. 1984. "Social Psychological Aspects of Computer-Mediated Communication." *American Psychologist* 39(10):1123-34.

Leavitt, H. J. 1951. "Some Effects of Certain Group Communication Patterns on Group Performance." *Journal of Abnormal and Social Psychology* 46:38-50.

MacCrimmon, K. R. and D. N. Taylor. 1976. "Decision-Making and Problem Solving." In *Handbook of Industrial and Organizational Psychology*, edited by M. Dunnett. Chicago: Rand McNally.

Moscovici, S. and C. Nemeth. 1974. "Social Influence II: Minority Influence." Pp. 217-50 in *Social Psychology*, edited by C. Nemeth. Chicago: Rand McNally.

Silver, S. D., B. P. Cohen, and J. Rainwater. 1988. "Group Structure and Information Exchange in Innovative Problem Solving." In *Advances in Group Processes*, Vol. 5, edited by E. J. Lawler and B. Markovsky. Greenwich, CT: JAI.

Steiner, I. 1972. *Group Processes and Productivity*. New York: Academic Press.

Wallach, M. and N. Kogan. 1965. *Modes of Thinking in Young Children*. New York: Holt.

Yetton, P. W. and P. C. Bottger. 1982. "Individual Versus Group Problem Solving: An Empirical Test of a Best-Member Strategy." *Organizational Behavior and Human Performance* 29(3):307-21.

PART III

DIFFERENTIATIONS,
INEQUALITIES,
AND ORGANIZATIONS

8

A General Theory
of Macrostructural Dynamics

JONATHAN H. TURNER

Micro- Versus Macroanalysis

One of the great debates in sociological theory revolves around the relationship between micro processes of interaction among individuals and the macro properties of "emergent" social structures. Indeed, there has been a recent frenzy of intellectual commentary on the issue (Alexander et al. 1986; Turner 1983; Knorr-Cetina and Cicourel 1981), with current opinion clearly swinging toward a micro emphasis. Increasingly, social structures are viewed as understandable in terms of micro interactions among individuals, thereby giving theoretical priority to behavior, action, interpersonal practices, human agency, and other topics. Indeed, some advocates of a micro perspective go so far as to view conceptions of macrostructures as mere reifications and hypostatizations.

There has, of course, been a long theoretical tradition devoted to macro-level analysis. Despite Weber's assertion that sociology is the study of meaningful action, Weberian sociology was decidedly macro; the same was true of Marx's, Spencer's, and Pareto's analyses of social dynamics. More recently, theorists such as Talcott Parsons and many others have insisted that social structures and systems represent emergent phenomena that require their own concepts and theories. The most extreme position in this regard can be found in the works of scholars like Blau (1977) and Mayhew (1981), who have argued for an analysis of structure that takes interaction as a given or, alternatively, as a statistical rate and even a random process.

A variety of approaches have sought to reconcile micro- and macro-analysis (e.g., Collins 1975; Giddens 1981, 1984; Alexander 1982-84), but my sense is that these lean toward either a micro or macro position. It is clear, then, that sociological theory has not resolved the question of whether theory should be micro, macro, or some combination of the two. For the present, the issue of micro- versus macroanalyses should, I think, be ignored. Far too much energy has been devoted to debating the question of which has theoretical priority instead of developing theories about either micro or macro processes. For the time being, it is wise to focus on developing abstract models and principles on those properties of the

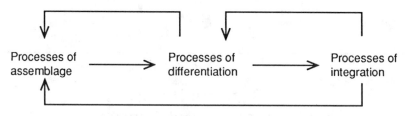

Figure 8.1. A Sensitizing Model of Macrodynamics

universe that are believed to be fundamental and generic. Before we seek reconciliation of the micro and macro, let us first develop more adequate theories about both. When this is done, we may find points of reconciliation and synthesis; or we may discover that micro and macro theories are not easily reconciled and that they simply provide different kinds of understanding of the social universe.

In this chapter, I will outline some of my ideas on macro processes. These ideas represent a "theory in progress," as the title of this book would suggest. To say the least, I have not fully developed the models and principles that will be presented, and so my analysis is only provisional. Indeed, over recent years I have been emphasizing micro processes (Turner 1986a, 1986b, 1987a, 1987b, 1988, 1989a, 1989b), but despite the gallant efforts of some (e.g., Blumer 1962, 1969), microanalysis cannot adequately conceptualize a basic fact of social life: Humans assemble and organize themselves into large-scale social patterns. True, we can examine such patterns by sampling interactions and micro situations (Collins 1975), but we will not fully understand such patterns in these terms.

A Sensitizing Model of Macrodynamics

In recent years, I have advocated a theoretical strategy stressing three levels of theoretical analysis: (1) simple sensitizing schemes, (2) more complex analytical models, and (3) abstract propositions and principles (Turner 1985, 1987a, 1987b). A sensitizing model denotes the properties of the social universe, and their basic causal connections, to be studied. Such models frame the topic and delineate the generic classes of variables that are to be incorporated into a theory. Sensitizing schemes should be simple because they do not represent theory per se, but only the subject matter of theorizing. Figure 8.1 presents one such sensitizing scheme for macrodynamics.

As is evident, I see three basic processes as critical to a theory of macrodynamics: (1) assemblage, (2) differentiation, and (3) integration. The concept of *assemblage* denotes those processes that "assemble" and "bring together" or, conversely, "disassemble" and "break apart" social units, whether individuals or collectivities. The unit of analysis in macro theory is thus an assembled population of individual or collective actors and their patterns of organization. *Differentiation* refers to those processes that create or eliminate distinctions among the social units of a population, whereas *integration* refers to those organizing processes that "connect" differentiated social units to one another. While the concepts of differentiation and integration have been associated with deficient forms of functional theorizing, they are nonetheless essential in macro theory. Without some understanding of those forces that lace together different kinds of units in a population, it would be impossible to analyze social organization. Thus macro theory must specify the conditions under which varying types of connections among differentiated social units are created, sustained, changed, or terminated.

As is obvious, the sensitizing model in Figure 8.1 is very old. We can trace its sociological origins back to Condorcet, but a more explicit origin of these ideas is Herbert Spencer ([1874] 1905), although Emile Durkheim ([1893] 1933) is usually given the credit for recognizing the importance of these interrelated issues. And, as is also evident, the basic variables in Figure 8.1 have been rediscovered and applied in diverse substantive fields, the most notable being organizational theory (e.g., Blau 1970). But we should not be snobbish about the basic processes denoted in Figure 8.1. They may not represent startling new insights, but they are fundamental to understanding the social universe. This is why they persist and keep reemerging in the analysis of social processes.

As I view these three properties, they are variables that can increase or decrease in value. Moreover, the arrows connecting them indicate that they are causally related. Changes in assemblage cause variations in differentiation that, in turn, affect integrative processes. And the reverse is true: Assemblage is constrained by the level of differentiation and integration, and differentiation is circumscribed by modes of integration.

One cautionary note should be introduced here. These three classes of variables were originally isolated in the analysis of social evolution, especially lineal portrayals of progressive change. I make no such assumptions; I assert only that if one wants to understand a population of actors, it is necessary to know about the processes that assemble (disassemble), differentiate (dedifferentiate), and integrate (or disintegrate) that population. As the first masters of sociological theory recognized, albeit with somewhat flawed evolutionary analyses, macrosociology is about the processes of assemblage, differentiation, and integration of human populations over time.

How, then, do we analyze these processes in more detail? My answer is that we need to develop the other two levels of theory: analytical models and propositions. An analytical model specifies in more detail the processes implicated in a property of the universe, but it is still abstract because it isolates only generic classes of variables and their basic causal effects on each other. While the term *model* is ambiguous in the social sciences, I am using it in a manner more typical of the natural sciences: a visual representation of elements and their interrelations. In sociology the resulting models are usually somewhat complex, involving paths of direct and indirect causality as well as lag, feedback, and cyclical effects.

An analytical model thus introduces some complexity into a sensitizing scheme like that in Figure 8.1. For each property of the universe isolated by the sensitizing scheme, we construct at least one analytical model and, if desired, additional submodels. The problem with models, however, is that their very strength — the capacity to see simultaneously configurations of causal effects among variables — makes them unwieldy and difficult to assess empirically. Hence models must be translated into propositions that specify the form of relationship among variables. In constructing propositions, more than simple decomposition of the model into more manageable units is involved. Certain variables and causal connections are selectively pulled out and viewed as more important than others. Moreover, new exogenous variables to propositions may also be added. There is, then, an additional element of theorizing when models are converted into propositions.

My view is that theorizing is most creative when it moves back and forth between analytical models and abstract propositions. It does not make a great deal of difference where one starts — that is, with a model or abstract principle. The critical activity is to translate principles into models in order to see the larger configurations of causal connections implied by a proposition or, alternatively, to convert models into laws or principles so that they can be made more testable. Such is the strategy that I will employ in examining macrodynamics.

An Analytical Model of Macro Processes

Figure 8.2 delineates what I see as the generic classes of variables for the processes of assemblage, differentiation, and integration (Turner 1987a). The arrows connecting these variables denote the important causal connections and paths. As presented, the model represents a composite of what are, in essence, three separate and more detailed models. Each of these three models is more complex than outlined in Figure 8.2, but for this "in progress" report, I have presented only the composite model. While some detail is lost in this portrayal, it highlights the crucial causal paths among the processes of assemblage, differentiation, and integration. Let me now turn to a more discursive review of these three processes.

THE PROCESS OF ASSEMBLAGE

In many respects, the process of assemblage is less theoretically interesting than either differentiation or integration. The bringing together of social units is often a matter of historical accident and hence not amenable to theoretical analysis, except in the manner depicted on the left side of Figure 8.2, where general classes of relevant variables are displayed.

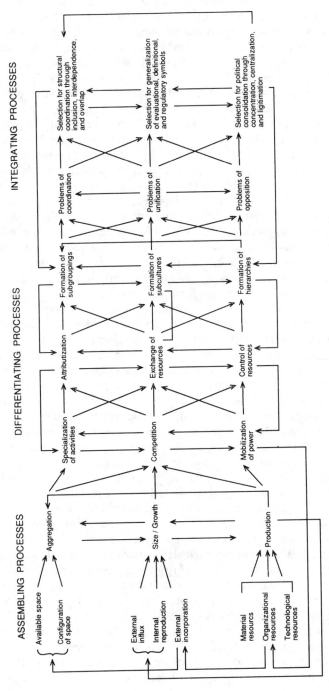

Figure 8.2. A Model of Macrodynamics

189

Aggregation denotes those processes organizing actors in space, especially with respect to the absolute amount of space occupied, the level of density, and the configuration of the spatial distribution, particularly in regard to (1) the relative proportions of actors in high-density spaces, (2) the number of densely populated locations, and (3) the degree of contact among both low- and high-density spaces. Indeed, urban sociology and social ecology are, as disciplines, devoted primarily to the empirical analysis of these classes of variables (e.g., Hawley 1950). The values for these aggregation variables are determined by those causal paths connecting other variables to aggregation. The most obvious variables are those at the far top and left of Figure 8.2, the availability of space and its geographic configuration. Equally important are the modes and levels of productive activity in a population as well as the absolute size and rate of growth in a population. In turn, as is denoted by the double arrows, these two classes of variables feed back and circumscribe the available space and the geography of space. There is also an important causal connection between a variable in the differentiation portion of Figure 8.2 and these aggregation processes: formation of subgroups as these are influenced by exchange, attributization, and subculture formation (these variables are discussed below). The differentiation of distinctive subgroups of actors is, on the one hand, caused by aggregation variables, but, on the other hand, the formation of subgroups feeds back and circumscribes the distribution, relative density, and level of contact among actors. Another crucial set of feedback effects comes from the mobilization of power, which can be used to increase directly the amount and configuration of space available to a population; and if the use of power involves the incorporation of new actors, then the density, distribution, and contact variables are also influenced by this mobilization of power (to be discussed in more detail below).

The next class of assemblage variables are those revolving around population size and its rate of growth. There are three basic variables affecting population size and growth: net immigration into a population, rates of reproduction of actors, and external incorporation of actors, especially under conditions of increased mobilization of power. Levels of productive activity also influence population size and growth by encouraging or discouraging external influx of, and internal increases in, the number of actors. There is also an important indirect causal path by which expanded production causes increased mobilization of power, which can then be used for external incorporation of actors.

The last assemblage variable is production, which denotes the use, conversion, and distribution of resources to sustain the activities of actors in a population. Production is influenced by the level of access to resources, the capacity to organize actors, and the knowledge base for gaining access to resources. Again, there is a crucial feedback loop from the mobilization of power that, on the one hand, is made possible by expanded production and the creation of a productive surplus but that, on the other, can provide organizational resources necessary to expand production. There is also a set of feedback processes, as denoted by the double arrows, among production and the capacity to develop material, organizational, and technological resources. This reciprocal synergy is particularly likely when population pressures (size and rate of growth) increase, encouraging the expansion of productive activity.

The causal connections among these assemblage variables is obviously more complex than I have outlined in this simple model. My point in addressing these processes is to examine them more theoretically than is typically the case. Most discussions of assemblage processes are descriptive, involving a historical/empirical scenario of a particular empirical case. Even the more abstract evolutionary analyses of Spencer ([1874-96] 1905) and Durkheim ([1893] 1933) tended to collapse these assemblage processes into a size/density variable that was interesting only because of its effects on social differentiation. Lenski's (1966) more contemporary analysis does somewhat better on this score, but here theoretical emphasis is primarily on the production variable. My view is that, while these are not particularly "glamorous" variables, they are fundamental to any theory of macrostructure. They profoundly influence the values of those variables that do interest theorists — power, inequality, exchange, subgroup formation, cultural heterogeneity, and the like. And they are not merely descriptive handles; in my view, they are generic variables and are, therefore, a proper subject of general theory as opposed to more middle-range models and theories of such processes as urban and political growth (e.g., Nolan 1979; Stephan 1971) or organizational dynamics (e.g., Hannan and Freeman 1977; Meyer 1972). Moreover, I have deliberately phrased these variables in highly abstract terms so that they can apply to more than societal units of analysis. Macroanalysis is not just about "society," although this is one type of macro unit. Rather, it is about populations of individual and/or collective actors organized in a variety of units, ranging from large groups to world systems. Thus, for example, the variable of "production" does not denote just economic activity in a societal system, although this is obviously one of the most interesting types, but all activities involved in gathering, organizing, using, and distributing resources to sustain the activities of actors. What I want to avoid, then, is the assumption that macrostructural analysis is a synonym for societal-level inquiry.

The processes of assemblage are thus relevant when theory addresses populations of actors. The portions of Figure 8.2 devoted to assemblage do not do complete justice to the complexity of this set of processes, but even in this truncated form, the model cannot be easily tested. As indicated earlier, in order to make a model more manageable and testable, it is desirable to use the model to create propositions, and vice versa. Table 8.1 lists some examples of principles that can be generated for processes of "population assemblage."

The important point about the propositions in Table 8.1 is that each element of these "laws" can be tested with just a little creative work by methodologists and researchers. They also illustrate my theoretical strategy, in that additional theoretical content appears in the propositions. For

Table 8.1 Elementary Principles of Population Assemblage

(I)   The Law of Population Density

The density in the distribution of a population is (a) an exponential and multiplicative function of constraints on available space and population size and (b) an exponential function of productive activity.

(II) The Law of Production

The level of productive activity for a population is (a) an exponential and multiplicative function of material, organizational, and technological resources; (b) a positive curvilineal function of population size; and (c) a positive curvilineal function of the mobilization of power.

(III) The Law of Population Growth

The size of a population in a population is (a) a lineal and additive function of the rate of external reproduction, the net rate of influx, and the extent of external incorporation, while being (b) a positive curvilineal function of productive activity and (c) a negative curvilineal function of political mobilization.

---

example, some assembling processes are considered more central to understanding macrodynamics than others — in this case, population density, population size, and population productivity. Moreover, some variables and their causal connections are seen as more important than others. And the hypothesized form of the relationship among the variables — lineal, exponential, additive, multiplicative, curvilineal, and so on — can be stated in a proposition. Of course, it may be necessary to reformulate the principles and redraw the analytical model on the basis of empirical assessment. But the essential analytical activity is to move back and forth among abstract models, propositions, and data. In fact, even these very simple propositions can be used to create more detailed analytical models, or submodels, on processes of assemblage.

Proposition I in Table 8.1 argues that population density is related to the size of population relative to the available space, hence making these two variables multiplicative in their effects on density. Expanding productive activity also increases density at an accelerating rate, for several reasons: (1) Material and technological resources tend to be concentrated, thereby encouraging the organization of actors in areas where resources are available; (2) expanded productivity requires the "economies of scale" that come with larger organizational units, thus again encouraging concentration of actors in space.

Proposition II in Table 8.1 sees production as increasing at an accelerating rate with the mutually reinforcing effects of expanded access to relevant material resources, development of new technologies or knowledge about how to manipulate the environment, and new mechanisms for organizing activity among actors. Growth in population size initially increases productive activity by creating pressures for expanded conversion of resources and their distribution to meet the needs of a greater number of actors, but as populations continue to grow, they eventually exceed the capacity of available material resources as well as the ability to organize actors for efficient production, thereby causing a decrease in production, at least in per capita productivity. The mobilization of power also bears a curvilineal relationship to production. Initial mobilizing of power increases the capacity to organize and coordinate actors as well as resources for production; but as power becomes highly concentrated and centralized, it is used to control and monitor, and, as a result, it becomes a detriment to expanded production (Pareto [1901] 1968; Spencer [1874] 1905).

Proposition III on population growth is perhaps self-evident, but nonetheless critical for understanding macro social dynamics. Internal reproduction of actors, net movement of actors (immigration less emigration), and incorporation of actors from other populations (e.g., conquest, annexation) obviously work to increase size in an additive manner. Production bears a more curvilineal relationship to population growth. Initial increases in the capacity to support actors through expanded production allow for internal growth, encourage immigration, and enable external incorporation through the use of power; but, as noted above, further increases in productivity require the capacity to organize actors efficiently and to sustain access to material resources, with the result that at some point production reduces incentives for further population growth. The mobilization of power initially involves considerable internal conflict and competition among social units, making it difficult to (1) increase production by providing organizational resources, (2) incorporate new actors from outside the population, or (3) expand the available space. But as power is increasingly mobilized, controlled, and concentrated, it can be used to increase population growth, either directly through external incorporation or indirectly via its effects on the level of organizational resources for production and on the amount of available space.

These propositions on density, production, and population growth are perhaps less interesting than those on differentiation and integration. Yet they are critical in understanding these other macro processes, for the degree of differentiation and integration among actors is very much influenced by their patterns of aggregation, levels of production, absolute size, and rates of growth. But, as noted earlier, the processes of assemblage, especially aggregation and growth, are somewhat less amenable to theoretical analysis than either differentiation or integration. Thus it is wise to leave this cursory analysis and concentrate for the remainder of the chapter on differentiation and integration, which are the basic organizing processes of human populations.

THE PROCESS OF DIFFERENTIATION

The concept of differentiation has been central to sociological theory since its inception (e.g., Smith [1776] 1937; Comte, 1830-42; Spencer [1874-96] 1905; Durkheim [1893] 1933), and more recent macro theories appear to view it as the fundamental structural property organizing populations of actors (e.g., Blau 1977; Parsons 1966, 1971). While all theorists can agree that the term *differentiation* refers to those forces creating "differences" in the attributes and activities of actors, there is still a surprisingly varied range of viewpoints on its most critical dimension(s). The middle portions of Figure 8.2 pull together the range of conceptualizations into one composite model.

In purely static and structural terms, I will define differentiation as the formation of subgroupings, subcultures, and hierarchies. That is, differentiation varies along three dimensions: (1) a "horizontal" dimension in which subsets of actors can be distinguished from each other in terms of their "grouping" patterns, such as rates of interaction and network structures; (2) a "cultural" or "symbolic" dimension in which differences in the "system of symbols" (Parsons 1966), "stocks of knowledge" (Schutz [1932] 1967), "collective conscience" (Durkheim [1893] 1933), and "generalized others" (Mead 1934) and other symbolic configurations among subsets of actors are evident; and (3) a vertical or "hierarchical" dimension whereby actors can be distinguished in terms of their respective shares of valued resources, particularly power but also including material and honorific resources. These three dimensions are viewed as variables in that the degree of subgroup formation (e.g., explicitness of boundaries, density of networks, rates of in-group interaction), degree of subculture formation (distinctiveness of values, beliefs, norms, stocks of knowledge, language), and degree of hierarchy (e.g., the number of hierarchies, their degree of inequality, and their extent of superimposition) can change, or vary.

Differentiation is also a process involving dynamic interconnections among these dimensions of differentiation. The existence of subgroupings encourages the formation of subcultures, and vice versa. When a subset of actors has high rates of interaction with each other, when these actors form dense networks of association, and when they reveal close physical proximity, then these actors are likely to develop distinctive configurations or systems of symbols, particularly with respect to those symbols that organize their patterns of association and interaction (i.e., language, styles of gesturing, norms, stocks of implicit understandings, empirical beliefs about their setting, and evaluative beliefs about what should and ought to exist or transpire in a setting). Conversely, the existence of such distinctive configurations of symbols encourages subgroup formation by (a) facilitating interaction and association among those sharing the same symbolic repertoire and (b) creating strained relations with those who do not share this repertoire. Similarly, the formation of hierarchies also encourages cultural distinctiveness between those who possess different levels of a given resource. Actors with power can control the activities of others and will, as a consequence, typically reveal patterns of demeanor, systems of beliefs, and other configurations of symbols that distinguish them from those with less or no power (Collins 1975). Moreover, those who possess large quantities of other resources, such as material wealth or honor and prestige, will also develop cultural patterns that differentiate them from those without these resources. Conversely, the creation of these distinctive subcultures among actors at different points in various hierarchies can become, itself, one of the resources used to sustain their place in a hierarchy. This is particularly likely to be the case in hierarchies revolving around honor, where types of "cultural capital" (demeanor, speech patterns, knowledge, and so on) are the critical differentiating resources.

Not only are there dynamic causal effects among the three dimensions of differentiation, but there are also critical causal paths to other variables. Both Spencer ([1874] 1905) and Durkheim ([1893] 1933) viewed "competition" among actors as promoting differentiation; and both saw population size, density, and productivity as important causal forces. It is not necessary, I think, to analyze such effects in evolutionary terms, as was the case for Spencer and Durkheim. Instead, we need only hypothesize that the level of competition in a population of actors is positively related to its absolute size, density of aggregation in space, and level of productive activity. Competition sets into motion two interrelated cycles that, in turn, feed back and increase the level of competition, at least up to a certain point. One of these cycles, as presented at the top of Figure 8.2, revolves around "specialization of activities," "attributization," and "exchange of resources." The other cycle, as outlined in the bottom of Figure 8.2, involves "mobilization of power," "control of resources," and "exchange of resources." The reciprocal and mutually reinforcing causal effects in these two cycles help explain why differentiation is difficult to stop, or reverse, once it is initiated.

Turning first to the upper cycle, competition will tend to produce exchange; and as all exchange theorists emphasize, exchange is inherently competitive (e.g., Homans 1961/1974; Emerson 1962, 1972; Blau 1964). Thus competition and exchange are mutually reinforcing. As Emerson (1972) and Blau (1964) have both stressed, these competitive exchanges produce specialization of activities among actors. For as actors compete and exchange resources, they tend to create a "division of labor" (Emerson 1972) in terms of (1) the resources that they supply for each other and (2) the activities that must be pursued to give or receive resources. Naturally, once such patterns of specialization exist, they become institutionalized niches in the macrostructure organizing a population, with individual actors gravitating toward those niches most commensurate with their resources. Specialization of activities creates what I term, for want of a better label, "attributization." Actors who pursue a particular line of activity, who exchange certain kinds of resources, and who experience similar outcomes in competition with others will tend to develop common attributes or characteristics with respect to modes of behavior, interaction demeanors, worldviews, beliefs, linguistic styles, consumption patterns, and other distinctive "attributes." In turn, these attributes will circumscribe what resources these actors can use in exchanges, how well they can do in competition, and what specialized activities they can pursue. As the long arrow in Figure 8.2 from assemblage processes indicates, however, attributization can also be influenced by the "external influx" or "external incorporation" of distinctive actors into a population, but once actors are part of the population, the processes denoted by the cycles in Figure 8.2 become operative. For example, patterns of ethnic antagonism often revolve around the incorporation or influx of actors with distinctive attributes who compete, exchange, and then assume specialized niches in a population (Turner 1986b).

Moving to the cycle at the bottom of Figure 8.2, competition produces mobilization of power, since actors seek to control their destiny vis-à-vis other actors; and the more intense the competition, the greater will be efforts at generating power. Moreover, intense competition creates pressures to develop regulatory agencies, or political authority, to mitigate the disruptive effects of competition that can potentially erupt into open conflict. The feedback loops from the right of Figure 8.2 to this mobilization variable underscore the tendency for competition per se to cause directly, or indirectly through the formation of hierarchies, the mobilization of power. Exchange escalates these tendencies for mobilization, especially if the attributes and activities of one actor are highly valued by others. For when actors value the resources of another but others cannot (1) reduce the value of these valued resources, (2) secure them elsewhere, (3) do without them, (4) coerce them, or (5) induce those possessing the resources into equitable exchanges, then differences in power between those who possess and those who desire these resources emerge (Emerson 1972; Blau 1964). This cycle of competition, exchange, and mobilization of power eventually leads to control of resources — especially power, material props, and honor — by those actors who "win" in competition and who possess those resources valued by others. As with specialization of activities, such control tends to become institutionalized and self-perpetuating once it is established, thereby giving actors who control resources the capacity to mobilize power, win in competition, and extract favorable exchanges. Moreover, as the feedback arrow from the formation of hierarchies to mobilization of power emphasizes, the creation of such hierarchies will structure the mobilization of power in ways that further institutionalize control of resources. Of course, as will be examined shortly, this cycle of mobilization, control, exchange, and competition inevitably generates opposition against those who use their hold over resources to exploit other actors in exchange or to regulate competition in ways that facilitates their control of power and other resources.

As outlined in Figure 8.2, these two cycles are what produce differentiation of subgroupings, subcultures, and hierarchies. In turn, as the double arrows and feedback loops indicate, differentiation along these

Table 8.2 Elementary Principles of Macrostructural Differentiation

(I)   The Law of Differentiation

The overall level of differentiation in a population is an exponential function of the degree of competition among actors, with the latter being (a) a logarithmic function of the density, size, and productivity of that population; (b) a multiplicative and gradual s-function of exchange, specialization, and attributization; and (c) a curvilineal function of mobilization of power and control of resources.

(II) The Law of Subgroup Formation

The number and distinctiveness of subgroups in a population is (a) an exponential function of population size; (b) a logarithmic function of the rate of external influx/incorporation of new actors into a population; (c) a multiplicative and gradual s-function of competition, exchange, specialization, and attributization; and (d) a logarithmic function of formation in subcultures and resource hierarchies.

(III) The Law of Subcultural Formation

The number and distinctiveness of subcultures in a population is (a) a multiplicative and logarithmic function of competition, exchange, attributization, and specialization; (b) an additive and gradual s-function of power mobilization and resource control; (c) a logarithmic function of formation in subgroups; and (d) a logarithmic function of the number of diverse hierarchies.

(IV) The Laws of Hierarchical Differentiation

(i) The number of distinguishable resource hierarchies in a population is (a) an inverse function of the mobilization of power and the control of resources, while being (b) a multiplicative and gradual s-function of competition and exchange.

(ii) The degree of consolidation and superimposition of resource hierarchies is (a) an inverse function of competition and exchange, while being (b) an additive logarithmic function of the mobilization of power and the control of resources.

---

three dimensions sustains the processes implicated in these cycles. Such need not necessarily be the case, especially if integrative problems ensue (to be discussed shortly), but once subgroups, subcultures, and hierarchies are clearly differentiated, they tend to increase the levels of specialization, attributization, competition, exchange, mobilization, and control to high levels. In turn, high values for these processes sustain patterns of differentiation among subgroups, subcultures, and hierarchies.

These complex causal paths among the variables implicated in the process of differentiation can be converted into propositions. Such an exercise allows certain causal connections to be emphasized, and at the same time enables speculation on the form of the causal relation. Moreover, the development of propositions can suggest leads for more detailed modeling of these processes implicated in differentiation. Table 8.2 summarizes what I see as the critical "laws" of macrostructural differentiation.

Proposition I argues that the overall level of differentiation — that is, the number and distinctiveness of subgroups, subcultures, and hierarchies — increases at an accelerating rate (at least up to a point) with increases in the level of competition. Such competition is fueled by assemblage processes of size/growth, density, and productivity in a logarithmic pattern. That is, initial increases in these assemblage processes escalate the level of competition dramatically, but at a decelerating rate. Thus initial increases in the size of a population, its level of density, and rate of productivity will have dramatic effects on competition and differentiation, as Spencer ([1874] 1905) and Durkheim ([1893] 1933) recognized a century ago. The process of exchange per se is inherently competitive; but eventually exchange relations become somewhat structured and routinized (Blau 1964), thereby causing the level of competition produced by exchange relations to level off. This leveling is particularly likely as the attributes and specialized niches of actors begin to dictate the resources being exchanged and the appropriate rates of exchange. Thus attributization and specialization are two processes by which actors are differentiated in ways that facilitate the structuring and routinization of exchange. Proposition I describes this relationship between competition on the one hand and specialization, attributization, and exchange on the other as multiplicative in the sense that an increase in any one of these latter variables will raise the value of the others in their effects on competition, at least up to the point where specialization, attributization, and exchange become highly routinized. The form of the relationship is portrayed as a gradual s-function because the multiplicative effects of exchange, attributization, and specialization on competition increase and then level off as exchange becomes institutionalized and regulated. It may be that the relationship is positively curvilineal, however, since institutionalization of exchange may actually decrease the level of competition as actors accept the attributes and the specialized niches determining the resources available for exchange. The relationship between mobilization of power and control of resources is unambiguously curvilineal.

The substantive rationale for this conclusion is that initial efforts to mobilize power and control resources escalate competition among those making such efforts, especially under conditions of exchange. But as more power is mobilized and used to gain control over resources, competition will decrease as those with power and other resources use them to control other actors directly, or indirectly, through the creation of unilateral monopolies in exchange relations (Emerson 1972).

Proposition II in Table 8.2 summarizes the critical processes influencing the degree of subgroup formation. Obviously, population size places limits on the number of subgroups that can be differentiated. This relationship between size and subgroups is exponential because, as population size increases, the number of potential associations and groups increases at an accelerating rate. The external influx (e.g., migration) and external incorporation (e.g., annexation, conquest) bear a logarithmic relationship to subgroup formation because those entering or being incorporated into the system usually bring with them distinctive group structures. Moreover, as a consequence of competition and exchange with members of the indigenous population, these new actors are typically forced into specialized niches that sustain their distinctive attributes, thereby maintaining subgroup formation. For both new and indigenous actors in a population, then, escalation of the rates of exchange and competition, as they affect each other as well as specialization and attributization of actors, gradually increases the number and distinctiveness of subgroups, at least up to the point where either the size of a population cannot be further subdivided or, more likely, the process of attributization and specialization in exchange relations has become stabilized and structured around actors organized into stable subsets of groupings where they accept their cost/reward outcomes in exchange relations. Such group processes are accelerated by the formation of distinctive subcultures, since the development of a common symbolic repertoire provides a means for unifying group members and consolidating group boundaries. Proposition II sees this relationship as logarithmic because group formation will be more rapidly achieved by the availability of a common symbolic legacy on which to elaborate group structures. Similarly, the elaboration of hierarchies creates converging shares of resources that actors can use to form group bonds. That is, those with a given level of resources are likely to be at similar positions in exchange networks (Emerson 1972) and thereby have greater opportunities to form group structures, especially if they are subordinate in a system of concentrated control of resources (Collins 1975).

Proposition III in Table 8.2 specifies the relationship between subculture formation and other differentiating processes. Competition and exchange, as they influence each other and the processes of specialization and attributization, increase subcultural formation logarithmically. The reasoning here is that common symbolic configurations, especially beliefs and components of worldviews, will form more rapidly than group structures. That is, those who find themselves in similar specialized niches in a system of competition and exchange will first develop a common culture *before* this culture is embellished and reinforced by increases in rates of interaction, network patterns, and group structures. Hence, unless preexisting group structures already exist and organize activity, subcultures will tend to emerge before clear group structures and boundaries, although as subgroupings begin to develop, they will immediately begin to stimulate subcultural development. A similar argument can be made for the formation of hierarchies, for as the distribution of resources among actors becomes more clearly differentiated, the respective shares of resources circumscribe the use of symbols, the degree of interaction, and the patterns of networks that produce and sustain subcultures. That is, hierarchies create structural levels that give actors similar resources and positions, thereby encouraging subcultural formation and, as indicated for Proposition II in Table 8.2, subgroup formation as well.

The final proposition in Table 8.2 is divided into two parts, one concerning the number of hierarchies and the other revolving around the degree to which actors hold similar positions across resource hierarchies (Blau 1977; Dahrendorf 1959). Turning first to Proposition IV(i), the mobilization of power and the resulting control of resources will decrease the number of resource hierarchies. As those with power gain control over resources, they will attempt to collapse hierarchies. Conversely, when the mobilization of power and the concentration of resources are less pronounced, no set of actors can hoard resources across hierarchies or collapse resource distribution into one hierarchy, with the result that more discrete hierarchies are likely to exist among the members of a population. Moreover, it is likely that the levels of inequality among actors at varying positions in these hierarchies will be less extreme than is the case when hierarchies are superimposed. Competition and exchange also promote multiple hierarchies, at least to that point where competition and exchange cause the mobilization of power and control of resources that are then used to (1) repress competition and open exchange and (2) collapse resource hierarchies. Thus competition and exchange have the ironic consequence of setting into motion those very dynamics that reduce the number of resource hierarchies, which, in turn, lessens open competition and free exchange (in fact, the relationship between competition/ exchange and hierarchies may be positively curvilineal rather than a gradual s-function).

With respect to the level of "consolidation" (Blau 1977) or "superimposition" (Dahrendorf 1959) among resource hierarchies, high rates of open competition and relatively free exchange lower the correlation among positions across hierarchies. For as long as actors can compete and exchange, they can move up and down a variety of hierarchies, but, as noted above, once competition and exchange create differences in power and monopolization of resources, it becomes possible to consolidate positions across hierarchies. For example, those with high levels of power can use this power to create or sustain a high position in resource hierarchies revolving around wealth and prestige, while those with wealth (and, to a much lesser extent, prestige) can use this resource to gain power.

In sum, then, Table 8.2 posits some "laws" of differentiation, although they might be better viewed as a series of tentative hypotheses. While the propositions in Table 8.2 are complex, each portion of given "law" is testable, at least in principle. And, as noted earlier, they can provide added theoretical content that can be used to construct more detailed analytical models.

INTEGRATION PROCESSES

The term *integration* now has unsavory connotations in sociological theory, being equated with the imputed deficiencies of functionalism (Turner and Maryanski 1978). Yet, we need some concept to denote the processes by which actors in a population are interrelated; therefore, I think that the concept of integration is still useful, indeed central, to sociological analysis. Integration denotes the degree and pattern of inter-relationship among social units or actors. There are, I believe, three variable patterns of interrelationship: (1) structural coordination among actors, or the degree to which goals and activities of social units are mutually facilitative; (2) symbolic unification among actors, or the degree to which the goals and activities of social units are organized in terms of reference to common configurations of symbols; and (3) political consol-idation, or the degree to which the goals and activities of social units are regulated by external actors possessing power. Thus the overall degree of integration in a population of actors is a joint function, obviously involv-ing interaction effects, of the degree of coordination, symbolic unifica-tion, and political consolidation. I am not asserting, of course, that high or low degrees of integration are "good" or "bad," as some have charged functionalists. Rather, my point is that populations vary in terms of their degree of structural coordination, symbolic unification, and political con-solidation.

There are, I contend, a limited number of forms for these three integrat-ing processes. For coordination processes, there are three interrelated patterns of variation: (1) the degree of "structural inclusion" (units inside of more inclusive units), (2) the degree of "structural interdependence" (units dependent upon, or coupled with, each other in their operation), and (3) the degree of "structural overlap" (units revealing common member-ship). For symbolic unification, there are also three variable types: (1) the degree of consensus over "evaluative symbols" (conceptions among ac-tors as to what is right/wrong, good/bad, appropriate/inappropriate), (2) the degree of consensus over "definitional symbols" (conceptions among actors as to what exists), and (3) the degree of consensus over regulatory symbols (conceptions among actors about the operative procedures for their activity). For political consolidation as well, there are three variable patterns: (1) the degree of "concentration of power" (number of units, as a proportion of the total, revealing the capacity to control other units), (2) the degree of "centralization of power" (ranking of power-holding units in terms of decision-making and controlling prerogatives), and (3) the degree of "legitimation of power" (acceptance by units of the right of power holders to make decisions and control their activities). Obviously, I have simply rephrased old ideas with somewhat new terms, but I have also ordered these ideas in a more comprehensive view of integrating processes. This view is summarized in Table 8.3.

Thus integration is a process that varies by degree along three basic axes: structural coordination, symbolic unification, and political consoli-dation. For each of these axes, a number of variable patterns or forms are evident. When the values for each of these patterns along all three axes are high, then a population is said to be integrated. Again, just whether this is "good" or "bad" is irrelevant to this conceptualization. With this defini-

Table 8.3 Variable Dimensions of Integration

| | Basic Integrating Processes | | |
	(1) Structural Coordination	(2) Symbolic Unification	(3) Political Consolidation
Variable Patterns of Integration	(a) inclusion (b) interdependence (c) overlap	(a) evaluative (b) definitional (c) regulatory	(a) concentration (b) centralization (c) legitimation

tional work out of the way, let me now return to the right-hand portion of Figure 8.2, where the causal dynamics of integration are outlined in a summary fashion.

Since Spencer's ([1874] 1905) early work, as it was later reinforced and supplemented by Durkheim ([1893] 1933) and then by Parsons (1966, 1971), the processes of differentiation and integration have been causally linked. The general argument is that increasing differentiation creates "problems of integration," which, depending upon the empirical circumstances, either "generates" new patterns of integration among actors in a population or sets into motion disintegration of that population. This argument need not be couched in evolutionary terms, as was the case for Spencer, Durkheim, and Parsons. Nor need it be viewed as an illegitimate teleology or tautology, as has often been argued. Instead, we need only invoke a "social selection" argument to avoid the problems of teleology and tautology (Turner and Maryanski 1978; Stinchcombe 1968). That is, the process of differentiation creates "selection pressures" for the activation of integrating processes; depending on the empirical circumstances, integrating processes can emerge, either by chance or through purposeful intent by actors. Alternatively, they may not emerge and the process of disintegration and, in all likelihood, dedifferentiation and disassemblage will ensue. These kinds of selection arguments are quite common in biology; they need not be troublesome in sociology, as long as it is recognized that integration is not inevitable. In fact, in the long run, all patterns of organization among a population of actors disintegrate.

The model on the right side of Figure 8.2 specifies in more detail the conditions produced by differentiation and the nature of the selection pressures that exist under these conditions. High levels of subgroup formation create problems of coordination among subgroups; increases in subcultural formation escalate problems of cultural unification; and the formation of hierarchies, especially their consolidation and superimposition (see Proposition III[ii] in Table 8.2), generates problems of opposition by those in nonprivileged positions in the hierarchy. Thus corresponding to the three axes of differentiation — subgroup, subculture, and hierarchy — are three sets of escalating integrative problems: coordination, unification, and opposition.

Each of these integrative problems creates "selection pressures" for its elimination, but whether actors can intentionally deal with these problems, or simply hit upon a solution by chance or trial and error depends, to some degree, upon the empirical/historical circumstances in which a population finds itself. Yet, as Table 8.3 underscores, I think that it is possible to specify the kinds of integrating processes that will emerge, *if* circumstances permit. Moreover, as the double or feedback arrows moving from the far right to left in Figure 8.2 suggest, once selection pressures have led actors to initiate integrative responses, these responses increase the likelihood that problems of coordination, unification, and opposition will be pursued further. For example, once some degree of interdependence, overlap, and inclusion exists in a population, these "solutions" to problems of coordination will typically encourage further efforts along these lines, even under adverse empirical circumstances. The same is true, I argue, for selection processes revolving around problems of symbolic unification and opposition. With this broad overview in mind, let me now turn to a more detailed analysis of these processes.

As problems of coordination increase as a result of (1) increases in the differentiation of subgroups/subculture, (2) escalating problems of symbolic unification, and (3) failure to generalize symbols, selection pressures for inclusion, interdependence, and overlap are initiated. Moreover, the problems of coordination created by a failure to create a system of generalized symbols set into motion selection pressures for such "symbolic generalization" (by which I mean the increasing abstraction of evaluative, definitional, and regulatory symbols). For diverse groupings to be coordinated requires not only a structural interlacing through inclusion, overlap, and interdependence but also, as Durkheim ([1893] 1933) recognized, an underlying symbolic basis. Yet, if such symbols are too specific under conditions of differentiation, they become irrelevant to actors operating in vastly different group situations. Differentiation and efforts to coordinate these differences thus escalate selection pressures for the creation of highly generalized systems of symbols — especially values, beliefs, and norms — that provide common ideas for actors who are otherwise very different. Of course, as Durkheim emphasized, if the structural coordination is not in place and problems of coordination and unification force symbols to generalize "prematurely," then "anomie" exists and the organization of a population disintegrates. But if interdependence, overlap, and inclusion can emerge, they increase pressures for symbolic generalization, thereby helping to resolve problems of symbolic unification (Turner 1981). Political consolidation also influences those selection pressures, especially interdependence and inclusion, that often emerge to resolve problems of coordination. As power becomes concentrated and centralized (through processes to be discussed shortly), efforts are made to (1) create control hierarchies, and hence inclusion, and (2) foster and regulate interdependencies among social units. Once such interdependencies and inclusion processes are operative, they feed back and help increase the level of political consolidation. And as structural coordination increases under these varied causal paths, it extends the capacity of a system to aggregate, grow, and expand its productive activity (see the long feedback arrow across the top of Figure 8.2).

Turning more directly and explicitly to problems of symbolic unification created by social differentiation, I argue that these problems exert strong pressures for the selection of generalized symbols. Moreover, in a less intense manner, they generate selection for structural coordination and political consolidation. In turn, as analyzed above, structural co-ordination stimulates further symbolic generalization, whereas political consolidation typically encourages efforts at legitimating power through highly generalized symbols, especially those revolving around evaluations and definitions. Thus as a system of general and abstract evaluative, definitional, and regulatory symbols emerges, it not only resolves problems of cultural unification, it also has important direct and indirect effect on those processes — structural coordination and political consolidation — that help resolve problems of coordination and opposition.

Shifting attention to problems of opposition generated by (1) the formation of hierarchies and their consolidation/superimposition, (2) the proliferation of subcultures and associated problems of cultural unification, and (3) the failure to generalize symbol systems, I argue that opposition encourages political consolidation. Initially, opposition causes the consolidation of power by each side in a potential conflict. But as such consolidation and/or conflict occurs, one party usually prevails; or, as is often the case, even more power is consolidated by a third party in an attempt to regulate, integrate, resolve, or repress opposition between those in opposition. The end result in either case is that power becomes consolidated. If such consolidation of power does not emerge, as has often been the case in actual historical systems, then all problems of integration in differentiating populations increase. For as opponents develop their own ideologies, generalization of symbols that cut across the entire population becomes difficult. And as the failure to consolidate power becomes manifest, structural coordination also becomes difficult. Yet, ironically, the failure to create political authority makes populations even more vulnerable to political consolidation, either by external conquest or by radical political movements within the population. And so, in the end, concentration and centralization of power will increase, at least for a while. However, if these two phases of political consolidation are not followed by political legitimation, especially with respect to generalized evaluational, definitional, and regulatory symbols, then such concentration and centralization of power will rely upon the use of coercive force, which, in turn, makes it even more difficult to achieve legitimation. Moreover, even without the extensive use of coercion, the long feedback loop at the bottom of Figure 8.2 underscores the fact that political consolidation, per se, sets into motion via a variety of causal paths among those differentiating processes that escalate integrative problems, especially the superimposition of hierarchies, the creation of disparate subcultures, and the formation of uncoordinated subgroupings. Such integrative problems increase the likelihood of even more political consolidation, which can escalate long-term integrative problems, particularly when (1) legitimation through generalized symbols does not occur and (2) structural coordination through noncoercive measures does not ensue. As is evident, then, there is a complex set of direct, indirect, and feedback causal paths among integrative processes in human populations. This brief discussion cannot fully explicate them all, but it is sufficient for using the model in Figure 8.2 to suggest a number of propositions on the process of integration in human populations. These are listed in Table 8.4.

Proposition I in Table 8.4 qualifies all of the remaining "laws" of integration. Processes of structural coordination, symbolic generalization, and political consolidation are activated by selection pressures created by social differentiation. They are not inevitable or inexorable outcomes of differentiation; rather, they mark the direction of integration *if* empirical conditions allow such integration to be initiated. Thus the "laws" of structural coordination, symbolic generalization, and political consolidation presuppose some degree of initial selection along these lines. If selection does not occur, then disintegration of a differentiating population is likely. That is, continual opposition and conflict will prevent political consolidation; symbols will remain tied to local constituencies and divide rather than unify a population; and the inability to regularize interdependencies will escalate problems of coordination among actors.

Proposition II(i) argues that structural inclusion initially increases with differentiation of subgroupings and subcultures, but as their number increases, it becomes increasingly difficult for inclusion to occur. Instead, clusters of subgroups and subcultures become differentiated from each other, thereby increasing selection pressures for other coordinating processes (as delineated in Propositions II[ii] and II[iii]). Structural inclusion is also influenced by political consolidation, especially concentration and centralization, at an accelerating rate, at least up to a point. As power is concentrated and as decision making is centralized, efforts to create lines and chains of authority involve embedding groups and subcultures in one another. Such inclusion processes are, however, constrained by those processes limiting the degree of concentration and centralization of power, with the result that attempts to create chains of authority will level off or perhaps even decrease.

Proposition II(ii) contends that the degree of interdependence among units is a positive curvilineal function of the number of subcultures and subgroupings. As their number increases, efforts to create exchange and other dependencies are likely, but as this number becomes high, it is impossible for interdependencies, even indirect ones, to exist among all units. Instead, interdependencies will be immediately facilitated, as Durkheim ([1893] 1933) recognized, by symbolic generalization. If symbols generalize, then it becomes immediately possible to create interdependen-

Table 8.4 Principles of Macrostructural Integration

(I)   The Law of Macrostructural Selection

The overall level of selection pressure in a population for structural coordination, symbolic generalization, and political consolidation is an exponential function of the degree of differentiation among actors in that population.

(II) The Laws of Structural Coordination

(i)   The degree of structural inclusion among the social units in a population is (a) a positive curvilineal function of the number of differentiated subgroupings and subcultures and (b) an exponential function of political consolidation, particularly the degree of concentration and centralization of power.

(ii) The degree of structural interdependence among the social units in a population is (a) a positive curvilineal function of the number of differentiated subgroupings and subcultures, (b) a logarithmic function of symbolic generalization, and (c) a gradual s-function of centralization and legitimation of power.

(iii) The degree of structural overlap in the membership of social units in a population is (a) a negative curvilineal function of the number of subgroupings and subcultures, (b) a logarithmic function of symbolic generalization, and (c) a negative curvilineal function of political consolidation.

(III) The Laws of Symbolic Generalization

(i)   The degree of generalization in evaluational symbols of a population is (a) a negative curvilineal function of the number of differentiated subcultures, subgroupings, and hierarchies; (b) a gradual s-function of structural coordination; and (c) a logarithmic function of political consolidation, especially legitimate processes.

(ii) The degree of generalization in definitional and regulatory symbols in a population is (a) a gradual s-function of the number of subcultures, subgroupings, and hierarchies and (b) a gradual s-function of structural coordination and political consolidation.

(IV) The Laws of Political Consolidation

(i)   The degree of concentrated power in a population is (a) a logarithmic function of superimposition among hierarchies, (b) a negative curvilineal function of opposition, and (c) a gradual s-function of structural coordination and symbolic generalization.

(ii) The degree of centralized power in a population is (a) a logarithmic function of opposition stemming from consolidated hierarchies and (b) a gradual s-function of structural coordination and symbolic generalization.

(iii) The level of political legitimation in a population is (a) an inverse function of opposition and/or concentration stemming from superimposed hierarchies, (b) a gradual s-function of structural coordination, and (c) a logarithmic function of symbolic generalization, especially evaluational symbols.

cies because there is an underlying set of evaluational, definitional, and regulatory presuppositions for otherwise different actors. Power has a more gradual effect on symbolic generalization. As power becomes centralized and as decision makers seek to legitimate their prerogatives, they employ generalized symbols that, in turn, can facilitate coordination of social units. But more directly, the effectiveness and legitimacy of power often rest on the ability of decision makers to lace subordinate units together in webs of interdependencies that can be centrally regulated and that create systems of mutual obligations that generate dependence, and hence a diffuse legitimacy, on regulatory authority.

Proposition II(iii) argues that structural overlap initially decreases with differentiation, and then with high levels of differentiation, structural overlap begins to increase again. Relatively undifferentiated systems almost always involve considerable overlap in membership of subgroupings, but initial differentiation tends to reduce this overlap, as groupings spread out in space and as power is mobilized to create hierarchies that divide a population in terms of inequalities. Yet, as differentiation increases further, rates of mobility also tend to escalate (Blau 1977) and fluctuating patterns of opposition create coalitions that increase overlapping memberships. Symbolic generalization accelerates these processes immediately, since it provides actors from different subgrounds and subcultures with common presuppositions that can facilitate those processes, such as mobility and coalition formation, creating overlapping memberships. Political consolidation initially decreases overlapping memberships as power is mobilized and consolidated to create hierarchies, but as power becomes more centralized, regulatory, and legitimated, it operates to encourage those processes, especially mobility and exchange, that can lead to overlapping memberships in subgroupings.

Proposition III(i) states that the generalization of evaluational symbols initially decreases with differentiation, as now separated clusters of actors create particularistic values and beliefs. With further differentiation, however, value generalization is increasingly likely, as problems of coordinating and regulating social units increases. Hence as processes of structural coordination are increasingly selected, they gradually generate pressures to create a common morality that can be used to facilitate such coordination. In contrast, political consolidation, particularly efforts to legitimate power, results in immediate efforts to generalize evaluational symbols so that all actors have a moral commitment to political authority.

Proposition III(ii) argues that definitional and regulatory symbols generalize in the same manner. Increases in the number of subcultures, subgroups, and hierarchies gradually escalate selection pressures for generalized symbols that can provide common definitions of situations where contact is made among differentiated actors and that can also specify the way actors should proceed in such situations. Such generalization of definitional and regulatory symbols is also facilitated by the development of structural interdependencies that increasingly require common definitions and procedural instructions. Moreover, as political consolidation occurs, the level of effectiveness in the use of power increasingly requires that those subject to authority possess similar definitions of, and expectations in, situations.

Proposition IV(i) on political consolidation states that the concentration of power, or the proportion of power by a given percentage of a population, will be high with superimposition of hierarchies. In fact, concentration of power is impossible without those controlling resources in one hierarchy also using this control to generate control of resources in other hierarchies. The degree of opposition bears a curvilineal relationship to concentrated power, because initially opposition involves the deconcentration of power as subpopulations mobilize against centers of power. Yet, in the long run, the level of concentrated power increases, regardless of whether opposition is successful. If successful, opposition groups must consolidate their gains, while holding off resistance by old centers of power; as a result, they concentrate power. If unsuccessful, the existing power structure will have had to concentrate its power to control opposition. Thus opposition will often decrease the concentration of power for a while, but in the end, it typically creates even more concentrated power. Efforts at structural coordination will also increase the concentration of power, but not at the same rate or degree as opposition. Yet, as efforts to regulate and coordinate subunit activities increase, there is inevitably some usurpation of power, but this trend toward concentration is typically gradual; it begins to level off, and perhaps even to decline (thereby making the relationship positively curvilineal rather than a gradual s-function), as differentiation of subunits increases beyond the point where further concentrations of power are effective or possible. Symbolic generalization can also influence the concentration of power by providing abstract legitimating symbols. Those who control resources inevitably seek to create systems of symbols that give them "moral right" to such control of power.

Proposition IV(ii) views the centralization of power, or the extent to which political decision making is controlled by a small elite, as likely to increase dramatically with opposition (Spencer [1874] 1905; Simmel 1903-04). For in order to mobilize and coordinate resources to deal with opposition, centralized decision making is essential. A more gradual impetus to centralization comes from pressures for structural coordination. As political authority seeks to resolve problems of coordination, it inevitably centralizes decision making. These efforts are facilitated when generalized symbols can legitimate centralization in the name of some other moral standard, such as "increased efficiency."

Proposition IV(iii) argues that such political legitimation is an inverse function of opposition, since opposition movements arise when the legitimacy of existing centers of power has been undermined. Structural coordination will gradually increase the legitimacy of political elites, for as relations among subunits are regularized, they come to have a vested interest in the maintenance of those centers of power facilitating their relations. And if abstract evaluational symbols can also be generated, they can be used to legitimate the moral right of political elites to consolidate their power. Indeed, legitimacy will increase very quickly if there is consensus over evaluational symbols.

In sum, the propositions in Table 8.4 provide some sense for the form and nature of key relations among the integrating processes delineated in Figure 8.2. Each "law" involves several subhypotheses that are testable in principle. Thus, as with the other propositions in Tables 8.1 and 8.2, those in Table 8.4 translate the complex configuration of causality in Figure 8.2 into more manageable theoretical statements. And as such statements are assessed in light of empirical cases, they can facilitate a redrawing of the analytical model.

Conclusion

As indicated several times, this chapter summarizes a "theory in progress." The analyses here should, therefore, be seen as only provisional. In fact, I view the chapter as an outline — indeed a very rough one — for a much larger project. Aside from providing this rough outline of a theory, my purpose in presenting ideas in this form has been to encourage a serious reconsideration of macro social theory and to advocate a particular strategy for building sociological theory. Let me conclude by elaborating on these two issues.

With just a few notable exceptions, sociological theory has clearly developed a micro bias. And even when macrostructural processes are considered legitimate, it is likely that they are seen to "emerge" out of micro processes, thereby giving theoretical primacy to the micro. In a sense, the return of microsociology represents a healthy movement, since sociological theory has had a macro bias for most of this century. Yet, as Figure 8.2 attempts to portray, there is still great analytical power in a purely macro approach, especially one that borrows from the legacy of the last century and early decades of this century. Moreover, I doubt if this macro level will ever be "reduced to," "translated into," or otherwise obviated by micro approaches. Conversely, this macro approach cannot provide much insight into the details of interaction among individuals. There is, then, always going to be a "gap" between micro and macro theory. Let us recognize this fact and build theory accordingly.

My strategy for doing so owes its inspiration to Comte, in this general sense: Sociology can be a natural science; it can isolate the universal and generic properties of the social universe; it can model these properties at an abstract level; and it can develop laws of their dynamic operation. Indeed, like Comte, I still prefer the term *social physics* to *sociology*. The strategy that I have adopted comes from trying to develop, to use Radcliffe-Brown's words, "a natural science of society." Whether one focuses on the process of interaction among individuals or the organization of populations of actors, the goals should be (1) to isolate *the* fundamental properties of the micro and macro universe, (2) to develop sensitizing models that highlight the general classes of causal relations among these properties, (3) to delineate abstract analytical models, and submodels, that explicate the configurations of causal paths among the variables used to conceptualize these properties, (4) to articulate abstract propositions that capture the form of relationship among variables, (5) to use the synergy between models and propositions as a source of creative insight, and, of course, (6) to check the plausibility of models and propositions in light of relevant data.

This strategy has led me to construct the composite model in Figure 8.2 and the propositions in Tables 8.1, 8.2, and 8.4. In a more elaborated approach, the composite model would be broken down into more detailed models of assemblage, differentiation, and integration. Moreover, the propositions would be more rigorously phrased and organized, and relevant data would be brought to bear on the propositions. Progress in sociological theory will ensue, I believe, only when theorists pursue a strategy that reveals the basic elements of the one illustrated in this chapter.

References

Alexander, Jeffrey C. 1982-84. *Theoretical Logic in Sociology,* 4 vols. Berkeley: University of California Press.

Alexander, Jeffrey C., Bernhard Giesen, Richard Münch, and Neil Smelser, eds. 1986. *The Micro-Macro Link.* Berkeley: University of California Press.

Blau, Peter M. 1964. *Exchange and Power in Social Life.* New York: John Wiley.

— — —. 1970. "A Formal Theory of Differentiation in Organizations." *American Sociological Review* 35(April):201-18.

— — —. 1977. *Inequality and Heterogeneity: A Primitive Theory of Social Structure.* New York: Free Press.

Blumer, Herbert. 1962. "Society as Symbolic Interaction." In *Human Behavior and Social Process,* edited by A. M. Rose. New York: Houghton Mifflin.

— — —. 1969. *Symbolic Interaction: Perspective and Method.* Englewood Cliffs, NJ: Prentice-Hall.

Collins, Randall. 1975. *Conflict Sociology: Toward an Explanatory Science.* New York: Academic Press.

Comte, Auguste. 1830-42. *System of Positive Philosophy.* Paris: Bachelier.

Dahrendorf, Ralf. 1959. *Class and Class Conflict in Industrial Society.* Stanford, CA: Stanford University Press.

Durkheim, Émile. [1893] 1933. *The Division of Labor in Society.* New York: Macmillan.

Emerson, Richard. 1962. "Power-Dependence Relations." *American Sociological Review* 17(February):31-41.

— — —. 1972. "Exchange Theory, Part II." In *Sociological Theories in Progress,* Vol. 2, edited by Joseph Berger, Morris Zelditch, Jr., and Bo Anderson. Boston: Houghton Mifflin.

Giddens, Anthony. 1981. *Central Problems in Social Theory.* London: Macmillan.

— — —. 1984. *The Constitution of Society: Outline of the Theory of Structuration.* Berkeley: University of California Press.

Hannan, Michael T. and John Freeman. 1977. "The Population Ecology of Organizations." *American Journal of Sociology* 82(March):929-64.

Hawley, Amos. 1950. *Human Ecology.* New York: Ronald.

Homans, George C. 1961/1974. *Social Behavior: Its Elementary Forms.* New York: Harcourt.

Knorr-Cetina, Karin and Aaron V. Cicourel, eds. 1981. *Advances in Social Theory and Methodology: Toward an Integration of Micro- and Macro-Sociologies.* Boston: Routledge & Kegan Paul.

Lenski, Gerhard. 1966. *Power and Privilege.* New York: McGraw-Hill.

Mayhew, Bruce H. 1981. "Structuralism Versus Individualism." *Social Forces* 59(3):627-48.

Mead, George Herbert. 1934. *Mind, Self and Society.* Chicago: University of Chicago Press.

Meyer, Marshall M. 1972. "Size and the Structure of Organizations: A Causal Analysis." *American Sociological Review* 37(August):434-41.

Nolan, Patrick D. 1979. "Size and Administrative Intensity in Nations." *American Sociological Review* 44(February):110-25.

Pareto, Vilfredo. [1901] 1968. *The Rise and Fall of Elites: An Application of Theoretical Sociology.* Totowa, NJ: Bedminster.

Parsons, Talcott. 1966. *Societies: Evolutionary and Comparative Perspectives.* Englewood Cliffs, NJ: Prentice-Hall.

— — —. 1971. *The System of Modern Societies.* Englewood Cliffs, NJ: Prentice-Hall.

Schutz, Alfred. [1932] 1967. *The Phenomenology of the Social World.* Evanston, IL: Northwestern University Press.

Simmel, Georg. 1903-04. "The Sociology of Conflict." *American Journal of Sociology* 9:490-525, 672-89, 798-811.

Smith, Adam. [1776] 1937. *An Inquiry into the Nature and Causes of the Wealth of Nations.* New York: Random House.

Spencer, Herbert. [1874-96] 1905. *Principles of Sociology.* New York: D. Appleton.

Stephan, Edward G. 1971. "Variation in Country Size: A Theory of Segmental Growth." *American Sociological Review* 36(June):451-61.

Stinchcombe, Arthur L. 1968. *Constructing Social Theories.* New York: Harcourt.

Turner, Jonathan. 1981. "Émile Durkheim's Theory of Integration in Differentiated Social Systems." *Pacific Sociological Review* 24(4):187-208.

— — —. 1983. "Theoretical Strategies for Linking Micro and Macro Processes: An Evaluation of Seven Approaches." *Western Sociological Review* 14(1):4-15.

— — —. 1985. "In Defense of Positivism." *Sociological Theory* 4(Fall):32-44.

— — —. 1986a. "The Mechanics of Social Interaction." *Sociological Theory* 4(Spring):95-105.

— — —. 1986b. "Toward a Unified Theory of Ethnic Antagonism: A Preliminary Synthesis of Three Macro Models." *Sociological Forum* 1(Summer):403-27.

— — —. 1987a. "Analytical Theorizing." Pp. 156-94 in *Analytical Theorizing,* edited by Anthony Giddens and Jonathan H. Turner. Cambridge, MA: Polity.

— — —. 1987b. "Toward a Sociological Theory of Motivation." *American Sociological Review* 52(February):15-27.

— — —. 1988. *A Theory of Social Interaction.* Stanford, CA: Stanford University Press.

— — —. 1989a. "A Behavioral Theory of Social Structure." *Journal for the Theory of Social Behavior* 18(4):354-72.

— — —. 1989b. "A Theory of Microdynamics." *Advances in Group Processes* 7:1-28.

Turner, Jonathan H. and Alexandra Maryanski. 1978. *Functionalism.* Menlo Park, CA: Benjamin-Cummings.

9

The Biased Net Theory
of Social Structures and
the Problem of Integration

THOMAS J. FARARO
JOHN SKVORETZ

(1) Introduction

Differentiation and integration are correlative general systems phenomena. Until an empirical entity exhibits differentiation into parts, there is nothing to integrate. And if differentiation occurs, then unless some degree of integration of the parts also occurs, there is no longer a single entity. Hence, to the extent that we have both a recognizable single entity and a multiplicity of parts, the whole enduring over time, we may seek for relations or mechanisms that account for the degree of integration. The focus on integration, therefore, emerges naturally in the study of the morphology or structural parts of *any* system.

Some theories treat social structure — a differentiated set of parts in some state of integration — as problematic in the sense of requiring production through some mechanisms of social interaction. The methodological individualism coupled with an exchange formulation by Homans (1974) provides an example. Other theories treat social structure as parametric for particular social interactions in the sense that the actors are *located* in terms of *given* parts that then condition the form and content of interaction. This is true of the strictly social system level of analysis in Parsons (1951) as well as the more recent work of Blau (1977). The present theory falls under the second type: structure as parametric to social interaction processes.

Our theory draws upon and complements another approach we have taken in which the concrete structural units of a social system are institutions (Fararo and Skvoretz 1984b). In that framework, an institution is a complex system of *unit-institutions*, each of which is a set of symbolic structures (in the strict sense) forming a stable design for social interaction that has the property of potential, and usually actual, *multiple embodiments* (Fararo 1981b) in a given social system. For concreteness, think of the factory as such a complex of unit-institutions. For Marx, as for us, systemwide aggregates of people exist by virtue of multiple embodiment: all the owners, all the workers, aggregated over the various embodiments, the factories in the system. Such a systemwide aggregate we will term a *collectivity*. Thus collectivities are nonlocalized aggregates of members of a social system, induced by the institutional structure of that system. (This formulation of a macrosociological starting point is similar to that of Etzioni 1968.) Such collectivities are, at least potentially, more than just statistical aggregates: Actual social associations are shaped by identifications of individuals as members of such collectivities. When all the collectivities induced by a given institution are considered, therefore, there is a problem of integration of such systemwide parts. This is one way to frame the starting point of the present chapter: The parts are collectivities and their integration is problematic.

In approaching this problem, we draw upon two ongoing research traditions, both of which have played a strong role in our earlier theorizing within the framework presented in this chapter. One tradition, now closely associated with the work of Blau (1977), conceptualizes parts as groups or strata of members. From our own point of view, these are collectivities that arise through social distinctions emergent with institutions. Such institutionally emergent distinctions (e.g., religion, political party, occupation, wealth) are purely classificatory, stratifying, or some combination of the two modes of specification. In this tradition, social integration rests on the formation of social associations between people in different collectivities, Blau's groups and strata. Associations that form between persons in the same collectivity — intragroup relations — are not integrative for the society as a whole. For Blau the formation of integrative associations is problematic due to the often observed tendency for people to associate (e.g., to marry, to become friends) with others like themselves; that is, relations tend to "inbreed" with respect to institutionally induced classificatory or stratifying dimensions. The basic idea in this tradition is to take the rates of intergroup social associations as "dependent" variables and thus, by extension, to take integration as a dependent variable, and to develop theoretical principles that relate (variable) properties of social structure to these rates. As is apparent, our institution foundation for the idea of systemwide collectivities connects to Blau's framework via the latter's presumption that we analytically can specify "parameters of social structure" (dimensions of differentiation or stratification) such that the equivalence classes generated by any *one* such dimension form a set of collectivities — men and women, blacks and whites, owners and workers, political elite and ordinary citizens, and so forth — usually with more than two collectivities per dimension.

The other tradition is associated with the "social networks" framework (Wellman 1983), in which social structural problems and properties are conceptualized with respect to the idea of a set of nodes tied to each other in one or more relations. Usually, in this approach, integrative problems are framed in terms of *paths* of ties linking nodes that do not necessarily directly associate. In particular, if a distinction is made between types of ties in terms of strength, an important principle in this framework is that

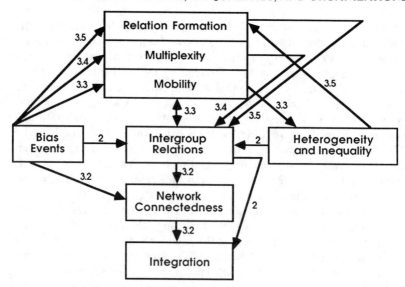

Figure 9.1. Components of the Theory
NOTE: Numbers on links refer to sections of the chapter.

weak ties constitute an important basis for integration of the network (Granovetter 1973, 1982). Another important idea in this tradition is that one can formulate "biased net" models in which a random net model functions as a generator of baseline expectations (Rapoport 1957; Fararo and Sunshine 1964).

In both traditions, it is a property of a relational network that "measures" the integration of the population spanned by the network. In the first, the key property is the extent to which relations join collectivities; in the second, it is the extent to which one node is reachable from another via indirect paths in the network. The two views on integration complement each other, occasionally coinciding in an intuitively clear way; for example, if no relations join collectivities, then any node in one collectivity cannot be reached from any node in other collectivities. One difference between the two traditions is the explicit concern of the first with how institutionally induced social structural properties — conceptualized in terms of differentiation and stratification — affect the associational network. But this difference is neither fundamental nor irremediable, as we show later.

Figure 9.1 summarizes the components of the theory we will discuss. As it makes clear, the theory addresses matters of long-standing interest to sociologists and has the potential to provide a rigorous, unified paradigm for their analysis.

The theory's scope is even broader than might first appear, for several reasons. First, the relational network to be modeled can be on different substantive levels of analysis as long as appropriately scaled relations and dimensions of differentiation can be discerned: Marriages between persons can be studied with the theory, but also mergers among organizations and trade relations among nations. Second, the theory is set out for a special type of relational network: The generating relation is symmetric and forms a uniform biased net, that is, (a) the biases affecting relations (e.g., an inbreeding bias that captures the tendency for people to choose as associates others like themselves) are invariant over collectivities distinguished by a social dimension, and (b) the average number of relations each node has is independent of collectivity membership. However, each of these restrictions could be relaxed and equations similar to those we will present could be derived. They would be more complicated but still usable in estimation and testing. For instance, if simple models fail on the grounds that inbreeding bias appears to vary over the relevant collectivities, all is not lost — more complex models that permit such variation can be developed (see Johnson 1980 for the case of religious intermarriage). Thus the theory can be developed to cover a variety of relation types, with the only loss being the elegance and simplicity of the theoretical relations.

Some linkages in the chart are explored in depth, while attention to the others is confined to exploration of theoretical consequences in simple types of networks. The chart also shows that the theory's basic explanatory concepts are heterogeneity (differentiation), inequality (stratification), and bias events. The former two concepts refer to population distributions over significant institutional dimensions and, more precisely, to properties of such distributions. The range of the "bias event" concept, on the other hand, is extended far beyond that initially required to formalize Blau's theory (like attracted to like): The theory also provides for outbreeding bias, stability bias, relation formation bias, multiplexity biases (which we term "pattern covariables" in a formalization of the diffuseness-specificity pattern variable) and "strength of weak ties" bias. These biases and their consequences mesh in an overarching formal-theoretical framework.

In effect, as in Blau (1964) there are two concepts or levels of social structure represented in the theory: One is *microstructure*, represented by the relational network among nodes; the other is *macrostructure*, represented by the distributions of nodes along institutional-level social dimensions defining systemwide collectivities (groups and strata) contingently connected via rates of association among members. The problem of integration is set up by the macrostructure's division of the population into collectivities. Integration of the collectivities, to the extent it occurs, is accomplished via the relational network. But properties of the network are, in turn, conditioned by the macrostructure. What is produced is either greater or lesser global integration as measured either by the extensiveness of intergroup relations or by the reachability of nodes from one another.

Part 2 of this chapter develops the basic ideas of the theory, which owe much to Blau (1977). In Part 3 we describe some current theoretical research in progress. In Part 4 we conclude with a discussion of the theoretical ideas presented in this chapter.

(2) Calculus of Heterogeneity and Inequality: Formalized Blau Theory

(2.1) INTRODUCTION

Consider a network in which (a) the number of nodes is very large, (b) there exist one or more bases of social differentiation of the nodes, and (c) these bases of differentiation yield nonrandomness in the patterning of relationships among the nodes. Our theory consists of a simple way to represent these facts and a variety of derived formulas that are used to explain various properties of structural data.

Either nodes or relations may be socially differentiated; there are classes or strata of members (collectivities) and types of ties between the nodes. In this section we consider networks with one or two dimensions of social differentiation of the nodes but treat the relationships as all of one kind. (In Sections 3.2 and 3.4, we discuss "multiple" networks with differentiated ties.) Given any one dimension of social differentiation of nodes, it may yield a classification of them or a stratification of them. For instance, the dimension of religion yields various religious collectivities, each of which contains all the "believers" of a given religion. The dimension of wealth yields stratified collectivities such as "the poor" and "the rich." Given any such dimension and given the meaning of the relation, the connection between relation and basis of differentiation may be random or biased. We assume, however, that institutionally grounded bases for social differentiation are nonrandomly connected to the relation. Hence we will postulate *bias parameters*, which are defined below.

In Section 2.2 we outline the basic definitions and analytic consequences for a single mode of differentiation or stratification. We do this with minor examples to help the reader follow a very compact statement that has been elaborated in discursive terms elsewhere, particularly in Skvoretz (1983) and Skvoretz and Fararo (1986). We distinguish these examples from applications to substantive explanatory contexts presented in Section 2.5.

In Section 2.3 we extend the results of Section 2.2 to the case of two bases of differentiation and/or stratification. The concept of "consolidation of parameters" arises here, typified by the cross-classification of members, the nodes. This consolidation is nothing but the correlation of the two bases of differentiation, but our model permits a very sharp demonstration of another use of a formalized theory: We deduce that the appropriate correlation measure is Goodman's and Kruskal's tau. In Section 2.4, we discuss certain issues in the testing of the theory. Finally, in Section 2.5, we discuss three applications of the formal theory. These applications involve the use of the formal calculus to account for anomalous findings (Section 2.5.1), logically to derive hypotheses already confirmed by data (Section 2.5.2), and to generate predictions (Section 2.5.3). These represent three of the ways in which a formalized theoretical apparatus can function in science. In Part 3, in contrast, we take on problems that are internal to the framework of biased network explanations of social structural regularities: modeling social integration via a synthesis of two formalized theories, modeling social mobility, representing and analyzing networks with an arbitrary number of types of ties, and modeling structural regularities from a relation formation viewpoint.

(2.2) NODE-DIFFERENTIATED/STRATIFIED 1-NETWORKS

A social network may be represented by a pair (M,R) such that M is a set of *nodes* and R is a set of *ties* between pairs of nodes. The nodes may be persons or they may be given other instantiations. When the network is represented in this way, no distinctions exist among nodes except that they differ in some way in terms of their patterns of ties (R). For our purposes it is necessary to begin with differentiated nodes. Hence we introduce one or more equivalence relations over M, each corresponding to a mode or dimension of differentiation. To initiate the presentation of our theory, we start with networks with one such mode of differentiation: We write (M,E,R) and say that this is a node-differentiated 1-network, where the 1 refers to the single equivalence relation or mode of differentiation. (Ties in R also may be differentiated, a topic to be discussed later in the chapter.)

Definition 1. Let (M,E,R) be a node-differentiated 1-network. Then the probability that two randomly selected nodes are differentiated is termed the *E-heterogeneity of the population M* and given by

$$H = 1 - \Sigma p_i^2 \qquad [1]$$

where p_i is the proportion of nodes in M in class i under E.

Example 1. Let E be gender differentiation, with 40% of M consisting of men, 60% of women, where E here induces two collectivities over a given system with membership M. Then H = .48 is the gender heterogeneity of M.

Definition 2. Let (M,E,R) be a node-differentiated 1-network. Then the probability that two nodes in relation R are differentiated is termed the *E-heterogeneity of the relation R* and given by

$$H_R = 1 - \Sigma r_i \qquad [2]$$

where r_i is the proportion of the ties in R in which both members are in class i under E.

Example 2. With E as gender differentiation, suppose that R is friendship — that is, a set of friendship ties among members in M. Suppose further that 90% of these ties are man-man or woman-woman; then H_R is .10. On the other hand, if R is marriage — a set of marriage ties — then $H_R = 1$.

Definition 3. Let (M,E,R) be a node-differentiated 1-network. Then the *salience* of E with respect to R is given by

$$S = H - H_R \qquad\qquad [3]$$

If $S \geq 0$, we term S *insalience* and if $S \leq 0$ we term it *outsalience*.

Example 3. Combining Examples 1 and 2, the salience of gender with respect to friendship is given by $S = .48 - .10 = .38$, a case of insalience. The salience of gender with respect to marriage is $S = .48 - 1 = -.52$, a case of outsalience.

Definition 4. A node-differentiated network (M,E,R) is termed random if, given M and E — given a population of differentiated members — ties in R are formed independently of each other and of E and with equal probabilities (subject to any formal constraints of particular random models).

> *Consequence 1.* In a random node-differentiated network (M,E,R) the E-heterogeneity of the relation is the same as the E-heterogeneity of the population, $H_R = H$, and so the salience of E with respect to R is zero.

Reasoning. Note that the event that two members of a tie both belong to class i has a probability r_i given by independence in a random network and each node has probability p_i of being in class i, so $r_i = p_i^2$.

Baseline model. A random network is a baseline model. The particular such model we employ is due to Rapoport (see Rapoport 1963; Fararo and Sunshine 1964). It involves the idea that the nodes are constrained to have an "element density a," meaning a is a parameter, interpretable as an average number of ties per node, which thus constrains the equal probability assumption to a form $P(aRb) = a/(m - 1)$. We have adopted the terminology of Mayhew and Levinger (1976) in speaking of "element density." Here m is the size of the population in M. For *symmetric* relations we add the constraint $P(bRa|aRb) = 1$.

Comment. A *biased network* is defined relative to this baseline model and our particular forms of bias are drawn from Fararo and Sunshine (1964). The basic bias parameters we employ initially are termed *inbreeding* (τ) and *outbreeding* (ϕ). These are defined implicitly in the following.

Definition 5. Let (M,E,R) be a node-differentiated 1-network in which E is insalient with respect to R. Then the *inbreeding bias parameter* τ is defined by:

$$P(E|R) = \tau + (1 - \tau)P(E) \qquad\qquad [4]$$

Since $P(E) = 1 - H$ and $P(E|R) = 1 - H_R$, we obtain the basic heterogeneity formula (insalience case):

$$H_R = (1 - \tau)H \qquad [5]$$

The baseline aspect is indicated by two consequences:

Consequence 2a. If the network is random, then $\tau = 0$ and we recover Consequence 1 as a special case, otherwise $H_R < H$.

Consequence 2b. The insalience is given by $S = \tau H$ (by Definition 3 and formula 2).

Comment. A thorough analysis of the theoretical implications of Consequence 2b is presented in Skvoretz (1983). Note that salience of E in respect to R is proportional to the E-heterogeneity of nodes. It should be noted that direct derivations of equation 5 and others in this part found in Skvoretz (1983) and Skvoretz and Fararo (1986) make clear that the formulas hold only if the relation forms a *uniform biased net* over the population; that is, the bias parameters are invariant over collectivities induced by E and each person has, on the average, about the same number of associations regardless of collectivity membership.

Example 4. In Examples 1 and 2, $H = .48$, $H_R = .10$ for friendship, and hence $\tau \cong .21$.

Definition 6. Let (M,E,R) be a node-differentiated 1-network in which E is outsalient with respect to R. Then the *outbreeding bias parameter* ϕ is defined by (with $\overline{E}$ the complement of E):

$$P(\overline{E}|R) = \phi + (1 - \phi)P(\overline{E}) \qquad [6]$$

Since $P(\overline{E}) = H$ and $P(\overline{E}|R) = H_R$, we obtain the basic heterogeneity formula (outsalience case):

$$H_R = \phi + (1 - \phi)H \qquad [7]$$

Consequence 3a. If the network is random, $\phi = 0$ and we recover the random baseline of Consequence 1, otherwise $H_R > H$.

Consequence 3b. The outsalience is given by $S = -\phi(1 - H)$.

Comment. A thorough analysis of outsalience is given in Skvoretz (1983), using the absolute value of S as the general measure of salience.

Example 5a. In Examples 1 and 2 for marriage, $H = .48$ and $H_R = 1$, so that $\phi = 1$.

Example 5b. Consider the interpretation of R as conflict, a symmetric relation between or within members of classes. It is plausible that we postulate a ϕ-bias and so with R replaced by C for conflict:

$$H_C = \phi + (1 - \phi)H$$

with ϕ thought of as a *loyalty-bias* parameter: If it vanishes, there is no real class conflict, since $H_C = H$, while higher values of ϕ more and more concentrate conflict to *between* classes, as measured by the heterogeneity of the conflict relation.

We now consider node-differentiated networks in which the differentiation is induced on a graduated basis: Each node has an *amount* of some institutionalized social resource, denoted X, and it is meaningful to speak of distances. We assume, further, that the analyst divides M into *strata* using X. Then we treat distance as zero within a stratum and assume that equal intervals exist between strata. Given these assumptions, we define concepts and derive formulas parallel to the heterogeneity analysis. We term (M,X,R) a node-stratified 1-network.

Definition 7. Let (M,X,R) be a node-stratified 1-network. Then the average distance between two nodes divided by twice the mean X is the *Gini inequality of the population M*:

$$G = \frac{E(D)}{2E(X)} \qquad [8]$$

where we find it useful to use expectation notation in theoretical work; we think of randomly choosing a pair of nodes and determining their values of X and their distance.

Example 6. Suppose we have the distribution of X over M with X scaled so that X = 1,2,3:

$$X = 1 \quad 2 \quad 3$$
$$P_X = .3 \quad .5 \quad .2$$

The E(X) = 1.9 and the distance distribution via random pairing is as follows:

$$D = 0 \quad 1 \quad 2$$
$$P_D = .38 \quad .50 \quad .12$$

The E(D) = .74. Therefore G = .195.

Definition 8. Let (M,X,R) be a node-stratified 1-network. Then the average distance between two nodes in relation R, divided by twice the mean X, is the *Gini inequality of the relation R* (which we also call the relation or network inequality):

$$G_R = \frac{E(D|R)}{2E(X)} \qquad [9]$$

where E(D|R) is calculated from a distribution in which the interpretation is that we randomly select a *tie* in R and find the distances between the two nodes so tied.

Consequence 4. If the network is random so that X is independent of R, then $G_R = G$.

Example 7. Let X and its distribution be as in Example 6, so that $E(X) = 1.9$. Assume that the following gives rates of associational ties, expressed as proportions of all ties:

$$
\begin{array}{c@{\quad}c}
 & \begin{array}{ccc} 1 & 2 & 3 \end{array} \\
\begin{array}{c} 1 \\ 2 \\ 3 \end{array} & \left(\begin{array}{ccc} .20 & .10 & .05 \\ .10 & .20 & .05 \\ .05 & .05 & .20 \end{array} \right)
\end{array}
$$

From this, we compute:

$$E(D|R) = 1(.20 + .10) + 2(.10) = .50$$

Hence $G_R = .153$.

Definition 9. Let (M,X,R) be a node-stratified 1-network. Then the *salience* of X with respect to R is given by

$$S = G - G_R \qquad [10]$$

If $S \geq 0$, we term S *insalience*; if $S \leq 0$, we term it *outsalience*.

Example 8. In Examples 6 and 7, we find that $S = .042$.

Note on the bias model. The baseline model remains the same, but there are choices in the formulation of the bias model. We assume the simplest model: $D = 0$ corresponds to E in the node-differentiated network, so we propose that the τ-bias or the ϕ-bias constructs apply, depending on the salience direction. With this assumption, for the τ case we have:

$$P(D = 0|R) = P(E|R) = \tau + (1 - \tau)(1 - H) \qquad [11a]$$
$$P(D = k|R) = (1 - \tau)P(D = k) \quad \text{(for k>0)} \qquad [11b]$$

Then for $E(D|R)$ we obtain:

$$E(D|R) = \Sigma k P(D = k|R) = (1 - \tau)\sum_{k>0} k\, P(D = k) = (1 - \tau)E(D) \qquad [12]$$

Hence, dividing by 2E(X), we obtain the basic inequality formula (insalience case):

$$G_R = (1 - \tau)G \qquad [13]$$

Consequence 5a. If $\tau = 0$, we recover Consequence 4 as a special case; otherwise $G_R < G$.

Consequence 5b. The insalience is given by $S = \tau G$.

Comment. A discussion of the implications of this consequence may be found in Skvoretz and Fararo (1986).

Example 9. Given G and G_R of Examples 6 and 7, $\tau = .216$, which is reflected in the main diagonal of the table of Example 7.

In treating the outsalient case, we have:

$$P(D = 0|R) = (1 - \phi)P(D = 0)$$
$$P(D = k|R) = \phi P(D = k|B_o) + (1 - \phi)P(D = k) \quad (k>0)$$

where B_o is the unobserved outbreeding bias event. Hence

$$E(D|R) = \phi \sum_{k>0} kP(D=k|B_o) + (1-\phi) \sum_{k>0} kP(D=k)$$

From this expression, we obtain the basic inequality formula (outsalience case):

$$G_R = [1 + \phi(Z - 1)]G \qquad [14]$$

Here $Z \geq 1$, where Z is the ratio of $E(D|B_o)$ to $E(D)$.

Comment. This formula is mainly of theoretical interest, since standing alone it involves two unknowns.

Consequence 6. If $\phi = 0$, then $Z = 1$ and $G_R = G$; otherwise $G_R > G$.

Figure 9.2 summarizes the basic formulas and shows how they logically derive from the concepts by using tree diagrams: To obtain H_R, sum all path probabilities leading to $\bar{E}$; to obtain G_R, sum all path probabilities leading to nonzero expectations (expressed as G or ZG).

(2.3) NODE-DIFFERENTIATED/STRATIFIED 2-NETWORKS

Consider now two simultaneous modes of differentiation of nodes. These can be of three types: both classificatory, both stratifying, or one of each. In any of the three cases, each mode of differentiation in connection with the relation R may be inbreeding or outbreeding. Hence there are six models to consider. Of these, we exhibit the logic of three of these six possibilities — for later reference, when we show how they account for certain phenomena. These are as follows:

- *Model M1:* two classificatory dimensions, both inbreeding
- *Model M2:* two graduated dimensions, both inbreeding
- *Model M3:* one classification dimension that is general (mixed) and one stratifying inbreeding dimension

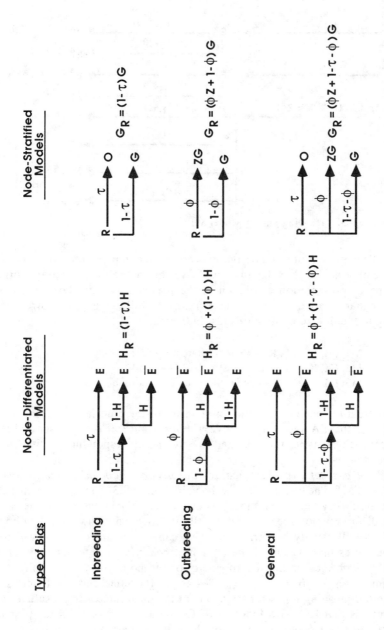

Figure 9.2. Diagram for Derivation of Basic Formulas

223

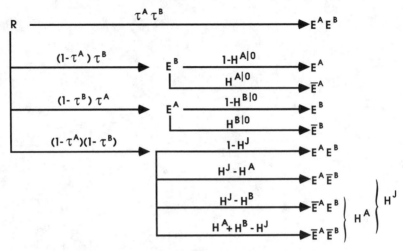

Figure 9.3. Tree Diagram for Model M1

The assumptions and derivations are more complex here, so we rely on tree diagrams to show the logic of the various models instead of the formal type of presentation employed in the previous section. For continuity, note that we are dealing with networks of the following types, corresponding to the three combinations just indicated:

- M1: (M, E^A, E^B, R) — a node-differentiated 2-network
- M2: (M, X, Y, R) — a node-stratified 2-network
- M3: (M, E, X, R) — a node-differentiated/stratified 2-network

We treat the node differentiation in terms of the criteria that define them, calling them A and B, respectively. For instance, if A is gender and B is occupational type, then E^A and E^B are the corresponding equivalences on M.

The case of two classificatory dimensions, both inbreeding. This is Model M1. The tree diagram is shown in Figure 9.3. The basic assumption of the theory here is that the *bias* events on distinct bases or dimensions of differentiation are probabilistically independent. However, the dimensions will usually be correlated. This can be explained in terms of new quantities that appear on the branches: *conditional heterogeneity* terms. $H^{A|0}$ is defined as the heterogeneity of the population, as classified by dimension A, *given* that the nodes are in the same class in B terms. A similar meaning holds for $H^{B|0}$. One of the most interesting results of our work is that $H^{A|0}$ is a function of Goodman and Kruskal's familiar tau statistics (see Skvoretz 1983 for the original derivation and Fararo and Skvoretz 1984a for another discussion). Namely, it can be shown that

$$H^{A|0} = H^A(1 - tau_{A|0}) \qquad [15a]$$
$$H^{B|0} = H^B(1 - tau_{B|0}) \qquad [15b]$$

$Tau_{A|0}$ is the PRE statistic in which we "predict" A, given B information, and $tau_{B|0}$ is in the other direction. From Figure 9.3 we compute three quantities that exhibit the connection between classes: H_R^A, the heterogeneity of relation R, along the A dimension; H_R^B, the heterogeneity of relation R, along the B dimension; and H_R^J, the heterogeneity of relation R, along the joint dimension $J = A \times B$ (the Cartesian product), where (recall formula 1 above):

$$H^J = 1 - \sum_{ij} p_{ij}^2 \qquad [16]$$

with p_{ij} the probability that a randomly selected node is in cell (i,j) of the cross-classification. To obtain H_R^A we simply compute the sum of all path probabilities leading to $\bar{E}^A$. To calculate H_R^B, we sum over paths to $\bar{E}^B$. For H_R^J we add over all paths except those leading to $E^A E^B$. Hence we obtain

$$H_R^A = (1 - \tau^A) [\tau^B H^{A|0} + (1 - \tau^B) H^A] \qquad [17a]$$
$$H_R^B = (1 - \tau^B) [\tau^A H^{B|0} + (1 - \tau^A) H^B] \qquad [17b]$$
$$H_R^J = (1 - \tau^A) \tau^B H^{A|0} + (1 - \tau^B) \tau^A H^{B|0} + (1 - \tau^A)(1 - \tau^B) H^J \qquad [17c]$$

Using equations 15a and 15b, we then obtain from equations 17a, 17b, and 17c:

$$H_R^A = (1 - \tau^A) H^A (1 - \tau^B tau_{A|0}) \qquad [18a]$$
$$H_R^B = (1 - \tau^B) H^B (1 - \tau^A tau_{B|0}) \qquad [18b]$$
$$H_R^J = H_R^A + H_R^B - (1 - \tau^A)(1 - \tau^B)(H^A + H^B - H^J) \qquad [18c]$$

Two stratifying dimensions, both inbreeding. This is Model M2. In Figure 9.4 we show the tree diagram for two inbreeding dimensions of stratification. The branches show a new concept, the Gini inequality of the population with respect to X, given equality with respect to Y, denoted $G^{X|0}$. Here *equality* means in the same class, and this, in turn, means distance zero in our representation. A similar meaning holds for $G^{Y|0}$. From the tree we obtain, by summing over all branches leading to some amount of X-inequality within R,

$$G_R^X = (1 - \tau^X)[\tau^Y G^{X|0} + (1 - \tau^Y) G^X] \qquad [19]$$

Similarly,

$$G_R^Y = (1 - \tau^Y)[\tau^X G^{Y|0} + (1 - \tau^X) G^Y] \qquad [20]$$

It can be shown that, with status J defined by a weighted summation over X and Y — that is, $J = w_1 X + w_2 Y$, so that $E(J) = w_1 E(X) + w_2 E(Y)$ — we obtain:

$$G_R^J = a(1 - \tau^X)\tau^Y G^{X|0} + b(1 - \tau^Y)\tau^X G^{Y|0} + (1 - \tau^X)(1 - \tau^Y) G^J \qquad [21]$$

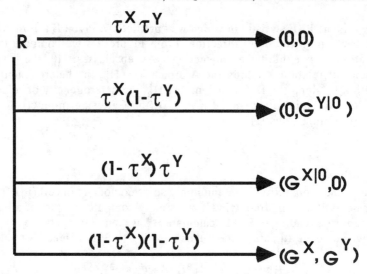

Figure 9.4. Tree Diagram for Model M2

where

$$a = \frac{w_1 E(X)}{w_1 E(X) + w_2 E(Y)}, \quad b = \frac{w_2 E(Y)}{w_1 E(X) + w_2 E(Y)} \qquad [22]$$

Hence we have obtained formulas for the inequality of the relation R in respect to dimensions X, Y, and J.

As in the case of the cross-classification by two dimensions, it turns out that the conditional Gini inequalities $G^{X|0}$ and $G^{Y|0}$ can be expressed in terms of a PRE statistic, but it is not one in common use. Namely, if we define

$$\text{beta}_{X|0} = \frac{G^X - G^{X|0}}{G^X} \qquad [23a]$$

$$\text{beta}_{Y|0} = \frac{G^Y - G^{Y|0}}{G^Y} \qquad [23b]$$

then we obtain

$$G_R^X = (1 - \tau^X)(1 - \tau^Y \text{beta}_{X|0})G^X \qquad [24a]$$
$$G_R^Y = (1 - \tau^Y)(1 - \tau^X \text{beta}_{Y|0})G^Y \qquad [24b]$$
$$G_R^J = a(1 - \tau^X)\tau^Y G^X(1 - \text{beta}_{X|0}) \qquad [24c]$$
$$+ b(1 - \tau^Y)\tau^X G^Y(1 - \text{beta}_{Y|0}) + (1 - \tau^X)(1 - \tau^Y)G^J$$

A general classificatory and an inbreeding graduated case. This is Model M3. Here one dimension, call it A, is classificatory and mixed as

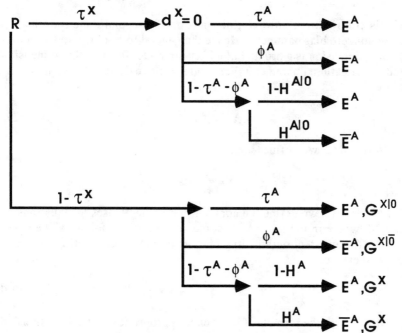

Figure 9.5. Tree Diagram for Model M3

to bias type, while the other dimension is an inbreeding stratifying one. Figure 9.5 shows the tree diagram.

We obtain:

$$H_R^A = 1 - \tau^A - (1 - \tau^A - \phi^A)[\tau^X(1 - H^{A|0}) + (1 - \tau^X)(1 - H^A)] \quad [25a]$$
$$G_R^X = (1 - \tau^X)[\tau^A G^{X|0} + \phi^A G^{X|\bar{0}} + (1 - \tau^A - \phi^A)G^X] \quad [25b]$$

Note that $H^{A|0}$ has the same meaning as in the case where the other dimension is classificatory. Recall also that $G^{X|0} = G^X(1 - \text{beta}_{X|0})$. While $G^{X|\bar{0}}$ can also be expressed in an analogous manner (see Fararo and Skvoretz 1984a), we simply write $G^{X|\bar{0}} = G^X K$, where K is a function of a correlation measure. Hence the last two equations become:

$$H_R^A = (1 - \tau^A)H^A(1 - \tau^X \text{tau}_{A|0}) + \phi^A[1 - H^A(1 - \tau^X \text{tau}_{A|0})] \quad [26a]$$
$$G_R^X = (1 - \tau^X)G^X(1 - \tau^A \text{beta}_{X|0}) + \phi^A(1 - \tau^X)(1 - K)G^X \quad [26b]$$

Analysis of Models M1, M2, and M3. The analysis of the implications of the derived equations for the three 2-network models is aided by the introduction of a new construct we term the *apparent bias*. The general idea is that the correlation of a second dimension with a given dimension produces a contribution to the salience of this latter dimension *even if* the dimension itself lacks any bias relation to the relation R. The effectiveness of this contribution, however, depends on the second dimension having some nonzero bias parameter. Hence the general form of the apparent bias on one dimension is a product of a bias parameter for the other dimension and a correlational parameter. For Model M1, we define the apparent bias $\bar{\tau}^A$ by:

$$\bar{\tau}^A = \tau^B tau_{A|0} \qquad [27]$$

For Model M2, we define

$$\bar{\tau}^X = \tau^Y beta_{X|0} \qquad [28]$$

For Model M3, we define the apparent inbreeding biases by equations 27 and 28, where in the latter τ^Y becomes τ^A and in the former τ^B becomes τ^X. For the apparent outbreeding bias we define, since $1 - K$ is a correlational measure,

$$\bar{\phi}^X = \phi^A(1 - K) \qquad [29]$$

Now we use the formulas for salience appropriate to differentiation and stratification — 3 and 10, respectively — replacing H_R and G_R terms from the derived equations for the three models with apparent bias terms also substituted. When all this is done, we obtain the formulas for salience in the three models:

- Model M1:

$$S^A = \tau^A H^A + (1-\tau^A)H^A \bar{\tau}^A \qquad [30]$$

- Model M2:

$$S^X = \tau^X G^X + (1-\tau^X)G^X \bar{\tau}^X \qquad [31]$$

- Model M3:

$$S^A = (\tau^A + \phi^A)H^A + [1 - (\tau^A + \phi^A)]H^A \bar{\tau}^A - \phi^A \qquad [32a]$$
$$S^X = \tau^X G^X + (1 - \tau^X)G^X(\bar{\tau}^X - \bar{\phi}^X) \qquad [32b]$$

Consider Model M1. Suppose that $\tau^A = 0$, so that E^A is independent of R. Nevertheless, the salience of A can be nonzero. Equation 30 for Model M1 shows that in such a case $S^A = \bar{\tau}^A H^A$. This result bears a formal resemblance to $S^A = \tau^A H^A$ for the 1-network. The difference is in the interpretation: In the 2-network context, we are saying that the bias term is only apparent, that is, it is induced by a correlation with a second mode of node differentiation. The general rule, obvious in equation 30, is that *apparent bias increases the salience of a mode of node differentiation that is inbreeding in respect to the relation.* Analogous results hold for stratification, by examination of formula 31. The results for Model M3 are more complex, but it is clear that in formula 32a an increase in apparent bias produces an increase in the salience of A and in 32b the apparent inbreeding bias increases salience, while the apparent outbreeding bias decreases it (thereby increasing outsalience). Note that formula 30 is a special case of 32a and that formula 31 is a special case of 32b.

(2.4) TESTING PROCEDURES

A difference arises in the testing procedures between classificatory and stratified dimensions. For the former, the dependent variable H_R is interpretable as the probability that a given relation is an interclass or intergroup one, thus a maximum likelihood estimation and testing framework may be used. For the latter, the dependent variable G_R cannot be interpreted as a probability, and current thinking on test procedures is to use a least-squares estimation and testing framework. This section briefly discusses both, using marriages as the relation of interest, as has been done in previous tests of Blau's original theory (Blau et al. 1982; Blum 1984; Rytina et al. 1988), with the focus being SMSA intermarriage rates as a function of the structural properties of SMSAs.

For node-differentiated 1-networks, let i index SMSAs where O_i is the observed number of outmarriages and I_i the observed number of inmarriages along some classificatory dimension, and H_i is the heterogeneity of the dimension in the ith SMSA. Since $(1 - \tau)H_i$ is the probability that any given marriage in the ith SMSA is an out-group one, $1 - (1 - \tau)H_i$ is the probability it is an in-group one, and the process may be viewed as Bernoulli. That is, the likelihood of exactly I_i inmarriages and O_i outmarriages under these probabilities is given by, for the ith SMSA:

$$L_i(\tau) = [(1 - \tau)H_i]^{O_i}[1 - (1 - \tau)H_i]^{I_i} \qquad [33]$$

The likelihood of the data over all SMSAs is given by multiplying the likelihoods within each:

$$L(\tau) = \Pi L_i(\tau) = \Pi[(1 - \tau)H_i]^{O_i}(1 - (1 - \tau)H_i]^{I_i} \qquad [34]$$

It is this expression that can be used to estimate τ by finding the value for τ that maximizes $L(\tau)$. Since the estimate is likely to be difficult to obtain analytically, an iterative approximation procedure, such as the one available in program P3R of the BMDP statistical package, must be used. The fit of a model may be assessed by the χ^2 goodness-of-fit statistic. Likelihood ratio χ^2 statistics may be used to assess the model in relation to two extremes: the baseline model in which, within an SMSA, marriages are held to form independently of the dimension; and the "saturated" model, in which the probability that a marriage is out-group is estimated by the relative frequency of outmarriages in that SMSA.

These procedures test a complex set of assumptions, any one of which could be at fault. The accuracy of the 1-network expression for the probability that a marriage is an out-group/in-group one depends on the assumptions (a) that the relation forms a uniform biased net in each SMSA; (b) that either other dimensions along which marriage is inbreeding are not correlated with the focal one or for those dimensions that are so correlated, marriage is neither inbreeding nor outbreeding; and (c) that gender is distributed independently of the focal dimension. If a simple 1-network model displays a serious lack of fit, any one or a combination of the above assumptions may be at fault. Conversely, satisfactory fit confirms their tenability.

For node-stratified 1-networks, the dependent quantity is not a probability, although the underlying model from which it is derived has a probabilistic basis and hence may also be estimated and tested at this level by maximum likelihood methods. However, to test it directly on the relational inequality quantities, a least-squares estimation technique appears suitable, in which the equation to be estimated is $Y = aX$, where Y is G_R, X is G, and $a = 1 - \tau$. Standard tests of fit are available, and again the accuracy depends on a similar set of assumptions so that lack of fit indicates that one or more are faulty.

(2.5) ILLUSTRATIVE APPLICATIONS

In this section, we want to display three ways in which the formal theory can be related to substantive problems. First, it can be used to explain findings that are anomalies from the standpoint of the nonformalized Blau theory; second, it can be used to derive a general hypothesis already confirmed by data; and third, it can be used to generate new predictions. These three types of applications are now illustrated.

(2.5.1) Intergroup Marriage: An Anomaly

Recent research on marriage by Blau and his colleagues (Blau et al. 1982; Blum 1984) confirmed, with one major exception, the basic claim embodied in equation 5 that heterogeneity is positively related to intergroup relations. The exception was the classificatory dimension of race: Although race was salient — that is, interracial marriages were well below chance expectations — no positive bivariate relation between racial heterogeneity of an SMSA and interracial marriage was found. Further exploration by Blau and his colleagues provided two complementary interpretations of the anomaly. The first attributed it to economic status — itself an inbreeding dimension with respect to marriage — being more strongly correlated with race in SMSAs where racial heterogeneity was greater. Blau et al. (1982) found a positive relation between racial heterogeneity and interracial marriage when the economic-race correlation was statistically controlled. The second interpretation, offered by Blum (1984), also attributed the anomaly to the positive association between racial heterogeneity and the economic status-race correlation, but went on to argue that the greater the correlation, the more salient would be race, and hence race would be more salient in SMSAs of greater racial heterogeneity. Thus the zero-order relationship between racial heterogeneity and interracial marriage would be attenuated.

Both views are derivable from our mathematical theory. The key equations are equation 26a, with the A dimension as race, the X as economic status, and $\tau_{A|0}$ representing the correlation of economic status with race, and equation 32a, with τ^A representing the apparent inbreeding bias on race induced by the correlation of economic status with race and the actual inbreeding bias along economic status. The equations are reproduced here (with $\varphi^A = 0$ and $\overline{\tau}^A = \tau^X$ tau $_{A|0}$):

$$H_R^A = (1 - \tau^A)H^A(1 - \tau^X tau_{A|0}) \qquad [26a]$$
$$S^A = \tau^A H^A + (1 - \tau^A)H^A \overline{\tau}^A \qquad [26b]$$

To derive the anomaly, note that the differential of H_R^A with respect to H^A is positive — increasing heterogeneity implies greater relational heterogeneity — that is, a greater probability that a marriage is interracial. But the differential of H_R^A with respect to tau$_{A|0}$ is negative — the greater the correlation of economic status with race, the smaller the probability that a marriage is interracial. Thus to the extent (a) racial heterogeneity and (b) the economic status-race correlation covary positively over SMSAs, the gain in interracial marriage produced by an increase in a is offset by the loss produced as a result of the corresponding increase in b. Thus at the bivariate level, no relationship between racial heterogeneity and interracial marriage may obtain.

That salience is implicated in the anomaly is derivable from the second equation. The differential of S^A with respect to H^A is positive, and so too is its differential with respect to tau$_{A|0}$ since the apparent bias τ^A is an increasing function of tau$_{A|0}$: The salience of race increases over and above the level implied by given increase in racial heterogeneity if the latter is accompanied by an increase in the economic status-race correlation. This means that intraracial marriages are more common and interracial marriages less common than can be accounted for by the degree of racial heterogeneity alone. Thus racial heterogeneity's association with interracial marriage is much weaker than it would be if the economic status-race correlation had no association with heterogeneity.

(2.5.2) Feld's Hypothesis

In a recent research note, Feld (1982) argues that much of what is often interpreted as "in-group preference" in the formation of social associations is actually due to "foci of activity." These foci, such as neighborhoods and work settings, he argues, are the initial conditions of the association process — an argument resembling that of Homans (1950) in regard to the "external system." Also, such foci tend to involve disproportionately homogeneous sets of people. Feld provides evidence of the latter hypothesis in terms of data on friendships in a factory where the foci are the various work departments and the homogeneity is with respect to age.

We now show that our mathematical theory implies this hypothesis, thereby both corroborating the theory and rationalizing the hypothesis. In this section, we derive Feld's empirically confirmed hypothesis.

The starting point involves noticing that a set of work departments constitutes a nominal characteristic, say B, whereas the intradepartment heterogeneity is with respect to a second nominal or graduated parameter (such as age in Feld's data source). So in terms of our framework Feld's Hypothesis, to be proved, states:

(1) The population homogeneity of A within categories of B tends to be larger than the overall population homogeneity of A;

(2) this tendency gets reflected in the association rate so that some part of the homogeneity of the relation $(1 - H_R^A)$ is *not* due to any inbreeding bias (τ^A) but to the fact above.

To derive part 1 of Feld's Hypothesis, note that $1 - H^{A|0}$ is the conditional homogeneity. Since $0 \leq \text{tau}_{A|0} \leq 1$, we know that $H^{A|0} \leq H^A$ from formula 15a, so that $1 - H^{A|0} \geq 1 - H^A$.

Next note that the greater the conditional homogeneity, the greater the value of $1 - H_R^A$, if $\tau^B \neq 0$, even if $\tau^A = 0$. This is part 2 of Feld's Hypothesis.

Feld's argument actually is an instance of the flexibility of interpretation of the τ-bias; we could not derive Feld's proposition if $\tau^B = 0$. What this means is that some underlying bias events make foci of activity germane to social associations and this is sufficient to generate $1 - H_R^A > 1 - H^A$, its random expectation, even if $\tau^A = 0$.

(2.5.3) Citation, Recognition, and Scientific Value

According to the literature on the sociology of science, rewards come in the "coin of recognition" (Merton 1957). And the concrete coins are most frequently identified as citations (Ben-David and Sullivan 1975). Hence there is a citation distribution in any population of scientists. Over this distribution of citations we can define the Gini inequality G^c. The status of a scientist may be defined in terms of the scientific value of his or her contributions, as determined by standing on the shared values that lead to evaluations of the contributions. Hence a "scientific status" distribution exists and we can define its Gini inequality G^s.

These two measures refer to the inequality of the population (of a scientific community). If we let R be a symmetric relation of association among these scientists, we have a node-stratified 2-network (M,c,s,R).

Let R and s be connected by insalience: Scientists tend to associate with others of similar status. Do scientists associate with others similar as to citations? Probably the answer is yes, but our hypothesis would be that R and c are unrelated directly. The explanation for any observed tendency for citations to be insalient with respect to associations then would be given by apparent bias depending on the consolidation of citations with scientific status.

Formally, we first write formula 30 in terms of c and s:

$$S^c = \tau^c H^c + (1 - \tau^c)H^c \overline{\tau}^c$$

where, from formula 28,

$$\overline{\tau}^c = \tau^s \text{beta}_{c|0}$$

Now our hypothesis is that in this instance $\tau^c = 0$, so that

$$S^c = \overline{\tau}^c H^c = \tau^s \text{beta}_{c|0} H^c \qquad [35]$$

Hence the salience of citations to associations is "purely apparent" in that it arises from the consolidation (correlation) of "symbols" (citations) with "reality" (value of scientific contributions) and the τ^s-bias, which links the latter status stratification to associations in science. A test of this prediction would involve examining associational data for a scientific community for which we can determine both the scientific status of members and their cumulative citation counts.

(3) Theoretical Models in Progress

(3.1) INTRODUCTION

In the previous section, we presented the fundamental formulas derived from the biased net representation of social structure, as motivated by the effort to contribute to the theoretical solution of the problem of integration of overlapping systemwide collectivities. In this part, we present the results of four theoretical investigations that have arisen in attempting to improve the theory by extending its scope, by integrating it with other theories, or by treating as problematic what it takes as given. In these investigations, then, the theoretical research program has exhibited what has been called "proliferation" (Berger et al. 1985). New constructs are introduced, novel problems emerge, fresh puzzles arise, and, as a result, there are more loose ends. The theory acquires the look and feel of being "in progress." Although the basic thematic focus is still the problem of integration of a system of overlapping collectivities, as defined earlier in Part 1, the various theoretical models differ in how directly they bear on this problem. In Section 3.2, the problem is very directly approached as we attempt to integrate formally the two strands of structuralist theorizing we described in Part 1, that deriving from Blau (1977) and that deriving from Granovetter (1973), by use of novel constructs and derivations within the biased net framework. (This unification, using a somewhat different formulation, is also reported in Fararo and Skvoretz 1987.) In Section 3.3, our attention turns to social mobility as represented in this framework in order to study how it affects the basic properties of social structure that enter into our fundamental formulas. In Section 3.4, we turn to multiplexity, treated in terms of what we call the pattern covariables of diffuseness-specificity, represented as bias parameters, in order to link our theory to the classic idea that increasing differentiation means, in part, increasing specificity, and then we ask how this relates to the social integration problem. Finally, in Section 3.5, we treat the relationship between the formal concepts E and R — the equivalence relation and the association relation in our network models of Part 2 — in a reversed fashion; now the focus is on terms of the form $P(R|E)$ rather than $P(E|R)$. We call this the relation formation point of view and derive a formula displaying how the τ-bias can be expressed as a function of structural parameters and the new "relation formation bias." In short, we present here four partially independent lines of formal-theoretical investigation (which can be read independently, we may add).

(3.2) SWT-τ THEORY AND THE DILEMMA OF INTEGRATION

The principle that networks be analyzed relative to a random baseline has been employed so far only in respect to biases that connect a mode of node differentiation or stratification to ties between nodes, such as τ-bias. A second type of bias parameter is defined with respect to the structure of the relation itself. Namely, assuming a symmetric relation R, we define "σ-bias" by the expression

$$P(aRb|cRa \text{ and } cRb) = \sigma + (1 - \sigma)P(aRb) \qquad [36]$$

The event of interest here is the existence of a tie between two nodes conditional on their both being related to a third node; or, we could say that σ is the chance that two "associates" of a node are themselves associates. In terms of the complementary event that the tie does *not* exist:

$$P(a\overline{R}b|cRa \text{ and } cRb) = (1 - \sigma)[1 - P(aRb)] \qquad [37]$$

In the context of a net with element density a, the term $P(aRb)$ is simply

$$P(aRb) = \frac{a}{m - 1} = d \qquad [38]$$

where d is the usual "density" — the fraction of all possible ties that actually exist. Hence formula 37 becomes

$$P(a\overline{R}b|cRa \text{ and } cRb) = (1 - \sigma)(1 - d) \qquad [39]$$

In our analyses, we always assume a very large population of the network and, by comparison with this population size, a very small element density a. Hence d is negligible and we can approximate the right-hand side of formula 39 by $1 - \sigma$ and interpret $1 - \sigma$ as (approximately) the *intransitivity bias*, since the probability of an intransitive event is, by symmetry of R:

$$P(a\overline{R}b|aRc \text{ and } cRb) = P(a\overline{R}b|cRa \text{ and } cRb)$$

Consider the a nodes tied to a typical node. There are $a(a - 1)$ pairs of them in which the typical node plays the structural role of c in the above expressions. Hence an expected $(1 - \sigma)a(a - 1)$ of these pairs are not "closed" in the sense that they are tied. If we divide this expression by a, we obtain a *reduced element density*, denoted α:

$$\alpha = (1 - \sigma)(a - 1) \qquad [40]$$

The meaning of α can be visualized in a *tracing*: Starting from an origin (t = 0) with one node, at step t = 1 we list the nodes tied to that node (and on the average there are a of these), then at step t + 1 list the nodes tied to those at t but not reached thus far in the tracing, for t = 1, 2, ... The average number of nodes *newly* reached at t = 2 will be α by formula 40, since each node at step 1 has $a - 1$ ties that *might* be listed at step 2 (since the node at step 0 is such a tie, we subtract one). Of these $a - 1$ nodes, σ of them will be tied to this typical node at step 1, via the meaning of σ-bias. Hence, on the average, the *reduced density* in tracing from step 1 to step 2 will be α. Of course, some of the previously reached nodes may be "targets" by chance.

Note that if $\sigma = 1$, then $\alpha = 0$; no new nodes are reachable at t = 2 so the network consists of a set of disjoint subnetworks, each of size a + 1. If $\sigma = 0$, then $\alpha = a$ and the network is generated by a random net model with element density a.

We define the *structure statistics* as the expected fractions of nodes reached for t = 0, 1, 2, ... There is a recursion equation for the structure statistics. Let P(t) be the expected fraction of nodes newly reached at step t and let X(t) be the expected cumulative fraction reached by step t. For a random net with element density a, it can be shown (Rapoport 1963) that

$$P(t + 1) = [1 - X(t)][1 - e^{-aP(t)}] \qquad (t \geq 0) \qquad [41]$$

Given a and P(0) — which is conveniently 1/m in the above example — then we calculate P(1). Given P(0) and P(1) as well as a, we calculate P(2), and so forth. It can be shown (Rapoport 1963) that the expected fraction reachable, denoted γ and called the *connectedness*, which is the limit of X(t) as t increases, is given by the following approximation formula:

$$\gamma \cong 1 - [1 - P(0)]e^{-a\gamma} \tag{42}$$

If P(0) is very small,

$$\gamma \cong 1 - e^{-a\gamma} \tag{43}$$

This expression can be solved numerically and yields values showing that γ is a monotone increasing function of a.

For the calculation of the structure statistics of a biased net model, prior publications have stated the principle that beyond the first step in the tracing, these statistics are the same as those of a *random* net with actual density α (Fararo and Sunshine 1964; Fararo 1981a, 1983). The more correct statement is as follows: Define a sequence P*(0), P*(1), . . . as follows: Let P*(0) = P(1), where P(1) is obtained from formula 41. Then generate the sequence of P*(t) via the following modification of formula 41:

$$P^*(t + 1) = [1 - P(0) - X^*(t)][1 - e^{-\alpha P^*(t)}] \quad (t \geq 0) \tag{41'}$$

where X*(t) = P*(0) + P*(1) + . . . + P*(t).

Then the expected structure statistics of the biased net are given by the sequence P(0), P(1), P(2) = P*(1), P(3) = P*(2), ... Also, $\gamma = \gamma^* + P(0)$, where γ^* satisfies equation 42 with P(0) replaced by P*(0) and a replaced by α. Since P*(0) = P(1) may *not* be "very small" even if P(0) *is* very small, we may not be able to use expression 43. Nevertheless, the general rule holds: The higher the value of the reduced density α, the greater the connectedness of the biased net. This yields the connectedness as a function of the σ-bias: The higher the σ-bias, the lower the reduced density α, and hence the lower the connectedness. Conversely, the larger the (1 − σ) bias, the greater the connectedness.

Our first aim is to prove a basic theorem of what we call "SWT theory," meaning "strength of weak ties theory," originated in a paper by Granovetter and in a restricted version derived from the biased net framework by Fararo (1983). Following this, we discuss how we can relate SWT theory and "τ theory" to generate one or more versions of an "SWT-τ theory."

As a prelude to the mathematical developments, we will summarize the basic ideas in Granovetter (1973). The *strength* of a tie refers, intuitively, to the spectrum from very minimal acquaintance to deep friendship and is reflected in such phenomena as time spent together, emotional intensity and intimacy of the relationship, and reciprocal services. For simplicity, one thinks of a relationship as either strong or weak, with *friendship* and *acquaintance* as the contrasting pair of terms.

The basic postulate is that when two people are strongly tied to a third they are likely to be either acquaintances or friends themselves. Granovetter's reasoning develops the implications of this postulate in its idealized form, in which "likely" becomes "certain." The fundamental consequence, which Granovetter develops in considerable detail, is that weak rather than strong ties provide the connections among local groups of strongly tied persons. This is illustrated in terms of such empirical contexts as diffusion studies, small world experiments, and a job-change study. In these contexts weak ties are strong in terms of connecting or integrating otherwise fragmented parts of a system.

In sum, the fundamental structural principle that is suggested is as follows: Weakness at the micro (local) level translates into strength at the macro (global) level in terms of integration. The dual principle is that strength at the micro level translates into weakness at the global level, since strong ties lead to fragmentation.

The problem is to derive this structural principle from the biased net framework. We assume a tie is either strong (ST) or weak (WT), so that relation R is the disjoint union of ST and WT. We postulate that σ-bias is a probability mixture of components: a weak term σ_w and a strong term σ_s. When node c is tied to a and b by strong ties, cSTa, cSTb, then σ_s is the bias probability of a tie, aRb. Similarly, if cWTa and cWTb, then σ_w is the bias probability of a tie, aRb. In the mixed situation typified by cWTa and cSTb, we assume a weighted combination yields the appropriate bias probability $p\sigma_w + (1 - p)\sigma_s$, so that p is the relative weight accorded a weak tie and $1 - p$ the weight accorded a strong tie in the probability of aRb given cWTa and cSTb.

The total probability of the bias event can now be written in the form:

$$\sigma = \omega_1\sigma_w + \omega_2[p\sigma_w + (1 - p)\sigma_s] + (1 - \omega_1-\omega_2)\sigma_s \qquad [44]$$

We postulate that transitivity is more likely for purely strong configurations than for purely weak configurations:

$$\sigma_s \geq \sigma_w \qquad [45]$$

From this postulate and formula 44 we obtain a simple expression if we first write

$$\sigma_s = \sigma_w + S \qquad [46]$$

where S is chosen to make this an identity. Note that $0 \leq S \leq 1 - \sigma_w$. The simple expression is:

$$\sigma = \sigma_w + (1 - \omega_1 - \omega_2p)S \qquad [47]$$

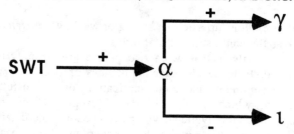

Figure 9.6. First Version of the Fundamental Diagram: The Dilemma of Integration

The final step in our derivation of the principle of SWT theory is to regard $1 - \sigma_w$ formally as the quantitative parameter corresponding to the strength of weak ties: *The strength lies in its intransitivity likelihood.* So let us write SWT for $1 - \sigma_w$. Then from formula 40 we obtain our derived formula for the reduced density:

$$\alpha = [SWT - (1 - \omega_1 - \omega_2 p)S](a - 1) \qquad [48]$$

We see immediately that the principle follows: As SWT increases, so does α and hence so does γ. The connectedness of the network is a monotone increasing function of the strength of weak ties. Thinking of γ as the global integration of the network, we need a corresponding concept for the local integration, around a node. We can take this to be the density (in the sense of proportion of possible ties) of the subnetwork defined by this node and the nodes tied to it. This local density is given by the ratio

$$\iota = \frac{2 + [\sigma + (1 - \sigma)d](a - 1)}{a+1}$$

Dropping the random component $(1 - \sigma)d(a - 1)$ in the numerator — recalling d is negligible for these large networks — we obtain

$$\iota = \frac{2 + \sigma(a - 1)}{a + 1} = \frac{a + 1 - \alpha}{a + 1} = 1 - \frac{\alpha}{a + 1} \qquad [49]$$

Thus microintegration is a monotone decreasing function of α. Thus we have what we call the *fundamental diagram of SWT theory* in Figure 9.6.

What the figure shows is that there is an inherent *dilemma of integration* built into social networks: The two loci of integration, micro and macro, are both functions of α, but in opposite directions.

We now link SWT theory to τ theory, that is, to that part of our earlier work in which inbreeding is the type of bias in relation to networks in which we have node differentiation or node stratification. The structure we are dealing with, then, is a network of the form (M,E,R), where R = ST ∪ WT and ST ∩ WT = Ø or an analogous form involving a stratifying dimension.

Table 9.1 Theory Construction Logic for SWT-τ Theory

| | Type of Network | | Structural Properties | |
| | | | Bias | Global |
	Nodes	Ties	Parameter	Integration
SWT theory	undifferentiated	differentiated	$1 - \sigma_w$	γ via formula 48
τ theory	differentiated	undifferentiated	τ	H_R via formula 5
SWT-τ theory	differentiated	differentiated	$1 - \sigma_w, \tau$	

Both SWT and τ have integrative effects, the former as depicted in the fundamental diagram. Our first task is to suggest a model by which we can express the effects of τ *on the same integration quantities*, γ and ι, of SWT theory. In addition, we want to relate these integration quantities to H_R, which corresponds to "intergroup association rate" in the work of Blau (1977), which considers an unspecified level of this element a necessary but not sufficient condition for social integration.

Our theoretical and formal problem will be apparent from Table 9.1, which shows that we now seek to combine two strands of theorizing with a focus on global integration. One strand, in the tradition of Granovetter, is SWT theory. This theory is one that differentiates relations but not nodes (except via induced structural roles, e.g., "bridge"). In our model, the fundamental bias parameter here is $1 - \sigma_w$ and the basic global integration measure is γ. The other strand of theorizing, in the tradition of Blau, is what we label τ theory, as developed in Part 2 above. Its basic bias parameter is τ and its measure related to global integration is H_R. This theory differentiates nodes but not relations (except in terms of rates between types of nodes). The new development is to be thought of as "SWT-τ theory," in which we postulate *both* bias parameters in one theoretical model. We list our problem focus by a question mark in the table, since we are asking for theoretical deductions related to the query, What is the nature of global integration in a network that is both node and relation differentiated?

Figure 9.7 shows the tree diagram for our first and simple model with this aim in mind. We postulate that

$$\theta \leq \theta' \qquad [50]$$

What the model asserts is that the probability (θ) that a homogeneous tie is weak is less than the probability (θ') that a heterogeneous tie is weak.

If we let $\theta' = \theta + c$, with $0 \leq c \leq 1 - \theta$, then

$$P(WT|R) = \tau\theta + (1 - \tau)[(1 - H)\theta + H\theta']$$
$$= [\tau + (1 - \tau)(1 - H)]\theta + (1 - \tau)H(\theta + c)$$

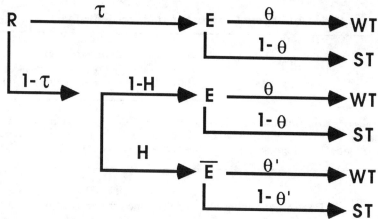

Figure 9.7. Tree Diagram for SWT-τ Model

Hence

$$P(WT|R) = \theta + H_R c \tag{51}$$

where we have used the basic heterogeneity formula valid for node-differentiated 1-networks with insalience (formula 5).

We are seeking to express ω_1 and ω_2 of SWT theory in terms of quantities in this model. Since ω_1 is the proportion of weak configurations, involving two weak ties, and ω_2 is the proportion of mixed configurations, this suggests the following postulates:

$$\omega_1 = [P(WT|R)]^2 \tag{52a}$$
$$\omega_2 = 2\,P(WT|R)P(ST|R) \tag{52b}$$

Note that $P(ST|R) = 1 - P(WT|R)$. Hence

$$\omega_1 = (\theta + H_R c)^2 \tag{53a}$$
$$\omega_2 = 2(\theta + H_R c)(1 - \theta - H_R c) \tag{53b}$$

Our first SWT-τ model, then, yields formulas 53a and 53b along with formula 48.

Using the fundamental diagram, we ask how the reduced density depends on the heterogeneity of the relation in order to answer the question of how the global versus local integration dilemma is affected by such heterogeneity. By partial differentiation of α with respect to H_R — where α is a function of ω_1 and ω_2 as shown in formula 48 and ω_1 and ω_2 are both functions of H_R as shown in formulas 53a and 53b, it can be shown that α is an increasing function of H_R. Also, by formula 5, the basic heterogeneity formula, H_R varies positively with the heterogeneity of the

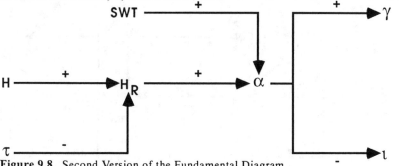

Figure 9.8. Second Version of the Fundamental Diagram

population, H, and negatively with τ-bias. All this is summarized in the extended fundamental diagram shown in Figure 9.8.

One theoretical implication of the extended diagram applies to the evolutionary or "modernization" sequence, in which a social system becomes more differentiated. This means, at least, that H increases. By the θ model, this will increase the relative frequency of weak ties and hence, as indicated in Figure 9.8, yield a positive contribution to the consequent change in α. If we assume that such a system also will yield a greater "opening up" of weak relationships so that SWT increases, then this contribution to change in α is reinforced via another positive contribution. And, if anything, τ-bias should either decline or remain stationary — producing still a third possible tendency to increase in α. The consequence is that global integration increases but local integration declines. We could think of the global type as Durkheim's organic solidarity, since it increases when heterogeneity increases. Similarly, we could think of ι as Durkheim's mechanical integration, since it increases with τ-bias, a similarity effect. Hence Durkheim's theoretical conjecture as to types of integration and their relative magnitudes in an evolutionary sequence is embedded in the extended fundamental diagram. (Another formal interpretation of Durkheim's idea will be given in Part 4.)

There is another way to relate the two strands of theory in the first two rows of Table 9.1. Namely, since WT and ST are disjoint and together exhaust R, we can easily show that

$$P(\overline{E}|R) = P(\overline{E}|ST)P(ST|R) + P(\overline{E}|WT)P(WT|R)$$

Then,

$$H_R = H_{ST}P(ST|R) + H_{WT}P(WT|R)$$

Now employing the θ model formula 51, we obtain

$$H_R = H_{ST}[1 - (\theta + H_R c)] + H_{WT}(\theta + H_R c)$$

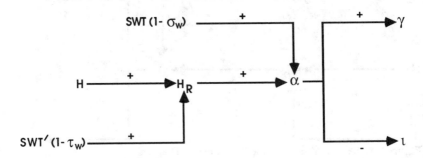

Figure 9.9. Third Version of the Fundamental Diagram

Next we apply the basic heterogeneity formula (5) to H_{ST} and H_{WT}, assuming distinct τ-bias terms, τ_s and τ_w, respectively:

$$H_R = (1 - \tau_s)H[1 - (\theta + H_Rc)] + (1 - \tau_w)H(\theta + H_Rc)$$

It seems reasonable to assume $\tau_s \geq \tau_w$. So let $\tau_s = \tau_w + T$ where $0 \leq T \leq 1 - \tau_w$. Hence

$$H_R = \frac{[(1 - \tau_w) - (1 - \theta)T]H}{1 - cTH} \qquad [54]$$

We can consider $1 - \tau_w$ another type of strength of weak ties, which is due to the fact that the greater this tendency for the τ-bias event *not* to occur, the greater the heterogeneity of the relation and so the greater the global integration given by connectedness γ. Note that if $\tau_w = \tau_s$, then $T = 0$ and $H_R = (1 - \tau)H$, reproducing the basic heterogeneity formula as a special case.

This suggests still a third version of the fundamental diagram with two "SWT-type" quantities — SWT = $1 - \sigma_w$ and SWT' = $1 - \tau_w$ — involved now in the impact on the integration dilemma (see Figure 9.9). From the figure we see the node differentiation (measured by H) and the strength of weak ties (measured by $1 - \sigma_w$ and $1 - \tau_w$) both act in the same direction: increasing global integration, but at the cost of reduced local integration.

(3.3) MOBILITY AND STABILITY BIAS

In his discussion of mobility, Blau (1977, p. 36) introduces an idea of special interest: The relational consequences of social structure may lead to a modification of that structure via the effect of a relational pattern on mobility, since the latter may alter the distribution of persons across classes of a dimension. But, in the present theory, this means social structural change. In this section we explore the relationship between mobility patterns and relational patterns from two directions: First, with social structure as parametric, the question is the effect of mobility on intergroup relations and thus integration; and, second, with relational patterns as parametric, the question is their effect on mobility patterns and thus indirectly on social structural properties.

In Blau's (1977) theory, the consequences of mobility for relations follow from one key assumption: "Established role relations are resistant to disruption" (p. 38), meaning that even if a person moves, some of his or her contemporary associations are based in past associations and thus will cross collectivity boundaries. Therefore, Blau asserts, "social mobility promotes intergroup relations" (p. 38). It is not immediately obvious how this assumption should be formulated within the mathematical theory. Fararo (1981a) introduces the notion of a residual inbreeding bias, but here we offer an interpretation that makes use of the theoretical machinery of Part 2.

The basic idea is to use the 2-network formalisms to conceptualize the problem, but in this context, both dimensions refer to the same characteristic at different points in time: A referring to past state or class occupied, and B referring to present state or class occupied such that τ^B refers to inbreeding bias based on similarity of present state occupied and τ^A refers to inbreeding bias based on similarity of past state occupied. It is the latter quantity that captures the idea that role relations are resistant to disruption: Having occupied a similar state of a dimension at some past point in time is a basis for inbreeding with respect to contemporary associations. (Despite the time element, the theoretical model in this section is not really dynamic; it is best thought of as comparative static.)

To go further, we limit discussion to node-differentiated networks and thus the formulas of interest are given by Equations 18a, 18b, and 18c, above. Mobility enters in through the various correlation measures: They are calculated over the cross-classification of present by past position and that cross-classification depends, in turn, on the pattern of movement connecting the past distribution over states with the present distribution. Hence the effect of mobility on relational patterns depends on how it affects the correlation of past and present position. The following results may be deduced, in which *ceterus paribus* means "for fixed values of H^B, τ^A, and τ^B."

(1) Ceterus paribus, relational heterogeneity at the second point in time, H_R^B, reaches its maximum value $[(1 - \tau^B)H^B]$ when $tau_{B|0} = 0$, that is, when present position is statistically independent of past position. Such a pattern of movement may be termed *the equal opportunity pattern*, since a person's chances of moving to a particular destination do not depend on his or her origin.

(2) Ceterus paribus, relational heterogeneity at the second point in time, H_R^B, reaches its minimum value $[(1 - \tau^B)H^B(1 - \tau^A)]$ when $tau_{B|0} = 1$. But there

are two distinct patterns of movement that produce a perfect correlation between present and past position: *perfect inheritance* of position so there is absolutely no mobility, and what we may term *scheduled mobility* in the special sense that all persons in a given position at the first time point move to the same other position at the second (as in the "promotion" of all pupils in a given grade to the next grade at the end of a school year). The commonality shared by both patterns is that in both a person's chances of moving to a particular destination are completely determined by his or her origin.

These results imply a general conclusion somewhat at variance with Blau's claim cited above: The more social mobility approaches the equal opportunity pattern, the more it promotes intergroup relations in the sense that the greater relational heterogeneity becomes. Note that it is not the amount of mobility that is important for integration via relational heterogeneity, but the extent to which it approximates the equal opportunity pattern. The difference between this conclusion and Blau's unqualified claim that social mobility promotes intergroup relations may be due to an unstated restriction on the scope of his claim deriving from certain actual patterns of mobility. These patterns tend to fall short of the equal opportunity pattern in the direction of greater position inertia — persons generally remaining in the same group or class from one time to another, with the extreme being no movement at all. Thus, up to a point, the more social mobility there is, the more it departs from this extreme in the direction of the equal opportunity pattern, and, therefore, the greater the chance that a relation is an intergroup one; thus intergroup relations are "promoted."

We may formalize this point and also initiate inquiry into the second question by directly formulating a model of how a relational pattern affects movements. Again, presentation is limited to node-differentiated networks. On this point, Blau (1977) theorizes that "associates in other groups or strata encourage and facilitate mobility into them" (p. 40). Presumably, as between two potential destinations, more movement would be expected to the destination where more intergroup associates are located. Also, there is the converse to the hypothesis: Associates in the same group or strata discourage and impede mobility out of it. A conceptualization that unites both points and contains the additional possibility that intragroup relations are stronger than intergroup relations and thus impede movement out more than intergroup relations facilitate it is given in Figure 9.10.

Here μ refers to what we will call *stability bias* and, in the event that the stability bias event does not occur, movement is proportional to the number of ties between origin and destination. Since this number is, in turn, determined by τ, the inbreeding bias, and by the distribution of the population into categories, the probability of movement is given by the probability of a relation between the members of the origin and destination classes or groups (see Figure 9.10).

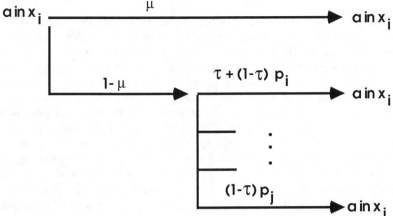

Figure 9.10. Tree Diagram for Mobility with Stability Bias

The model has the following implications (in which the first statement is needed to derive the others):

(1) The proportions in the various groups or classes are stable over time. That is, it can be shown that the proportion in group i at t_1, p_i is equal to the proportion in group i at t_2, $p_{.i}$, for all i.

(2) The correlation between position at t_1 and position at t_2 measured by tau, which in this case is symmetric, is a function of μ, the stability bias and τ, the inbreeding bias; in particular:

$$tau = [\mu + (1 - \mu)\tau]^2 \qquad [55]$$

Analysis of equation 55 yields some further results.

(3) The larger the stability bias — that is, the greater the ability of ties to likes to impede movement relative to the ability of ties to dissimilars to enhance it — the greater the over-time correlation of position.

(4) The stronger the inbreeding bias, the greater the over-time correlation of position.

(5) Even if there is no stability bias (i.e., $\mu = 0$), the assumption that movement to a destination is proportional to the ties connecting origin and destination ensures a nonzero over-time correlation of position. Positions can be uncorrelated over time only if there is neither a stability bias nor an inbreeding bias; movement then follows the equal opportunity pattern.

Of these results, the first is the most problematic, although it is derived from a model that captures reasonably well Blau's main theoretical points regarding relations and mobility. It does imply that to the extent that nonstationarity holds for the proportions in various classes, mobility must be modeled with more than relational ties as determinants.

Setting aside this limitation in the Figure 9.10 model, it can be used to investigate one of Blau's more interesting assertions about the effects of movement on structure, namely, that mobility increases the correlation between dimensions of differentiation. The intuitive logic of this claim is that people will move to positions where there are ties to occupants so that, for example, in the two-dimensional case, they are likely to move to positions along the first dimension occupied by those with whom they share some ties, but they are more likely to have such ties with those who occupy the same position on the second dimension. Thus movement is apparently likely to occur in such a way that persons who are alike on one dimension but different on the other become alike on both, with the net result being an increase in the correlation between the two dimensions. Hence the question is whether the correlation claim would hold *if* movement were determined only by relational ties.

To investigate this claim in the simple two-dimensional case requires that four dimensions be considered: A and B at each of two points in time. Further, to extend the model of Figure 9.10, we now have two stability biases, μ^A and μ^B, which we assume operate independently of each other. For example, if both stability biases occur — the chance is $\mu^A\mu^B$ — then the person is sure to remain in the same joint state $z_{ij} = (x_i, y_j)$; if neither occurs — the chance is $(1 - \mu^A)(1 - \mu^B)$ — then the person moves to a particular destination, including possibly the origin, with a chance proportional to the number of relations between origin and destination, which, in turn, reduces to the chance of a relation between origin and destination as determined by the 2-network node-differentiated τ-bias model. The question is how the correlation between A and B at t_1 is related to the correlation between the two at time t_2 if the model adequately describes the mobility process. The logical derivation is too complicated to present here, but the basic conclusion can be easily stated:

(6) In an apparent contradiction to Blau's claim, if movement is determined only by relational ties, mobility *decreases* the correlation between dimensions of differentiation as long as the stability and inbreeding biases are not perfect — that is, are less than unity. Further, repeated iteration of the process reduces the correlation between dimensions to zero. The logic of the derivation can be illustrated by considering a case of perfect correlation between dimensions in which, for the sake of convenience, all cases fall on the main diagonal of the table cross-classifying A and B. If the inbreeding biases are not perfect, then there will be some relations between those in state z_{ii} and those in state z_{jj}. Further, if the stability biases are not perfect, then there is a chance that a particular individual will be subject to the stability bias on dimension A but not on dimension B and thus a chance that he or she will move from state z_{ii} to some state z_{ij}. As a result, at the second time point, individuals are no longer all found on the main diagonal, but begin in greater or lesser numbers to move out to previously empty cells. But this means that the correlation between A and B at this later point in time is less than its original, perfect value. Hence mobility has decreased the correlation between the two dimensions.

Thus if movement were determined solely by relational ties, then the correlation between the two dimensions would decline rather than increase as Blau claims. The contradiction between our analysis and Blau's may have originated in two ways. First, Blau may have drawn the wrong conclusion as a result of his informal reasoning. Second, he may have been implicitly assuming some additional determinants of movement that, when combined with relational determinants, produce increasing correlation between dimensions over time. However, in either case, a generalization of our model is in order because actual systems are not likely to exhibit the stationarity the provisional model implies. This is one more aspect of the "in progress" character of our work.

(3.4) MULTIPLEXITY AND PATTERN COVARIABLES

Although Section 3.2 differentiated two types of ties, strong and weak, these were disjoint modes of relation so that any pair of nodes is tied by at most one link, in that formal representation. But social relationships are often multiplex, that is, consist of multiple ties or relations of a distinct qualitative nature — for example, a father employing his son in a family business constitutes both a kinship relation and an employment relation. The purpose of this section is to initiate extension of the theory to multiplex relationships. Formally, to node differentiation we now add relation differentiation. The extension is developed for a simple case: node-differentiated 1-networks in which R is differentiated in terms of two relations denoted R_1 and R_2 — that is, $R = R_1 \cup R_2$ where R_1 and R_2 are not disjoint; that is, two persons can be both R_1 and R_2 related to each other. To simplify matters, the scope condition that the densities of R_1 and R_2 are equal — that is, $P(R_1) = P(R_2) = d$ — is also assumed.

Under these circumstances, we can define two multiplexity bias models, one based on a *diffuseness bias*, denoted λ, and the other on a *specificity bias*, denoted λ^* and defined as follows:

$$\text{diffuseness bias model: } P(R_1|R_2) = \lambda + (1 - \lambda)P(R_1) \quad [56a]$$
$$\text{specificity bias model: } P(\overline{R}_1|R_2) = \lambda^* + (1 - \lambda^*)P(\overline{R}_1) \quad [56b]$$

In these models, λ represents the extent to which there is a greater than chance tendency for relationships in the population to be diffuse (that is, for pairs to be connected by multiple ties), while λ^* represents the extent to which there is a greater than chance tendency for relationships to be specific (that is, either R_1 or R_2, but not both).

We may term the pair (λ, λ^*) *pattern covariables* since they represent the intuitive sense of a pair of disjunctive elements characterizing relational patterns (as in Parsons 1951). The dichotomy now, however, is not between two values of a single classificatory variable, but between two *variables* (i.e., bias parameters) such that only one characterizes a given composite relational structure R composed of R_1 and R_2. In this sense, we are suggesting one way to formalize this intuitively appealing but often empirically inapplicable Parsonian idea.

Further analysis may be motivated by the following interpretation: Let H indicate the heterogeneity of occupation (division of labor) and R_1 refer to affective ties and R_2 to instrumental ties. A social structure in which R_1 and R_2 are related by a diffuseness bias is one in which affective-instrumental *fusion* exists while a social structure in which the two are related by a specificity bias is one in which affective-instrumental *differentiation* exists. The interpretation of R_1 with respect to the division of labor suggests that it is governed by a τ-bias: People tend to seek out others in the *same* occupational class for such ties. The interpretation of R_2 suggests ϕ-bias: People tend to seek out others in a *different* occupational class in carrying out instrumental tasks.

Omitting details of the derivations, these two models for the pattern covariables of multiplexity yield the following consequences:

Diffuseness:

$$H_R = \frac{(1 - \tau)H + \phi + (1 - \phi)H - [\lambda + (1 - \lambda)d](1 - \tau)[\phi + (1 - \phi)H]}{2 - [\lambda + (1 - \lambda)d]} \quad [57a]$$

Specificity:

$$H_R = \frac{(1 - \tau)H + \phi + (1 - \phi)H - (1 - \lambda*)d(1 - \tau)[\phi + (1 - \phi)H]}{2 - [1 - \lambda*]d} \quad [57b]$$

Analysis by partial differentiation yields the following conclusions:

(1) In both models, relational heterogeneity is an increasing function of population heterogeneity.

(2) In both models, relational heterogeneity is an increasing function of the ϕ-bias of relation R_2.

(3) In both models, the effect of a change in τ-bias on relational heterogeneity depends on the value of the ϕ-bias in relation to a critical value ϕ_c, which is a function of the density (d), the populational heterogeneity (H), and the bias (λ or $\lambda*$):

(3a) If $\phi < \phi_c$, then H_R is a decreasing function of τ,

(3b) if $\phi = \phi_c$, then H_R does not vary with τ,

(3c) if $\phi > \phi_c$, then H_R is an increasing function of τ.

(4) If the ϕ-bias of relation R_2 is not too small and if the τ-bias of R_1 is less than one-half, then the heterogeneity of the relation R is an increasing function of specificity (in the specificity model) and a decreasing function of diffuseness (in the diffuseness model). But if τ exceeds one-half, then these relationships are reversed; for instance, the heterogeneity of R becomes a *decreasing* function of specificity.

The complexity of these results leaves us with a feeling that more analytical and interpretive work needs to be done with these models before we can be confident about their meanings. For the present, we merely note their relevance to the problem of integration in the perspec-

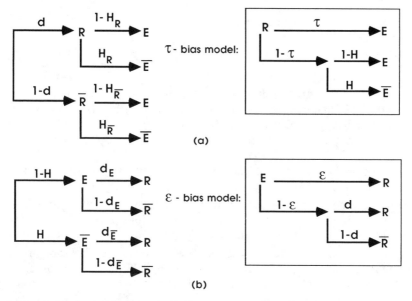

Figure 9.11. Derivation of Relation Formation Model (b) Based on Analogy with the τ-Bias Model (a)

tive of a Durkheim-derived idea of the consequences and correlates of an increasing division of labor.

(3.5) RELATION FORMATION

The theory developed so far provides no account for the formation of relations and how that formation may itself be subject to inbreeding or outbreeding biases. The analysis is post hoc with respect to relations: Given that a relation forms, the questions addressed have to do with its tendency to be an in-group or out-group relation or a relation in which members are closer to or further from each other in status than chance would dictate. The main idea of this section is to explore a model in which the biases operate at the level of relation formation. We pursue the idea in the context of a node-differentiated inbreeding 1-network.

In order to derive our approach to this problem, we try to "imitate" the model in Part 2 (see Figure 9.11). Tree a in the figure shows the logic of the τ models, in which we generate the probability $P(\overline{E}|R) = H_R$, the heterogeneity of the relation, based on the population heterogeneity H and the inbreeding bias. In the new model, with an analogous tree, we postulate a process to account for $P(R|E)$ in terms of the density d and the *relation formation bias*, denoted ε-bias. That is,

$$d_E = P(R|E) = \varepsilon + (1 - \varepsilon)P(R) = \varepsilon + (1 - \varepsilon)d \qquad [58]$$

From this postulate we obtain

$$d_{\overline{E}} = \frac{d - [\varepsilon + (1 - \varepsilon)d](1 - H)}{H} \qquad [59]$$

Hence, if $\varepsilon = 0$, then $d_E = d\overline{E} = d$, as in a random net. Further, if $0 < \varepsilon \le 1$, then $d_E > d\overline{E}$, that is, the relation is denser as between pairs of individuals of similar background than as between pairs of individuals of different background, reflecting the effect of similarity, ε-bias, on the formation of relations.

It should be pointed out that there is an implicit constraint relating values of ε, d, and H by virtue of the fact that $d_{\overline{E}}$ in equation 59 must lie between 0 and 1. The constraint is that a specification of values for two of the quantities, ε, d, and H determines a lower limit (or upper depending on the quantity) for the third quantity, beyond which $d_{\overline{E}}$ exceeds its boundaries. For example, if $\varepsilon = .5$ and $H = .5$, then $d \ge .333$, although d is free to vary between this lower limit and its upper limit. If d were assumed to be less than this lower limit, $d_{\overline{E}}$ would become negative. The constraint can be stated in empirical terms: A network in which $\varepsilon = .5$, $H = .5$, and $d \ge .333$ is empirically impossible and will *never* be observed. Put in still another way, if a net in which $H = .5$ and $d < .333$ is observed, then ε must be below .5 on logical grounds alone. (The same type of constraint pattern is at work in the τ-bias model since the quantity $H_{\overline{R}}$ must also lie between 0 and 1. That is, a specification of values of any two of the quantities τ, d, and H determines limits for the third beyond which $H_{\overline{R}}$ exceeds its boundaries.) The point here is not one of inconsistency in the model but one of "boundary value" interdependency among theoretical quantities.

With ε and H regarded as fundamental — particular pairs of values placing a limit on the value d can assume, but not implying a particular value — this approach can be related directly to the τ-bias model. An expression for τ in terms of ε, H, and d may be derived:

$$\tau = \left(\frac{1 - H}{H}\right)\left(\frac{1 - d}{d}\right)\varepsilon \qquad [60]$$

This equation also illustrates the boundary value interdependence; for example, the logically incompatible set of parameter values $H = .5$, $\varepsilon = .5$, and $d < .333$ would imply that τ is greater than unity.

Analysis of this equation produces the following results:

(1) As the density of the network increases, the value of τ declines, that is, inbreeding bias in the sense of τ declines.

(2) As the relation formation bias increases, so does inbreeding bias in the sense of τ; further, if $\varepsilon = 0$ then $\tau = 0$.

(3) As the heterogeneity of the population increases, τ declines, that is, inbreeding bias declines.

The expression for τ in terms of more fundamental quantities has further implications for the original questions of the effects of population heterogeneity on relational heterogeneity and on the salience of a dimension of differentiation. In particular, it can be shown via the partial differentiation of the equation obtained by substituting the derived expression for τ in equation 5 that

(4) as the density increases, relational heterogeneity, that is, the probability that a relation is an intergroup one, increases;

(5) as the relation formation bias increases, relational heterogeneity declines;

(6) as population heterogeneity increases, relational heterogeneity increases; and

(7) as population heterogeneity increases, the salience of the corresponding dimension of differentiation decreases. (This follows from Consequence 2b in Part 2 by substitution, using expression 60.)

This last conclusion is in striking contrast to the result obtained when τ is taken as a fundamental quantity — there salience increases as population heterogeneity increases. The disparity is due to the fact that τ, expressed as a function of H, d, and ε, declines with increases in population heterogeneity and this negative, indirect effect of an increase in H outweighs its positive, direct effect. When τ is taken as fundamental, it is assumed constant as H increases, hence salience increases uniformly with increases in H. Put another way: To assume that τ remains constant with increases in H is to assume that increasing population heterogeneity is empirically associated with either declines in d, the density of the relation, or increases in ε, the relation formation bias. In any event, the salience prediction is a clear difference between the two approaches and one that can be adjudicated empirically. Existing evidence on the question supports the τ-bias approach with salience increasing as a function of heterogeneity (Rytina 1982, Table 4.4 — the numbers in this table must be used to recalculate salience in our sense).

(4) Discussion

The problem of integration has been an item long on sociology's agenda, but without formal conceptual definitions of the problem, progress on it has been left to intuition and insight. The theory we have presented provides a formal framework that can be a basis for the analysis of integration, but the mode of integration captured in the framework is that of patterns of relations or associations, a Simmelian mechanism, rather than that of value consensus or functional interdependence, the Durkheimian mechanisms.

Blau (1977, pp. 198-203) criticizes the latter ideas in his discussion of Durkheim's concepts of mechanical and organic solidarity. He first points out that Durkheim uses, in effect, two opposite assumptions to explain integration: In societies with little differentiation, common background promotes solidarity, while in societies with much differentiation, different background promotes solidarity via interdependence. But he then notes that the change in assumption is not necessary, since as the division of labor advances, a population becomes more occupationally heterogeneous and this, in itself, will tend to increase interoccupational association; that is, there will be proportionally more associations that cross occupational boundaries in more differentiated societies as opposed to less differentiated ones even when in both the attraction to those with common occupational backgrounds is equally strong. Hence he concludes that interdependence need be given no special attention as a mechanism by which complex social orders are held together.

But it is doubtful that either common values or interdependence mechanisms should be discarded. Mere association is only sociation, the highly generic process of synthesizing or integrating parts, a necessary but not sufficient condition for the integration of a complex system of collectivities. Common values arise from similarities in social positions and are part of the basis for the formation and endurance of associations among people in such positions. But then, in one interpretation, the τ-bias that tends to join or bond members of the same systemwide collectivity is mediated by such common values. One can think of this in microanalytic terms as an underlying interpersonal balancing process, an ABX configuration, in each concrete relationship; the common values are then the similarly signed orientations to items X (see, for instance, Davis 1966). Hence the common value mode of integration seems to be modeled by the τ-bias. And interdependence can be modeled by the ϕ-bias: Certain relations among persons in different collectivities are governed by systematic out-group preferences, which (by postulation) are due to functional interdependence of the institutionalized positions of the members. Then Blau's idea that interdependence can be discarded could be tested given appropriate data. If more differentiated societies had more intergroup relations than could be accounted for by their greater level of differentiation alone, then some form of out-group bias (i.e., the interdependence mechanism) may be at work. This, of course, would be a very difficult proposition to test and not just because of the difficulty of obtaining a proper data set. The relational pattern characterizing a society is not a simple function of the heterogeneity along a single dimension and its associated inbreeding and/or outbreeding biases. Heterogeneity along other nominal dimensions and inequality along graduated dimensions figure in, as well as the patterns of consolidation and correlation between and among dimensions. In addition to these considerations first noted by Blau (1977), there are ones we have introduced: the multiplexity of relations, the consequences of mobility, the problem of relation formation bias, and the distinction between strong and weak ties, all of which can affect the development of a society's relational network. And all this still does not treat the *whole* society as a collectivity in its own right, with its potential for action in concert. Indeed, such concerted action of collectivities (emphasized by Etzioni 1968) is outside the scope of this theory.

Clearly, to have any hope of sorting out these factors as they bear on the integration problem, we must treat the matter formally. Substantively, the main idea is that τ-bias is the analytical element corresponding to mechanical (common value) integration and φ-bias is the element that corresponds to organic (interdependence) integration and that both elements are the bias components of the explanation of a structure of associations that also reflects the impact of heterogeneity, inequality, and consolidation.

Although the problem of integration is at the very core of the discipline's classic heritage, for theoretical sociology it has been difficult to edge this problem away from ideological obfuscations and exaggerations as well as from the conceptual obscurity that often accompanies novel ideas. There are clear analogues in our work for constructs and principles in the theories, say, of Durkheim, Simmel, Homans, and Parsons, not to mention the more explicit relations to Blau's ideas. In our discussion above, we have indicated the τ/φ analogue of mechanical/organic modes of integration. We do not have the space to present other such links with the classic and more contemporary theoretical heritage. Nor is our theoretical apparatus sufficiently mature to permit an unambiguous formulation in answer to every conceptual or theoretical problem that may arise from these traditions.

Instead, we close with some general remarks. There are at least two levels at which integration can be addressed in analytical terms. At one level, the key concept is institution, meaning stable design of social action and interaction. The concrete parts are human acts and the sheer potentiality of incomprehensibility and chaos in the coordination of acts of distinct individuals is the problem to which institutional integration responds. This is the focus of the other part of our joint work (Skvoretz et al. 1980; Fararo and Skvoretz 1984b). The formal mode of representation is generative, both in the sense of involving a process or mechanism generating observable normal patterns of institutionalized interactions of persons in roles and in the sense of involving a set of grammarlike internalized cultural structures that, when activated, constitute this mechanism.

At another level, the meanings of acts and their integration into stable designs are taken as givens, and the problem shifts: The integration of a network containing a set of overlapping systemwide collectivities brought into being by institutions is the problem focus. Following Parsons (1966), we may term this the problem of the integration of a general *social* system, implying *givenness* of institutional structures as contrasted with the former problem of the integration of a general *action* system (implying that the stable design of social action and interaction is problematic). For *this* problem, we have constructed the present biased net framework and models: The mode of representation is intrinsically statistical by virtue of aggregating ties over multitudes of individuals. In this way we have made firm contact with recent "structuralist" ideas — such as weak ties in relation to global integration — within a formal theory. The aim, common to all science, is that of comprehending the surface complexity of particular empirical cases in terms of the interrelations of simpler theoretical constructs. Our work, incomplete though it is in many respects, is a step in this direction.

References

Ben-David, J. and T. Sullivan. 1975. "Sociology of Science." Pp. 203-222 in *Annual Review of Sociology*. Palo Alto, CA: Annual Reviews.

Berger, J., D. Wagner, and M. Zelditch, Jr. 1985. "Introduction: Expectation States Theory — Review and Assessment." In *Status, Rewards, and Influence: How Expectations Organize Behavior*, edited by J. Berger and M. Zelditch, Jr. San Francisco: Jossey-Bass.

Blau, P. M. 1964. *Exchange and Power in Social Life*. New York: John Wiley.

— — —. 1977. *Inequality and Heterogeneity*. New York: Free Press.

Blau, P. M., T. C. Blum, and J. E. Schwartz. 1982. "Heterogeneity and Intermarriage." *American Sociological Review* 47:45-62.

Blum, T. C. 1984. "Racial Inequality and Salience." *Social Forces* 62:607-17.

Davis, J. A. 1966. "Structural Balance, Mechanical Solidarity, and Interpersonal Relations." In *Sociological Theories in Progress*, Vol. 1, edited by J. Berger et al. Boston: Houghton Mifflin.

Etzioni, A. 1968. *The Active Society*. New York: Free Press.

Fararo, T. J. 1981a. "Biased Networks and Social Structure Theorems." *Social Networks* 3:137-59.

— — —. 1981b. "Social Activity and Social Structure: A Contribution to the Theory of Social Systems." *Cybernetics and Systems* 12:53-81.

— — —. 1983. "Biased Networks and the Strength of Weak Ties." *Social Networks* 5:1-11.

Fararo, T. J. and J. Skvoretz. 1984a. "Biased Networks and Social Structure Theorems: II." *Social Networks* 6:141-75.

— — —. 1984b. "Institutions as Production Systems." *Journal of Mathematical Sociology* 10:117-82.

— — —. 1987. "Unification Research Programs: Integrating Two Structural Theories." *American Journal of Sociology* 92:1183-1209.

Fararo, T. J. and M. Sunshine. 1964. *A Study of a Biased Friendship Net*. Syracuse, NY: Syracuse University Youth Development Center and Syracuse University Press.

Feld, S. L. 1982. "Social Structural Determinants of Similarity." *American Sociological Review* 47:797-801.

Grannovetter, M. S. 1973. "The Strength of Weak Ties." *American Journal of Sociology* 78:1360-80.

— — —. 1982. "The Strength of Weak Ties: A Network Theory Revisited." In *Social Structure and Network Analysis*, edited by P. V. Marsden and N. Lin. Beverly Hills, CA: Sage.

Homans, G. C. 1950. *The Human Group*. New York: Harcourt, Brace.

Homans, G. C. 1974. *Social Behavior*, rev. ed. New York: Harcourt, Brace, & Jovanovich.

Johnson, M. 1980. *Religious Assortative Marriage in the United States*. New York: Academic Press.

Mayhew, B. H. and R. L. Levinger. 1976. "Size and Density of Interaction in Human Aggregates." *American Journal of Sociology* 82:86-110.

Merton, R. 1957. "Priorities in Scientific Discovery." *American Sociological Review* 22:635-59.

Parsons, T. 1951. *The Social System*. New York: Free Press.

— — —. 1966. *Societies: Evolutionary and Comparative Perspective*. Englewood Cliffs, NJ: Prentice-Hall.

Rapoport, A. 1957. "A Contribution to the Theory of Random and Biased Nets." *Bulletin of Mathematical Biophysics* 19:257-71. (Reprinted in *Social Networks: A Developing Paradigm*, edited by S. Leinhart. New York: Academic Press, 1977.)

— — —. 1963. "Mathematical Models of Social Interaction." In *Handbook of Mathematical Psychology*, Vol. 2, edited by R. D. Luce, R. R. Bush, and E. Galanter. New York: John Wiley.

Rytina, S. 1982. "Structural Constraints on Intergroup Contact: Size, Proportion, and Intermarriage." Pp. 81-100 in *Social Structure and Network Analysis*, edited by P. V. Marsden and N. Lin. Beverly Hills, CA: Sage.

Rytina, S., P. M. Blau, T. C. Blum, and J. E. Schwartz. 1988. "Inequality and Intermarriage: A Paradox of Motive and Constraint." *Social Forces* 66:645-675.

Skvoretz, J. 1983. "Salience, Heterogeneity and Consolidation of Parameters: Civilizing Blau's Primitive Theory." *American Sociological Review* 48:360-75.

Skvoretz, J. and T. J. Fararo. 1986. "Inequality and Association: A Biased Net Theory." In *Current Perspectives in Social Theory*, edited by J. Wilson. Greenwich, CT: JAI.

Skvoretz, J., T. J. Fararo, and N. Axten. 1980. "Role-Programme Models and the Analysis of Institutional Structure." *Sociology* 14:49-67.

Wellman, B. 1983. "Network Analysis: Some Basic Principles." In *Sociological Theory 1983*, edited by R. Collins. San Francisco: Jossey-Bass.

10

Processes of Allocation
to Open and Closed Positions
in Social Structure

AAGE B. SØRENSEN

Certain sociologists may, at times, doubt whether or not they are in fact engaged in sociology. Quantitative sociologists, relying heavily on sample surveys, tend to use individuals as units of analysis, and they pursue the causal analysis of individual outcomes determined by individual-level antecedents resulting from past experiences and demographic characteristics. It is often difficult, if not impossible, to differentiate the sociologists engaged in such pursuits from social psychologists when the focus is on mental states and from economists when the focus is on socioeconomic outcomes.

The boundary between sociology and social psychology is blurred for a number of reasons other than the design of survey research. Even when that boundary is emphasized, social psychologists can usually be counted on to cooperate and to collaborate, rather than to compete, with sociologists for grants, recognition, and academic resources. This is not so with respect to economists. Here the boundary is sharp. There are few shared areas in curricula, in publication outlets, or in research personnel. To make matters worse for sociologists, economists are known to consider economics the queen of the social sciences, and some economists have

Author's Note: This chapter was originally published in *Zeitschrift für Soziologie* 12(1983):203-224. Reprinted by permission. This chapter was completed while the author was guest professor at the Zentrum für Umfragen, Methoden und Analysen in Mannheim, Germany. Additional support was obtained from the Graduate School Research Committee at the University of Wisconsin — Madison. The research was supported by the Institute for Research on Poverty, University of Wisconsin — Madison, with a grant from the Department of Health and Human Services pursuant to the Economic Opportunity Act of 1964, and by a grant from the National Institute of Education (Grant No. NIE-6-81-0009) to the Wisconsin Center for Education Research. Valuable comments on an earlier draft were received from Karl Ulrich Mayer, Natalie Rogoff-Ramsøy, Rachel Rosenfeld, Annemette Sørensen, and Arthur Stinchcombe. The opinions expressed here are those of the author.

been heard whispering that there are few sociological problems that a bit of economic theory could not straighten out.

Grand sociological theory sees the economy as a subsystem of the social system. But grand sociological theory usually does not deal with individual-level outcomes; it is here that the boundary problem is most acutely felt. A large and important sociological literature that contains this problem has come into being over the last 15 years. The literature concerns the determinants of socioeconomic outcomes of individuals, measured in occupational status, income, or earnings. The first wave of this research focused on the intergenerational transmission of personal resources that are important for individual socioeconomic outcomes. Its beginning is usually dated to Blau and Duncan (1967). The second — and current — wave emphasizes the importance of labor market structures, in the form of dual or segmented labor markets, for socioeconomic outcomes. In this research, "structural" variables are added to the background variables that were employed in the first wave of sociological attainment research. (For a review, see Kalleberg and Sørensen 1979.)

Socioeconomic attainment research has been a successful enterprise in sociology, and it is perhaps the closest thing to "normal science" in the discipline. There is a substantial amount of cumulation of knowledge, publications replicating earlier research or introducing additional variables, and disputes over measurement procedures and the proper role of variables in causal sequences. The area has its critics and detractors: It has been argued that the emergence of labor market research to replace status attainment research represents a change of paradigm (e.g., Beck et al. 1980). It seems, however, that the second wave of attainment research consists primarily of the addition of a new set of variables. No fundamental change in the structure of models employed, or in the basic conception of what takes place, seems to be implied by the new sociology of labor markets. In fact, that research and the earlier status attainment research share the failure to give attention to conceptual problems regarding what accounts for observed effects of structural as well as of individual-level variables (Baron and Bielby 1980; Sørensen 1983). Most theory in the sociology of labor markets is about the organization of the economy into dual and other divisions, and not about what models should look like and which mechanisms generate observed outcomes.

The neglect of specification of mechanisms accounting for observed outcomes and the nature of the dependent variables makes sociological attainment research vulnerable to imperialistic forays by economists. The economic nature of the dependent variable is clear with respect to earnings and incomes, which are increasingly employed as dependent variables in sociological attainment research. Socioeconomic status is usually not seen as an economic variable; it is a somewhat nebulous concept. Despite the frequent use of "prestige," a relational concept, to denote this variable, Goldthorpe and Hope (1972) have convincingly argued that prestige is not what is measured. It seems instead to refer to a quality of "goodness" of occupational positions. If economics is about the allocation of scarce resources and goods, then socioeconomic status is an economic variable.

The proposition that sociological attainment research concerns an economic process that can be specified by economic theory is admitted in one of the few explicit statements on the subject, presented by Berg (1981), who asserts that the sociology of labor markets is about the specification of the demand side of labor markets. A similar implication follows from the discussion represented by Grannovetter (1981). This certainly appears to be what most economists believe sociologists are doing.

There is, however, another way to perceive the matter. The classic sociological idea of seeing the economy as a subsystem should mean that sociologists have something to say about the boundaries for the operation of market mechanisms and about alternative mechanisms for the allocation of valued resources and goods. This chapter endeavors to perform that task. It argues that basic sociological concepts and ideas provide the ingredients for a theory about nonmarket allocation mechanisms that are of particular relevance for the study of attainment processes. Of course, if all allocation processes are seen as economic, then this theory is also an economic theory. It is, however, a theory about what should happen when markets are of only indirect relevance for allocation. This seems to be a situation quite difficult for standard economic theory to depict.

The basic ideas derive from Weber's distinction between open and closed relationships, which he presents in *Economy and Society* ([1925] 1968).[1] This distinction is applied in this discussion to positions in the social structure. Open positions are seen as characterizing competitive markets with the properties assumed in neoclassical economic theory, and the mechanisms that allocate people to positions in such markets are those described by orthodox theory. The main task of this chapter is to specify the allocational mechanisms operating when positions are closed, so that market mechanisms cannot operate. The mechanism argued to govern allocations when positions are closed — not easily accessible to out-siders — will be referred to as *vacancy competition*. I shall try to show that vacancy competition differs from market competition in three important ways: with respect to the specification of models for attainment processes, with respect to the interpretation of observed effects of independent variables on attainment, and with respect to the measurement of variables.

The next section will develop more fully the idea of closed and open positions. It is followed by a description of the vacancy competition mechanism allocating people to positions in a closed system. In this discussion, many of the illustrations are labor market examples. I then give an explicit treatment of the labor market application of these ideas. Because it seems useful to show that the ideas are not specific to this particular area of application, I shall illustrate how the ideas of closed positions and vacancy competition also can be used in the analysis of school systems and the educational attainment process.

Several of the ideas presented in this chapter are drawn from other sources. Some of the characteristics of the allocational mechanisms that operate in closed-position systems have been described by Boudon (1974) and Thurow (1975). The latter's notion of job competition is quite close to the idea of vacancy competition. The vacancy concept and the idea that vacancy chains define the opportunity structure of organizations are derived from White (1970). Important ideas about the operation of internal labor markets — the main labor market structure thought to have the property of a closed-position system — are owed to Doeringer and Piore (1971) and, especially, Williamson (1975). Hirsch's (1976) notion of "positional goods" is also similar to the ideas presented here.

This chapter emphasizes to a greater degree than in previous work the importance of ideas concerning how empirical research is to be conducted. It is ultimately difficult to argue that suggestive ideas are important if they do not have operational consequences. A few empirical results are available to illustrate these consequences; examples are described more fully elsewhere (Sørensen 1979; Sørensen and Hallinan 1982), and elements of the theoretical development have also been reported in other works (Sørensen 1977; Sørensen and Kalleberg 1981).

Systems of Closed and Open Positions

This chapter is concerned with mechanisms of access to positions in labor markets and educational structures. These positions should be conceived of as defining tasks and activities for incumbents to carry out. In labor market applications, the positions are jobs. In educational applications, positions are places in instructional groups or classrooms. The labor market application shall be used here in the development of the main arguments. The schooling application, which requires certain modifications and elaborations, will be described in the context of the labor market application.

Incumbents of positions are assumed to receive benefits in return for execution of the tasks and activities of positions. The benefits may be a direct payment for the execution of a specific task or a stream of payments over a period of time in the form of wages, or they may consist of opportunities for future rewards resulting, for example, from participation in educational activities. Tasks and activities associated with positions, and benefits and rewards obtained as a result of occupying positions, make individuals care about which positions they occupy. They are assumed to have interests and preferences related to the distribution of benefits and the distribution of individuals among positions (in particular themselves).

Thus the concern here is for hierarchically organized positions where individual attainment of unequally distributed rewards and opportunities depends on obtaining access to positions. The process of acquiring access will be argued to depend on whether positions are open or closed. Weber (1968) defines the concepts of open and closed social relationships as follows:

> A social relationship, regardless of whether it is communal or associative in character, will be spoken of as "open" to outsiders if and insofar as its system of order does not deny participation to anyone who wishes to join and is actually in a position to do so. A relationship will, on the other hand, be called "closed" against outsiders, so far as, according to its subjective meaning and binding rules, participation to certain persons is excluded, limited, or subjected to conditions. (p. 43)

Weber goes on to argue that competitive markets are characterized by open relationships, while the establishment of the worker's right to and possession of particular jobs is an example of a closed relationship. The characterization of market relationships as open, and of closed relationships as involving control over access to positions, is basic for the arguments that are developed here.

Whereas Weber speaks of closed and open "relationships," here the terms *open* and *closed* will be applied to positions. No change in meaning is implied. Positions are nodes in social relationships and are defined by these relationships. The terms *closed* and *open positions* thus refer to the ease of access to the basic relationships defining the position. In labor market applications this means access to the employment relationship.

The distinction between open and closed positions or relationships is used here in a more specific sense than that provided by Weber. Positions are referred to as closed when they are available only after being vacated by the previous incumbent. This means that in closed-position systems new allocations can take place only when positions become vacant, so that the timing of allocation is governed by the timing of the occurrence of vacancies. In contrast, incumbents of positions in open-position systems can be replaced at any time, and the occurrence of vacancies has no bearing on the timing of new allocations.

The causes of the emergence of closed-position systems are here illustrated by specific applications. Certain general properties of such systems are noted because of their relevance for the allocational process. Three properties have particular relevance: (1) the predetermined and well-specified nature of positions in closed-position systems, (2) the indefinite duration of matches between people and positions when positions are closed, and (3) allocations to closed-position systems that represent the outcomes of authority decisions rather than market exchanges.

The predetermined and well-specified nature of positions in closed-position systems means that those systems have "more structure" than open-position systems. In labor market systems this results from interdependencies among jobs in different divisions of labor, from the existence of training ladders and on-the-job training arrangements, from the existence of promotion ladders, and from the nature of such systems as hierarchically organized authority systems. Some of these features are linked to the reasons causing positions to be closed (on-the-job training arrangements); others may be seen as consequences of closed-position systems (promotion ladders). Regardless, these features mean that relationships among positions are so well established that positions come to exist independently of people. In Simmel's apt formulation in 1908 (1950), in his discussion of super- and subordination or authority relationships:

> The division of labor is everywhere correlated with the codification of actions and conditions. The *a priori* elements of the relationship are no longer individuals with their characteristics, out of which the social relationships develop, but, rather the relations themselves, as objective forms, as "positions," empty spaces or contours (as it were) which must merely be "filled" by individuals. (p. 293)

Simmel goes on to discuss one of the main issues of this chapter: "The inevitable disproportionate distribution of qualifications and positions."

It is the predetermined and well-specified nature of the positions in closed systems that makes it meaningful to speak of vacant positions to be filled. It should further be noted that the linkages among positions in closed systems imply that in general it is impossible to adjust in a fluid manner the number of positions to cycles in product markets (or funding levels) or to changes in the supply of candidates for positions. The existence of a single position is linked to the existence of other positions so that single positions usually cannot be created or eliminated at will.

It follows from the definition of *closed* that the duration of matches in the closed-position system reflects the fact that no one can have access to a position unless there is a vacancy. In closed-position labor market systems, new allocations can be made only when the previous incumbent has left voluntarily. Unless the incumbent is forced to retire, voluntary departures should be made only to move to a better position: In closed systems, the duration of matches will therefore be governed by upward mobility regimes, or promotion systems. It will be shown in the next section that these mobility regimes are organizationally and historically specific. The timing of new allocations is generally not under the control of the authority (employer) who makes the allocation. This has two important consequences. First, new matches usually cannot be established when changes in individual performance, or the availability of a candidate with qualifications believed to be superior to an incumbent, would make it desirable. Second, when a new match is established, there is considerable uncertainty about how long it will last.

The indefinite duration of matches in closed-position systems and the constraints on the creation of new positions combine to produce only a limited number of vacancies in a system at any given moment. Also, a limited and usually well-defined set of candidates will exist for these vacancies as a result of the supervisory, technical, incentive, and learning relations that exist among positions. The authority decisions that establish matches between individuals and positions in closed-position systems are thus single decisions involving the choice between a limited set of candidates in a particular system.

Open-position systems, being markets, are polar opposites to closed systems in terms of the attributes described above. Specifically: (1) Open-position systems lack "structure," that is, positions cannot be said to exist independent of incumbents; (2) the duration of matches in open-position systems is short and definite; and (3) matches are established in market exchanges rather than as a result of authority decisions.

Open-position labor markets are like markets for other goods. Buyers, who are employers, offer wages for the execution of specific tasks and activities. Sellers, who are workers, decide how much leisure time they are willing to give up at the going wage rate in order to perform tasks for employers. This results in schedules of work demanded at given wage rates and work supplied at given rates. The intersection of these two schedules establishes a market wage rate or price for the particular type of work transacted for. The conception of labor market that is implied by this application of standard price theory is one where transactions result in employment contracts that are like sales contracts for ordinary goods (see Simon 1957). Employments are established for the (brief) periods of time it takes to complete specific tasks. New tasks produce new transactions or employment contracts. In other words, matches between individuals and tasks are reestablished continuously. Positions, conceived of as sequences of tasks, are open because new contracts, available to anyone, will be established for each new task in the sequence of tasks.

In labor markets that conform to this conception, the separation of individuals and positions is of little relevance. The number of positions is determined by the amount of work demanded at given wage levels. In a labor market that is in equilibrium, no more work will be demanded at the given wage and it makes little sense to speak of vacant positions. The level of employment and hence the number of positions respond in a fluid manner to changes in the market. Positions are assumed to be unrelated to each other, or "unstructured."

Market transactions result in matches of individuals to well-specified tasks. New matches are established when tasks are completed, and these new matches need to involve the same persons. Durations of matches are therefore short and definite. There is no uncertainty about how the task is to be carried out, and no need to be able to predict future performance, since the match is of short duration — or can be made of short duration without adverse consequences.

The market transactions that allocate people to positions in open-position systems are exchange relations rather than authority decisions, as in closed-position systems. In the neoclassical economic conception of labor markets, a very large number of such transactions are assumed to occur simultaneously and independently of each other. They establish market prices or wage rates for different types of labor, and no one is prevented from working at some wage rate. No single transaction will influence these wage rates. Employers can rely on competition among workers to minimize labor costs, and workers can rely on competition among employers to ensure they get the market wage. While they cannot influence that market wage, they can increase their earnings by working more or by supplying a different and higher quality of work.

Open and closed positions are end points on a continuum: No labor market is completely open; there is involuntary unemployment. Nor is any labor market structure completely closed; dismissals do take place, and they sometimes are carried out because a candidate with better qualifications than the incumbent is available. Nevertheless, it is the contrast between open and closed that matters for the allocational process. For the open-position scenario, this allocational process is well described by standard economic theory. The mechanisms that govern allocations in closed-position systems are described in the next section.

Those who apply the open-position market assumption to labor markets are likely to argue against the importance of the distinction made here. They would claim that closed-position systems are short-term imperfections; that the arguments presented here ignore the role of competition; and, in the long run, competition will eliminate whatever implications are drawn from the nature of closed positions. Two comments are in order. First, it is unreasonable to see competition as a monopoly of markets. In fact, a great believer in markets, Hayek (1948), has argued that if markets completely conform to what is assumed in (neo)classical economic theory, there would be no competition according to the definition provided by Samuel Johnson, "the action of endeavouring to gain what another endeavours to gain to at the same time" (p. 96). Complete information, uniform and well-specified goods, and other attributes of perfect markets would make this action quite infeasible.

Competition for access to positions in a closed system can indeed be ferocious; one has only to ask French students. In the long run, the argument here is that the distinction between open and closed positions determines the structure of the processes allocating people to positions. Once determined, it is difficult if not impossible to imagine why basic mechanisms would change from one form to another over a long time.

Second, it is not argued here that competition in product markets does not exist, or that firms could not behave as they are supposed to with respect to equating the marginal productivity of some aggregate of their labor force to the wage bill. Of interest is the internal pricing and allocation of labor, for these elements are observed in research on the socioeconomic attainment process.

Vacancy Competition:
Mobility Regimes and Queues

The indefinite duration of matches in closed-position systems and the limited number of vacancies, and candidates for vacancies, appearing at any moment are of fundamental importance for the nature of the allocation process that emerges in such systems. These attributes imply that occurrences of new allocations, created by vacancies, are governed by mobility regimes in systems of closed positions; and that outcomes of allocation will be determined by ranking candidates, who, for this reason, may be seen as forming queues for the opportunities presented by vacancies.

New vacancies are created when people leave the system or when new positions are added. New vacancies may set in motion vacancy chains (White 1970). When a vacancy is created, either a person from outside of the system fills the vacancy or a person from within the system moves, or is moved, into it. The latter creates a new vacancy, which again may be filled from the outside or from within. Vacancies filled from within may be filled by a person either at the same level or from the level below. In the latter case a promotion occurs. In a hierarchically organized system, the filling of vacancies from within the system may be conceptualized as a process in which a vacancy moves down as a person moves up. The chains thus formed are then vacancy chains moving in the opposite direction of promotions, to be terminated by someone entering from the outside, or by a position being eliminated.

The rate at which new vacancies are created either by people leaving the system or by new positions being added, together with the distribution of positions, determines how many vacancies are created in a period of time. This quantity and its distribution form the opportunity structure of the system — that is, in Simmel's terms, the number of empty spaces to be filled at the various levels.

There are two important aspects of this conception of opportunity structure. First, as already noted, the timing of the creation of vacancies has nothing to do with the performances and qualifications of the candidates for these vacant positions, or with whatever changes take place in qualifications and performances. One may work hard for a promotion but not get it because there are no promotions to be had. One may also work not so hard and still get a promotion because one was at the right place at the right time. In open-position market systems, one can move freely to whoever offers more for one's additional qualifications; and one should do so, to get the benefits of market competition. In an open-position system, life-cycle changes in socioeconomic outcomes reflect additions to one's productivity. In a closed-position system, life-cycle changes in socioeconomic outcomes may come about without any changes in performance, skills, or knowledge.

Second, the opportunity structure in a closed system reflects the past history of the system or organization to which one belongs. People do not leave closed-position systems randomly over time, but tend to leave in certain age intervals (for retirement). Growth in the number of positions follows cycles in product markets or in funding levels (for public bureaucracies). This will strongly influence the rate at which vacancies are created and induce accidental differences in the age distributions at various job levels. The organizational and historical specificity of the opportunity structure again contrasts to the situation in open-position systems, where turnover is independent of past business cycles. In market systems, a person's attainments in no manner depend on what happened to his or her employer in the past or on the composition of the particular labor force of the employer.

It is difficult to characterize the opportunity structure in concrete empirical systems. Information on vacancies is often not available; the impact of history and the organization of positions may be difficult to specify. A considerable amount of work has been done, however, on the mobility regimes of organizations (see, for example, Bartholomew 1973), particularly in the area of human resources and educational planning.[2] Using strong and simplifying assumptions, it is possible to characterize the opportunity structure by a single parameter. This will be described in the next section.

Specifying the mobility regime does not answer the question of who will take advantage of the promotion opportunity. The simple, but important, answer is that it depends on the set of candidates. Because of the indefinite or arbitrary duration of matches, there is considerable uncertainty about future performance. This uncertainty is reduced by relying on past performance, which is one reason vacancies tend to be filled from within rather than from the outside. The decision by the authority performing the allocation has the objective of finding, among those available, the most qualified candidate for the vacant position (in labor markets, unions may interfere in this by insisting on seniority principles). Therefore, the available candidates are ranked and the position allocated to whomever ranks first.

Ranking may seem an innocuous operation, but the use of rankings has important substantive and methodological implications. Rankings have no metrics for the distances between them and provide no information on these distance. A person may work hard to change his or her qualifications and performance, but the effort may not change that person's rank order, because the unmeasurable distance to the next person in the queue is too great (or because the decision maker used a weighting scheme that did not give enough weight to the particular performance displayed). Rankings also imply that the outcomes of people's efforts become interdependent. Thus the efforts of other candidates become a very important consideration. Displaying a great deal of effort to obtain a promotion provides a strong incentive to others to increase their efforts, in order to maintain their rank order. This is one reason promotion systems are to be conceived of as incentive devices. For the very same reason, however, there can also be an incentive to convince others to reduce effort. Rankings bear no relation to overall effort levels. The same outcomes in terms of career changes may come about at very low and at very high effort levels. This does not affect the outcome of the allocational process, and presumably this is what matters to individuals; but it does affect the performance of the organization. The strategic behaviors toward reducing efforts by some collective, though informal, agreement may be more serious the more stable the group of candidates. The stability of the group depends on the rate of promotion. One way to increase this rate, since little can be done about the creation of vacancies by people leaving the system, is to increase the number of job levels. Promotion systems therefore become more elaborate than dictated by technical considerations or chains of command.

Allocation decisions are authority decisions about whom to select for a particular vacancy among a small group of candidates. These decisions therefore pose a "small numbers problem" (Williamson 1975). The candidates will present themselves in their best light, and, in fact, have incentives to present themselves in a better light than reality may justify. Such opportunistic incentives are checked in market transactions, because of the large number of transactions and the short duration of each match. In closed-position systems there are no similar checks. One result should be heavy reliance on "objective" characteristics, such as educational credentials, and visible attributes, such as race and sex, believed to provide information about future performance (the latter is the source of what has been labeled "statistical discrimination" by Thurow 1975 — a group attribute is believed to provide information on individual members of the group). There is, in other words, a potential for inequality of opportunity and discrimination inherent in the allocation of people to vacancies in closed-position systems — a potential not present in open-position markets, where competition eliminates discrimination (Becker 1971).

The small numbers problem diminishes in the case of internal promotions, and is therefore argued by Williamson to be one cause of the emergence of closed-position internal labor markets. With hirings from the outside the problem does arise. It is possible that some systems can rely on market competition in entry positions; this is widely believed to take place in internal labor markets (Doeringer and Piore 1971). But for certain organizations this may not be feasible. If new positions are added, recruits from the outside may also be needed at higher job levels.

Rank orders are irrelevant in open-position systems, and small numbers opportunism checked, as noted, by the market, which provides a price system for individual attributes through an interval metric, that is, money. And the efforts of one can be changed independently of the efforts of others, because outcomes are established in independent transactions.

The use of rankings in vacancy competition has important methodological implications. The measurement strategies employed in research on the attainment process should reflect the mechanisms and procedures governing allocation processes. Conventionally used metrics are not informed by a concept of the allocational process in closed-position systems — for example, education measured in years of schooling. Empirical examples of the usefulness of this insight will be provided below.

Simmel's problem, the inevitable disproportion between the distribution of qualifications and the distribution of positions, is solved by the use of rankings, which may be fitted to any outcome distribution. This use of rankings also resolves a classic problem in the study of income distributions dating back at least to Pigou (1932): How can the well-known skew in the income distribution be compatible with the presumed normality of the ability distribution? [3] If incomes are allocated according to vacancy competition, the problem ceases to exist, for the ability distribution is used without interval metrics.

Simmel points to another solution. One may not even specify the qualifications of the position, but assume that the position makes the person. "Whoever God gives an office, He also gives the mind necessary for it." This proverbial piece of optimism about the human fate is, in fact, the rationale for internal labor markets provided by Thurow (1975), though there the minds are created by on-the-job training. It is a good rationale for promotion by seniority. According to Simmel, this solution attains its ultimate form in the Catholic clergy, where consecration creates the special qualifications for the position to which it calls the individual.

The use of rankings — and in some cases, perhaps, consecrations — to fill vacancies created by idiosyncratic mobility regimes is then the main feature of vacancy competition. System size may be seen as a variable that, to some extent, interacts with the vacancy competition mechanisms. In large systems, vacancies may be more predictable and occur at a more frequent rate. The number of candidates for these vacancies is larger. As a result, the number of allocations to be performed is larger. It is therefore conceivable that, in large systems, the prediction from market mechanisms corresponds more closely to predictions from vacancy competition. The importance of this qualification should not be exaggerated, for large systems are often aggregates of smaller systems. The next section will describe empirical results obtained from an analysis of vacancy competition in national labor markets.

Vacancy Competition in Labor Markets

There are long-standing disagreements on the nature of labor markets and the appropriateness of applying the open-position concept to them. As early as 1848, Mill argued that labor markets were not completely homogeneous and open, and pointed to the importance of "noncompeting" groups that present barriers to entering certain pursuits; an example is occupational groups. In fact, the empirical existence of such imperfections was earlier suggested by Adam Smith. Institutional economists dominated labor economics through the 1950s, and were much occupied by the structural aspects of labor markets (e.g., Dunlop 1957; Kerr 1950). They ceded their dominant position in the 1960s to neoclassical economics, particularly human capital theory. This meant a return to the concept of labor markets as open and homogeneous. This change in turn provoked reaction from neoinstitutionalist and radical economists, and later from sociologists of the labor market (for a review see Kalleberg and Sørensen 1979; an important critique of the reaction is provided by Cain 1976).

The criticism of neoclassical labor economics has largely been directed at the assumption of market homogeneity. A barrier to entry is, nevertheless, not very interesting; it may give rise only to different supply and demand schedules inside and outside the barrier. This does not in itself mean that market mechanisms do not account for the attainment process. Such mechanisms need open positions behind barriers. This is, of course, quite possible. It is when barriers are posed to closed positions that the arguments of this chapter become relevant. Closed-position systems are described in the extensive literature on internal labor markets, which refers to the causes of closed-position systems in labor markets. Of particular relevance are Doeringer and Piore (1971), Williamson (1975), and Thurow (1975).

THE CAUSES OF CLOSED LABOR MARKET POSITIONS

Williamson (1975) considers the difficulty of establishing market contracts for the employment relationship in jobs that are idiosyncratic in nature. He sees this difficulty as the cause of the emergence of internal labor markets. Idiosyncratic jobs are those where most of the skills and knowledge needed to perform a job are acquired on the job. Further, amounts of uncertainty and complexity that are not trivial characterize these tasks, making standard sales contracts for employment impossible (see also Simon 1957). Therefore, the essential feature of open-position systems — many transactions that are independent and of short duration — does not obtain. Combined with the incentives to behave opportunistically created by the employee's special skills and knowledge, individual-level contracts are unenforceable. The result is collective employment relationships that are authority relations: Wages are attached to jobs and not to individuals.

The absence of individual wage bargaining in internal labor markets poses an incentive problem. Supervision is costly and is limited by information problems. As already suggested, the result is the establishment of promotion structures as incentive devices. The use of promotion as a motivational device, emphasized by Stinchcombe (1974), in fact goes back to Weber's analysis of bureaucracy.

The link between jobs for which needed skills and knowledge are acquired on the job and internal labor markets, where employees have a great deal of job security, has been argued by several authors. The classic formulation of human capital theory by Becker (1964) sees specific on-the-job training as having the effect that individuals will not be paid the competitive market wage and that employers (who have to pay for specific training that cannot be used elsewhere) have an incentive to retain the employee as long as possible to obtain the greatest return for the cost of that training. A more extreme formulation is provided by Thurow (1975), who conceives of practically all skills as acquired on the job, so that internal labor markets form a system of consecration. The implication is that it becomes impossible to make a distinction between individuals and jobs (for reasons contrary to those in open-position systems). Thurow also emphasizes the need for job security, or closed positions, to induce trainers to train the workers through on-the-job training ladders. A broader formulation, also stressing interdependence of jobs and the importance of collective action for closed employment relations, is provided by Sørensen and Kalleberg (1981). Whatever the formulation, there is substantial agreement that certain job structures generate matches of people to jobs that are usually dissolved only by the employee (mandatory retirements excepted).

The role of promotion systems as incentive devices reinforces the closed nature of jobs in internal labor markets. If promotions are to provide incentives, there must be a chance for everyone to obtain them. This is not the case when there is a high frequency of involuntary dismissals or other attempts by the employer to take advantage of market changes in the qualifications of candidates. Nonindividual wage bargaining is also reinforced by promotion systems. If those at the same level in the promotion hierarchy do not obtain approximately the same job rewards, the incentive of promotions is diminished.

The closed nature of jobs does not prevent business cycles in product markets from curtailing production. In firms that can be assumed to have closed-position internal labor markets, it is indicative that unemployment typically takes the form of layoffs, in which the individual usually retains the right to the job. Furthermore, when layoffs do occur, they follow seniority.

Doeringer and Piore (1971) link the existence of internal labor markets to labor market segmentation. The so-called primary labor market consists of internal labor markets, while secondary markets are conceived of as open-position, competitive markets. This dualism of labor markets has been much cited by sociologists, but it is usually linked to the dual-economy concept (Hodson 1978; Beck et al. 1978), and the earnings models used do not mirror internal labor market mechanisms. It is relevant for the specification of the vacancy competition model, described next, that the secondary market usually is considered a low-attainment market, while the primary market, consisting of a set of internal markets, is associated with differentiated, including high, levels of attainment. In other words, most of the variation in attainment is produced by internal labor markets, hence by vacancy competition.

It should be noted, finally, that internal labor markets provide efficiency gains. This point is much stressed by Williamson (1975) — and by Weber. They are thus sustained and reinforced by competition in product markets and not aberrations, as some seem to believe.

A SPECIFICATION OF VACANCY COMPETITION IN LABOR MARKETS

A main problem is how to obtain evidence to support the idea that different mechanisms work in internal versus competitive labor markets. Neoclassical labor economists have been imaginative in reinterpreting evidence to support scenarios that are alternatives to the open labor market model; or they have been able to point to methodological problems with the evidence for alternative scenarios (Cain 1976). This indicates in part that very little has been done to operationalize ideas about allocational mechanisms in internal labor markets. Relying on earlier work (Sørensen 1977, 1979), a specification of the vacancy competition model and some empirical support for that specification will now be presented.

The standard of comparison is, of course, human capital theory. It assumes open-position systems and obtains impressive support for some of its predictions. Human capital theory concerns schooling and training decisions, which are conceived of as investment decisions. Their outcomes depend on the earnings that the market returns to additional training and schooling. Market returns are assumed to be calculated from lifetime earnings streams, which provide a link between the amount of human capital and the earnings of individuals.[4] The theory accounts only for the supply side of the supply and demand mechanisms that determine wages in open-position markets: The predictive power of human capital models depends on the degree to which markets are homogeneous, which is why so much attention has been devoted to this issue.

A major empirical study of the earnings attainment process, informed by human capital theory, is presented by Mincer (1974). With cross-sectional census data, Mincer accounts for a substantial amount of variance in earnings (56%), using only three variables. This is as much, or more, variance explained as in sociological earnings models that use a large number of "structural" variables in addition to numerous individual attributes. One of Mincer's variables, weeks worked, primarily represents an accounting relation (an important one, as the theory relies on market theory of prices or wage rates; this relation is nevertheless ignored in much of the sociological research that is critical of human capital research). The other two variables are education and experience. Human capital theory is usually seen to center on education, and its relationship to earnings is assumed to reflect the acquisition of skills in schools. The market returns to these skills should cover the costs of acquiring them, for anyone doing so. A major portion of the costs are earnings forgone by staying in school, and these costs are roughly proportional to number of years spent in school. Measuring educational attainment in years of schooling therefore provides an appropriate metric.

Education actually accounts for only a modest portion of the variance explained in earnings. Work experience is much more important, using the somewhat ambiguous criterion of variance explained. Experience accounts for earnings variation, according to human capital theory, because it represents additional skills and knowledge acquired on the job (and transferable to other jobs so that individuals have to pay the costs of training themselves). Because of finite lifetimes in the labor force, and because investments become more costly as earnings increase, the rate of investment will be highest in the younger years and gradually taper off. Earnings should therefore show the same nonlinear growth by time in the labor force, though vacancy competition also can account for this. It is important to note that in human capital theory experience reflects changes in individuals that can be observed in the cross section, as the process is assumed to be in equilibrium.

A specification of the vacancy competition model should capture such empirical observations and will, it is hoped, provide new insights into the process. The specification described by Sørensen (1977) relies on strong, but not completely unrealistic, assumptions. One is that attainment levels are exponentially distributed. This is an assumption concerning the distribution of empty spaces or positions, not about individuals. Nevertheless, the distribution of individuals corresponds roughly to the distribution of positions, as most positions are filled. In a discrete variable representation of attainment levels, the exponential distribution corresponds to the geometric distribution, often assumed to describe hierarchical structures where there is a fixed ratio of superiors to subordinates.

If y denotes the attainment level, the distribution of jobs thus can be characterized by the distribution function $F(y) = 1 - e^{\beta y}$, where β is assumed to be negative. The parameter governs the shape of the pyramid. The larger β is in absolute magnitude, the fewer positions will exist at higher levels of attainments. In this distribution, vacancies are assumed to be created at all levels and at a constant rate by people leaving the system. The rate at which vacancies are created is characterized by a parameter, h.

Vacancies not immediately filled from the outside set in motion vacancy chains, providing opportunities for people in the system to move up. Positions are assumed to be closed and downward moves to be infrequent, and so ignored. The exponential distribution and the assumption of a constant rate result in a very simple mobility regime. It can be derived that, at each level, new vacancies will arrive at a constant rate, q, where q further can be shown to be $q = -h/\beta$. The quantity q thus represents the opportunities for advances in attainment, or promotions, that are present at each level. It is determined by the shape of the distribution (governed by β), and the rate at which new vacancy chains are created (governed by h).

People are not equally likely to take advantage of the mobility or promotion opportunities present at their level. Their qualifications are taken into account in promotion decisions. Assuming that these qualifications do not change over time after entry into the labor force (in sharp contrast to human capital theory), the probability of a discrepancy between a person's current level of attainment and these qualification should be highest at the start of the career. For all individuals at a given attainment level, individual rates of getting promoted should sum to the overall rate at that level, q. If this rate is denoted r(t), then

$$\int_0^\infty r(t)dt = q \qquad [1]$$

A simple specification of r(t) that will solve this integral equation for the individual rate is as follows:

$$r(t) = e^{bt} \qquad [2]$$

where t is time since entry into the labor force, or experience as conventionally measured. The parameter b is equal to β/h and measures the magnitude of opportunities for gains in attainment provided by the system. The smaller b is in absolute magnitude, the more opportunities for gains the system provides. In empirical research using these ideas, major attention is focused on this interpretation of b.

Moves to higher levels are jobs shifts, and the number of shifts in a period of time can be derived by integration of equation 1. A person will start with a certain level of attainment y(0). By time t, attainment can be shown to be:

$$y(t) = \frac{z}{t} (e^{bt} - 1) + e^{bt} Y(0), b < 0 \qquad [3]$$

Here, z is a measure of a person's resources or qualifications, as determined, for example, by educational credentials. This attainment model has some of the same features, though not the same functional form, as Mincer's human capital model. The human capital model does not include y(0), since it assumes that the earnings attainment process is in equilibrium at all times. Both models provide the same general prediction about the shape of the attainment curve by time in the labor force. It is nonlinear, rapidly growing in the early years and then gradually tapering off.

Since the human capital theory assumes equilibrium, it can be estimated from cross-sectional data. The parameters of equation 2 cannot be identified unless data on change in attainments are used. Equilibrium attainments, which will be maximum attainments because of the absence of downward mobility, can be obtained by letting $t \to \infty$. This produces:

$$y(e) = -\frac{z}{b}$$

This expression can be made to look like a conventional attainment model by expanding z linearly in measures of individual attributes, so that $y(e) = -1/b (c_0 + \Sigma c_i x_i)$. The ratio $d_i = -c_i/b$ is estimated as coefficients in this additive model, assuming the process is in equilibrium. The observed effects of independent variables thus confound the contribution of individual attributes to a person's overall level of resources and the number of opportunities determined by b.

EMPIRICAL RESULTS

Information about the usefulness of the vacancy competition model in this specification is not obtained by observing the effect of education on attainment, or by demonstrating the shape of the life-cycle attainment profile. These features could equally be explained by human capital theory. More information is provided by obtaining evidence for the validity of the interpretation of parameters, the explanatory power of the model, and the implications of the vacancy competition theory for metrics of variables.

The mathematical specification of the vacancy competition model assumes an exponential distribution of attainments. Socioeconomic status can be seen as a comprehensive measure of the rewards provided by positions in the social structure. It has, as usually measured, an ordinal metric (though it also usually is treated as an interval-level variable). The assumption about the exponential distribution can easily be implemented. Nothing prevents assigning a metric to socioeconomic status that generates this distribution, as long as this metric preserves rank order. This results in a metric called SAS; its derivation is described in Sørensen (1979).

The distributional assumption is of course not essential for the conception of vacancy competition, though it is essential for the mathematical specification. The conception of vacancy competition implies that attributes of individuals used in allocating them to vacant positions are used to form rankings; thus only ordinal metrics are implied for these variables. The mathematical specification does, however, need a measure with a stronger metric. One may assign these variables a metric reflecting the outcome distribution, that is, the exponential distribution, provided the metric preserves rank orders.

In the vacancy model, education should be considered a key individual attribute in allocating people to closed positions. The measurement of education in years of schooling has a justification only in human capital theory. In vacancy competition, education only establishes rank orders.

There has been a dramatic secular change in educational attainment in recent history. This means that the rank order, or competitive advantage, provided by a given level of educational attainment, say high school, has declined. This can be captured by standardizing the educational distribution by cohorts of entrants into the labor market. Using this strategy, and imposing the exponential distribution on the educational attainment distribution for each (five-year) cohort, results in a metric for education called EDR (Sørensen 1979). This metric measures competitive advantage, assuming that most people compete with those who enter the labor force at roughly the same time (these are not cohorts of people born in the same period because of the considerable differentials in school-leaving ages). The metric assigns higher values to, say, high school education for those who entered years ago and who compete with others having lower levels of education than to high school education in more recent cohorts.

In these new metrics the correlation between education (EDR) and socioeconomic status (SAS) is .625 for a very large sample of white men aged 20-64 in 1970 (Sørensen 1979).[5] In the conventional metrics of Duncan's SEI and years of schooling, the correlation is .552. It should be noted that this correlation, assuming a linear relation, is a misspecification of the vacancy competition mode. It assumes the process to be in equilibrium, presumably not the case for the youngest age groups. Still, the difference is noteworthy in support of the vacancy competition model, for most of the difference is due to the treatment of education — the correlation between EDR and SEI is .600.

A conventional status attainment model with only two variables, education and experience, produces results consistent with the zero-order correlations. The R^2s in the new metrics are .394, as opposed to .328 in the conventional metrics. The R^2s are higher than any reported in the status attainment literature for models that include measures of family background. These models do not include experience. In Sørensen (1979), both a linear and a squared term for experience are included in models in both metrics, and experience has a substantial effect. Still, the metrics provided by the vacancy competition model produce a larger R^2 than obtained in a status attainment model that includes age and age squared (Bielby et al. 1977).

It may be argued that, at the outset, I said that the standard of comparison would be human capital models in terms of earnings. Cross-sectional earnings models have not been estimated using the vacancy competition model, and in any event the use of the vacancy competition model as specified in equation 2 would be a misspecification of data such as those used by Mincer (1974). Nevertheless, the status and earnings attainment models are structurally equivalent, even though status attainment research cannot be said to be informed by human capital theory. The relation between education and socioeconomic status, seen as measures of the "goodness" of jobs, should be explained by human capital theory if it explains attainment processes, with education measured in years of schooling.

Performance, measured by R^2s, is dependent on population variances and measurement reliabilities. A more informative test of the usefulness of the vacancy competition model would be obtained by direct estimation of the parameter b, assumed to measure the number of opportunities in closed-position systems. Using information on change in attainments from 1965 to 1970, such estimates are presented in Sørensen (1979) for national samples of population groups defined by sex and race. Racial and sexual inequalities are widely believed to reflect differences in opportunities. This estimation therefore provides a way of validating the interpretation of b.

The predicted differences occur. For white men, b is estimated to be .222; for white women, b = −.264; for black men, b = −.282; and for black women, b = −.324. Interestingly, the opportunity structure for black women seems the most unfavorable of all, even though they have average levels of attainment higher than those for black men. The reason for the discrepancy is that black women have higher levels of education than black men. Their higher resources thus compensate for their less favorable opportunities.

These estimates again pertain to status attainment. For earnings, direct estimates of b are presented by Rosenfeld (1980), who finds the same differences among racial and sexual groups as those reported here. She does not find the same pattern for status attainment, but she does not use the appropriate metrics for status.

Direct estimates of rates of job mobility provide another way of obtaining empirical support for the model. Such work is reported in Sørensen and Tuma (1981) and in Sørensen (forthcoming a). The same impact of change in metrics has been established for analysis of rates of upward shifts in status as measured by the fit of the continuous-time stochastic process model used in the analysis of job shifts (Sørensen forthcoming a).

Of particular interest are the results obtained in the research on job shifts regarding the role of experience. In human capital models, experience measures skills. In the vacancy competition model, experience is simply amount of exposure to mobility or promotion processes; no change in performance is implied. Job shifts can be seen as generated by the discrepancy between the current level of attainment and the ultimate level that is determined by a person's resources (given the opportunity structure). In vacancy competition, time in the labor force is an indicator of the magnitude of this discrepancy. Hence, with the proper specification of the effect of current job rewards and individual resources on the rate of shift, experience should have no effect. This is indeed observed when models where only experience is included (like equation 1 here) are compared to models including measures of current rewards and resources (Sørensen and Tuma 1981).

Overall, there seems to be some support for the vacancy competition model in labor markets. The illustrations, however, all pertain to national labor markets. Though this can be justified as focusing on the aggregation of internal labor markets, the historical and organizational specificity of mobility regimes is lost. Other research on organizational mobility suggests the importance of this; see, for example, Konda and Stewman (1980) and especially Rosenbaum (1979), who shows the importance for career trajectories of growth and decline periods of organizations.

Vacancy Competition in School Systems

There are strong similarities between the educational attainment process, conceived of as a flow among closed positions in educational structures, and the socioeconomic attainment process, conceived of as a flow among closed positions in labor market structures. The conception of educational systems as structures of closed positions is not common in sociological research on the educational attainment process. The notion of schools as hierarchies of instructional groups is usually not made explicit, either. These concepts will first be specified.

SCHOOLS AS HIERARCHICAL EDUCATIONAL STRUCTURES

The conception of a school as a structure sees instructional groupings as the elements or positions in the structure. The empty spaces to be filled are places in these instructional groups as they appear when groups are formed or reorganized. Grouping of students is a universal feature of formal schooling. All school systems use some form of classroom grouping, at least in the form of age grading. But a number of other grouping systems exist, over and above those of classrooms and age grades. If a group of students assigned to a curricular unit is seen as the basic unit in educational systems, these units may be organized in one of several ways. They may be organized to form tracks or programs, as in U.S. high schools, or to form separate schooling systems, as in traditional European systems. Groupings within classrooms may be performed with some differentiation among groups in curricula. This kind of ability grouping will provide our empirical example of the allocational process in schools, described below.

Grouping students for instructional purposes forms a structure. Two types of relations can be defined among instructional groups. One is the curriculum relations that link instructional groups, since it is necessary to cover some particular material before going on to some other material (e.g., in a sequence of mathematics); or different parts of a curriculum are taught in specific combinations to implement the school's instructional goals. The second type of relations consists of the flow of students created by their movement in definite patterns among curricular units. These flows often reflect curriculum relationships.

The relations that thus define the educational structure are temporal ones. It appears, therefore, that educational structures differ from labor market structures, where static relations, such as those of authority, are usually emphasized. Labor market structures could also be described as mobility patterns that are promotion schedules, but the static relations existing among positions in labor market structures usually identify the hierarchical nature of such systems. Among educational structures, the hierarchical characteristic resulting from temporal relations needs to be defined.

One may describe flows of students in an educational structure in a matrix resembling a population matrix: Rows and columns are instructional groups identified by listings of classrooms, ability groups within classrooms, tracks, or courses at higher educational levels. One row denotes the "outside" of the school system that eventually absorbs the process. The elements of the matrix are the quantities of a_{ij}, which measure the probabilities that students will move from one group to another in the period of time that defines the minimum lifetime of an instructional group (an academic year or a semester).

Using well-known results from the mathematical theory of Markov chains (e.g., Kemeny and Snell 1960), one may, from such matrices, define a fundamental matrix $(I - A)^{-1}$, where A is the matrix of a_{ij}'s and I is the identity matrix. This matrix reveals several properties of the system. In particular, it can be used to calculate quantities technically referred to as expected time to absorption, or, in this application, the number of years to school leaving. Such quantities, c_{ij}'s, can be defined for any instructional group and would, for each group, reveal the career consequences of being assigned to that group. In principle this could be done for all instructional groups in a school system (for a simple example, see Sørensen forthcoming b). Since the educational attainment level is heavily dependent on time spent in the system, the c_{ij}'s measure the educational ranks of instructional groups and thus provide a metric for assigning a vertical dimension to the educational structure.

For many instructional groups, these elaborate procedures are not needed. In ability grouping, it is usually clear what is up and what is down. High school tracks, such as college preparatory programs, leave little doubt about their intended career implications. There are, however, grouping systems where the career assignments are not explicitly defined, nor are they widely communicated to students. For these systems the more elaborate procedure is needed.

The educational rank of an instructional group provides the measure of the "reward" provided by a match of a student to an instructional group. It is the analogue to the job reward in labor market structures.

CAUSES OF CLOSED POSITIONS
IN EDUCATIONAL STRUCTURES

In the general discussion of closed and open positions, three aspects of closed-position systems were emphasized as particularly relevant for the allocation process: (1) The number of positions within them is predetermined, (2) duration of matches of individuals and positions is indefinite, and (3) the allocational decisions are authority decisions. The reasons that the first two of these properties emerge in educational systems differ somewhat from the situation in labor markets.

The predetermined numbers and types of instructional groups result from the particular characteristics of educational systems. First, educational ideologies, as implemented in curriculum requirements fixed by governments and educational authorities, imply that a minimal set of curriculum units should be provided. Resources, in the form of number and qualifications of teachers, set other constraints. Most educational systems also require that the number of students in instructional groups not go below or above certain limits. Moreover, the physical layout of school buildings constrains the number of places available in instructional groups, and the available equipment sets other constraints. Together, these constraints limit the ability of schools to vary the kinds of instructional groups that may be offered and the number of places in the groups.

Schools usually draw their students from a specific geographical area. Considerable variation may exist in the composition of student bodies with respect to abilities and interests. The size and type distributions of instructional groups usually do not closely reflect this composition. The number, types, and sizes of instructional groups is determined quite, though not totally, independent of the characteristics of those who are to fill the empty places. This proposition should not be controversial as applied to classroom and track groupings in most primary and secondary schools (higher education may to some extent be an exception, though student interests do not solely determine course offerings either). It is, perhaps, more intriguing that in the case of groupings within classrooms, the size distribution of groups is independent of the student body from which ability groups and the like are formed.

When teachers form groups within classrooms, they can in principle let the number and sizes of groups accommodate the composition of students in the class. In ability grouping, this implies that the size distribution of groups mirrors the ability distribution of students. Ability groups are of unequal sizes (unless by some fiat the ability distribution is uniform), as small or large as needed to maximize homogeneity. But that arrangement runs counter to other considerations the teacher must take into account. One is the ability to manage inattention, which precludes large groups or too many groups. The other consideration is the need to divide instructional time roughly equally among students and groups. These considerations mean that there are few, not many, groups within the classroom (three to five, it appears) and that the groups are of roughly equal size. There is evidence that managerial considerations in fact override any attempt to make the size distribution of ability groups mirror the ability distribution of students (Hallinan and Sørensen 1982; Eder 1979). In other words, instructional groups formed within the classroom may be seen as representing a set of predetermined places to be filled by students when they become vacant.

The relative independence of the instructional grouping system and the composition of the student bodies allocated to these groups is a necessary, but not a sufficient, condition for places in instructional groups to be considered closed positions. The closed nature of instructional groups reflects curriculum relations and organizational constraints on mobility among existing groups.

If instructional groups are arrayed by their educational ranks, as defined earlier, access to higher groups from lower groups is often prevented by curriculum differences between high and low groups. This holds true both for between-classroom and within-classroom groupings. In the latter case, the very rationale for ability grouping usually is to accommodate teaching materials to the aptitudes of students.

Downward moves from high to low groups during the year are not always prevented by different teaching materials in different groups. Nevertheless, there are strong limits to how frequently it can be done. Creating downward mobility alone would change the size distribution of instructional groups. Too many moves are prevented by the forces that initially created this distribution. In addition, there is the influence of parental pressures and uncertainty about the reliability of performance fluctuations, making it uncomfortable for teachers to demote students. These organizational constraints on mobility after groups are established have been documented for within-classroom groupings by Hallinan and Sørensen (1982). In fact, in her qualitative study, Eder (1979) found that teachers would rather reinterpret performance than move students. Rosenbaum (1976) appears to provide a picture of much onward mobility among high school tracks, but confounds moves within and between academic years. The process might as well be described as a promotion system that leaves more and more students without chances for promotion, in a process that Rosenbaum refers to as "tournament mobility."

In sum, once assigned to instructional groups, students are unlikely to be reassigned. Their stay in these groups is not indefinite, as it is in labor market positions, where jobs are vacated only when incumbents leave because of promotion. But the duration of a match is arbitrary in relation to the performance and efforts of students.

The analogy between the closed nature of positions in labor market structures and the closed nature of positions in schools may be strengthened. Recall that the relations defining educational structures are temporal. One may define particular temporal configurations of instructional groups, or educational trajectories, as elements of this structure. These trajectories may be considered relatively closed for two reasons.

First, the curriculum relations existing between instructional groups constrain and define assignments over time, including before and after the times instructional groups are formed. Earlier curricula are requirements for later curricula. This prevents access to "higher" trajectories from "lower" trajectories over the schooling period. Movement in the other direction is perhaps more feasible, though again the basic constraints imposed by the inflexibility of the size distribution of instructional groups are of some importance. This still provides a concept of schools as characterized by mobility in the opposite direction of what is observed in closed labor market structures, where promotions are the rule. However, when we move from lower to higher educational levels we also move from more comprehensive instructional groups to less comprehensive groups. Those groups with the highest rank thus typically have the most elaborate requirements. Viewed in this manner, the sorting of students in schools may be seen as a promotion system.

Second, early assignments provide signals about competencies and abilities that influence later allocations to instructional groups, even when formal curriculum requirements are not present. As in other closed systems, the ability to predict performance is of the essence in assignments to instructional groups of different educational ranks. Those performing assignments are subject to considerable uncertainty and, in some cases, much outside pressure. Past assignments form one, apparently reliable, indicator of what the student can do, and they create expectations in students and parents that teachers can be made aware of.

Perfectly closed educational trajectories run counter to ideology, especially in the United States. Schools may institute procedures to modify the long-term effects of early assignments on later assignments. Even though it is common to change teachers at every grade level in U.S. schools, the receiving teachers obtain information from the previous teachers. Eder (1979) reports that first-grade teachers rely heavily on information provided by kindergarten teachers when forming reading groups in first grade.

The use of elective assignments at secondary educational levels is another device to reduce the effect of early assignments on later assignments. Nevertheless, the freedom of choice may appear greater than it is in reality. Cicourel and Kitsuse (1963) vividly describe the strong influence in high school that counselors and teachers have on student choices, and show how they direct these choices so that available places are filled without changing the size distribution of instructional groups. To this is added the role of curriculum requirements, discussed earlier.

ASSIGNMENT TO INSTRUCTIONAL GROUPS AS VACANCY COMPETITION

Configurations over time in sizes of instructional groups define opportunities for students as they move through the educational structure. There are particular historical and organizational circumstances that may strongly influence these opportunities. Variations among schools in curricula and size distributions of instructional groups interact with student body composition to produce historical and organizationally specific opportunity structures. For example, a student with a given level of ability may achieve placement in a college-bound trajectory in one setting and not in another, simply because the number of places providing access to higher education differs in the two settings; or, differences in the compositions of student bodies may make access to a particular set of instructional groups easier in one setting than another.

The interdependence of one's own career and the careers of colleagues reflects the use of rankings in the vacancy competition operating in schools. A specific and limited number of places has to be filled, and there is a limited number of candidates for those places. Prediction of performance is important; opportunism is likely. Schools therefore like to rely on "objective" tests when making the most important assignments. Though these tests may have stronger metric properties than ordinality, they are inevitably used to produce percentiles, so that cutoff points can be established corresponding to the number of available places.

Strangely enough, few of these theoretical factors have been incorporated into research on the educational attainment process. The extensive literature on school effects does not look at how schools evaluate and channel students into educational trajectories, but at how much variance global school characteristics add to individual-level attributes in explaining levels of academic achievement.

There is some research on the effect of tracking (e.g., Alexander and McDill 1976), but it focuses on additive effects in models that do not reflect the interaction between educational trajectories and rankings in vacancy competition. Qualitative research does suggest the usefulness of some of the ideas presented here (e.g., Rosenbaum 1976).

A simple example can illustrate the metric implications of vacancy competition (Sørensen and Hallinan 1982). In a study of the assignment of students to reading ability groups in 34 classrooms, one question addressed was the effect of race. These classrooms varied considerably in racial composition. Using as the dependent variable the probability of getting assigned to a high-ability group, logit models were estimated. The analysis first fitted a "conventional" model, where the probability of being assigned to the high group was seen as determined by the reading achievement of the student (measured at the start of the school year) and the race of the student. The reading achievement variable was first measured in the usual metric for such tests (standardized scores, using national norms).

In the "conventional" model the results appear to be (1) a strong effect of reading achievements, (2) a major race effect in favor of nonblacks, and (3) a strong interaction effect between race and achievement. The interaction effect presumably means objective reading achievements are used differently for blacks and nonblacks in the assignment to reading ability groups. Further analysis established strong, but difficult to interpret, effects of classroom characteristics, such as racial composition and grade level.

A change in metric produced dramatically different results. The vacancy competition concept implies that teachers use student rankings in particular classes when making assignments to reading groups. To capture this, within-classroom achievement distributions were obtained and the percentile ranks in these distributions were used as the metric for achievement. This produced a significantly better fit of the model (for example, the chi-square for a model with only race and reading achievement in the conventional metric was 699.8; with the percentile metric it was 639.5; and the degrees of freedom were the same, 573). With the change in metric, the interaction between race and achievement disappeared; in fact, the effect of race on assignment disappeared altogether. The first results were an artifact created by using the wrong metric. The metric also eliminates the classroom effects that are difficult to interpret. Part of this results from the incorporation of another variable, inspired by the vacancy competition model, that measures the relative sizes of the high-ability groups in the various classrooms, or the number of empty places to be filled.

These results show the usefulness of elementary ideas inspired by the vacancy competition concept of the allocation of students to places in instructional schools. The findings obviously need elaboration and extensions in future research.

Research on assignment processes in schools and on educational careers is not the only area where vacancy competition ideas may be useful. The interdependence of outcomes created by the allocation of a limited number of students to a predetermined number of places should have consequences for the efforts of students. As already noted, the same set of outcomes can be produced in vacancy competition at high effort levels and at low effort levels. Schools may be less concerned than firms about overall performance, and are therefore not likely to invent elaborate incentive devices by complicated promotion systems. This poses performance problems to which solutions are proposed by turning schools into open-position market structures in voucher systems. Whether this is feasible remains to be seen. However, despite a considerable amount of research on peer group effects and the like, little is known, except for the possible existence of "frog pond" effects, about how the interdependence of allocational outcomes creates strategic behaviors of students and collective manipulations of effort levels in schools.

Conclusion

I would like to point to a few consequences of the discussion presented here for our understanding of common concepts in sociological attainment research. *Opportunity, inequality of opportunity*, and *inequality* are terms very frequently used in that research. The nature of the phenomena they denote and the interrelations among these phenomena depend on whether systems consist of open or of closed positions.

Opportunity has a well-defined meaning in closed-position systems. An opportunity is an empty space or a vacancy to be filled by someone. Upward mobility predominates in such systems, and each vacancy represents a favorable occasion for someone. This seems to be the sense in which opportunity is usually understood. There is an interesting and important relation between the number of opportunities a system provides, in a period of time, and the degree of inequality of the system. This can be seen from the specification of the vacancy competition model described above. An exponential distribution of positions by the attainment level they provide is assumed. The variance of this distribution, as defined before, is $(-1/\beta)^2$, where β is negative. Hence the closer β is to zero, the more inequality there is in the system. But the number of opportunities provided by the system is characterized as $b = \beta/h$.[6] Hence, for given h, the more inequality there is, the more opportunities there are for growth in socioeconomic attainment.

More unequal systems provide more promotion opportunities, at least if they have the hierarchical structure assumed here. Promotion opportunities represent incentives. One may see the considerable amount of inequality in personal attainments found in labor markets (inequalities due to capital are another matter) created in large organizations as deliberate devices to move employee performance from perfunctory to excellent. Ironically, extreme inequalities are often seen as products of the market. They instead reflect the impossibility of using market mechanisms in certain job structures, and the incentive problem thus created.

The relation between individual attributes and ultimate attainments reflects the opportunity structure. In specifying the vacancy competition model, it was shown that the contribution of an individual attribute to the ultimate level of attainment is measured by $d_i = -c_i/b$. Here, c_i measures the weight or contribution to the qualifications of the individual of a single attribute used in the rankings performed in vacancy competition. The observed effect on ultimate attainment will also be dependent on b, measuring how many times the individual was ranked. The more opportunities provided by a system, the stronger will be the observed effects of individual attributes on ultimate attainment. This has a methodological implication. Much of the sociological research on labor markets looks for "structural" effects that are added to individual-level effects, but if structural effects are produced by internal labor markets, the effects are not additive but interaction effects. The relationship between observed effects of individual attributes and the opportunity structure also has an important substantive implication. If any ascriptive characteristics influence the allocational process, the effect will be magnified the more opportunities there are. More inequality produces more opportunities for growth that may result in more observed inequality of opportunity.

Inequality of opportunity need not occur in vacancy competition, depending on how individual attributes are used in ranking candidates for new vacancies. But there is, as noted, a tendency toward inequality of opportunity in such systems created by the limited number of vacancies and of candidates for these vacancies at a given moment. Rankings reflect ascriptive characteristics, and if they do so in a consistent manner across promotions, there is no automatic mechanism that will eliminate inequality of opportunity in such systems. One can only observe the performance one has created by past allocation in a particular system.

The nature and interrelation of opportunity, inequality of opportunity, and inequality are very different in open-position markets. The concept of opportunity is not well specified in markets, and systematically created favorable occasions do not exist in perfect markets. This is the rationale for the argument by Hayek on the impossibility of competition in perfect markets, already noted. Opportunities are, when they do occur, market imperfections. But such imperfections are at least thought to be transient. They have no long-term effects on the attainments of individuals; they merely create error terms in attainment models, and indeed the attainments of individuals are not influenced by their past attainment histories. Markets in equilibrium are static systems providing wage rates that measure the performance of individuals at the time at which they are observed. Inequalities are produced outside of the market, in the acquisition of human capital and in genetic endowments. The importance of individual attributes is not cumulative, and there is no need to establish incentive procedures. Wage rates are attached to individuals, so no one is paid more than markets say they contribute. It is difficult to imagine a relation between the number of market imperfections, supposed to be transient, and the degree of inequality in the attainment distribution. Such a relationship may exist between the opportunities for acquiring human capital in institutions outside of the market, in particular from the family, and inequality. This presents a major rationale for concern over the intergenerational transmission of socioeconomic resources. It is to be noted, however, that most of the opportunities for acquiring human capital are provided by closed-position school systems, where vacancy competition also governs outcomes.

It is well known that markets are supposed to eliminate inequality of opportunity. Employers who use attributes of individuals in the allocational process that do not reflect productivity will be punished by the market. There are automatic checks to eliminate discrimination. The number of opportunities in the system and the degree of inequality of opportunity are unrelated. What appear to be inequalities of opportunity are produced outside of markets in ascriptive allocations of human capital and genetic endowments.

Closed-position systems, because of the interdependence of outcomes and ranking, idiosyncratic mobility regimes, and strong effects of past histories, are perhaps both more interesting and more frustrating than markets. Perfectly competitive markets are not very interesting; in them one has only oneself to blame for one's attainment.

Notes

1. I am indebted to John Myles for first pointing out to me the usefulness of Weber's distinction for the analysis of mobility processes. Our collaboration resulted in the work

published in Myles and Sørensen (1975), which points out some of the implications of the distinction between closed and open positions for the analysis of intergenerational mobility.

2. It is interesting to note that most of this work has been carried out in Europe, where the conceptualization of phenomena in terms of markets is less widespread.

3. One solution to the problem is to argue that ability is not normally distributed, but is only observed in a metric producing a normal distribution. Mincer (1970) resolves the paradox using human capital theory, keeping the assumption of normally distributed abilities.

4. There are strong assumptions involved in the derivation of the human capital earnings model employed by Mincer (1974) and many others. It is assumed that lifetime earnings are equal for everyone, regardless of educational attainment, as all current earnings differences compensate for training cost differences. Without this assumption the earnings equation is not identified and coefficients to education do not measure rates of return (Rosen 1977).

5. The sample used in Sørensen (1979) was obtained from the Public Use Sample of the 1970 U.S. Census. From the 1-in-100 PUS file, samples of white men, white women, and black women were obtained. Sample sizes varied from 18,000 to 30,000.

6. Recall that the smaller b is in absolute magnitude, the more opportunities there are.

References

Alexander, K. L. and E. L. McDill. 1976. "Selection and Allocation Within Schools." *American Sociological Review* 41:963-80.

Baron, J. N. and W. T. Bielby. 1980. "Bringing the Firms Back In: Stratification, Segmentation, and the Organization of Work." *American Sociological Review* 47:175-88.

Bartholomew, D. J. 1973. *Stochastic Models for Social Processes*, 2nd ed. New York: John Wiley.

Beck, E. M., P. M. Horan, and C. M. Tolbert. 1978. "Stratification in a Dual Economy: A Sectoral Model of Earnings Determination." *American Sociological Review* 43:704-20.

— — —. 1980. "Social Stratification in a Dual Economy: Further Evidence for a Structural Alternative (reply to Hauser)." *American Sociological Review* 45:712-19.

Becker, G. S. 1964. *Human Capital*. New York: Columbia University Press.

— — —. 1971. *The Economics of Discrimination*, 2nd ed. Chicago: University of Chicago Press.

Berg, I. 1981. Introduction. In *Sociological Perspectives on the Labor Market*, edited by I. Berg. New York: Academic Press.

Bielby, W. T., R. M. Hauser, and D. L. Featherman. 1977. "Response Errors of Black and Nonblack Males in Models of the Intergenerational Transmission of Socioeconomic Status." *American Journal of Sociology* 82:1242-88.

Blau, P. M. and O. D. Duncan. 1967. *The American Occupational Structure*. New York: John Wiley.

Boudon, R. 1974. *Education, Opportunity, and Social Inequality*. New York: John Wiley.

Cain, G. G. 1976. "The Challenge of Segmented Labor Market Theories to Orthodox Theory." *Journal of Economic Literature* 14:1215-57.

Cicourel, A. V. and J. I. Kitsuse. 1963. *The Educational Decision Makers*. Indianapolis: Bobbs-Merrill.

Dahrendorf, R. 1959. *Class and Class Conflict in Industrial Society*. Stanford, CA: Stanford University Press.

Doeringer, P. B. and M. Piore. 1971. *Internal Labor Markets and Manpower Analysis*. Lexington, MA: D. C. Heath.

Dunlop, J. T. 1957. *The Theory of Wage Determination*. London: Macmillan.

Eder, D. J. 1979. "Stratification Within the Classroom: The Formation and Maintenance of Ability Groups." Unpublished Ph.D. dissertation, Department of Sociology, University of Wisconsin — Madison.

Goldthorpe, J. H. and K. Hope. 1972. "Occupational Grading and Occupational Prestige." In *The Analysis of Social Mobility: Methods and Approaches*, edited by K. Hope. Oxford: Clarendon.

Grannovetter, M. 1981. "Toward a Sociological Theory of Income Differences." In *Sociological Perspectives on the Labor Market*, edited by I. Berg. New York: Academic Press.

Hallinan, M. T. and A. B. Sørensen. 1982. "The Formation and Stability of Instructional Groups." Paper presented at the annual meetings of the American Sociological Association, Toronto, 1981 (revised 1982).

Hayek, F. A. 1948. "The Meaning of Competition." In *Individualism and Social Order*. Chicago: University of Chicago Press.

Hirsch, F. 1976. *The Social Limits to Growth*. Cambridge, MA: Harvard University Press.

Hodson, R. D. 1978. "Labor in the Monopoly, Competitive and State Sector of Productions." *Politics and Society* 8:429-80.

Kalleberg, A. L. and A. B. Sørensen. 1979. "The Sociology of Labor Markets." *Annual Review of Sociology* 5:351-79.

Kemeny, J. G. and J. L. Snell. 1960. *Finite Markov Chains*. New York: Van Nostrand.

Kerr, C. 1950. "Labor Markets: Their Characteristics and Consequences." *American Economic Review* 40:278-91.

Konda, S. L. and S. Stewman. 1980. "An Opportunity Labor Demand Model and Markovian Labor Supply Models: Comparative Tests in an Organization." *American Sociological Review* 45:276-301.

Mill, J. S. 1848. *Principles of Political Economy*, Vol. 1. Boston.

Mincer, J. 1970. "The Distribution of Labor Incomes: A Survey." *Journal of Economic Literature* 8:1-26.

— — —. 1974. *Schooling, Experience and Earnings*. New York: Columbia University Press.

Myles, J. F. and A. B. Sørensen. 1975. "Elite and Status Attainment Models of Inequality of Opportunity." *Canadian Journal of Sociology* 1:75-88.

Ossowski, S. 1963. *Class Structure in the Social Consciousness*. London: Routledge & Kegan Paul.

Pigou, A. C. 1932. *The Economics of Welfare*, 4th ed. London: Macmillan.

Rosen, S. 1977. "Human Capital: A Survey of Empirical Results." In *Research in Labor Economics*, edited by R. G. Ehrenberg. Greenwich, CT: JAI.

Rosenbaum, R. E. 1976. *Making Inequality: The Hidden Curriculum of High School Tracking*. New York: John Wiley.

— — —. 1979. "Organizational Career Mobility: Promotion Chances in a Corporation During Periods of Growth and Decline." *American Journal of Sociology* 85:21-48.

Rosenfeld, R. A. 1980. "Race and Sex Differences in Career Dynamics." *American Sociological Review* 45:583-609.

Simmel, G. [1908] 1950. *The Sociology of Georg Simmel*, translated and edited by K. H. Wolf. New York: Free Press.

Simon, H. 1957. "The Employment Relation." In *Models of Man*. New York: John Wiley.

Sørensen, A. B. 1977. "The Structure of Inequality and the Process of Attainment." *American Sociological Review* 40:456-71.

— — —. 1979. "A Model and a Metric for the Intragenerational Status Attainment Process." *American Journal of Sociology* 85:361-84.

— — —. 1983. *Conceptual and Methodological Issues in Sociological Research on the Labor Market* (Discussion Paper 718-83). Madison: Institute for Research on Poverty, University of Wisconsin.

— — —. Forthcoming a. "Career Patterns and Job Mobility: Toward a Theory of Opportunity and Attainment." In *Social Stratification in Japan and the United States*, edited by D. Treiman and K. Tominaga. Greenwich, CT: JAI.

— — —. Forthcoming b. "The Organizational Differentiation of Students in Schools." In *Multilevel Aspects of the Educational Process*, edited by H. Oosthoek and P. v. d. Eeden. London: Gordon & Breach.

Sørensen, A. B. and M. T. Hallinan. 1982. "Race Effects on Assignment to Ability Groups." Paper presented at the Conference on Student Diversity and the Organization of Instructional Groups, Madison, WI, May.

Sørensen, A. B. and A. L. Kalleberg. 1981. "Outline of a Theory for the Matching of Persons to Jobs." In *Sociological Perspectives on the Labor Market*, edited by I. Berg. New York: Academic Press.

Sørensen, A. B. and N. B. Tuma. 1981. "Labor Market Structures and Job Mobility." In *Research in Social Stratification and Mobility*, edited by D. J. Treiman and R. V. Robinson. Greenwich, CT: JAI.

Stinchcombe, A. L. 1974. *Creating Efficient Industrial Administrations*. New York: Academic Press.

Thurow, L. C. 1975. *Generating Inequality*. New York: Basic Books.

Weber, M. [1925] 1968. *Economy and Society*, Vol. 1. New York: Bedminster.

White, H. C. 1970. *Chains of Opportunities*. Cambridge, MA: Harvard University Press.

Williamson, O. E. 1975. *Markets and Hierarchies: Analysis and Antitrust Implications*. New York: Free Press.

Wright, E. O. 1979. *Class Structure and Income Determination*. New York: Academic Press.

11

Expectations, Shared Awareness, and Power

YITZHAK SAMUEL
MORRIS ZELDITCH, Jr.

The purpose of this chapter is to develop a theory of expectations about interpersonal power. *Power* in the present sense means control over rewards and/or penalties that give one actor, A, the capacity to induce otherwise unwilling compliance by a second actor, B. A theory of expectations about power is concerned with assumptions by both A and B about its future use and compliance with its use.

If A repeatedly promises a reward r to B if B will do X, and threatens a penalty to B if B does not do X, B will come in time to have expectations about (1) A's preferences — what A will wish, request, demand, or direct; (2) what A will promise for compliance and/or threaten for noncompliance; and (3) the probability that A will or will not carry out such promises and threats. In turn, A will come in time to have expectations about (4) B's preferences — what B will easily do, what B will resist; (5) the probability that B will or will not comply with A's wishes; and (6) what B will do in retaliation for A's promises or threats.

With sufficient time, A and B each may further elaborate such "first-order" expectations by coming to have expectations about the other's expectations. A may come to expect that B expects certain preferences and resources, and believes certain probabilities about their use. B may come to expect that A expects some particular rate of compliance and/or retaliation. Thus second-order expectations also emerge.

But past experience of A with B and B with A is not the only way in which expectations emerge. Expectations are transmissible, and hence need not depend on direct experience. In fact, expectations arise in at least four ways: (1) by direct experience of B with A and A with B; (2) by report

Authors' Note: This research was supported by NSF Grant No. SOC-7817434. We wish to thank Sanford M. Dornbusch for helpful comments on an earlier draft.

of a third party, C, telling B about A or A about B; (3) by generalizing direct experience with people *like* A or B; and (4) by socialization into traditions about people like A or B.

The only theory of power to treat expectations about power at all is the subjective expected utility (SEU) theory of power (Nagel 1968, 1975; Pollard and Mitchell 1972; Tedeschi et al. 1973). An SEU theory is a decision theory in which choice among alternatives is determined by their relative SEU. The SEU of an alternative is the sum of the products of the utility (i.e., subjective value) of each possible outcome of the choice weighted by the subjective probabilities of the outcomes. That alternative is preferred that has the highest SEU. Obviously, subjective probabilities are a kind of expectation (for example, about the likelihood that promises or threats will be carried out). But SEU theories neglect any other kind of expectation.

SEU theories explain some important properties of power relations that are more difficult to explain using other theories of power. Nagel (1968, 1975), for example, is motivated to make SEU central to his theory in order to explain Friedrich's (1937, 1963) "law of anticipated reactions," in which the rate of compliance by B is determined by B's expectations about A's exercise of power (as distinct from A's actual exercise of power). Nevertheless, the neglect of other kinds of expectations leads even SEU theories to understate the speed with which expectations about power come to define power relations, the amount of power they create, and the stability of power (i.e., its rate of change), and to overstate the visibility of power (i.e., the overt use of directives, promises, threats, and retaliations).

Thus our purpose in constructing a theory of expectations about power is to derive implications about emergence, amount, stability, and visibility of power that go beyond existing theories of interpersonal power. Put slightly differently, we frankly admit that we are guided by certain intuitions about power, derived from our own observations, with which others may or may not agree. These intuitions are as follows:

(1) Power is in some sense "sticky"; that is, in time the amount of power of A over B becomes stable unless disturbed by exogenous forces.

(2) This implies that there is a process through which such stability emerges. But emergence sometimes appears instantaneous, at other times not. Both kinds of emergence require explanation.

(3) As stable power emerges, it increases in effect; it tends to become amplified, the same resources creating more compliance.

(4) At the same time, power becomes less and less visible; that is, there is less overt expression of preferences, promises, and threats, and less actual use of penalties.

In other words, we regard as unsatisfactory any theory that does not imply these intuitions about power; the goal of constructing an alternative theory is to explain these four properties.

This chapter is divided into four parts. In the first, we very selectively review the existing literature on interpersonal power. This may prove tedious for the reader already familiar with it, who may wish to skip directly to the second section. However, the purpose of the first section is largely to motivate the second, that is, to show that in fact existing theory does not adequately explain what we intuitively believe about the stability, emergence, amount, or visibility of power. In the second section we formulate a theory of expectations about power, and in the third we derive from it implications about stability, emergence, amount, and visibility of power. Finally, we consider some of the factors that increase or decrease the magnitude of the effects that expectations have on power.

Theories of Interpersonal Power

CONCEPTS OF POWER

We need to locate the sense in which we use the term *power* in relation to the large literature on the subject before going any further. Few words have more meanings: For Russell (1938), power is simply the capacity to pursue and accomplish a goal (individual or collective) — a sense sometimes referred to as the "power to." This sense of the term recurs in Hawley (1963) and Parsons (1963), for whom it means the power to pursue collective goals, and again in Poulantzas (1973) and Lukes (1974), for both of whom it is the capacity of a class to realize its interests. (This kind of power is called "macro" power by many, e.g., Lehman 1969.) It is used in quite a different sense by Weber (1947) and Dahl (1957), who both use it to refer to interpersonal power, often referred to as "power over." Weber uses it to refer to potential power (what one actor *could* do to another), while Dahl refers to actual power (power use), but both use the term very broadly to refer to any kind of change in behavior of one actor caused by another. Hence persuasion, inducement, coercion, authority, manipulation, and force are all "power." In French and Raven (1959) we find some of these kinds of power distinguished from others because persuasion behaves differently from rewards and punishments, which behave differently from authority. It is for this reason that Festinger (1953) uses the term more narrowly for "forced" or "unwilling" compliance, compliance that is public but not private, and Harsanyi uses it to refer to compliance induced by desire for rewards or fear of penalties (as opposed to persuasion or acceptance of authority), both of which are extrinsic, as distinct from intrinsic, motives for compliance. It is in the Festinger-Harsanyi sense that we use the term in this chapter.

THEORIES OF POWER

Preliminaries

It will help to bring some order into the confusion of contemporary theories of interpersonal power to distinguish first of all between theories of *acts of compliance* and theories of *power-dependence relations*. The latter, of which Emerson's power-dependence theory is the most important (Emerson 1962, 1972; Cook and Emerson 1978), is essentially a structural theory and does not deal with tactics, acts, or even sequences of acts (as pointed out forcefully by Bacharach and Lawler 1980, 1981). The former, on the other hand, is concerned with units of action, not structure, and analyzes power as choice (in decision theories) or as particular instances of compliance to particular instances of the exercise of power (in field and behavioral theories).

While power-dependence theory stands more or less in a class by itself as an analysis of relations, there is a considerable profusion of theories of compliant action. These fall into three groups: Field theories, which conceptualize acts such as compliance in terms of the state at a given moment of a field of forces (in the psychological sense) and power as the capacity to affect the forces, or valences, in the field (as in Cartwright 1959; or French and Raven 1959); behavioral exchange theories, which conceptualize behavior such as compliance in terms of reinforcement contingencies and power in terms of control over these contingencies (as in Homans 1961, chap. 5); and decision theories, which conceptualize behavior as choices determined by the value or utility of outcomes, weighted in some instances by the probability of the outcomes, and power by control over these outcomes (as in Blau 1964, chap. 5; Harsanyi 1962; Tedeschi et al. 1973; Thibaut and Kelley 1959).

In practice it has proved difficult to distinguish empirically among field, behavioral, and decision theories of power. There are substantial similarities in their underlying structure, and they differ little in their implications (Crosbie 1975, pp. 344-55; Schopler 1965). More useful are distinctions among various kinds of decision theory, some of which define value objectively and some subjectively, some of which define choice deterministically and some stochastically, some of the latter defining probability objectively and some subjectively. There are material differences, for example, between theories like (1) Thibaut and Kelley's (1959), which are deterministic, objective, "value" theories, and (2) theories like Harsanyi's (1962), which are subjective, or "utility," theories although also deterministic; between both these kinds of theories and (3) stochastic value models like March's (1955) or (4) stochastic utility theories like Alker's (1973), in which the probabilities are objective; and between all these and (5) subjective expected utility theories, like Tedeschi et al.'s (1973), in which value is subjective, choice is probabilistic, and the probabilities are subjective.

In reviewing this literature our only purpose is to motivate interest in four problems to which we believe expectations are a solution. For this purpose, it is sufficient to review selectively just three kinds of theory of power: (1) power-dependence theories, (2) deterministic utility theories, and (3) subjective expected utility theories. Our interest in these theories is in how little power-dependence theory has to say about these problems and how much utility and subjective expected utility theory underestimate

(1) the emergence, (2) the amount, and (3) the stability of power, and overestimate (4) its visibility.

Power-Dependence Theory

Power-dependence theory treats power in such a way that its use is invisible, its amount often greater than any particular promised reward or threatened penalty, and its emergence instantaneous. These are all properties that we, in effect, claim a theory of power ought to have. But the theory predicts that power is stable only if it is equal, which seems to us highly improbable, and it is a somewhat unsatisfactory solution to the questions of use, amount, and emergence because it tends to rise above rather than answer them. It is a theory of structure, not action; its principle difficulty is in fact in linking acts to structure (Bacharach and Lawler 1980, 1981).

Power-dependence theory is founded on a theory of exchange relations. It is concerned with two actors, A and B; two acts, x and y; and four subjective values, Ax, Ay, Bx, and By. If X is the amount of x that is traded by A to B for the amount Y of y, an exchange at a given price (ratio of values of amounts traded) occurs if and only if $AyY - AxX > 0$ and $BxX - ByY > 0$. If exchange between A and B acquires both a past history and a prospective future, Ax;By is an *exchange relation*. It is the concept of an exchange relation that sets Emerson's power-dependence theory apart from theories of compliant actions. Emerson's sociology is a study of social relations, not of acts or persons.

Power in an exchange relation depends on resources and their control. A *resource* is any act, attribute, or object that is instrumental to accomplishing the ends of an actor. Power depends on the fact that resources are sometimes controlled by others. Its amount depends on the extent of B's *dependence* on A, which in turn depends on two factors: It increases as the subjective value to B of a resource of A's increases, but decreases as the number of alternative sources of the resource increases. Power is of course a reciprocal relation, hence each actor is to some extent dependent on the other. Therefore, a second factor decreasing A's power over B is A's dependency on B. But the less dependent actor is the more powerful: Thus the basic principle of the theory is that $P(AB) = D(BA)$, where $P(AB)$ is the power of A over B and $D(BA)$ is the dependence of B on A. Assuming that A is the less dependent, more powerful actor, the *power advantage* of A over B is $P(AB) - P(BA)$ or, equivalently, $D(BA) - D(AB)$. It is this advantage (which can be 0) that drives all behavior in the theory.

This power advantage refers, however, to *potential* power, not power in use (see Molm 1985). The basic theorem of the theory is true only if (1) one assumes all potential power is used or (2) one uses it to refer only to structure. Cook and Emerson (1978), for example, assume use is equal to potential in deriving steady-state transactions between A and B at the point at which $AyY - AxX = BxX - ByY$. Their experiments are constructed to eliminate constraints on the actual use of power. But there is clearly a difference between power at any point (except the equilibrium) and the steady state because both A and B undergo changes in the subjective value of a resource as the number of transactions increases. Nor can the theory predict actual use of power even at the steady state. It simply is not a theory about the *use* of power in the sense of making demands, making promises, making threats, giving rewards, or penalizing others. Michaels and Wiggins (1976) and Burgess and Nielson (1974) (all of whom are in the Emerson tradition) argue, we believe correctly, that the theory is purely a structural theory, describing characteristics of relations, and the "balancing" operations Emerson incorporated into it do not in fact logically derive from it without further assumptions about use of power. Emerson himself, in discussing power "use," makes it clear that what he means by "use" is not use in the sense of using or withholding rewards contingently (which is Molm's attempt to define use in power-dependence terms), but, essentially, the amount of exploitation, however brought about (see Emerson 1972).

The "balancing operations" just mentioned refer to various means by which inequality in power can be reduced, for example, by forming coalitions or differentiating status. Emerson carries the idea of reactance, that the exercise of power creates resistance (Brehm 1966), to its logical conclusion: A power advantage of A over B is defined in Emerson as an "imbalance," and the theory supposes that power relations tend toward balance. Asymmetric relations are therefore unstable, giving rise to pressures toward change until an equilibrium state is reached at which $P(AB) - P(BA) = 0$.

Thus power in power-dependence theory is inherently unstable. It has a certain stability by comparison with any theory of compliant actions because it deals with potential, rather than actual power, with relations rather than acts, and is therefore issue-free. It does not vary with the utility of X at any particular time to either A or B, nor with the amounts of r and t exchanged on particular occasions. But there are at least four ways in which, nevertheless, potential power is unstable. First, the objective stock of A's resources may change over time as they are consumed by B. Second, some resources, like information, change the value of $D(BA)$ over time because they are *not* consumed in use, but their transfer is irreversible, hence they become resources of B (Palmier 1963). (Both factors are true in any theory of power whatever, not only power-dependence theory.) Third, motivational investments, on which dependence rests, change with time. And fourth, imbalanced relations are in any case unstable, giving rise to changes in power that continue until A and B are equal in power.

Stability is the one question, however, that power-dependence theory addresses directly. We have already said that it is essentially silent on use. Power is invisible in the theory because it is not about acts. The same can be said for amount and emergence of power. The theory deals more satisfactorily with the problem of the amount of power than any other because it focuses on potential rather than actual power. But the amount of potential power, P(AB), is in 1:1 correspondence with the amount, utility, and sources of A's resources. Repeated use creates no "amplification" of the amount over time. And emergence is instantaneous largely because there is no action in the theory.

Bacharach and Lawler (1980, 1981) have attempted to fill the gap between structure and action by linking Emerson's power-dependence hypotheses to acts in bargaining relations. They argue that the development of tactical implications of power-dependence theory depend on the cognitive (as distinct from behavioral) side of dependence, which they deduce from the factors that determine behavioral dependence and use to predict choices among tactical options. Earlier studies of perceived power had led Bacharach and Lawler to conclude that the perceived power of A and B is an increasing function of the values of the alternatives (to each side) and a decreasing function of the number of alternatives available (to each side). (See Bacharach and Lawler 1976; Lawler and Bacharach 1976, 1979; Michener et al. 1973.) Such perceived power determines tactical choices by anticipating probable choices by the other, likelihood of success, and so on.

But the implication of Bacharach and Lawler's method is that perceived power is in 1:1 correspondence with dependence, and hence with power. Its properties are therefore like the properties of power-dependence relations: not very visible, and immediately emergent, but the amount of power is unstable and emergence adds nothing to the amount. In a sense, Bacharach and Lawler do not take enough advantage of their basic idea: The only factors that enter their equations are those of power-dependence analysis. Subjective probability, for example, which had been introduced into this kind of analysis by Michener et al. (1973), drops out of Bacharach and Lawler's later analysis of perceived power. This results in a too-limited analysis of the process by which perceptions and expectations emerge and come to govern the exercise of and compliance with power. Among the elements that are missing are (1) effects of reputations for power on perceived power, hence (2) perceptions of power that are not linear functions of objective amounts of resources and alternatives, and (3) subjective probabilities of power use and compliance that are determined by indirect as opposed to direct experience and are therefore not linear functions of objective probabilities.

Deterministic Utility Theories

The elements of a utility theory of power are actors, A and B, their acts, X and Y, and unique outcomes of these acts. The outcomes have values that are rewards if they benefit actors and penalties if they disbenefit them. (Penalties forgone are rewards and rewards forgone are penalties.) The motivation to engage in any activity (including interaction itself) depends on the relative utility one expects to gain from it, where the utility of an act is the algebraic sum of the rewards and penalties associated with it. Given a choice between acts X and Y, every actor chooses that course of action that yields the greatest utility. Interaction between A and B is governed by the same principle, and hence occurs if and only if it yields *each* actor the greatest available utility. But the important thing about "choice" in a utility theory is the *comparison* of alternatives: What looks to an observer like an unattractive course of action may be chosen by A or B because it is preferable to its alternatives.

This is an important fact in understanding power and compliance, which often involves choice between the lesser of two evils. "Power" flows from control over rewards and costs, from the capacity to induce acts by promise of reward or threat of penalty. In Harsanyi's theory, for example, which is probably the most elegant utility theory, A offers reward r to B if B will increase the rate at which B does X from p_1 to p_2 $(p_2 > p_1)$ and threatens penalty t if B persists in performing X at rate p_1. B's compliance is proportional to $(r + t)/x$, where x is the disutility to B of doing X. That is, it is a monotonically increasing function of the rewards for doing X and penalties for not doing X and a decreasing function of the disutility to B of X. B will therefore perform X at the rate p_2 if and only if $r - p_2 x > -t - p_1 x$.

But power is even more unstable in utility theories than in power-dependence theory. There is no balance assumption in utility theory, no endogenous pressure for change. But utility theory has most of the same sources of instability as power-dependence theory and at least one that power-dependence theory does not have.

There are three sources of change in the amount of power in utility theories (aside from differences in $u[X_i]$): First, the values of r and t change with time (as they also do in behavioral exchange theories such as that of Homans 1961 — see the analysis by Crosbie 1972). The whole point of a utility, as distinct from a value, formulation is the law of marginal utility. The value of r decreases with the frequency of r. The behavior of t is complicated by the fact that if it consists of withholding r its value may increase rather than decrease with frequency but it nevertheless fluctuates with time. Second, the supply of rewards and penalties changes over time. If A uses them without replacement, the stock decreases. But as the stock decreases, the marginal cost to A of a promise or threat increases. But, third, the impermanence of power is even greater in utility than in power-dependence theories because the effects of power are determined by the amount of r and t on each specific occasion. The unit of analysis is the act, not the relation. Each act is independent of any other act, is without reference to either the past or the future, except for frequency. Saturation (in behavioral terms) or marginal utility (in decision theory terms) determines the value of r and t, but in all other respects each unit act occurs as if it had no past and holds no consequences for the future.

Unlike power-dependence theory, utility theories imply (or, perhaps more exactly, require) a high level of visibility of power. Because of the focus on a unit act, the process is described as an act by B in response to a threat/promise by A, which depends on an actual reward/penalty by A.

Throughout, no matter now often the sequence has been repeated in the past, compliance occurs because of a demand by A and depends on actual use of power. There is no potential power, no law of anticipated reactions, no compliance without overt exercise of power.

The process does not even depend on A's stock of resources, except as it affects A's costs by depletion. Each act is determined entirely by $(r + t)/x$. There are theories (like Parsons's theory of power as a system of credit, 1963) in which resources are pyramided by the reputation they create, the faith they build up, and the resources obtained from others by previous use of power, but none of these factors operates in a deterministic utility theory of power, which depends only on the value at a given instant of r, t, and x. For the same reason, power may be thought of in such theories as power instantaneously created and instantaneously dissipating. One cannot speak of it as "emergent": It is a continuous process in time (as opposed to a process that creates "expectations" that, when activated, determine behavior).

Subjective Expected Utility Theories

A subjective expected utility theory is a stochastic theory of power in which the values and the probability of outcomes are both subjective (Nagel 1968, 1975; Pollard and Mitchell 1972; Tedeschi et al. 1973). Thus utility affects choices to an extent weighted by the subjective probability that the outcome to which the utility is attached will occur. A utility of, say, 100 will have less effect than one of, say, 10 if the probability that 100 occurs is .001 while the probability that 10 occurs is 1.00 because $(.001 \times 100) < (1.00 \times 10)$. As Nagel (1968) notes, an SEU theory makes it possible to reason that B complies with A's "demands" without A openly promising rewards or threatening penalties because B, based on prior experience, is able to anticipate A's reactions (captured by the subjective probability of an outcome). B infers A's probable future behavior based on a knowledge of A's preferences and B's subjectively held beliefs about the probability of a reward for compliance or penalty for noncompliance. (This hypothesis is confirmed by Ford and Zelditch 1988.) Furthermore, A is as capable of inferring B's probable future conduct as B is A's. Therefore, power is less overtly exercised. It is less needed not only from B's point of view, it is also less needed from A's. In a deterministic utility theory, A exercises power every time A believes he or she will gain from B's compliance. The rate at which power is exercised is an increasing function of the utility of an outcome of B's actions to A and a decreasing function of the cost to A of the exercise of power (in terms of alternatives forgone, for example). In an SEU theory of power, A exercises power whenever the SEU of its use is greater than the SEU of not using power (Tedeschi et al. 1973). But the factors determining the use of power include the utility to A of B's compliance, the costs to A of B's noncompliance, the costs of exercising power, the probability of success if power is exercised, and the probability of retaliation if B resists compliance. In consequence, there is a law of anticipated reactions for A just as for B (pointed out by Dahl 1956, 1961); and A may be supposed (1) not to make demands that cannot be enforced and (2) not to make promises/threats openly when B will comply without overt exercise of power.

An SEU theory therefore predicts much less visibility of power than deterministic utility theories do, and it also implies more stability. Subjective probabilities are beliefs that, once formed, are capable of persistence; knowledge of preferences also persists. Together, they imply that power fluctuates less from occasion to occasion than deterministic utility theories imply.

But SEU theory faces serious measurement problems and applications of the theory in practice tend to undermine its more powerful implications. (For a review of these measurement problems see Coombs et al. 1970, pp. 129-37, 145-47.) In practice, it is typically assumed that "the average of the subjective utilities and subjective probabilities should approximate the objective values and probabilities" (Tedeschi et al. 1973, p. 57). In practice, therefore, investigators tend to lose sight of the distinctive value of the theory. Of even more far-reaching consequence is the fact that the theory assumes subjective probability is founded in the specific history of the AB relation (except Nagel 1968). The result is that many other sources of expectations for A's and B's behavior are treated as insignificant. The theory therefore implies that at each new encounter between previously unacquainted A and B the process begins as if it had no history. It takes time for subjective estimates of another's preferences and probable actions to emerge. And it remains true, as in deterministic utility theories, that A's stock of resources plays no role in the theory except that its depletion affects A's costs.

Thus SEU theories depend more on past events and expectation of future events than deterministic utility theories, hence are not committed to analyzing power in terms only of unit choices, and they incorporate a kind of expectation (subjective anticipations of reactions) that increases stability and decreases visibility of power. But they still tend to underestimate the effects of expectations because they begin sequences of events between A and B as if history begins always at the beginning. One of the important ways in which an expectation, once introduced, makes a difference is that it can be transmitted to others, hence can operate on them before the specific history of a relation has even begun.

Summary and Conclusions

We regard a theory of power as satisfactory if it can explain four features that we intuitively believe to be true of power:

(1) It is relatively stable,
(2) sometimes emerging instantaneously, but sometimes not,
(3) amplifying the amount of power as it becomes stable, and
(4) at the same time decreasing its visibility.

Power-dependence theory predicts instant emergence and virtual invisibility of power, but no amplification of the amount of power, and assumes pressures toward instability of asymmetric power. Thus it does not explain those instances in which emergence is not instantaneous, perhaps outdoes our intuitions about visibility, and understates both the amount and stability of power. Bacharach and Lawler's (1980, 1981) attempts to link power-dependence relations to particular acts of compliance, although taking perceptions of power into account, have the same tendency to understate stability and amount of power.

In utility theories there is no stability at all, no emergence, no amplification, and power is always visible. Thus they explain none of the properties we intuitively attribute to power.

SEU theories match our intuitions better than other theories, but still underestimate stability, have only one kind of emergence (explaining it only when it is comparatively slow), underestimate the amplification of power created by emergence, but still overestimate the visibility of power.

Expectations, Shared Awareness, and Power

We shall model a process in which one actor, A, directs another, B, to do X. By hypothesis, B attaches sufficient disutility to X that B would not do X were it not for promises of reward, r, for doing X or threats of penalty, t, for not doing X, or both. A's requests or directives, promises and/or threats, rewards and/or penalties are referred to as A's *exercise*, or *use*, of power and B's behavior is referred to as B's *compliance*, if B does X, or *noncompliance*, if B does not do X. B also may use power, as retaliation for A's threats and/or resistance to A's directives.

Both A's and B's behavior are thought of in the theory as choices among alternative courses of action. That is, it is assumed that each alternative is in principle possible; any alternative could in principle occur. Perfectly institutionalized behavior is outside the scope of this kind of theory, and alternatives that are made impossible by a given social structure are not among the alternatives the theory treats. Hence the probability of a "choice" is to begin with neither 0 nor 1.

The choice of a course of action by A and by B is assumed to depend in the first instance on the subjective expected utility of the outcomes associated with each action. That is, each alternative X_i is associated with one or more outcomes, O_{ij}. Each outcome, O_{ij}, is associated with a subjective value, called a *utility*, $u(O_{ij})$. If there is a unique outcome for each alternative, it is assumed that each actor chooses the alternative that has the most preferred outcome, that is, for which $u(O_i)$ is greatest. (If the actor is indifferent as to alternative outcomes, it is assumed that he or she alternates equally among them.) But alternatives may have more than one outcome; that is, choice may only probabilistically determine the outcome. While there may be a true probability distribution over the outcomes, in SEU theory it is assumed that actors do not know this distribution. They do, however, have *subjective probabilities* associated with each possible outcome of each possible choice, which we denote by ψ_{ij}. But it is assumed that if the "outcome" of a choice is itself decomposable into parts, the utility of a choice is a linear combination of (1) the utility of each outcome, (2) weighted by its subjective probability, that is, $\Sigma\psi_{ij}u_j$. If we accept as axiomatic the principle that actors choose the alternative that has the most preferred outcome, it seems reasonable to suppose that in the probabilistic case they choose that alternative that has the best *expected* outcome. That is, they should be expected to choose the alternative that is associated with the largest value of $\Sigma\psi_{ij}u_j$.

Although virtually all decision theories will have this same basic framework, it is worth noting that they differ considerably in what elements enter the choice function and how the function itself is formulated. In particular, virtually any theory of "choice" in one way or another assumes that the actor is driven to choose X_i by all the positive features associated with it but is driven away from X_i by all its negative features. Consequently, one may also think of the actor as driven toward X_i by all the negative features of its alternatives. In Camilleri et al. (1972), this idea underlies how gains are computed. But there are obviously many functions that might represent this idea. That is, in *any* choice theory the choice of X_i depends as much on what the actor does *not* like about its alternatives as on what the actor *does* like about X_i. But in the simplest such function, which is the one we have adopted as our starting point, this is implicit rather than explicit. We do not ourselves have any interest in the question of what choice function is best, and believe that our theory will have the same implications regardless of which is chosen. What we like about the function we are using is simply that it is so transparent.

If, as we are supposing, A prefers that B do X while B prefers not to do X, it follows that whether or not B actually does X depends on the utilities of r and t and the probabilities with which r follows compliance and t follows noncompliance. That is, B should do X if and only if the expected utility of r + t exceeds the difference in utility between X and its most preferred alternative, $u(\overline{X}) - u(X)$. (Without loss of generality we can speak simply of two alternatives.) For in general, B will do X if and only if $\Sigma\psi_{ij}u(X) > \Sigma\psi_{ij}u(\overline{X})$. Assuming that, absent r and t, $u(\overline{X}) > u(X)$, B will therefore do X if and only if $u(X) + \psi u(r) > u(\overline{X}) - \psi u(t)$.[1] Equivalently, B will do X if and only if $\psi u(r) + \psi u(t) > u(\overline{X}) - u(X)$.

On A's side, whether A actually attempts to use power to compel compliance by B will depend in the first instance on the subjective expected utility of X to A and on the cost of obtaining B's compliance. (*Cost* here refers simply to the marginal utility to A of r and t.) This should depend in part on the probability that B complies, because the actual use of r and t depends on whether B complies or not. If the subjective probability of B's compliance is ψ_x, A should exercise power over B if and only if $u(X) - u(\overline{X}) > \psi_x u(r) + \overline{\psi}_x u(t)$.

Thus, taking SEU theory as a starting point, we make the following assumption.

Assumption 1 (SEU assumption). For given X, r, and t:

(1) B complies with preferences of A that he or she do X if and only if

$$\psi u(r) + \psi u(t) > u(\overline{X}) - u(X)$$

(2) A promises r to B for doing X and/or threatens t if B does not do X if and only if

$$u(X) - u(\overline{X}) > \psi_x u(r) + \overline{\psi}_x u(t)$$

where ψ is B's subjective probability that A actually rewards compliance, which may or may not differ from B's subjective probability that A actually penalizes noncompliance, and ψ_x is A's subjective probability that B actually complies with the directive to do X and $\overline{\psi}_x = 1 - \psi_x$.

If now we assume that this interaction is repeated a number of times, or that others like it are reported to A and B, or that traditions about it are transmitted from the past to A and B, we can also assume that A and B develop *expectations* about what the other will want and will do. We refer to these as *first-order* expectations when we speak of (1) B's expectations about A's preferences, A's resources (i.e., A's stock of rewards/penalties), the probability that A uses these resources, and the probability that A complies with B's own preferences (for example, if B attempted counterthreats); and (2) A's expectations about B's preferences, B's resources, B's use of these resources, and the probability of B's compliance with A's preferences.

Without introducing the idea as an assumption of our theory, we note that the concept of an expectation implies that some elements at least of the power/compliance relation are stable. For expectations change if and only if behavior is incongruent with them. But expectations, once formed, are important determinants of behavior and the behavior that they determine is congruent with expectations. They tend, therefore, to maintain themselves once formed.

Expectations do not change the conditions under which compliance occurs, but they do change the rate at which A openly expresses preferences, promises rewards, and/or threatens penalties. Thus the second assumption we adopt is Friedrich's (1937, 1963) "law of anticipated reactions" (LAR) (also see Ford and Zelditch 1988).

Assumption 2 (LAR). For given X, r, and t:

(1) If B expects in advance that $\Sigma \psi_{ij} u(\overline{X}) > \Sigma \psi_{ij} u(X)$, then B complies with A's preferences independently of any overt expression of preferences, promises, or threats by A.

(2) If A expects in advance that $\Sigma\psi_{ij}u(\overline{X}) > \Sigma\psi_{ij}u(X)$, then A does not express preferences, promises, or rewards, or threaten penalties to B with respect to X.

That is, Assumption 2 holds both (1) that A *need* not exercise power to cause compliance if B knows already what A prefers and that $\psi_{ij}u(r) + \psi_{ij}u(t)$ exceeds the disutility of compliance and (2) that A will not demand X of B if it is highly likely that B will resist and the costs of using power exceed the expected gain.

Note that not only will compliance often occur without A overtly voicing demands, promises, or threats, but in the case of coercion A does not even overtly use penalties.

A and B may each, in addition, form expectations about the other's expectations. These we refer to as *second-order* expectations, consisting of (1) A's expectations about B's expectations about A's preferences, A's resources, the probability that A uses them, and the probability of A's compliance with any preferences of B; and (2) B's expectations about A's expectations about B's preferences, B's resources, the probability that B uses them, and B's compliance with any preferences of A's. When such expectations form on both sides, we refer to this as *shared awareness* of the components that go into determining use of and compliance with power.

About shared awareness, we assume that when first- and second-order expectations are either absent or *incongruent*, power becomes more overt, more visible. If A knows that B knows exactly what A will do to compel X, there is no need for A to express preferences, promise rewards, or threaten penalties (which follows from the LAR). But if A expects that B expects more or less than A will do, it becomes necessary to exercise power overtly. This will be necessary if B expects less because B is therefore less likely to comply. If B expects more, it will be necessary to renegotiate terms of exchange. Similarly, if B knows that A knows exactly what reward or penalty will induce B to do X, B will do X without a murmur if B expects that $\psi_{ij}u(r) + \psi_{ij}u(t)$ exceeds $\overline{u}(X) - u(X)$. But if B does not know what A expects him or her to expect, or believes that what A expects is less than B will actually take to do X, then noncompliance or renegotiation of terms, either of which is likely to lead to open struggles, is more likely. (In B's case, incongruence that promises too much reward probably does not lead to any renegotiation on B's side.)

Thus we assume, in addition to the LAR, a "law of shared awareness": *Assumption 3* (LSA). For given X, r, and t:

(1) If A knows B's expectations for A, overt expression of preferences, promises, and/or threats by A occurs if and only if A's second-order expectations are incongruent with A's actual preferences and willingness to use resources.

(2) If B knows A's expectations for B, noncompliance and retaliation occur if and only if either
(a) the SEU of noncompliance exceeds that of compliance or
(b) B's second-order expectations for A are less than B's actual preferences and terms of compliance.

Thus not only does A not need to express preferences, promises, and threats overtly or use penalties overtly, A *knows* that they are not necessary. Hence their overt use is less likely. Overt power on either side is more likely when one, the other, or both either do not know what the other expects or believe that they do know (correctly or not) but believe that the other's expectations are wrong.

Implications

At least four implications may be logically derived from shared awareness: (1) Power is less visible than SEU theory would predict, (2) it is more stable, (3) the process itself amplifies power, and (4) under some conditions instant emergence of expectations is possible.

VISIBILITY OF POWER

The most immediate implication of the LAR and LSA assumptions is that overt exercise of power is seldom visible once expectations form, especially when A has more power than B. If A has more power than B, and expects that, at $\psi u(r)$ and $\psi u(t)$, the utility of X exceeds that of $\overline{X}$, A expects B to comply with A's preferences; whereas B expects A to reward B with r in return for compliance or penalize him or her with t for noncompliance. Given these first-order expectations, A is unlikely to express directives, threats, or promises in order to attain B's compliance; it will be unnecessary. By the same token, B is unlikely to express threats of retaliation or demand a specific reward, r, for his or her compliance.

Given second-order expectations (i.e., A knows that B knows, B knows that A knows, and so on), A is even less likely to penalize B and B is less likely to retaliate than otherwise, since they both share the same expectations — that is, expectations and behavior are congruent, and, therefore, both correctly anticipate behavior and outcomes.

As a result especially of shared awareness, power therefore plays an almost invisible role in interpersonal relations. Neither acts of power nor acts of counterpower (retaliation) need to be exercised overtly by either party. The theory predicts, in fact, that if A has more power than B, A exercises overt power only when B is not expected to comply but the value of u(X) to A is greater than the costs of exercising power; or when A has no second-order expectations about B's expectations; or when A's second-order expectations are incongruent with A's actual u(X), $\psi u(r)$, and $\psi u(t)$.

On B's side, B openly struggles with A only if B expects that $\psi u(r) + \psi u(t)$ is less than the difference between $u(\overline{X}) - u(X)$, or B has no second-order expectations about A's expectations, or when B's second-order expectations are incongruent with B's actual $u(X)$, $u(r)$, $u(t)$, and probability of compliance. From this theoretical viewpoint, it is no wonder that open threats or promises are rarely expressed in work relations between superordinates and their subordinates in conjunction with routine assignments and task performance. The invisibility of power in such cases is mainly a result of shared awareness concerning both sides' preferences, resources, and probabilities of action. It appears, however, that exercise of power and retaliatory attempts are quite common in parent-child relations. This pattern of visible power may be mainly due to the fact that parents doubt the emergence of first-order expectations in younger children.

STABILITY OF POWER

Our theory of expectations predicts that power is much more "sticky" than any other theory would have suggested. *Stability* refers in the first instance to the stability of the expectations underlying power/compliance, which are stable if and only if the expectations with which an exchange begins are unchanged by its outcome. This should be reflected in stability of the observable behavior of A and B, that is, of their use of and compliance with power, with respect to X through time. Stability in power relations is a property that emerges from two underlying trends: continuity and regularity. Continuity is the length of time that a given power-dependence relationship between two or more persons persists. Regularity is the amount of variation in A's and B's modes of behavior over time, hence the extent to which participants are likely to behave in a predictable way at any given point of time. Both are positively affected by shared awareness of mutual expectations.

Without the effect of expectations, four forces are likely to drive power relations to discontinuities: (1) Actual resources are subject to considerable fluctuations due to changes in both the actors' stocks of resources and the external conditions under which they operate; (2) the utilities attached to outcomes decline as a function of repetitive transactions; (3) frequent use of threats and promises exerts pressure from which actors attempt to escape or that generates resistance; and (4) each exercise of power is independent of its past and future.

Not all of these are affected by expectations. Nevertheless, expectations change at a much slower pace than actual resources. The basic property of any "expectation" concept is that it causes behavior that is congruent with itself. While changes in expectations will occur (probabilistically) if behavior is incongruent with them, incongruent behavior is in fact unlikely to occur except for the effects of exogenous factors. If the law of shared awareness holds, only incongruence between an actor's second-order expectations and actual preferences, resources, and likely reactions gives rise to change in expectations. Expectations therefore introduce a quite stable element into the otherwise fluctuating power of A over B. They do not counteract the changing marginal utility of u(X), u(r), and u(t), but they do introduce a past and a future into the AB relation, and because they decrease its visibility they also reduce the resistance created by the overt exercise of power.

Thus the effect of expectations is to increase the continuity of the relation A > B. They also increase regularity, because by definition they increase predictability. There are fewer unexpected, provocative acts by either actor, less need to test the credibility of either's promises or threats. Each can anticipate in a predictable way the consequences of his or her acts in terms of the other's likely behavior.

THE EMERGENCE OF EXPECTATIONS

Of the four ways that actors can form expectations for each other, three are indirect. The fact that expectations can be created by means other than direct experience implies that actors A and B can enter a new relationship with already formed expectations. Therefore, the level of dependence, expected compliance, expected sanctions, or expected retaliation that determines both exercise of power and compliance can be determined instantaneously. Such predetermined expectations, then, motivate both actors, A and B, to behave in a specific manner at the outset of their relation. Preformed expectations probably play such a role mainly in well-structured social contexts, as in organizations, in which rules, procedures, ranks, and symbols reduce the level of ambiguity. Similarly, in traditional families spouses may come to their marriage with strictly defined expectations concerning, among other things, their relative power and its derived modes of behavior. Thus a causal chain of effects may be postulated among structural settings, instantaneous expectations, and the exercise of power, compliance, and retaliation. That there is sometimes less than instantaneous emergence is due to variations in the extent to which expectations are preformed.

AMPLIFICATION OF POWER

Expectations in fact appear often in the literature on power as "reputational" effects of power (e.g. Gamson 1966). One of the important consequences of reputations for power is that they amplify the amount of A's power over B. That is, as expectations emerge, the rate of B's compliance with A's preferences increases even if the actual stock of A's resources does not.

This effect occurs for three reasons. First, one effect of expectations is that at least t is seldom actually required. While expenditures of r will be necessary, the total costs of the exercise of power are reduced by the fact that threats seldom need to be carried out. In cases where the only inducement employed is threats, expectations in fact preserve the stock of resources relatively unchanged. This inflates the actual stock of A's resources by comparison with models in which there are no expectations for power. But second, because expectations are "reputations" for power, they also add a resource to A's stock. The effect is not unlike that Parsons (1963) attributes to power in the collective, "power to" sense, though it will in general not be true that interpersonal power is therefore a variable-sum quantity. (That is, even amplified power will be zero-sum for "power over.") A given stock of resources makes possible something like the extension of "credit"; that is, more power can be created by the same actual resources as reputations for power emerge. Hence reputations pyramid the amount of power. Third, stability itself amplifies power. Actual resource stocks fluctuate more than expectations do. Expectations therefore introduce a steadying hand on the flow of power, but are especially significant in maintaining the reputed level of resources when they are in fact decreasing. So long as the decrease is not secular — that is, a long-term decline — the correction of downside fluctuations has the effect of increasing A's overall power over B.

Contingencies

The fact that expectations "emerge" suggests the obvious possibility that at different stages of their emergence expectations differ in how certain the actor is of them. Furthermore, that they emerge in different ways and have different sources may give rise to additional uncertainties. We must therefore think of expectations as weaker or stronger, in the sense of being more or less certain. And the magnitude of the effects claimed for expectations in the preceding section should be proportional to their certainty.

EFFECTS OF UNCERTAINTY

One way to think of what *emergence* means (in the context of power) is that expectations begin to form that, with time, become both stronger and more widely shared. Hence, to the extent that expectations are not at first certain, the rate of emergence is slower, and the greater the uncertainty the slower the rate of emergence ought to be.

A slower rate of emergence immediately implies, of course, that the amount of power created by uncertain expectations should be less than that created by certain expectations, hence there should be less amplification of the amount of power.

On the other hand, visibility will be greater with uncertainty, for, in part, it is visible power that creates expectations. There are actually two somewhat different ways power may be made visible, of course: by "real" use and by symbolic use. One can think of a kind of gestural politics in which A and B give off cues to each other (and to other parties) about their preferences, resources, and probable reactions, *in order to* create expectations, in the way that President Reagan's aides continually spoke of "giving signals" to Gorbachev. Uncertainty should increase visibility by increasing one or the other of these kinds of public displays of power.

Finally, uncertainty should decrease stability of power relations. That is, not only will stability take longer to emerge, which follows from the conclusions already reached about emergence, but the weaker the expectations at any given point the greater the likelihood that some kind of change will take place. This follows simply from the fact that the weaker the expectations, the greater the likelihood of behavior incongruent with expectations, hence the greater the endogenous pressures for change.

Despite its importance, we have made no attempt to study exhaustively all the factors that give rise to certainty or uncertainty in expectations. However, we wish to call attention to at least four: (1) consensus, (2) sources of expectations, (3) validation of expectations by others, and (4) sharing of symbols of power.

CONSENSUS, CONGRUENCE, AND CERTAINTY

To the extent that B's first-order expectations for A are the complement of A's first-order expectations for B, we can say that their first-order expectations are *congruent* and they share a *consensus* about expectations. B's expectations for A complement A's expectations about B when, for example, if A supposes that he or she is superior in power to B then B at the same time supposes that B is inferior in power to A. (This can be made more precise in terms of actual SEU values, but greater precision is unnecessary for our present purposes.) If A supposes that A and B are equal, then B complements A if B also supposes that they are equal. Finally, if A supposes that B is superior in power to A, B is the complement of A if B supposes that A is inferior to B.

To the extent that A and B do not share a consensus about their respective roles in the relation, behavior caused by expectations should be incongruent with the expectations of at least one of them. This, in turn, should induce a higher level of uncertainty about the actor's expectations for the other, driving the process toward some change in expectations. Thus dissensus should have the effect of slowing emergence, deflating power, inducing more visible exercise of power, and decreasing stability.

The role of consensus, however, is not limited to first-order expectations. An important form of it, mentioned in the preceding section, is congruence between second-order expectations and actual preferences, resources, and reactions. One may in fact think of a triadic relation among one actor's *actual* state (say A's), the other's first-order expectations of that state (say B's), and the first actor's second-order expectations about the other's expectations. This triadic relation is illustrated in Table 11.1, in which the "actual" level is denoted the "0th" level.

Table 11.1 Congruence Between Expectations at Different Levels

	Actor	
Level of Expectations	*A*	*B*
2	A expects that B expects that u(X), ψ (r,t)	
1		B expects that u(x), ψ(r,t)
0	u(x), ψ(r,t)	

It should be evident from the table, however primitive its representation of the features in actual power/compliance situations, that consensus depends on similarities not only in first-order expectations but also across levels. If A and B do not share a first-order consensus, this will be evident to *each* of them, if second-order expectations exist, because of incongruence between second-order expectations and what each actor expects of him- or herself. As a result, uncertainty of expectations about the other should be greater. If second-order expectations do not exist, the LSA assumption implies that the "consensus" is incomplete, which will have the same effect. The result in either case will be more visible use of power, slower emergence, less amplification of power, and less stability.

THE EFFECT OF DIFFERENCES
AMONG SOURCES OF EXPECTATIONS

Some point was made in the section on implications of the fact that there are a number of different sources of expectations in addition to direct experience. One may therefore think of the more indirect sources as differing in both the quantity and the quality of the "information" they provide the actor. Some of them are highly institutionalized and therefore probably unquestioned and unquestionable. Some of them are unique, and therefore idiosyncratic, to the particular source.

While a rather complicated theory of this subject could probably be developed, one obvious starting place is to think simply of the amount of certainty that can be created by (1) the number and consistency of sources that provide the same information and (2) the credibility of the source, for example, its status value. If a large number of well-placed people consistently believe in A's power, for example, the certainty with which B believes in the expectations they transmit about A should increase, which should accelerate emergence, inflate power, decrease visibility, and increase stability.

SOCIAL VALIDATION,
SOCIAL SUPPORT, AND CERTAINTY

To the extent that objective reality itself is not sufficient to validate the "information" provided by individual and cultural sources, its reality is "social" (i.e., depends on the beliefs of people around A and B). If C is a third party to the relation of A to B, to the extent that C shares the same expectations, acts by C that are consistent with them socially validates them for A and B. Thus other people are not only the sources, they are also the guarantors of expectations about power.

But over and above the impact of C on the certainty with which A and B hold expectations for each other, there is the fact that third parties imply a new kind of expectation, *expectations of support by C.* Interpersonal relations typically take place in larger social contexts. An important effect of parties like C is more or less support for the use of power by A and B's compliance with it. Support will frequently be expected, by both A and B, for exercises of power by A that are within culturally defined limits. On the other hand, noncompliance, even resistance, by B will often be supported by C if it appears justified by circumstances. For example, noncompliance is likely to be supported in cases of child abuse, sexual harassment, or immoral demands.

We are not trying to offer a theory of the causes of social support. It may derive from legitimacy, from material interest, from sentiments (such as liking for A or B), or any number of other motives. What matters is that both A and B have expectations about who and what C will and will not support.

These third-party expectations will in the first instance affect A's and B's actual behavior. If C is expected by A to support B's noncompliance, A is less likely to use power. If C is expected by B to support noncompliance, B is less likely to comply. Because they are a factor in A's and B's behavior, third-party expectations affect the congruence between behavior and expectations. Hence validation is a source of certainty not only directly, because of its effects on expectations, but also indirectly because of its effects on behavioral congruence with expectations. If C's behavior, and A's and B's expectations of C's behavior, are incongruent with A's and B's first-order expectations for each other, the effect is to increase uncertainty first of all because A's and B's expectations have less social validity and second of all because they have less anticipated support, changing actual behavior. The two effects taken together will decrease stability, deflate power, and increase visibility.

THE EFFECT OF SYMBOLS OF POWER ON CERTAINTY

The process of emergence is frequently associated with "gestural" politics, that is, public displays of power the purpose of which is to create (or maintain) expectations about intentions, resources, and willingness to use them. Sometimes this involves actual use of power — overt demands, promises, threats, rewards, penalties — used less to induce compliance than to create or maintain expectations about future use of, support for, or compliance with power. But sometimes what it involves is symbolic power ritually displayed.

Some of these displays are symbols of the potential use of power, like such symbols of police power as visibly worn sidearms, clubs, and handcuffs. Some are symbols of deference, of potential compliance with power, such as the military salute. By means of such symbols and rituals, such as reveille and retreat on a military base, expectations are transmitted to new members and maintained for already socialized members. These symbols affect, first of all, the actual or potential objects of power, but they also are important for the actual or potential users of it, for they also create expectations that one has power to use and that others support its use.

While some symbols and rituals are well institutionalized, like reveille and retreat, some are less widely shared, even unique to a particular A and B. The gavel will probably create immediate understanding of who is in authority in a courtroom, but in a delinquent gang it would be understood with a different meaning entirely, adding nothing to authority.

Ceremonial display of less institutionalized rituals and symbols will create less certain expectations in either users or objects of power. To the extent that less well-institutionalized symbols or rituals create less certainty, they should decelerate emergence, deflate the amount of power, and create less stable power. The effect on the visibility of power is perhaps more complicated because symbol and ritual are themselves significant only to the extent that they visibly display power. But there are nevertheless two ways in which more widely institutionalized symbols and rituals of power reduce its visibility. First, visible symbols of the institutions of power, like police weaponry, so widely diffuse expectations and give them so much certainty that no particular exchange between any particular A and B is required to establish them. Hence particular gestural politics are not needed. Second, when particular gestural politics do occur it is possible to carry them on at a largely symbolic level, reducing the visible use of "real" powers, such as firing weapons or wielding clubs.

Summary and Conclusion

Our starting point is a subjective expected utility theory of interpersonal power. By *power* we refer to the use of rewards and/or penalties to induce or coerce compliance. In an SEU theory, power is used if the gain from its use exceeds the cost. The gain depends on the sum of the subjective values, or utilities, of the various possible outcomes of using power, each multiplied by the subjective probability of the outcome. Costs are obtained in the same way, depending in part on how likely it is that the other complies. Compliance itself occurs if the sum of the SEU of rewards and penalties exceeds the difference in SEU between noncompliance and compliance.

The subjective probabilities of an SEU theory are one kind of expectation about probable future use of rewards/penalties and compliance. Relative to SEU theories, we further complicate the expectations involved in power by introducing more sources, kinds, and levels of them. Sources include not only direct experience of A and B with each other but also various indirect sources such as socialization to a pregiven tradition. Kinds include not only expected reactions but also preferences and resources. Levels include not only first-order but second-order expectations. (First-order expectations includes A's expectations about the preferences, resources, and reactions of B and B's expectations about the preferences, resources, and reactions of A. Second-order expectations include A's expectations about B's expectations about A and B's expectations about A's expectations about B.)

A system of expectations that is complete (i.e., all first- and second-order expectations exist) and about which A and B are certain implies (1) that expectations in any particular instance emerge instantaneously; (2) that the amount of power created by a given stock of resources is amplified, that is, that expectations induce a greater amount of compliance; (3) that the amount of power they create is relatively stable, creating the conditions of its own persistence; but (4) that power is much less visible than any other theory of compliant actions predicts.

But the magnitude of these effects depends on the certainty and completeness of the expectations. The less certain and complete they are, the slower the emergence, the less they amplify power, the less stable power is, and the greater its visibility.

No attempt is made to treat all sources of certainty exhaustively, but four that are important are as follows: (1) consensus between the expectations of A and B and congruence of their behavior with these expectations; (2) the status, number, and consistency of third parties, C, who transmit expectations to A and B; (3) the extent of social validation and expected support by third parties, C, once expectations are formed; and (4) the extent to which symbols that communicate about power are institutionalized in the system of which A and B are part.

Note

1. We assume that the utility of penalties is negative. We omit subscripts for $\psi u(r)$ and $\psi u(t)$ but note that they may or may not take the same value of ψ.

References

Alker, H. 1973. "On Political Capabilities in a Schedule Sense: Measuring Power, Integration, and Development." Pp. 307-73 in *Mathematical Approaches to Politics*, edited by H. R. Alker, K. W. Deutsch, and A. H. Stoetzel. San Francisco: Jossey-Bass.

Bacharach, S. B. and E. J. Lawler. 1976. "The Perception of Power." *Social Forces* 55:123-34.

– – –. 1980. *Power and Politics in Organizations.* San Francisco: Jossey-Bass.

– – –. 1981. *Bargaining, Power, Tactics, and Outcomes.* San Francisco: Jossey-Bass.

Blau, P. 1964. *Exchange and Power in Social Life.* New York: John Wiley.

Brehm, J. W. 1966. *A Theory of Psychological Reactance.* New York: Academic Press.

Burgess, R. L. and J. M. Nielsen. 1974. "An Experimental Analysis of Some Structural Determinants of Equitable and Inequitable Exchange Relations." *American Sociological Review* 39:427-43.

Camilleri, S. F., J. Berger, and T. Conner. 1972. "A Formal Theory of Decision-Making." Pp. 21-37 in *Sociological Theories in Progress*, Vol. 2, edited by J. Berger, M. Zelditch, Jr., and B. Anderson. Boston: Houghton Mifflin.

Cartwright, D. 1959. "A Field Theoretical Conception of Power." Pp. 183-220 in *Studies in Social Power*, edited by D. Cartwright. Ann Arbor: University of Michigan Press.

Cook, K. and R. Emerson. 1978. "Power, Equity and Commitment in Exchange Networks." *American Sociological Review* 43:712-39.

Coombs, C. H., R. M. Dawes, and A. Tversky. 1970. *Mathematical Psychology.* Englewood Cliffs, NJ: Prentice-Hall.

Crosbie, P. 1972. "Social Exchange and Power Compliance: A Test of Homans' Propositions." *Sociometry* 35:203-22.

– – –. 1975. "Interpersonal Power." In *Interaction in Small Groups*, edited by P. Crosbie. New York: Macmillan.

Dahl, R. A. 1956. *Preface to Democracy.* Chicago: University of Chicago Press.

– – –. 1957. "The Concept of Power." *Behavioral Science* 2:201-15.

– – –. 1961. *Who Governs?* New Haven, CT: Yale University Press.

Emerson, R. 1962. "Power-Dependence Relations." *American Sociological Review* 27:31-41.

– – –. 1972. "Exchange Theory." Pp. 38-87 in *Sociological Theories in Progress*, Vol. 2, edited by J. Berger, M. Zelditch, Jr., and B. Anderson. Boston: Houghton Mifflin.

Festinger, L. 1953. "An Analysis of Compliant Behavior." Pp. 232-56 in *Group Relations at the Crossroads*, edited by M. Sherif and M. O. Wilson. New York: Harper.

Ford, J. and M. Zelditch. (1988) "The Law of Anticipated Reactions." *Social Psychology Quarterly* 51:164-71.

French, J.R.P. and B. Raven. 1959. "The Bases of Social Power." Pp. 150-67 in *Studies in Social Power*, edited by D. Cartwright. Ann Arbor: University of Michigan Press.

Friedrich, C. 1937. *Constitutional Government and Politics.* New York: Harper.

– – –. 1963. *Man and His Government.* New York: McGraw-Hill.

Gamson, W. A. 1966. "Reputation and Resources in Community Politics." *American Journal of Sociology* 72:121-31.

Harsanyi, J. C. 1962. "Measurement of Social Power, Opportunity Costs, and the Theory of Two-Person Bargaining Games." *Behavioral Science* 7:67-80.

Hawley, A. H. 1963. "Community Power and Urban Renewal Success." *American Journal of Sociology* 68:422-31.

Homans, G. C. 1961. *Social Behavior.* New York: Harcourt, Brace & World.

Lawler, E. J. and S. Bacharach. 1976. "Outcome Alternatives and Value as Criteria for Multistrategy Evaluations." *Journal of Personality and Social Psychology* 34:885-94.

– – –. 1979. "Power-Dependence in Individual Bargaining: The Expected Utility of Influence." *Industrial and Labor Relations Review* 32:196-204.

Lehman, E. W. 1969. "Toward a Macrosociology of Power." *American Sociological Review* 34:453-65.

Lukes, S. 1974. *Power: A Radical View.* New York: Macmillan.

March, J. G. 1955. "An Introduction to the Theory and Measurement of Influence." *American Political Science Review* 49:431-51.

Michaels, J. W. and J. A. Wiggins. 1976. "Effects of Mutual Dependency and Dependency Asymmetry in Social Exchange." *Sociometry* 39:368-76.

Michener, H. A., E. J. Lawler, and S. B. Bacharach. 1973. "Perception of Power in Conflict Situations." *Journal of Personality and Social Psychology* 28:155-62.

Molm, L. 1985. "Relative Effects of Individual Dependencies: Further Tests of the Relation Between Power Imbalance and Power Use." *Social Forces* 63:810-37.

Nagel, J. H. 1968. "Some Questions About the Concept of Power." *Behavioral Science* 13:129-37.

— — —. 1975. *The Descriptive Analysis of Power.* New Haven, CT: Yale University Press.

Palmier, L. H. 1963. "The Impermanence of Power." *Human Relations* 16:199-205.

Parsons, T. 1963. "On the Concept of Political Power." *Proceedings of the American Philosophical Society* 107(3).

Pollard, W. E. and T. R. Mitchell. 1972. "Decision Theory Analysis of Social Power." *Psychological Bulletin* 78:433-46.

Poulantzas, N. 1973. *Political Power and Social Classes.* London: NLB.

Russell, B. R. 1938. *Power.* London: Allen & Unwin.

Schopler, J. 1965. "Social Power." Pp. 177-214 in *Advances in Experimental Social Psychology*, Vol. 2, edited by L. Berkowitz. New York: Academic Press.

Tedeschi, J. T., B. R. Schlenker, and T. V. Bonoma. 1973. *Conflict, Power, and Games.* Chicago: Aldine.

Thibaut, J. and H. H. Kelley. 1959. *The Social Psychology of Groups.* New York: John Wiley.

Weber, Max. 1947. *Max Weber: The Theory of Social and Economic Organization*, translated by A. M. Henderson and T. Parsons. New York: Oxford University Press.

12

Power Structures:
Derivations and Applications
of Elementary Theory

DAVID WILLER

BARRY MARKOVSKY

TRAVIS PATTON

A decade of research has shown that structures of social relations can determine the exercise of power and the incidence of phenomena such as exploitation and domination. One theory active in this endeavor is "elementary theory" (Willer and Anderson 1981). The theory's "elementary" label is based on the fact that conceptual elements, relatively simple and few in number, are used to generate more complex theoretical models. In Fararo's (1984, 1987) terms, elementary theory is *generative*. Specifically, (1) the basic elements are used to compose social actions into relationships and relationships into structures, and (2) dynamic models are produced by introducing theoretic actors in the structures. This chapter will not repeat the first steps through which the conceptual parts were built, as these have been published elsewhere (Willer 1981, 1984, 1987). Instead, the focus will be on structural conditions of power.

Again in Fararo's terms, elementary theory is *neoclassical*. It is founded on the view, common to Marx ([1867] 1967) and Weber ([1918] 1968), that the interests that actors pursue are produced by social relationships and the conditions under which they are pursued are determined by social structures. The theoretical works of Marx and Weber form an important orienting perspective. For example, both recognize that the rate of exchange of work for wages is conditioned by unemployment — that is, by the *exclusion* of some job seekers from work. In theory, this exclusion undergirds the power relations of capitalist societies. As we will show below, analogous exclusions produce power relations in the experimental investigations of exchange networks.

Though sometimes confused with exchange theory, elementary theory is a multilevel theory of actors in relations conditioned by structures. Exchange relations and structures are included within its scope, in addition to coercion and conflict phenomena. Despite some common ground, however, elementary theory and exchange theory have distinct points of departure in their origins, concepts, strategies, and methods.

Expressed in terms of its neoclassical roots, the theory presumes that actors are capable of engaging in meaningful social action, in the sense used by Weber. By building step by step through relations to structures, the aim is to investigate Marx's claim that power relations in social structures allow structures to reproduce themselves. If Marx was correct, the theoretical task of specifying the structural conditions of power remains to be accomplished (see Poulantzas 1973; Isaac 1987).

No single structural condition determines power. Though all of the structural conditions thus far discovered will be presented, this chapter places special emphasis on the development of formulations and tests for the effects of exclusion. At the level of actors in relations, "resistance theory" is used to generate dynamic models of exchange. At the level of relations in structures, graph theoretic procedures are used to locate high, low, and equipower positions, and points of network instability.

Critical tests have long been a measure of maturity in exact sciences. Elementary theory and power-dependence theory (e.g., Emerson 1972a, 1972b; Cook et al. 1983) identify different conditions for power, and so provide opportunities for critical testing. When applied to the same networks, the two theories frequently identify different positions as high and low in power. A central point in this chapter is to show how theory is used to develop the critical tests.

Power

In the classical tradition, power was a relational concept. For Marx, capitalist exploitation occurs through the exchange relation of labor for wages. For Weber ([1918] 1968), the relation of domination, whether based on coercion or exchange, always involved "a certain minimum interest of the subordinate in his own obeying" (p. 945). Wrong (1968, 1979) has added clarity to the concept of power by distinguishing its dispositional and episodic aspects, a usage also followed in power-dependence theory from the early works of Emerson. For Emerson the term *power* has always been dispositional. That is, power is a potentiality, not an actuality. The actuality of any power episode is referred to as "power use." We share the view that this is a crucial distinction.

Although space does not allow a comprehensive review of the many definitions of power, those of Dahl and Lukes are exemplary:

My intuitive idea of power, then, is something like this: A has power over B to the extent that he can get B to do something that B would not otherwise do. (Dahl 1957, pp. 202-3)

A exercises power over B when A effects B in a manner contrary to B's interests. (Lukes 1974, p. 34)

Both definitions express widely shared implicit meanings. To apply Dahl's idea we need to know what B would otherwise do. To apply Lukes's idea we need to know B's interests. A formalized, relational conception of power can supply both pieces of information.

Following its classical roots, elementary theory views power as relational. In the exchange relation, power use is usually indicated by the deviation of exchange outcomes from equality or some baseline value. Since that deviation is in the interest of one actor and contrary to the interest of the other, it is power in Lukes's sense. Below we will show how structural conditions also permit one actor to get another to do something that he or she would not otherwise do. Thus our conception of power also conforms to Dahl's. In addition to the views of Dahl and Lukes, however, the relational conception of power developed here addresses the concerns of many other formulations (see Van Doorn 1962; Luckenbill 1979; Layder 1985; Mann 1986).

Power-dependence theory also conceptualizes power use as deviation from a baseline — from a balanced division of profit points. It is because both approaches use relational conceptions of power and power use that the predictions and results of elementary and power-dependence theories can be compared.

Exchange Theory

For elementary theory, exchange occurs under certain specifiable conditions. For example, following Marx and Weber, private property is a condition of exchange. Historical study has found that four types of private property rights are essential to the occurrence of exchange (Gilham 1981; Willer 1985): Actors must have (1) an *exclusive* right to the object of exchange, (2) the right to *alienate* their exclusive right, (3) the right to *appropriate* the right of the other(s), and (4) their agreements to alienate and appropriate governed by a *right of reciprocity*. This means that exchange is a joint transferal of exclusive rights that may or may not be accompanied by actual transferal of the objects of exchange. This also means that exchange is historically contingent and is not, as Polanyi (1957) recognized, the product of some inherent human propensity to "truck and barter," a propensity that economic historians have long held to be a non sequitur.

That exchange is historically contingent, not innate, follows immediately from the negation of the four rights. Imagine a social structure in which no actor has the right to exclude, to alienate, or to appropriate, and with no reciprocity rights. In theory, these are the conditions of *communal property relations* and studies have shown that, with communal property, the transfer of goods does not take the form of exchange (Loukinen 1981; Hansen 1981).[1] Since the kinds of social relations in which people engage vary, private property rights must be initial conditions to produce exchange in experiments. For enforcement of the rights, the experimenter plays the role of the state.

In contrast, the operant formulations underpinning exchange theory view exchange as a product of psychological processes. The reinforcement principles producing exchange are considered to be innate and immutable properties of the human organism. Though more systematic, power-dependence theory's point of departure can be traced to Homans's operant exchange theory. Homans's basic propositions imply that, because people act on the principle of positive reinforcement, relations occur only if the acts of each are rewarding to the other. According to Homans (1967):

> Either two persons reward one another in more than one way, like each other
> on more than one count, and increase their interaction, or they will hurt one
> another in more than one way, dislike one another, and decrease interaction.
> (p. 46)

Homans (1974, p. 26) and Blau (1964, p. 224) have both noted that punishment is an ineffective reinforcer.[2] This statement is, however, technically incorrect. In operant psychology, reinforcers increase frequency of a behavior, and punishments decrease that frequency. Homans and Blau confound punishment with negative reinforcement. In so doing, only mutually rewarding exchanges are allowed (Willer and Anderson 1981, pp. 9ff.). This misinterpretation accounts for the constricted scope of exchange theory, in particular for its exclusion from consideration of relations such as coercion and conflict. Both coercion and conflict contain negatives. Since exchange theory holds that negatives simply decrease interaction, both are transitory and only exchange relations have life spans of sufficient duration to permit their study. The recent effort to extend exchange theory to include negatives (Molm 1987) has not included a coherent formulation for coercive structures or the recognition of structural similarities between coercive and exchange structures (Willer 1984, 1987).

Homans's psychological reductionism eliminated structure, then reconstituted it on psychological grounds—an approach also taken by Emerson (1972a, 1972b). Connecting exchange relations affects reinforcement schedules. For instance, Homans (1967) discusses a centralized network in which "Person" and "Third Man" are not connected, but both are connected to "Other." Both provide Other the same kind of reward. According to Homans's (1967) Proposition IV:

> The more often in the recent past a person has received a particular reward, the less valuable any further unit of that reward becomes to him. (p. 37)

By receiving rewards from two sources, Other moves more rapidly toward satiation than either Person or Third Man. Both of the latter must increase the rate at which they reinforce Other if they are to maintain a given rate of reward from him. Thus the ratio of rewarding acts changes over time, with the rate at the periphery increasing relative to the rate at the center. While Homans designated this as an instance of Other's power, power-dependence theory — formulated some time later — called this a "negative connection." Among exchange theories, only power-dependence theory has investigated experimental structures. The discussion to follow will therefore focus on that theory.

Experiments conducted within the power-dependence tradition (Stolte and Emerson 1977; Cook and Emerson 1978; Cook et al. 1983) all refer to Emerson's (1962) stipulation that $P_{AB} = D_{BA}$ and $P_{BA} = D_{AB}$. In words, the power of actor A over actor B is equal to B's dependence on A and similarly for B's power over A. Drawing from Emerson (1972a, 1972b) with minor modifications, all studies used the following definition of dependence:

> The dependence of A on B in a dyadic exchange relation (e.g., Ax;By) is a joint function (1) varying directly with the value of y to A and (2) varying inversely with the availability of y from alternative sources. (Cook et al. 1983, pp. 284-85)

This stipulates how dependence varies within and between relations. The connection between these two types of relations is explained only in Emerson's 1972 papers. For a given situation (S_j), "the magnitude of dependence is the strength of S_j as a conditioned reinforcer" (1972a, p. 50). Thus D_{AB} is determined by the strength of B's conditioned reinforcer on A, and D_{BA} by the strength of A's reinforcer on B. A may be connected to more than one exchange relation, and so the value of D_{AB} can be affected by the other relation(s). However, this is so only if the relations are in the same exchange domain, defined as follows:

> Given a set of exchange relations connected at A, and given the set T of all transactions A might initiate during an extended time period, in the same or different relations, an *exchange domain* is a subset d of T such that any transaction in the subset increases satiation for all other transactions in that subset. (Emerson 1972a, p. 50)

This definition has two implications. First, A's exchanges in one domain do not affect exchanges in another. Second, since "any transaction" increases satiation within a domain, satiation begins with the first trans-action. It follows that satiation should be observable even in relatively brief experiments.

Emerson applied his theory to unilateral monopolies. In a unilateral monopoly, A is connected to a number (N) of Bs and all exchanges occur in the same domain (1972b, pp. 76ff.). Assume that, initially, $D_{AB} = D_{BA}$ and that A's exchanges are uniformly distributed across Bs. Since A exchanges N times more frequently than the average B, A approaches satiation more rapidly than the Bs. After the first A-B exchange, $D_{AB} < D_{BA}$ "by virtue of the principle of satiation (Proposition 2)" (1972b, p. 70). Thus A has a power advantage because *satiation reduces dependence* for A more rapidly than for the Bs.

A's power advantage produces imbalanced relations in which "the 'exchange ratio' changes in favor of the party with the power advantage" (1972b, p. 66). Emerson does not assert that A gains greater benefit by using power. As in Homans's similar case, the exchange rate changes because the value of the Bs' reinforcers declines. Since this suggests that A's total reward is constant, power cannot be defined by an increase in A's reward. But the Bs' costs are increasing and thus A's use of power can be defined by these costs (Emerson 1972b, p. 65, Definition 16).

The unilateral monopoly is an instance of *negative connection*:

Two exchange relations, A;B and A;C are *connected at* A if the frequency or magnitude of transactions in one relation is a function of transactions in the other relation. (Emerson 1972b, p. 70)

Since each B is a source of reward for A, the Bs are

alternative relations negatively connected at A, and the Bs are in effect competing with one another for access to x_i from A. (1972b, p. 76)

Alternative relations in the same domain are negatively connected. But if the exchanges are not in the same domain they are not alternative relations and are said to be positively connected (1972b, p. 72, Rule 4). Later, Stolte and Emerson (1977, p. 124) introduced the idea that, for positively connected relations, "an increase in one relation is associated with an increase in the other."

Though new terminology has been introduced, the parallel between power-dependence theory's treatment of a unilateral monopoly and Homans's discussion of the "Third Man" indicates that both views derived social structure from reinforcement in the same way. As Emerson (1972b) noted, "The concept of *power advantage* has little importance in the case of bilateral monopoly" (p. 69). Instead, power advantages emerge because actors have alternative relations. Since satiation reduces dependence in each relation, the dependence of the central actor varies inversely with the number of alternatives. Over time, the rate of reinforcements emitted by the central actor declines, the connection is negative, and the central actor exerts power over the peripherals. Call this the operant formulation of power-dependence theory.

From an Operant to a Branching Formulation

Later statements of power-dependence theory fundamentally altered the meaning of dependence and other basic concepts. Initially the theory asserted that different rates of satiation produce differences in dependence, which then produce differences in power use. In 1972 the theory integrated the individual and structure by relating changes of dependence within relations to exchange alternatives. In 1978, Cook and Emerson stated: "One of the variables governing dependence (*alternatives*) is represented in the number of high-value exchange relations the position provides. The other variable is held constant by controlling resource value" (p. 726). Thus in 1972 dependence within relations was *determined* by dependence between relations, whereas in 1978 dependence within and between relations were *independent* variables. Dependence within relation was held constant in the 1978 version by controlling resource allocation (numbers of profit points) and dependence between was changed by varying the relative number of alternative relations available to each position. But this contradicted the 1972 view that dependence within relations varies due to satiation stemming from numbers of alternative relations.

As formulated in Emerson (1972a, 1972b), alternative relations in the same domain are negatively connected because of A's satiation. But since 1978 negative connection can no longer be due to satiation because it is introduced as an *initial* condition. For example, in 1983 it was stated that

each person was allowed to complete only one transaction per period. Therefore, the network created in the laboratory was negatively connected. (Cook et al. 1983, p. 290)[3]

Emerson (1972b) defined power use *only* in terms of the costs that a power holder can induce on others (Definition 14) and said that "to use power is to impose cost" (p. 65). Oddly, power does not benefit power holders. On the contrary, the benefit to power holders is constant because increased numbers of rewards are balanced by increased satiation of the power holder. But later, according to Cook et al. (1983), power "is conceived as a potential for gaining increased benefit at the other's expense" (p. 287).

Between 1972 and 1978 the meanings of *dependence, negative connection,* and *power* apparently changed without acknowledgment. In fact, it has been claimed that later definitions are consistent with earlier formulations (Cook and Emerson 1978; Cook et al. 1983). Adding further confusion, a recent paper has explicitly returned to operant formulations (Yamagishi et al. 1988, p. 838). But from these changes at least one result is clear: By 1978 a new *branching formulation* for dependence was introduced.

In the branching formulation, the dependence of a position is determined by the number of other positions to which it is connected. For example, if A is connected to B_1, B_2, and B_3, none of whom is connected to any of the others, A is less dependent than any B because A is connected to more than one B, whereas each B is connected only to A. Since $D_{AB} < D_{BA}$, it follows that $P_{AB} > P_{BA}$. That is, A will be high and the Bs will be low power positions. A will then receive favorable exchanges and the Bs unfavorable exchanges. This prediction based on branching is like the prediction based on satiation. In fact, the operant and branching formulations produce similar predictions for the early power-dependence experiments. Their predictions, however, need not be identical.

The First Critical Test

The networks in Figure 12.1 were investigated by Stolte and Emerson (1977) and Cook and Emerson (1978) and can be analyzed using the operant version of power-dependence theory. "Exchange" was operationalized as the division of profit points between connected positions.[4] Solid lines represent high-profit relations; dashed lines indicate low-profit relations. In the 1977 study, 13 profit points were available in high-profit relations, and 3 in low-profit relations. In the 1978 study the values were 24 and 8. A 1-exchange rule limited each position to a single exchange per bargaining round.

Since A was guaranteed a high-profit exchange every round, and the Bs had such an opportunity on the average of only one-third of the time, A could receive more profit points than any B. It followed from the operant formulation that, through satiation, the value of the profit points should decline more rapidly for A than for any B making $D_{AB} < D_{BA}$ and, theoretically, $P_{AB} > P_{BA}$. In fact, As received much larger payoffs per exchange than the Bs. In contrast, every subject in the 12.1b network had the same opportunity to receive points and satiation should have occurred at similar rates. For any (i,j) pair, $P_{C_iC_j} = P_{C_jC_i}$ and, as expected, the observed profit point divisions were approximately equal.

The branching formulation of power-dependence theory gives the same predictions as the operant formulation, though for different reasons. Considering high-profit relations in 12.1a, branching occurs only at A. Since A has high-profit alternatives and the Bs do not, A is less dependent than any B and will be a high power position. In 12.1b each of the C positions has the same number of alternatives, thus all are equally dependent and equally powerful. Like the operant version, the branching approach is consistent with experimental results.

(a)

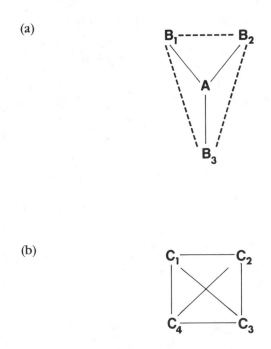

(b)

Figure 12.1.

Now consider the Figure 12.2 structures reported by Brennan (1981). In each network, A was permitted a maximum of three exchanges per round. From the perspective of the operant formulation of power-dependence theory, As should have (on average) equal satiation rates in each of three structures. Therefore the rate of change of D_{AB} should be constant across all of the structures. In the experiments, subjects rotated to new positions after four periods of bargaining, a new subject occupying the central position after each rotation. This rotation procedure was introduced for systematic control of differences among subjects. Operant dependence predicts, for all three structures, that (1) during the time each subject occupies the central position, A's rate of exchange[5] should increase (as he or she becomes satiated) and (2) after each rotation the rate of exchange should move to equality. The overall effect is oscillation between power and nonpower conditions.

The branching formulation, because it is independent of satiation, does not predict such oscillations. Instead, it predicts that A will be high and the Bs low in power in all structures. In each structure A has alternatives that reduce dependence, whereas the dependence of each B, not having been reduced by branching, will be higher than that of A. Thus $P_{AB} > P_{BA}$.

The elementary theory's predictions differed from those of the operant and branching formulations. No power advantages were expected in

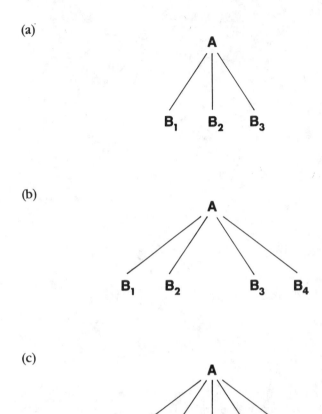

Figure 12.2.

12.2a. Instead a stable, balanced exchange rate was predicted for all A-B relations. Only the 12.2b and 12.2c networks were expected to produce power differences. The rate for both structures was expected to favor A increasingly. It was predicted that the rate of change of the exchange rate in the 12.2c structure would be twice that of 12.2b. Since satiation was not a consideration, no effects were predicted for subjects rotating among positions.[6]

The Figure 12.2 networks provided a critical test, the results of which supported elementary theory and refuted the predictions from both versions of power-dependence theory. The exchange rate for the 12.2a structure was stable both within and between rotations; the rate for the other structures approached that maximally favorable for A; the rate of change of the exchange rate for 12.2c was nearly twice that of 12.2b; and only 12.2b and 12.2c were power structures. Neither power-dependence version could account for these results.

Structural Exclusion

Consider *exclusion* as a structural condition of power in exchange networks. Note the structural similarity between 12.1a and the 12.2b and 12.2c networks. In each case at least one B was necessarily excluded from exchanging with A in every bargaining round. In 12.1a, the 1-exchange rule meant that two Bs were excluded. In 12.2b and 12.2c, the 3-exchange rule excluded one and two Bs, respectively. As a consequence, Bs are forced to bid against one another, either implicitly or explicitly, in order to avoid exclusion from exchange.[7] By contrast, there are no exclusions and no power differences in 12.2a.

Elementary theory views this bidding process as the dynamic underlying A's power. In the critical test, bidding was observed in the 12.2b and 12.2c structures but not in 12.2a. We have also found bidding in other networks conditioned by the 1-exchange rule (see below). These results support the inference that exclusion, a structural condition not explicitly recognized by power-dependence theory, produces the power observed in experiments.

The clearest statement of the power-dependence approach has been provided by Cook et al. (1983), and there exclusion may play an implicit role. These authors provide explicit definitions for the key concepts of power, dependence, and connection, and explicit hypotheses regarding the distribution of power in selected networks. However, unlike the 1972 version, the theory's use of the concept of negative connection implies exclusion from exchange. Furthermore, the use of the 1-exchange rule in experiments created exclusion. The key question is, Are the exclusions created by negative connections sufficient to produce power?

Cook et al. provide no definitive answer to this question. The first part of their paper implies that negative connections are sufficient to produce power since they limit alternatives within domains, thus modifying dependence, thus determining power. The second part of their paper introduces a preliminary measure of network vulnerability that implies otherwise — that the network analyst must take into account more than just whether connections are negative; he or she must also consider configurations of more remote positions. The vulnerability measure, however, has been refuted on both logical and empirical grounds (Willer 1986; Markovsky et al. 1988). Power-dependence theory then leaves unanswered the question of whether exclusion is sufficient for power.

Later we will show that exclusion is necessary but not sufficient to produce power in exchange networks. It is necessary in that a position cannot exert power unless it can exclude one or more of its alternatives. It is not sufficient because, even if alternatives are excluded, those alternatives will not engage in bidding if they have guaranteed alternatives of their own.

Resistance

Elementary theory addresses power as an agency-structure problem. At issue is how structures delimit or determine actors' pursuits of their interests. When interests conflict, how do structures influence their resolution? The theory is multilevel (Markovsky 1987) in that it spans actor, relational, and structural conditions. Rather than assuming that innate, immutable actor properties produce relationships and structures, our models connect the decision processes of actors through relations to structural conditions, none of which is subsumable by the others.

If the problem to be addressed here were limited to dyadic bargaining, Nash's (1950, 1953) or similar methods could be used to find a compromise rate of exchange, and Zeuthen's (1930) to interpret the bargaining process of concessions that lead to that solution. But when the potential for exclusion exists, bidding — not bargaining — occurs among those potentially excluded. When one actor or set of actors structurally excludes others and is not excluded in return, exchange rates are not settled by compromise; they become maximally stratified. Though it may be that some bargaining model could be adapted to cover dyads and exclusionary structures (see Rapoport 1970; Young 1975), there are further power conditions to consider. Later we discuss inclusive exchange structures and coercive structures. Since coercion involves the threat of force, it is considered by at least some game theorists to be amorphous (see Pen 1975, p. 169). It seems doubtful, then, that any established theory of negotiation can cover the full range of relevant phenomena.

Resistance theory is a general procedure for deriving rates of exchange and power events under a variety of conditions. The procedure is consistent with the foundations of elementary theory in Marx and Weber, for it arrives at rates by interpreting the interests of actors in relations and structures. In this section resistance is first applied to the isolated dyad and then to exclusionary branch structures. We offer other applications below.

The theory of resistance (Willer 1981, 1984, 1987; Heckathorn 1980) explicates actors' interests and actions. In brief, actors have two interests: I_b, an interest in gaining maximum outcome (P_{max}) from the exchange, and I_c, an interest in avoiding the worst possible outcome (P_{con}) at nonexchange or "conflict." (P_{con}, the benefit in the absence of exchange, is here set equal to zero.) The extent to which these interests are fulfilled by an actual offer, P, is quantified by the differences between P_{con}, P_{max}, and the offer:

$$I_b = P_{max} - P$$
$$I_c = P - P_{con}$$

The resistance of actor A to offer P_A is then given as

$$R_A = I_b(A)/I_c(A)$$
$$= \frac{P_{max}(A) - P_A}{P_A - P_{con}(A)}$$

and similarly for actor B. Since both seek to minimize the value of I_b and maximize the value of I_c, resistance to an offer is minimal as P_A approaches $P_{max}(A)$ and maximal as P_A approaches $P_{con}(A)$. If P_A and P_B are initially set at zero, a pair of actors will exchange only if $P_A > 0$ and $P_B > 0$. Thus for any exchange that can occur, the worst system state possible is nonexchange where $P_{con}(A) = P_{con}(B) = 0$. Then it must be the case that $P_i > P_{con}(i)$ for any exchange.

Power-dependence networks use an exchange-analogue relation in which resource pools are divided between adjacent actors. In the case of A and B bargaining over 24 profit points,

$$R_A = \frac{(23 - P_A)}{(P_A - 0)}$$

If a division takes place, A could gain at most 23 points. If no deal is made, A receives nothing. Any offer from B (i.e., P_A) is considered in light of these best and worst possibilities. The same holds for B such that

$$R_B = \frac{23 - (24 - P_A)}{(24 - P_A) - 0}$$

where $(24 - P_A) = P_B$ is the amount B receives when A gets P_A.[8] Resistance predicts that agreements are reached when, through negotiation, a P_A and P_B are obtained that make $R_A = R_B$. As can be calculated, $R_A = R_B$ at a 12/12 division.

Now consider the models for the critical test. The Figure 12.2 structures are composed of a number of exchange relations connected at A. For each relation, A is initially allocated 11 resource units, any number of which can be transmitted to a B. Each B is allocated 10 resource units, which can be transmitted to A as an "all or none" block. A values all resource units equally; Bs value only the resources that A can provide. A's best possible outcome would be to obtain the block of 10 points from B while giving up only 1 point, a net profit of 9 for A. Thus $P_{max}(A) = 9$, and P_B would equal 1. No exchange would mean no profit increment, so $P_{con}(A) = 0$. From B's perspective, A could conceivably offer up to

9 points in trade for B's 10. (A has no interest in giving 10 or 11 to get 10 from B.) Therefore, $P_{max}(B) = 9$, at which point $P_A = 1$. Also, $P_{con}(B) = 0$.

The exchange rate $X_{A/B} = P_A/P_B$ is based on A's profit increment over B's, where "profit" is the net amount gained in an exchange. A seeks to maximize — and B to minimize — $X_{A/B}$. The range of possible exchange rates for the relationship is $1/9 \leq X_{A/B} \leq 9/1$. For the 1/9 rate to occur, A gives up 9 units and receives 10 for a net profit $P_A = 1$. At the same time $P_B = 9$ due to the 9 units obtained from A. For the 9/1 rate, A must give up 1 unit to receive 10 from B for a net of 9, while B gains only the 1 unit.

Under these conditions A will initially seek $X_{A/B} = 9/1$ and Bs will seek $X_{A/B} = 1/9$. To open the bargaining, A should offer 1 unit for B's 10, but B will request 9. Subsequently, each will concede until $R_A = R_B$, that is, until

$$\frac{P_{max}(A) - P_A}{P_A - 0} = \frac{P_{max}(B) - P_B}{P_B - 0}$$

In this example, P_B is always equal to $10 - P_A$, making it possible to solve for the P_A and P_B values satisfying the equality. For each A-B relation, $P_A = P_B = 5$ at equiresistance and the predicted exchange rate is 5/5. In short, the isolated dyad engages in a bargaining process, the end point of which is compromise at equiresistance. The resistance theory predicts that the sequence of offers and counteroffers will be hyperbolic in form. In fact, the bargaining patterns reported by Siegel and Fouraker (1960) resemble hyperbolas.

In extending resistance to branching structures, it will be assumed that actors have full information concerning ongoing offers and past exchanges and may take this information into account in determining their actions. These conditions were in fact met in the experiments on the Figure 12.2 structures.

The 12.2a branch connects three relationships at A. Since A can now exchange with three Bs, A's resources are multiplied by three. Though A now has alternatives, this does not affect bargaining processes in any of the relationships. The completion of an exchange in one relation is irrelevant to exchanges in others, and the resistance equations may be applied for each A-B. As above, $X_{A,B} = 1$ for each pair at the point of equiresistance. The repetition of bargaining rounds has but one consequence: Actors' initial offers may reflect concessions made in prior rounds.

In the 4-branch of Figure 12.2b, A is still limited to exchanging with three of the Bs in any single round. Assume that the first round unfolds as predicted for 12.2a; A and three of the Bs bargain to compromise at $X_{A/B} = 5/5$. Thus $P_B = 5$ for three of the Bs, but 0 for the fourth. In the next round, the excluded B knows that A has no interest in accepting a fourth offer for which $X_{A/B} \leq 5/5$. Therefore, all $X_{A/B} \leq 5/5$ are no longer viable. Although it was initially the case that $P_{max}(B) = 9$, after the first round $P_{max}(B) < 5$, that is, $P_{max}(B) = 4$.

Now $R_B = 0$ for the previously excluded B. Resistance of that B shifts to zero for the following reasons. Since $P_{max}(B)$ has dropped to 4, the best offer possible for that B is $X_{A/B} = 6/4$ at which P_B is also equal to 4. Then $P_{max}(B) - P(B) = 4 - 4 = 0$ and $R_B = 0$. Thus the 6/4 offer is made by that B with zero resistance. When that offer is made, all other Bs face the possibility of exclusion and must generate offers of 6/4 or better to avoid exclusion. These offers, like those of the previously excluded B, are also made at zero resistance. Thus is generated a *bidding process*, the outcome of which quickly approaches 9/1, the rate most favorable to A.

The bidding process is generated because R_B shifts to zero at each new rate of exchange. It is sustained because of concomitant changes in A's resistance. Initially, $P_{con}(A) = 0$ within each of A's relations. However, given the multiple offers, $P_{con}(A) = 5$. That is, nonexchange with one B does not entail forgoing profits, since another B is available. Thus, for any further offer of $X_{A/B} = 5/5$, $P_A - P_{con}(A) = 0$ and R_A goes to infinity; A is infinitely resistant to further offers of $X_{A/B} = 5/5$, then to offers of 6/4, and so on. The rate moves toward $X_{A/B} = 9/1$, for which $P_A = P_{max}(A)$.

The same bidding process is predicted for 12.2c as for 12.2b. Now, however, two Bs are excluded. The bidding process should go more rapidly and the rate of change of $X_{A/B}$ will be greater.

The interaction processes predicted by resistance were observed in the experiments. In 12.2a all agreements were reached through a bargaining process. But in 12.2b and 12.2c the Bs offered a sequence of bids such that the rate moved rapidly toward the extreme most favorable to the A. In fact, the modal rate in 12.2c was $X_{A/B} = 9/1$ (Brennan 1981).[9]

The resistance formulation may be used to analyze the 12.1a structure that was experimentally investigated by power-dependence theorists. Since these experiments were run under a 1-exchange rule, two of the three Bs are excluded from exchanging with A in each round. As in 12.2b and 12.2c, the Bs should bid and the division of profit points moves toward the extreme favoring A. Assume that $X_{A/B} = 17/7$. Now any B_i can offer a 7/1 split to another B_j in hopes of gaining as many profit points from B_j as are available from A. Four-way bidding will now develop such that two Bs will reach an equal division in the low-profit relations at $X_{B(i)/B(j)} = 4/4$, while $X_{A/B(k)} = 20/4$ for A and the remaining B.

In 12.1b, all of the C positions are connected by high-profit relations and all bid to even divisions. Alternatively, were the Cs to pair off, bargaining to compromise at $R_{C(i)} = R_{C(j)}$ would also produce 12/12 divisions.

The application of resistance to the power-dependence networks allows us to offer an interpretation to account for the somewhat less extreme rates found in those experiments as compared to our more complete information studies. The theory of resistance suggests that the rate of change of profit point divisions in the 12.1a structure will be slowed by restrictions on the information available to actors. It seems that only A could know all ongoing offers in the high-profit relations, while each B knew only the offers in its own relations. This means that the resistance of the Bs in the A-B relations could not go to zero, as in the 12.2b and 12.2c structures. However, since A knew all ongoing A-B offers, its resistance could still be very high (as in 12.2b and 12.2c) — in fact, infinite for any $X_{A/B}$ worse than an exchange rate achieved in a prior exchange. Thus A could act on its positional advantage, but the Bs — not necessarily aware of their disadvantage — could react only to incoming offers. Whereas it is frequently assumed that limiting the information of those low in power favors the powerful, in this case A's exercise of power was hindered by the Bs' limited information.

A Simple Power Index

Resistance shows how exclusion produces power in simple exchange structures. By analyzing a network to determine where exclusions can occur, one may predict each position's power. Cp is a simple exclusion-based index of power used in earlier versions of elementary theory (Willer 1981). Cp differentiates "strong" branches in which power emerges from "weak" branches in which it does not. In strong branches the central position excludes at least one peripheral position. In weak branches no exclusion occurs.

Let M_i be the number of 1-step paths from (i.e., positions connected to) position i, and N_i the number of exchanges i is allowed. Then

$$Cp_i = M_i/N_i$$

In the weak Figure 12.2a branch, $Cp_A = 3/3$; 12.2b is a strong branch with $Cp_A = 4/3$, and in 12.2c, $Cp_A = 5/3$. Considering only high-profit relations in 12.1a, $Cp_A = 3/1$. In general, Cp > 1 for central positions in strong structures. That is, Cp > 1 when at least one position is structurally excluded and Cp = 1 when there is no exclusion. In all Figure 12.2 structures Bs were limited to one exchange, hence $Cp_B = 1$. Thus power occurs in a branch when $Cp_A > Cp_B$, but not when $Cp_A = Cp_B$. It is also the case that $Cp_A = Cp_B$ in isolated dyads. That Cp = 1 for all positions in dyads and weak branches indicates their structural similarity.

The rate of change of an exchange rate is $\Delta X_{A/B} = k(Cp_A - Cp_B)$, where k is an empirical constant determined by the experimental setting and information conditions. This equation successfully predicted the relative rates of change in tests of the three Figure 12.2 structures. Applying the equation to dyads or the weak 12.2a structure, $\Delta X_{A/B} = 0$, meaning that the rate of exchange will be stable and no power use develops. Applying the equation to the 12.1b structure, since Cp = 3 for all positions, $\Delta X_{Ci/Cj} = 0$ for any pair and no power use develops. This conclusion is consistent with Stolte and Emerson (1977) and may be consistent with Cook and Emerson (1978) (see Willer and Patton 1987).

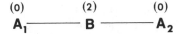

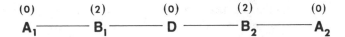

Figure 12.3.

The Cp index has certain limitations when applied to larger and more complex networks. Two are especially critical. First, Cp > 1 is necessary but not sufficient for i to exercise power (Willer and Patton 1987). Also, in some cases Cp = 1 for *both* disadvantaged and equipower positions, as with the Bs in 12.2a and 12.2b. The resistance analysis, however, implies that the B positions in the two networks are structurally different.

These limitations follow from the calculation of Cp: The number of positions connected to i is compared to the number with which i can exchange. When i is central in a branch, this ratio is based on the number of peripherals excluded per round. But consider the 4-position line of Figure 12.3 under a 1-exchange condition. Cp = 1 for the As and Cp = 2 for the Bs. No position has a structural advantage, however, because none is necessarily excluded. Similarly, in the 5-position line, Cp = 2 for D. But D cannot develop power over the Bs given that each has an adjacent A with which it can seek to exchange.

Willer and Patton (1987) offered alternative procedures to analyze simple networks. Taken together, however, these were still scope restricted. A more desirable solution is one that, like Cp, would be sensitive to branching, but also takes into account the effects of more remote network connections.

The limitations of earlier procedures are overcome by considering the effects of longer paths from i. For example, in strong branches a given B_i is disadvantaged only when a B_j *two* steps away is bidding against it. If we allow the 1-path B_i-A to add one to B_i's index, then the presence of a "rival" B_j two steps away should reduce B_i's index by one. A more general index applied to strong structures would then generate a value of zero for Bs. This method does not change the values for A positions in branches since A has no paths longer than one. Similarly, for the 4-position line of Figure 12.3, the path from B_1 to B_2 is negated by the path from B_2 to A_2. Because there is no path beyond the adjacent A_1, the count on that side contributes +1. Summing paths to the left and right of B_1 yields $1 - 1 + 1 = 1$, not 2 as it was for Cp.

The p Index

The p index predicts the relative power of network positions. From the standpoint of predicting power use in complex networks, the resistance analysis is a generative theory-modeling dynamic process. It will yield predictions for relative power, but only by "playing out" or simulating all negotiations and exchanges that take place in the network over a series of rounds. The p index, on the other hand, predicts the outcome of this dynamic process based only on network connections and a relatively small number of calculations. Thus the p index is consistent with the resistance analysis but eliminates resistance calculations when one wishes to determine only the relative power positions as opposed to exact points of compromise.

The analysis focuses on how structures create and eliminate positional exclusions; that is, the conditions under which a position, based on its connections (and its connection's connections, and so forth), generates a bidding process leading to differences in power use, or a process of bargaining with adjacent positions, implying equality of structural power.

The power index applies to all networks examined by power-dependence theorists. The scope conditions of power-dependence networks include the division of replenishable resource pools and the 1-exchange rule. Since exchange consists of a division of points between adjacent actors, resources cannot flow through positions and affect the decisions of actors remote in the network, and power use can occur only between adjacent positions.

Let m_{i1} be the number of 1-paths (direct relations) stemming from i and, in general, m_{ik} the number of nonintersecting k-paths (paths of length k). Two (or more) k-paths stemming from i are *nonintersecting* only if i is the only position common to them. For these networks, that

only nonintersecting paths are counted in the calculation of i is a consequence of the 1-exchange rule. The reasons for considering only nonintersecting paths will be more fully explicated in the applications below.

The $p(1)_i$ index (i's power under a 1-exchange rule) is now expressed as

$$p(1)_i = \sum_{k=1}^{g} (-1)^{(k-1)} m_{ik}$$

$$P(1)_i = m_{i1} - m_{i2} + m_{i3} - \ldots \pm m_{ik}$$

where g is the length of the longest path(s) stemming from i. Even
in networks such as 12.1b, where paths connect back to themselves,
g remains finite due to the nonintersecting path restriction. From this we
may construct a simple index for i's power relative to j's:

$$P(1)_{ij} = p(1)_i - p(1)_j$$

For now we may suppress the number of exchanges parameter and refer
to the index as simply p_i.

In Figure 12.3, p_i values are shown near their corresponding network
positions. We will assume that 24 points are available to each pair of
actors in adjacent positions. In the dyad, A_1 and A_2 both have a 1-path, but
none longer. Thus for both, $p_A = 1$ and $p_{AA} = 0$, and the actors will bargain
to a 12/12 compromise. For the 3-position line, A_1 has a 1-path to B and
a 2-path to A_2. Since the network is symmetric, A_2's path lengths are the
same as A_1's. Therefore $p_A = 1 - 1 = 0$. B has two 1-paths and none longer,
so $p_B = 2$ and $p_{BA} = 2$. These values mean that the low-power As will offer
bids to the high-power B and the division of points will move toward that
most favorable to B. Using the earlier terms, this is a strong 2-branch.

In line networks all paths are nonintersecting and, under the 1-
exchange condition, an analytic shortcut is available. For either A in the
4-position line we may simply sum while counting along the line +1, 0,
+1. Thus $P_A = 1$. For either B the count is +1 to the adjacent A, and
counting in the other direction, +1, 0. Summing the two counts, $P_B = 1$.
Since $P_{AB} = 0$ for all adjacent actors, no power advantages exist in this
network.[10] In the 5-position line the count for either A is +1, 0, +1, 0, and
$P_A = 0$. For the Bs it is +1 in one direction, while counting in the other it
is +1, 0, +1, and summing $P_B = 2$. For D the count is +1, 0, in one
direction, and +1, 0, in the other. Therefore, $P_D = 0$. Since $P_{BD} = P_{BA} = 2$,
D and the As will offer bids to their adjacent Bs, who will gain increasingly favorable profits.

It is evident that in the case of lines, the relative power of *all* positions
is changed by the addition (or deletion) of a *single* relationship. The
3-position line is simply a dyad with an additional position connected to
one end. Now the end positions can no longer bargain but must bid against

one another for exchange with the central position. The 4-position line is the 3-position line with one added position. One of the inner positions, previously an end-point of the line, will now have an alternative to bidding against the other end position. This removes the power advantage from the position that was previously central. However, adding one more position to the end of the line reestablishes power in the even-numbered positions. The Bs in the 5-position line are never structurally excluded from exchange, while D or an A must be excluded in every round of exchange. In general, all lines with an odd number of positions have alternating high and low power positions, but lines with an even number of positions have no high and low power positions.

In some structures, p_i values will change within a given round of exchange. Consider the 5-position line and assume that B_1 exchanges before B_2. If the B_1-A_1 exchange is made, a 3-position line remains within which B_2 has the advantaged position. B_2 will receive bids from D and A_2. However, if the first exchange is B_1-D, then only a B_2-A_2 dyad remains, with $p_B = p_A = 1$, $p_{AB} = 0$, and the two will bargain to compromise. Whether B_1 or B_2 exchanges first is assumed to be indeterminate. Therefore, over a series of exchanges the Bs are still expected to have power, even though one or the other need not always receive high profit in a given round. In fact, in empirical contexts we may expect that in the case of odd-length lines, the greater the length, the more rounds will be needed for positions to "sort themselves out" before consistent power differences and bidding processes emerge.

Figure 12.4 shows two of the Cook et al. (1983) networks with p_i values given for each position. As in the above analysis of 12.1a, low-profit relations (dashed lines) do not affect the location of high and low power positions — only the amount of power use that will develop. Thus only paths containing exclusively high-profit relations are counted in the calculation of p_i. In 12.4a each A has one 1-path to its adjacent B, one 2-path to D, one 3-path to the other B, and one 4-path to the other A, and so $p_A = 1 - 1 + 1 - 1 = 0$. Each B has two 2-paths (one to D and one to its adjacent A), one 2-path to the other B, and one 3-path to its nonadjacent A. Therefore, $p_B = 2 - 1 + 1 = 2$. Finally, D has two nonintersecting 1-paths and two nonintersecting 2-paths, so $p_D = 2 - 2 = 0$. This network is structurally identical to the 5-position line analyzed above. The B positions will achieve profit advantages at the expense of D and the As.

The Figure 12.4b network can be used to justify the nonintersecting requirement. D has three nonintersecting 1-paths and three nonintersecting 2-paths, and so $P_D = 3 - 3 = 0$. From D's perspective, the presence of three Bs implies the possibility of excluding two in any round of exchange, thereby starting a bidding war among the Bs. However, a B with *even one* A as an alternative exchange partner need not participate in the war. From D's point of view, a single A removes D's advantage, that is, the "+1" that the B *would* have provided. In the case of 12.4b, all Bs in

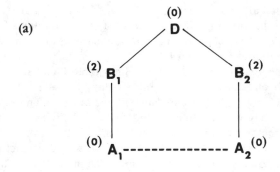

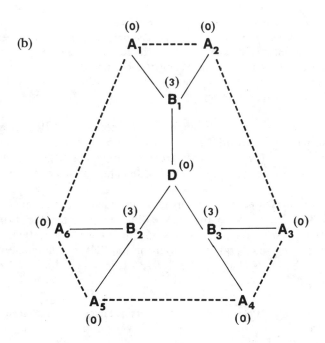

Figure 12.4.

fact have two such alternative partners. But whether B has one, two, or a hundred As is irrelevant to D, since it takes just one to remove D's power advantage. Thus *only one of the As is counted*, and this is done by counting only *nonintersecting* 2-paths from D.

Continuing the analysis of 12.4b, each B has three 1-paths, one nonintersecting 2-path, and one nonintersecting 3-path: $p_B = 3 - 1 + 1 = 3$. Each A has nonintersecting 1-, 2-, 3-, and 4-paths (one of each), and so $p_A = 0$. In terms of relative power, 12.4b is analogous to 12.4a, with the positions adjacent to the center having power over the others. However, since p_{BA} and p_{BD} are greater for 12.4b than for 12.4a, we would predict a more rapid increase in power exercise in the former than in the latter. The Cook et al. (1983) experimental results for the 12.4a network and their simulation results for the 12.4b network concur with our conclusions.

Structural decompositions. It is not always the case that high and low power positions will alternate along paths. In some structures high power positions are adjacent to one another, though they do not exercise power over each other. In theory, such networks are unstable and will decompose into substructures. To analyze networks of this type we offer the following extension of our theory. (See Markovsky et al. 1988 for a formal statement.)

- *Axiom 1:* Given by the $p(1)_i$ equation above.
- *Axiom 2:* i seeks exchange with j if and only if i's power is greater than j's or if i's power relative to j equals or exceeds that of any of i's other relations.
- *Axiom 3:* i and j can exchange only if each seeks exchange with the other.
- *Axiom 4:* If i and j exchange, then i receives more resources than j if and only if i has more power than j.

In Axiom 2, "i seeks exchange with j" means that offers from i will compete with other offers (if any) received by j. The axiom claims that this occurs when (1) i's power is greater than j's and (2) i's power is less than j's *and* j's power is the same or less than that of other positions related to i.[11]

Axiom 3 does not claim that any two actors seeking exchange with each other will exchange — only that they will not exchange without first seeking exchange with one another. Axiom 4 claims that potential power determines the use of power, an assertion implicitly assumed above.

Of the theorems that can be derived from the axioms we note the following:

- *Theorem 1:* If i has no alternative relations, then i seeks exchange with j.
- *Theorem 2:* If i does not seek exchange with j *or* if j does not seek exchange with i, then i and j do not exchange.
- *Theorem 3:* Actor i does not seek exchange with j if and only if i's power is less than or equal to j's *and* i has a better alternative to j.

- *Theorem 4:* If i's power is less than or equal to j's and i has a better alternative to j, or if j's power is less than or equal to i's and j has a better alternative to i, then i and j will not exchange.

Consider the application of Theorem 4 to the Figure 12.5 networks. In 12.5a, D_1 has D_2 as a better alternative to B and so D_1 will not exchange with B. This network decomposition is represented in 12.5b and the p_i values of all positions are recalculated. B is then the sole high power position. In 12.5c both Bs have better alternatives than each other and the network decomposes as shown in 12.5d.

The Second Critical Test

Network 12.5a serves as a critical test between the elementary theory and the power-dependence theory. In 1983, Cook et al. introduced the concept of vulnerability, which "in a negatively connected network locates points of minimum dependence, equivalent to maximum network-wide power" (p. 300). To determine i's vulnerability, first i and its relations are removed. Second, the maximum possible flow of resource points is determined for the resulting network. Then i and its relations are replaced, and the procedure is repeated for every position. Those positions whose removal produces the greatest reduction in resource flow (relative to the case where no positions are removed) are high power positions.

Applying vulnerability to 12.5a finds that the maximum number of profit points obtainable in the network as a whole is 48, since up to two divisions (24 points in each) may take place in one round of bargaining. Removing either A still leaves two resource pools to be divided. However, removing B, D_1, or D_2 reduces the number of possible exchanges and the maximum resource flow becomes 24. Thus B, D_1, and D_2 are all high power positions (Willer 1986).

In 1986, Cook et al. published a modification of the vulnerability procedure and applied it to the 12.5a network. They found that B should be most powerful, followed by D_1 and finally by D_2, A_1, and A_2. It was not clear whether they meant that the latter three positions are equal in power or ordered from high to low in power. Nevertheless, the assertion that D_1 is more powerful than D_2 means that the 12.5a network still provides a critical test.

We have tested the 12.5a network, with results supporting the p_i predictions and disconfirming both versions of the vulnerability procedure (Markovsky et al. 1988). There were five experimental groups, each having 20 bargaining rounds — a total of 100 exchange opportunities in the entire study. As expected, the structure was unstable. A predicted split between B and D_1 obtained, with only three B-D_1 exchanges observed across the 100 opportunities. As predicted, the D_1-D_2 division of profit

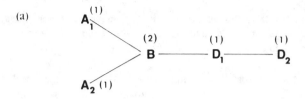

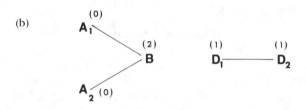

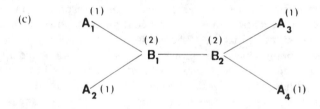

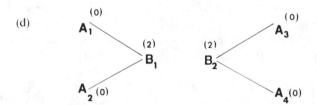

Figure 12.5.

points was almost exactly 12/12 and occurred through a bargaining process. The division of profit points between B and its adjacent As moved
toward, and on occasion reached, the 23/1 extreme, averaging about 20/4
for the study as a whole. Thus D_1 and D_2 were not high power positions

as predicted by application of the 1983 vulnerability procedure and D_1 was not higher in power than D_2 as predicted by the 1986 version.

Multiexchange Networks

The 1-exchange rule may now be relaxed as follows. Let i be permitted to complete e exchanges in a given round, each exchange involving a different partner. That is, all of i's exchanges must be *unique*. All other conditions are identical to those of power-dependence networks. That is, "exchange" consists of the division of replenishable resource pools by adjacent positions, all actors have relatively full information, and so on. It follows that when e = 1, e-exchange networks are power-dependence networks.

The concept of *domain* simplifies the location of power. When e > 1, it is possible for autonomous domains or independent subnetworks to exist. Power and exchange processes in one domain have no channel through which to influence the processes in another. Calculation of p is simplified since it is now obtained by considering only domain configurations rather than entire networks.

Domains are defined by the positions they contain, and these contents are determined by the following rule:

Given an e-exchange network; positions i and j on a path; positions $V = \{v_1, v_2, \dots\}$ on the path between i and j: i and j are in the same domain if and only if (1) $V = \{0\}$, or (2) $m_1 > e$ for all v_i.

By this definition, adjacent positions (for which $V = \{0\}$) are always in the same domain. If $m_1(i) = e(i)$ for each adjacent position, then those positions form a *dyadic domain*. No structural exclusion occurs in dyadic domains, so members cannot have power advantages over one another.

The definition also asserts that if all positions between i and j have more 1-step relations than opportunities to exchange (i.e., $m_1 > e$), they reside in a *power domain*. The whole power domain is the set of all adjacencies satisfying the $m_1 > e$ condition. There are structural changes that may be introduced at i that will affect j's relative power — a phenomenon demonstrated above for line networks under 1-exchange conditions. When all positions in a network are in the same domain, that network is said to form a *unitary domain*. Isolated dyads are unitary, as are all networks when e = 1. In other words, power-dependence networks always form unitary power domains.

Figure 12.6 illustrates both types of domains under the following conditions. Let e = 2 for D and the Bs, and e = 1 for the As. (In fact, e cannot be larger than one for the As because they have only one adjacent position.) Note that all adjacent positions reside in the same domain, as required by the criteria given above. But for each D-A path there is a B, and $m_1(B) = e(B)$. Therefore, no A is in the same domain as D. Since

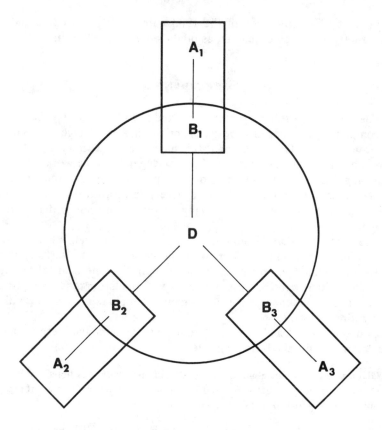

Figure 12.6.

$m_1(A) = e(A)$ and $m_1(B) = e(B)$, all A-B pairs form dyadic domains, indicated by rectangles in Figure 12.6. D and its adjacent Bs form a power domain, indicated by the circle.

Having isolated these network substructures, p(e) calculates the relative power of positions within each of their domains. p(e) is formulated much the same as p_i. The p(e) function is given by:

$$p_{id}(e_d) = (1/e_d)\sum_{k=1}^{h_{id}}(-1)^{(k-1)}m_{idk}$$

where $p_{id}(e_d)$ is i's index *within domain d*, H_{id} is the length of i's longest nonintersecting path in that domain, e_d is the number of exchanges i uses in the domain, and m_{idk} is the number of nonintersecting paths of length k stemming from i in the domain. The $1/e_d$ factor gives p(e) the same range as p_i: $p(e) > 1$ for all high power positions in a domain, and $p(e) < 1$ for positions low in power. For clarity we eliminate subscripts on $p(e)$.

For many networks the calculation of $p(e)$ is simpler than that of p_i since many paths are truncated by domain boundaries. Consider its application to the Figure 12.6 network. B_1 has two exchanges and, given the unique exchange rule, no more than one can be offered to either A_1 or D. Thus B_1 has no power to exclude A_1 and the two bargain to equal profit point divisions. In fact, in all dyadic domains $p(e)_A = p(e)_B = 1$, but in the power domain $p(e)_B = 0$ and $p(e)_d = 3/2$. Thus when B_1 tries to use its second exchange opportunity to bargain with D, B_1 finds that it must bid along with B_2 and B_3, as D has only two exchanges to spend among three adjacent positions. Therefore, B bargains at equal power with A, but must bid as a low power position with D.

Several logical consequences derive from the scope conditions, definition of domain, and axiom for calculating $p(e)$:

If $m_{i1} = e_i$, then i has (1) e_i domains, (2) e_i $p(e)$ values, and (3) one exchange opportunity within each domain.

In Figure 12.6, $m_{i1} = e_i$ for positions A and B. Each A is in one domain, has one $p(e)$ value, and can exchange only once in its domain. Further, each B is in two domains, has two $p(e)$s, and an exchange opportunity in each of its domains.

If $m_{i1} > e_i$, then i has (1) one domain — a power domain, (2) one $p(e)$ value, and (3) e_i exchange opportunities within the domain.

In the Figure, $m_{D1} > e_D$. D is in a single power domain, has one $p(e)$ value, and may use its two exchanges within the domain.

If d is a dyadic domain then both members will have equal power in that domain.

This was found to be the case for each A-B dyad.

To summarize, $p(e)$ is calculated by first determining domains, and then counting, signing, and summing paths within domains as specified in the $p(e)$ function. Then theorems are applied within domains.

The $p(e)$ procedure is applicable to networks like those in Figure 12.2. Recall that $e_A = 3$ for all three networks. By the definition of domains, Figure 12.2a contains three dyadic domains. $p(e)_A = p(e)_B = 1$ in each dyadic domain, hence all positions have equal power. Figures 12.2b and 12.2c, however, are each unitary power domains. In 12.2b, $p(3)_A = 4/3$ and since every B has one nonintersecting 1-path and one nonintersecting 2-path, $p(1)_B = 0$. Therefore, $P_{AB} = 4/3$. In 12.2c, $p(3)_A = 5/3$ and again $p(3)_B = 0$ and so $p_{AB} = 5/3$. These results concur with the resistance analyses conducted earlier.

For lines, when $e(i) = m_{i1}$ for all positions, the ends exchange once and all interior positions exchange twice. Therefore all lines form a sequence of dyadic domains and each interior position exchanges in two domains. Since $p(e) = 1$ for all positions on the line, there would be no bidding and no power use. Instead, all positions bargain to compromise in their domains. We have not studied lines under these conditions, but this derivation receives indirect support in the experiment to be reported next.

The Third Critical Test

To test the $p(e)$ formulation, the Figure 12.6 structure was studied under 1- and 2-exchange conditions (Markovsky et al. 1988). Each experimental session was divided into two phases. Half of the sessions permitted one exchange per bargaining round in the first phase and then two per round (for D and the Bs) in the second phase. Consistent with the unique exchange condition, A positions always had just one exchange to offer. The other half of the sessions reversed the order; the 2-exchange phase was followed by the 1-exchange condition. Every subject experienced both phases and, within each phase, every network position. At issue was whether there was a change in the distribution of power as it was affected by the 1- and the 2-exchange conditions.

Since the 1-exchange rule is not a theoretic scope condition of experiments by power-dependence theorists, the change in numbers of exchanges between the two phases of this experiment offered a third critical test between the elementary theory and power-dependence theory. In Cook et al. (1983), simulation results for the Figure 12.6 network (with the As connected by low-profit relations) suggested that the Bs are high in power, a conclusion supported by the vulnerability analysis. In that paper, and contrary to our derivation for the 2-exchange condition, it was suggested that there is a " 'decentralization' principle such that networks tend to form into systems organized around multiple foci of power" (p. 302; also see Cook and Emerson 1984). Contrary to the formulations for domains, it was asserted that networks have "system-wide dependence" (p. 299).

In the 1-exchange condition, $p_B = 2$ and $p_A = p_D = 0$. The Bs are high power positions and the rest are low. However, when D and the Bs may exchange twice per round, as derived above, in the power domain $p_D = 3/2$ and $p_B = 0$, while in the dyadic domains $p_A = 1$ and $p_B = 1$. Thus with the change from one to two exchanges (1) the power and profit advantage is predicted to shift to the D position, (2) the three Bs bid for D's two available exchanges, and (3) all A-B dyads bargain to equal profits.

All of these predictions were supported. Under the 1-exchange condition, the Bs achieved high profits at the expense of D and the As. Under the 2-exchange condition, the A-B pairs bargained to compromise, with the average division of profit points being very close to 12/12. In the D-B relations, the division of profit points moved toward the rate maximally preferred by D. Since D was the only high power position the decentralization principle was not supported.[12] Thus the results supported all derivations from the $p(e)$ formulation. The change from 1-exchange to 2-exchange condition shifted the power status of all positions in the network. Since p_i is simply $p(e)$ for the 1-exchange condition, both sets of derivations followed from one general formulation.

The power distribution shifts shown in this experiment demonstrate that power is not determined solely by the shape of networks, but also by conditions such as the number of exchanges allocated to each position. Taken together, these factors determine the distribution of structural exclusions in the network and thus the distribution of power. It follows that the results of the many experimental studies on 1-exchange networks are less general in their implications than has been previously assumed. Finally, the experimental results do not support broad generalizations like the decentralization principle or that all networks have systemwide dependence.

Inclusion and Power

The idea of structural *inclusion* complements that of exclusion. Exchanges in a branching structure are inclusive when, for the central actor, profit can be realized only if more than one exchange is completed. A wide variety of "natural" exchange networks appear to be conditioned by inclusion. For example, households must provide food, clothing, *and* shelter to their members, and the purchase of one cannot substitute for the purchase of any other(s). Imagine a firm that assembles e parts into a marketable whole. If all parts are needed and if each can be obtained from only a single supplier, then the firm is in an inclusive branch for which $e = m_1$. Common to the two examples is the nonsubstitutability of the valued resources. As will be seen, the need to complete all exchanges in the branch adversely affects the resistance of the central actor, producing power at the periphery.

In this section we will show that the direction of the effect of inclusion is opposite that of exclusion, while the strength of inclusion's effect is not as great. Although we do not yet have a satisfactory general method of solving inclusive networks, resistance models provide a generative theory of the negotiation processes that transpire in branching structures with inclusive conditions, and it is these situations with which we are concerned below.

First, consider the "all-inclusive" branch. While peripheral positions receive profit from any exchange they complete, the central actor must exchange in *all* the relations of the branch to realize profit. Let B represent the central position, and we will consider three or five As at the periphery.

Recall that resistance for any actor A is

$$R_A = \frac{P_{max}(A) - P_A}{P_A - P_{con}(A)}$$

As before, the cost of not exchanging is set equal to zero for all positions. That is, if A and B cannot agree to exchange, they are in confrontation, and $P_{con}(A) = 0$. Thus for A resistance reduces to

$$R_A = \frac{P_{max}(A) - P_A}{P_A}$$

Now consider the resistance of the central B after completing the first exchange. If the second exchange is not completed, profits from the first will be lost. It follows that, for the second exchange, $P_{con}(B) = -P_B$.[13] Since failure to complete the third exchange means the loss of the value of the previous two, $P_{con}(B) = -2P_B$ and for the eth exchange $P_{con}(B) = -(e - 1)P_B$. Therefore, the resistance of B is

$$R_{B(P)} = \frac{P_{max}(B) - P_B}{P_B - [-(e - 1)P_B]}$$

and, simplifying,

$$R_{B(P)} = \frac{P_{max}(B) - P_B}{eP_B}$$

If B exchanges in sequence, then B's resistance for any given offer will decline with each new negotiation. Thus with the first A, $e = 1$ and for that exchange B and A bargain to compromise at an equal-profit rate exactly as they would in a branch with no exclusion or inclusion condition. But for the second exchange $e = 2$, B's resistance is lower for any offer, and the compromise rate at $R_{B(P)} = R_A$ will be more favorable to A — and increasingly so up to the eth exchange. Thus for sequential exchanges in any inclusive branch, the rates of exchange will increasingly favor the peripheral As, with the eth A having the most favorable rate of exchange relative to B.

In actual exchange settings, B may exchange in sequence only if the As reach agreements sequentially with B. After the first exchange, however, each A will "discover" that those who exchange later gain better rates than those who exchange earlier, and so each A has an interest in being B's e^{th} exchange partner. If all As act on that interest, however, each will wait until the last instant, all will exchange simultaneously, and each can receive the rate of the eth exchange. Assuming that As exchange simul-

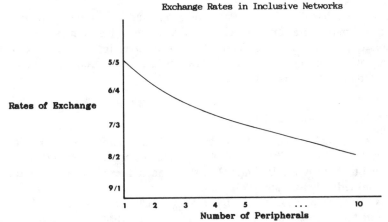

Figure 12.7.

taneously, as the number of branches increase the rate of exchange becomes increasing favorable to all peripherals. For this condition of simultaneous exchange, Figure 12.7 gives the rate for all exchanges in e-branches derived from the resistance equation. Note that unless e is very large, inclusive branches produce less power at the periphery than do exclusive branches at the center.

Inclusive structures with three and five branches have been investigated experimentally (Patton and Willer 1987). For the 3-branch the average observed exchange rate was 7.2/2.8, and for the 5-branch the average observed rate was 7.4/2.6, both favoring peripheral positions. As predicted, (1) both rates exceeded the 5/5 rate predicted for equipower, (2) the 5-branch rate exceeded that of the 3-branch, and (3) the rate of exchange for inclusive branches was not as extreme as the rate observed in prior research for exclusive branches.

Future research will take two directions. First, an index analogous to p(e) must be developed to help investigate a wider variety of network forms. Second, mixed structures containing both inclusive and exclusive conditions will be investigated. We expect that, for at least some branches, the effect of exclusion will wipe out the effect of inclusion. Furthermore, knowledge gained in the theoretical analysis of these opposed conditions should greatly increase the theory's applicability to networks outside of the laboratory.

Other Theoretical Directions

Exclusion produces power structures in which one or more actors exercise power because others are excluded from exchanging. Inclusion produces power structures in which some actor(s) are low in power because more than one exchange must be completed for value to be realized. In addition to exclusion and inclusion, the effects of hierarchies, mobility, coercion, and coalition formation have been investigated. Next we will summarize work in these areas. Following this, an important new theoretical direction will be discussed.

HIERARCHY/MOBILITY

Hierarchical exchange structures were studied using a network with a central A and six peripheral Bs. A was allocated resource units that were valued by both A and B, while Bs were allocated resources that could be transmitted only as a unit of 10 and were valued only by A. The range of possible exchange rates was $9/1 \leq X_{A/B} \leq 1/9$. Since $X_{A/B} = P_A/P_B$, A prefers higher rates and the Bs lower rates. No positions were structurally excluded from exchange, and each B could exchange with A once per negotiation round.

For all structures the rates of exchange were stratified by dividing the A-B exchanges into two subsets. The first subset contained the first two exchanges in the negotiation period. Of these two, the first could be for any rate mutually agreed upon by A and one of the Bs, while the second rate was restricted so as to be greater than or equal to the first.

The second subset contained the four remaining exchanges. The restriction here was that A had to receive a minimum of two units more than from the first exchange. For example, if the first exchange was for 3/7 (3 for A, 7 for B), then the second exchange could be for 3/7 or 4/6, and so on, and the four remaining exchanges could be for any rate 5/5 or greater. Alternatively, if the first exchange was 7/3, the second could be for 7/3, 8/2, or 9/1, and all remaining exchanges had to be 9/1.

The experimental networks were run under two conditions. Under the *fixed* condition, positions B_1 and B_2 had to exchange with A first and second, respectively. Positions B_3 through B_6 could then exchange with A, subject only to the restrictions in the previous paragraph. Under the *mobile* condition, any B position could be the first, second, third, and so on, to exchange with A. In sum, both fixed and mobile conditions had two strata, with one privileged relative to the other. For the fixed condition two of the actors had exclusive right to positions in the privileged strata, but in the mobile condition any actor could gain either position in the privileged strata.

The p(e) index helps to analyze these situations. In the fixed condition, A-B_1 negotiates an exchange, followed independently by A-B_2. Each substructure operates as an independent dyad with p(1) = 1 for each position—hence no power advantages. For the remaining exchanges, A has four relations and four exchanges to offer, hence $p(4)_A = 1$, and p(1) = 1 for the remaining Bs. Thus the fixed structure should not produce power differences. In experiments on the fixed structures, all rates of exchange were a consequence of bargaining, with the average rate for the first exchange being approximately 3/7 while the rate for the third through sixth exchanges was approximately 5/5 (Willer 1987).

In the *mobile* condition, all Bs had an interest in competing for the first exchange with A, since profit from subsequent exchanges was limited by that of the first. Initially, then, six Bs competed for one exchange, and so $p(1)_A = 6$, whereas $p(1)_B = 0$. For the second exchange there were five Bs competing for the exchange and $p(1)_A = 5$. After the first two exchanges, each further exchange should have had no effect on the profit available from those to follow. In experimental tests, the Bs actively bid for the first opportunities to exchange. As a consequence, the rates offered to A increased rapidly such that the average rate for the first exchange was approximately 6.4/3.6 and the average rate for the third through sixth exchanges was slightly higher than 8.4/1.6. Note that the more privileged rate of the mobile structure was less favorable to the Bs than the less privileged rate of the fixed structure (Willer 1987).

Structures with hierarchy and mobility permit differential power, while hierarchical structures without mobility do not. For applications outside the laboratory, these results suggest that stable power relations found in bureaucracies, what Weber called domination, may be due to mobility of officials in the bureaucratic hierarchy. This is consistent with Weber's extensive investigation of appropriation of office as a condition for power.

COERCIVE STRUCTURES

Willer (1987) has formulated models for coercive structures. These are composed of coercive relations, for each of which there is a coercer who holds a negative sanction and a coercee who holds positive sanctions. The interests of the relationship lead the coercer to attempt to extract all or some part of the coercee's resources by threat of transmission of the negative. All coercive relations are power relations. Some structural conditions, however, can augment, diminish, or even remove that power.

In a strong coercive network, the central position must transmit at least one negative sanction to one of the peripherals in each round of negotiations. In a weak coercive structure, the number of transmittable negative sanctions controlled by the central position equals the number of peripheral positions. Resistance analyses and experimental investigations show that with a central coercer, strong and weak coercive networks produce high and low rates of coercive exploitation, respectively. When the coercee is central, investigations show low and near-zero rates of coercion in weak and strong networks, respectively. Thus, even though coercive relations differ from exchange relations in key respects, at least some structural effects in coercive structures mirror those observed in exchange networks.

COALITION FORMATION IN
EXCHANGE AND COERCIVE STRUCTURES

The designs of coalition formation experiments by power-dependence theorists and elementary theorists have differed. For example, Cook and Gillmore (1984) countervailed the power of a branch by restricting negotiation and exchange of the central position to only one peripheral. By eliminating branching, the effect, according to power-dependence theory, was to balance the rate of profit point division. Their design also eliminated structural exclusion and, as we would predict, exchange rates equalized. However, the elimination of exclusion was irrelevant from the point of view of power-dependence theory.

Yet to be published are coalition formation studies on structures like those of Figure 12.2. For 12.2b and 12.2c, with one and two exclusions respectively, it was observed that peripherals who were allowed to form coalitions decided to take turns at self-exclusion. Since the central position had three exchange opportunities with only three peripherals negotiating, it was observed that the rates of exchange were settled by bargaining, not bidding, and power was countervailed. The countervailing of power was not impeded by the other branches as would have been expected by power-dependence theory. Also counter to that theory, there was no power in the 12.2a structure. Since there was no power to countervail, it was not surprising that coalition formation had no effect on exchange rates.

Willer (1987) also reported investigations of coalition formation in coercive structures. The resistance analysis of these structures allowed predictions of the amount of collective benefits received. In general, the experiments supported the derivations.

FLOW NETWORKS

Thus far the scope of the theory has been restricted to situations in which resources obtained from one exchange relation cannot be used in a second — what we call a "discrete" exchange condition. This scope condition places certain bounds on the applicability of our theory beyond the laboratory.

Since power use is defined in terms of rates of exchange, a necessary condition for power and power use between any pair of positions is that the two be linked by a resource flow. The discrete condition restricts power and power use to adjacent positions. In "flow networks," however, if A has power over B and B has power over C, A can have power over C. At issue is the determination of the conditions under which power will be transitive. A necessary condition for power transitivity among three or more positions is that resources flow from the first, *through* the second, to the third. Since these are exchanges, there also must be a flow from the third, through the second, to the first.

Power transitivity in flow networks may be investigated under any of the structural conditions we have discussed. To illustrate, the Figure 12.8 networks use exclusion. The 12.8a network serves as a baseline to which the others can be compared. Resource i is provided to A and resource j to C. Exchange will occur if A values j more than i, C values i more than j, and B either (1) values both i and j or (2) values only one resource but recognizes that the other has exchange value.[14]

Retaining exchange conditions analogous to those used earlier, assume rounds of bargaining for which i and j are replenished at A and C, and only one exchange may be made for a given resource. B needs only an initial resource allocation, after which exchanges with A and C supply the rest.

All exchanges in 12.8a should occur at equal power, since no position has the capacity to exclude any other position from exchanges without itself suffering a loss of profit. In 12.8b, given the 1-exchange rule, A may exchange only with one of the Bs, and each B only with one of the Cs in a given round. This should generate bidding within each branch: The Cs bid to exchange with their B, and the Bs bid to exchange with A. The rates of exchange should then move toward the extreme most favorable to A. As A gains an advantage, the Bs receive fewer units of i from A, and the Cs receive fewer i units from the Bs. Also, units of j should accumulate at A. Thus power transitivity is predicted.

Networks 12.8c and 12.8d illustrate different types of transitivity. In 12.8c, though each B is in a nonpower relation with its adjacent C, the bidding of the Bs in their exchanges with the As should move the rate of exchange toward the extreme most favorable to the A. That is, each B-C pair is equal, and together they are low in power, with A being the sole high power position. This suggests that the rates of exchange in the 12.8c structure will be identical to the rates in 12.8b. In contrast, A and B in 12.8d are equal, and together they are high in power relative to the Cs. A and B share in the benefits of the Cs' bidding.

A Note on Confirmation Status

In evaluating the confirmation status of the elementary theory, we must consider the relationship of this theory to both its tests and its alternative formulations. We agree with Toulmin (1953) that a few successful studies ranging over a wide scope are more important to the confirmation status of a theory than a large number of studies over a narrow range. We also agree with Popper (1968) that a theory is preferable to its alternatives if it has greater precision, explains more, provides more detailed explanations, survives tests that alternatives have failed, suggests test not considered by alternatives, and unifies previously unrelated problems.

Assessing the confirmation status of the elementary theory is complicated by its programmatic structure. As a *research program* (Lakatos

(a)

(b)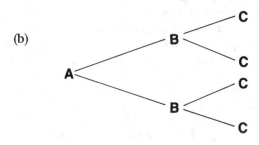

(c)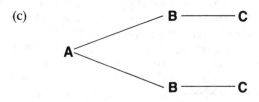

(d)

Figure 12.8.

1970, 1978), the theory is characterized by a relatively static "core set" of concepts, assumptions, strategies, and findings, and a more dynamic "protective belt" of theory in progress and research activity.

If there were rival programs with identical aims, it would be a simple matter to declare which was the most successful. In actuality, some of the branches of the elementary theory (e.g., the p formulation) have alternatives against which they may be compared (e.g., Marsden 1983; Bonacich 1987). Some of those alternatives are explicitly integrated in larger theory programs with divergent scope (Marsden's case) and some stand in relative isolation as specialized formulations (Bonacich's case). Other branches of the elementary theory, however, simply have no alternatives developed to a degree that is sufficient to permit critical testing. Empirical tests (against null hypotheses) then provide the only available mode of corroboration. In such cases, the elementary theory again fares well (see Willer and Anderson 1981; Willer 1987).

In brief, then, systematic scope expansions, empirical tests of derivations, and critical testing all strengthen the elementary theory vis-à-vis Toulmin's and Popper's criteria for confirmation. Tests of formulations in each new empirical domain (e.g., dyadic bargaining, coercive relations, discrete network exchanges, multiexchange networks) have been few but carefully chosen. In addition, the theory has generated precise, falsifiable predictions for those tests and, whenever possible, alternative formulations have been fairly assessed under controlled conditions.

Summary and Conclusions

Power and related phenomena have been structurally produced in exchange networks by conditions of exclusion, inclusion, and hierarchy/mobility. Conditions affecting power in coercive structures have also been examined and successfully tested. Critical tests between the elementary theory and power-dependence theory indicate that power has not been produced by satiation-dependence or branching-dependence and that power positions cannot be accurately located by vulnerability. This is not to say that power-dependence experiments did not have structurally produced power relations. However, the critical tests indicate that those power relations were produced by exclusion processes and not by the processes claimed in the power-dependence formulation.

Unlike the pure structural forms and conditions that may be generated in the laboratory, some if not all structures found outside the lab contain multiple conditions for power. For example, while a firm exchanges in inclusive conditions with its suppliers, it may be able to choose among multiple suppliers for some of its needed resources. If suppliers of like resources compete among themselves, the advantage that they could gain from the inclusive connection to the firm is lost. But if competing suppliers merge (i.e., form a coalition), they can profit from the inclusive condition. The decision to merge, however, may not be made by owners who will benefit directly from increased profits, but by officials whose position in a structure of hierarchy/mobility might be threatened by a merger. The act of merging might be opposed by workers concerned that they might join the unemployed, who are currently excluded from earning a wage. To deal with instances of this kind requires a theory that recognizes multiple bases of power. We hope in future research to use our theory to learn how actors attempt to control the conditions of power in structures.

We see future work with the elementary theory as moving step by step through the investigation of flow networks and structures with multiple power conditions toward applications to power structures outside the laboratory. There is no doubt that additional structural conditions of power remain to be discovered. With these, the scope of the theory will be broadened even further.

Notes

1. To cover varying historical conditions, Willer (1984, 1985, 1987) has differentiated social and economic exchange. In this chapter, *exchange* refers to what has elsewhere been called *economic exchange*: Actors transmitting valued goods suffer losses and those receiving valued goods enjoy gains. Also see Ekeh (1974) for the scope limits of exchange theory.

2. Blau's (1964) work in exchange has both rational and operant formulations. See Blau (1987) for his recent views on the scope of limits of exchange theory.

3. Cook and Emerson (1978) state, "The connection is *negative* if exchange in one is contingent upon non-exchange in the other" (p. 725). How this relates to the 1972 satiation-based definition is not explained.

4. Note that the division of profit points introduced by power-dependence theorists for their experiments does not involve the alienation and appropriation of valued goods. Thus their experiments did not need to include property as an initial condition. Though the division of profit points is not an exchange relation, its payoff matrix is similar to exchange and thus can be used as an analogue for it.

5. Throughout this chapter, "i's exchange rate" refers to i's net profits from exchange relative to i's exchange partner. Thus a high exchange rate for i means that i's net gain is high relative to the partner's.

6. The following sections show how these predictions were derived.

7. Here and elsewhere, *exclusion*, in reference to networks drawn by power-dependence theorists, means exclusion from high-profit relations. As will be seen below, low-profit relations do not affect the distribution of power.

8. The way that P_A and P_B enter into the same equation may suggest that we are making direct comparisons not simply of scores, but of utilities. Though economists object to interpersonal utility comparisons, the comparisons here are between theoretic actors. In any case, the same solutions as those derived here can be found graphically without interpersonal comparisons.

9. In Brennan, the rate of exchange in the A-B relation was expressed as a ratio of flows, not P values.

10. The B positions may exercise power by organizing their exchanges so as to form a coalition against the As. However, in such a case the effective shape of this network changes and the equal-power prediction no longer applies.

11. After an extended series of exchanges, an actor with p = 0 should seek to exchange in *all* its relations, regardless of power differences. That is, in order to avoid exclusion, the actor will offer to accept a rate minimally better than confrontation to all adjacencies. Since this actor is no longer negotiating, only offering a fixed rate, this does not violate Axiom 2.

12. Given profit point divisions it is, of course, impossible for power to occur between any but adjacent positions. Thus the initial conditions particular to power-dependence networks can produce decentralization. But it would be wrong to infer that this is a general tendency in exchange networks. For example, the flow networks considered below have no such tendency.

13. This derivation is a special case based on a simplifying assumption. Actually, $P_{con}(B)$ for the second exchange is equal to the profit that could be lost from the first exchange, $P_{con}(B)$ for the third exchange is equal to the sum of the profit lost in the first and second exchanges, and so on. By assuming that each of these losses is $P(B)$, a more parsimonious model results. While this assumption is manifestly false for the sequential case in question, it may fit the simultaneous case below.

14. Let j_A/i_A be A's relative valuation of the resources and similarly for C. Then it can be shown that the minimal condition for flow through the network is $j_A/i_A > i_C/i_C$ — given condition 1 or 2 for any B(s) between A and C.

References

Blau, Peter. 1964. *Exchange and Power in Social Life*. New York: John Wiley.

— — —. 1987. "Microprocess and Macrostructure." In *Social Exchange Theory*, edited by Karen Cook. Newbury Park, CA: Sage.

Bonacich, Phillip. 1987. "Power and Centrality: A Family of Measures." *American Journal of Sociology* 92:1170-82.

Brennan, John S. 1981. "Some Experimental Structures." In *Networks: Exchange and Coercion*, edited by David Willer and Bo Anderson. New York: Elsevier/Greenwood.

Cook, Karen S. and Richard M. Emerson. 1978. "Power, Equity and Commitment in Exchange Networks." *American Sociological Review* 43:721-39.

— — —. 1984. "Exchange Networks and the Analysis of Complex Organizations." In *Research in the Sociology of Organizations*, Vol. 3, edited by Samuel Bacharach and Edward J. Lawler. Greenwich, CT: JAI.

Cook, Karen S., Richard M. Emerson, Mary R. Gillmore, and Toshio Yamagishi. 1983. "The Distribution of Power in Exchange Networks: Theory and Experimental Results." *American Journal of Sociology* 89:275-305.

Cook, Karen S. and Mary Gillmore. 1984. "Power, Dependence and Coalitions." In *Advances In Group Processes*, Vol. 1, edited by Edward Lawler. Greenwich, CT: JAI.

Cook, Karen S., Mary Gillmore, and Toshio Yamagishi. 1986. "Power and Line Vulnerability as a Basis for Predicting the Distribution of Power in Exchange Networks." *American Journal of Sociology* 92:445-48.

Dahl, Robert. 1957. "The Concept of Power." *Behavioral Science* 2:201-18.

Ekeh, Peter. 1974. *Social Exchange Theory*. London: Heinemann.

Emerson, Richard M. 1962. "Power-Dependence Relations." *American Sociological Review* 27:31-41.

— — —. 1972a. "Exchange Theory, Part 1: A Psychological Basis for Social Exchange." In *Sociological Theories in Progress*, Vol. 2, edited by Joseph Berger, Morris Zelditch, Jr., and Bo Anderson. Boston: Houghton Mifflin.

— — —. 1972b. "Exchange Theory, Part 2: Exchange Relations and Network Structures." In *Sociological Theories in Progress*, Vol. 2, edited by Joseph Berger, Morris Zelditch, Jr., and Bo Anderson. Boston: Houghton Mifflin.

Fararo, Thomas J. 1984. "Neoclassical Theorizing and Formalization in Sociology." *Journal of Mathematical Sociology* 10:361-94.

— — —. 1987. "Generativity in Theoretical Model-Building." In *Advances in Group Processes*, Vol. 4, edited by Edward J. Lawler and Barry Markovsky. Greenwich, CT: JAI.

Gilham, Steven A. 1981. "State, Law and Modern Economic Exchange." In *Networks: Exchange and Coercion*, edited by David Willer and Bo Anderson. New York: Elsevier/Greenwood.

Hansen, Knud L. 1981. " 'Black' Exchange and Its System of Social Control." In *Networks: Exchange and Coercion*, edited by David Willer and Bo Anderson. New York: Elsevier/Greenwood.

Heckathorn, Douglas. 1980. "A Unified Model for Bargaining and Conflict." *Behavioral Science* 23:73-85.

Homans, George C. 1967. "Fundamental Social Processes." In *Sociology: An Introduction*, edited by Neil J. Smelser. New York: John Wiley.

— — —. 1974. *Social Behavior: Its Elementary Forms*, rev. ed. New York: Harcourt Brace Jovanovich.

Isaac, Jeffrey. 1987. *Power and Marxist Theory: A Realist View*. Ithaca, NY: Cornell University Press.

Lakatos, Imre. 1970. "Falsification and the Methodology of Scientific Research Programmes." In *Criticism and the Growth of Knowledge*, edited by Imre Lakatos and Alan Musgrave. New York: Cambridge University Press.

— — —. 1978. *The Methodology of Scientific Research Programmes*. New York: Cambridge University Press.

Layder, Derek. 1985. "Power, Structure and Agency." *Journal for the Theory of Social Behavior* 15:131-49.

Loukinen, Michael. 1981. "Social Exchange Networks." In *Networks: Exchange and Coercion*, edited by David Willer and Bo Anderson. New York: Elsevier/Greenwood.

Luckenbill, David. 1979. "Power: A Conceptual Framework." *Symbolic Interaction* 2:97-114.

Lukes, Steven. 1974. *Power: A Radical View*. London: Macmillan.

Mann, Michael. 1986. *The Sources of Social Power*, Vol. 1. Cambridge: Cambridge University Press.

Markovsky, Barry. 1987. "Toward Multilevel Sociological Theories: Simulations of Actor and Network Effects." *Sociological Theory* 5:101-17.

Markovsky, Barry, David Willer, and Travis Patton. 1988. "Power Relations in Exchange Networks." *American Sociological Review* 53:220-36.

Marsden, Peter V. 1983. "Restricted Access in Networks and Models of Power." *American Journal of Sociology* 88:686-717.

Marx, Karl. [1867] 1967. *Capital*. New York: International Publishers.

Molm, Linda. 1987. "Linking Power Structure and Power Use." In *Social Exchange Theory*, edited by Karen Cook. Newbury Park, CA: Sage.

Nash, John F. 1950. "The Bargaining Problem." *Econometrica* 18:155-62.

— — —. 1953 "Two-Person Cooperative Games." *Econometrica* 21:128-40.

Patton, Travis and David Willer. 1987. "Power in Centralized Networks." Paper presented at the annual meetings of the American Sociological Association, Chicago.

Polanyi, Karl. 1957. *The Great Transformation*. Boston: Beacon.

Pen, Jan. 1975. "A General Theory of Bargaining." In *Bargaining: Formal Theories of Negotiation*, edited by Oran Young. Urbana: University of Illinois Press.

Popper, Karl. 1968. *Conjectures and Refutations: The Growth of Scientific Knowledge*. New York: Harper & Row.

Poulantzas, Nicos. 1973. *Political Power and Social Classes*. London: New Left.

Rapoport, Anatol. 1970. *N-Person Game Theory*. Ann Arbor: University of Michigan Press.

Siegel, Sidney and Lawrence Fouraker. 1960. *Bargaining and Group Decision Making*. New York: McGraw-Hill.

Stolte, John and Richard M. Emerson. 1977. "Structural Inequality: Position and Power in Exchange Structures." In *Behavioral Theory in Sociology* edited by Robert L. Hamblin and John H. Kunkel. New Brunswick, NJ: Transaction.

Toulmin, Stephen. 1953. *The Philosophy of Science*. New York: Harper & Row.

Van Doorn, J. A. 1962. "Sociology and the Problem of Power." *Sociologia Neerlandica* (Winter): 3-51.

Weber, Max. [1918] 1968. *Economy and Society.* Berkeley: University of California Press.

Willer, David. 1981. "Quantity and Network Structure." In *Networks: Exchange and Coercion*, edited by David Willer and Bo Anderson. New York: Elsevier/Greenwood.

— — —. 1984. "Analysis and Composition as Theoretic Procedures." *Journal of Mathematical Sociology* 10:241-70.

— — —. 1985. "Property and Social Exchange." In *Advances in Group Processes*, Vol. 2, edited by Edward J. Lawler. Greenwich, CT: JAI.

— — —. 1986. "Vulnerability and the Location of Power Positions." *American Journal of Sociology* 92:441-44.

— — —. 1987. *Theory and Experimental Investigation of Social Structures.* New York: Gordon & Breach.

Willer, David and Bo Anderson, eds. 1981. *Networks: Exchange and Coercion.* New York: Elsevier/Greenwood.

Willer, David and Travis Patton. 1987. "The Development of Network Exchange Theory." In *Advances in Group Processes*, Vol. 4, edited by Edward J. Lawler and Barry Markovsky. Greenwich, CT: JAI.

Wrong, Dennis H. 1968. "Some Problems in Defining Social Power." *American Journal of Sociology* 73:673-81.

— — —. 1979 *Power: Its Forms, Bases and Uses.* Oxford: Basil Blackwell.

Yamagishi, Toshio, Mary R. Gillmore, and Karen S. Cook. 1988. "Network Connections and the Distribution of Power in Exchange Networks." *American Journal of Sociology* 93:833-51.

Young, Oran, ed. 1975. *Bargaining: Formal Theories of Negotiation.* Urbana: University of Illinois Press.

Zeuthen, Frederik. 1930. *Problems of Monopoly and Economic Warfare.* London: Routledge & Sons.

13

The Theory of the Distributive-Justice Force in Human Affairs: Analyzing the Three Central Questions

GUILLERMINA JASSO

In studying the operation of what has come to be called the distributive-justice force, three sets of questions are central:

(1) What do individuals and collectivities think is just?
(2) What is the magnitude of the perceived injustice associated with given departures from perfect justice?
(3) What are the behavioral and social consequences of perceived injustice?

Each set encompasses many questions and unsolved problems. Moreover, some of the questions in each set are related to questions in the other sets and related as well to the questions of other theories, that is, to the operation of other forces. For example, one of the important elements in distributive-justice theory — the individual's *actual reward*, which aggregates to form the collectivity's actual distribution of resources — arises by the operation of other forces (forces that are studied in social stratification, biology, labor economics) and arrives to play a part in the second set of questions; at the same time, phenomena analyzed by the third set of questions include the alteration of actual rewards. At first blush, it would appear not only that distributive-justice phenomena contain a generous share of the mysterious, but also that their connections to other fields of study consign us to confusion and ambiguity.

But confusion and ambiguity are not the future for the theory of the distributive-justice force. Since 1972 — the watershed year marking publication of the landmark paper by Berger, Zelditch, Anderson, and Cohen (in Volume 2 of *Sociological Theories in Progress*) — the questions have begun to fall, one by one, to statement with precision and clarity. If as yet there are few answers, we know that it is simply a matter of time; for now many of the questions can be stated precisely.

This chapter will provide a comprehensive summary of the current state of the theory of the distributive-justice force. The goal is to provide a guide to what is known and what is unknown (the latter of necessity constrained by current vision) and to express mathematically both what is known and what is unknown. Thus many substantive questions will be seen to resolve to mathematical problems, the solutions to which are possible partly by theoretical reasoning and partly by empirical investigation. As will be seen, distributive-justice theory yields a wealth of interesting unsolved problems.

The underlying premise of the theory of the distributive-justice force is that all observed human behavioral and social phenomena may be usefully regarded as the product of the joint operation of many forces and that the distributive-justice force may be one of these forces. The theory provides a mathematical description of the process whereby individuals compare their holdings of the goods they value (such as beauty, intelligence, or wealth) to holdings deemed just or appropriate for them, experiencing a fundamental instantaneous magnitude of the *Justice Evaluation* (J), which captures their sense of being fairly or unfairly treated in the distributions of the natural and social goods. This process generalizes to include judgments about the justice or injustice of another person's situation. As in the classical literature, this instantaneous experience of being fairly or unfairly treated (or of another's being fairly or unfairly treated) in the distributions of the natural and social goods is regarded as having the most wide-ranging and diverse consequences for virtually every area of human individual and social behavior.

The theory has a two-part structure, the first part containing the postulates and the second containing the predictions.[1] A short initial assumption set — consisting of one postulate, one measurement rule, and one identity — yields a refined formula for J, which immediately enables derivation of predictions for such diverse phenomena as crime, migration, illness, and leisure-time activities. Introduction of additional postulates, some of which highlight aggregations — over valued goods, over time, and across persons — of the basic quantity J, enables derivation to other wide arenas, producing predictions concerning population size, economic growth, income inequality, conflict within and between groups, the emergence of sanctions, societal divorce rates, and the rise of religious orders.[2]

The predictions obtained to date have been derived from the skeleton of the theory, that is, from the basic formula for J at the individual level, and the mean and dispersion of the instantaneous distribution, both under the simplest conditions. Yet, even as we may prize the parsimony of the reasoning yielding these predictions, we recognize the need for richer and more precise statement of the postulates, for greater fidelity to the complex world we observe. This assessment of the theory, in light of the attempt to achieve greater fidelity and precision, is organized by returning to the schema with which this chapter began and examining separately the three central sets of questions that arise in the study of distributive justice.

The First Set of Questions:
What Is Just?

What do individuals and societies think is just? What is the just reward for an individual of specified characteristics? What is the just distribution of resources? These questions have a long and intellectually rich history, the many highlights of which include the foundational accounts of commutative justice and distributive justice in Plato and Aristotle, Julius Caesar's principle of observing the battlefield behavior of his soldiers so as to reward them justly, Cervantes's story of the division of spoils among a band of thieves, and St. Antoninus's homilies on the just wage.

THE MODERN FOUNDATION:
THE BERGER ET AL. REFERENTIAL STRUCTURE

The modern formulation of the basic question — What is viewed as just? — begins with Berger et al.'s path-breaking contribution. Berger et al. (1972, pp. 133-35) postulated the theoretical entity they named the "referential structure," describing it thus:[3]

> For a distributive-justice process to unfold, [the observer must have access to] a referential structure [with] the following four components:
>
> (a) Generalized individuals,
> (b) who possess given states of given characteristics,
> (c) to which are associated given states of given goal-objects,
> (d) where the characteristics and goal-objects are all status-valued.
>
> . . . The referential structure must have three fundamental properties: (a) It must be unitary. (b) It must be differentiated. (c) It must be balanced.

Berger et al. (1972) showed that in the absence of a referential structure with its Just Reward it is impossible to distinguish justice from injustice and impossible to distinguish injustice of the underreward type from injustice of the overreward type. They argued that the referential structure provides a way to incorporate not only cardinal information (e.g., wages) but also ordinal information (for example, "high" and "low" states of characteristics and goal-objects) and qualitative information (e.g., race, sex) (pp. 127-29, 133-35).

Table 13.1 Four Forms of the Berger et al. Just Reward Function, Obtained by Combining Cardinal and Ordinal Just Rewards with Cardinal and Ordinal Inputs

	Just Reward	
Inputs	Cardinal	Ordinal
Cardinal	$JR = h(X_1,...,X_K)$	$\alpha_{JR} = h(X_1,...,X_K)$
Ordinal	$JR = h(\alpha_1,...,\alpha_K)$	$\alpha_{JR} = h(\alpha_1,...,\alpha_K)$

GENERAL MATHEMATICAL EXPRESSIONS OF THE BERGER ET AL. JUST REWARD FUNCTION

Berger et al. described the referential structure with such precision that its translation into mathematics is immediate, as shown by Jasso (1983a), and directly yields two concepts fundamental in the study of commutative and distributive justice — the Just Reward and the Just Reward Function — and, by simple aggregation, a third fundamental concept — the Just Reward Distribution.

In the general mathematical expression of the instantaneous observer-specific Just Reward Function (JRF), the Just Reward (JR) for any rewardee (including the observer him- or herself) is expressed as a function of K reward-relevant variables, denoted X, where JR is strictly monotonic in each argument, and where the JR and the inputs may be represented either cardinally or ordinally by the associated ranks α. For example, Jasso (1983a, pp. 193-97) presents the cardinal-inputs form of the Berger et al. Just Reward Function,

$$\text{Just Reward} = h(X_1, \ldots, X_k), \quad [1]$$

and the ordinal-inputs form,

$$\text{Just Reward} = f(\alpha_1, \ldots, \alpha_k), \quad [2]$$

where the arguments α_k are the *ranks* on the reward-relevant characteristics X_k. Table 13.1 displays the four possible forms obtained by combining cardinal or ordinal inputs with cardinal or ordinal JR. Note also that ordinal and qualitative input variables can be represented in a cardinal-inputs form by sets of binary variables; and mixed forms can combine cardinal, ordinal, and qualitative variables.

CONTENT OF THE BERGER ET AL.
JUST REWARD FUNCTION

Any good may be the subject of the Just Reward Function. Thus the class of goods includes both the natural and social goods.[4] The major distinction relevant to scientific work is whether the Just Reward Function is expressed in terms of theoretical quantities or observable quantities.

Theoretical Statement of the JRF

The Just Reward may be expressed as a function of theoretical terms. The set of theoretical reward-relevant variables X_k proposed in the literature includes, but is not limited to, the following: need, merit, scarcity, supply, demand, marginal product, investment, effort.

Observable Statement of the JRF

In this case, an observable term, such as just wage, is expressed as a function of observable arguments. The set of observable X_k proposed in the literature includes, but is not limited to, the following: age, sex, schooling, type of job, work intensity, seniority, marital status, number of dependents.

Second-Order Versions of the JRF

Following the Berger et al. foundational reasoning, the Just Reward Function is specified as a function whose arguments are reward-relevant characteristics. But notice that, in the vocabularies of both an observer and a theorist, sometimes the argument of the Just Reward Function consists of *another reward* rather than of reward-relevant variables. The hallmark of this *other reward* is that it assumes a magnitude in the reward's domain. It may appear in two versions: first, as the Actual Reward of a specified person and, second, as a parameter of the Actual Reward Distribution.

To illustrate the first of the two second-order versions of the Just Reward Function found in the literature, consider the following JRF specifications. Shepelak and Alwin (1986) specify the Just Reward as a function of own Actual Reward; Mirowsky (1987) specifies the Just Reward as a function of spouse's Actual Reward; and Markovsky (1988) specifies the Just Reward as a function of co-worker's Actual Reward. In all these cases, one can reason that the given Actual Reward is a proxy for the right-hand side of an implicit Just Reward Function. Hence such versions may be considered second-order versions of the Just Reward Function.

The second kind of second-order version of the Just Reward Function arises when the JRF'S right-hand side contains a parameter of the Actual Reward Distribution, most commonly the mean reward (as in Jasso 1980), but potentially also other parameters such as the median, lower and upper extreme values, and transformations thereof. Note that the particular case of the mean reward may also be regarded as a proxy for a (set of) reward-relevant variable(s) constant in the population.

MATHEMATICAL FORM OF
THE BERGER ET AL. JUST REWARD FUNCTION

What is the mathematical form of the Just Reward Function? At the present time, there does not appear to be any theoretical reasoning advancing a particular mathematical form for the JRF. Building an a priori argument for the mathematical form of the JRF is an important task. In the meanwhile, the literature (of which I am aware) contains six distinct mathematical forms. Four of these were proposed as estimates of empirical Just Reward Functions; the other two arise via mathematical simulations. The empirical forms are a constant function (Lerner 1974), a linear function (Alves and Rossi 1978; Alves 1982), a square-root function (Jasso and Rossi 1977), and an exponential function (Jasso 1978).[5] The hypothetical forms are a power function (Jasso 1983a) and a function containing an integral (Jasso 1983a). The six forms are displayed in Table 13.2.

THE MATCH BETWEEN THE JUST REWARD FUNCTION
AND THE JUST REWARD DISTRIBUTION

Suppose that each individual member of a society is judged to be perfectly justly rewarded in the distribution of a socially valued good (such as income). Does it necessarily follow that the observer making the judgment will also judge the resultant probability distribution of that good to be a just distribution? This question was posed by Brickman in a compelling series of papers (see Brickman et al. 1981). Jasso (1983a) shows that the Just Reward Function and the Just Reward Distribution (JRD) are linked together in an exact mathematical relationship that includes the probability distributions of the reward-relevant characteristics and, hence, that at a single point in time the JRF and the JRD imply each other.

Over time, however, if the distributions of the reward-relevant characteristics change, the match between JRF and JRD is destroyed, and a new matched pair of JRF and JRD must be found. But there is an important case when the original match between JRF and JRD is not destroyed — the case where the JRF is expressed in ordinal-arguments form. Thus the ranks version of the JRF constitutes the unique solution to the intertemporal version of the micro-macro problem posed by Brickman.

UNSOLVED PROBLEMS

Berger et al.'s contribution set the research agenda with respect to the Just Reward and the Just Reward Function. Berger et al.'s idea of the

Table 13.2 Mathematical Forms Underlying Just Reward Functions in the Literature

---

A. Just Reward Functions Estimated Empirically

    1. **Constant Function: Equality** (Lerner 1974)

$$Just\ Reward\ =\ C$$

    2. **Linear Function** (Alves and Rossi 1978; Alves 1982)

$$Just\ Earnings\ =\ a + \sum b_k X_k$$

    3. **Square-Root Function** (Jasso and Rossi 1977)

$$Just\ Earnings\ =\ \frac{-b\left[b + \sqrt{b^2 - 4a(c + \sum d_k X_k)}\right]}{2a}$$

    4. **Exponential Function** (Jasso 1978)

$$Just\ Earnings\ =\ P\left(\prod e^{b_k X_k}\right)$$

B. Just Reward Functions Derived by Theoretical Simulation

    1. **Power Function** (Jasso 1983)

$$Just\ Earnings\ =\ Pa X^{b/c}$$

    2. **Integral Function** (Jasso 1983)

$$Just\ Earnings\ =\ P\left\{1 - F_N\left[a + b\ln\left(\frac{x}{c}\right)\right]\right\}^{-d}$$

NOTE: The symbol F_N denotes the cumulative distribution function of the standard normal distribution

referential structure made it possible to pose the classical questions with unprecedented clarity. The following are among the most important unanswered questions in the first set of distributive-justice questions:

(1) *Classes of rewards:* Does the Just Reward Function vary systematically by reward class?

(2) *Set of reward-relevant variables:* For each class of reward, what are the reward-relevant variables?

(3) *Functional form:* For each class of reward, what is the best approximation to the functional form?

(4) *Observer's repertoire of Just Reward Functions:* For each class of reward, is there a repertoire of JRFs (Merton and Rossi 1950; Berger et al. 1972)? What is the size of the repertoire? The dispersion in the Just Reward? What activates one JRF in the repertoire?

(5) *Relevant groups in ordinal case:* When the JRF assumes an ordinal form, what is the group within which the ranks are calculated?

(6) *Observer effects:* Do the foregoing five elements differ by observer? If so, what are the relevant characteristics of the observer and of the observer's social, political, and informational environment? How much does the Just Reward vary across observer? How does the JRF change, if at all, when the rewardee is the observer him- or herself?

(7) *Relationship between the Just Reward Function and the Actual Reward Function, within and across observers:* Under what conditions, if any, does the Just Reward Function mimic the Actual Reward Function (Homans 1976)? Under what conditions, if any, does the Actual Reward Function mimic a Just Reward Function? How may we fruitfully describe the process by which an actor or collectivity wages a campaign to change an Actual Reward Function, and hence a steward's Just Reward Function, in order to bring it into conformity with the actor or collectivity's Just Reward Function?

(8) *Collective Just Reward Function:* How do particular JRFs spread among observers and become normative? How, in turn, are they attacked and discarded? If, under a Rawlsian veil of ignorance, the observer-specific JRFs converge, what is the relation between this collective JRF and the JRF reasoned by theologians to be the deity's JRF?

Evidently, much of the entire first set of questions is encompassed by a single equation, the Just Reward Function:

$$JR_{grots} = h_{grots}(\mathbf{X}_{grots}; \mathbf{B}_{grots}), \qquad [3]$$

which contains three sets of unknowns — (1) the vector of reward-relevant variables $\mathbf{X}$, (2) the parameter vector $\mathbf{B}$, and (3) the functional form h — and where the subscripts *grots* denote, respectively, the reward (or good), the rewardee, the observer, the time period, and the society.

For any combination of reward, rewardee, observer, time period, and society, once the Just Reward Function is known — that is, once the reward-relevant variables and the equation's functional form and parameters are known — the probability distribution of the Just Reward can be solved for, using information or assumptions on the joint distribution of the X_k. Moreover, theoretical simulations can investigate the classes of JRDs that would be produced from alternative JRFs, given the joint distribution of the X_k.

The Second Set of Questions: The Justice Evaluation Function

What is the magnitude of the injustice associated with specified departures from perfect justice? The theory of the distributive-justice force answers this fundamental question with the Justice Evaluation Function, which combines two terms — the Actual Reward and the Just Reward — to produce the instantaneous Justice Evaluation J,

$$J = h(\text{Actual Reward, Just Reward}). \qquad [4]$$

In its currently most tenable and fruitful form, the Justice Evaluation Function (JEF) is, by postulate, specified as the logarithm of the ratio of the Actual Reward to the Just Reward:

- *Postulate of Logarithmic Specification:* The Justice Evaluation J varies as the logarithm of the ratio of the Actual Reward to the Just Reward:

$$J = \ln[(\text{Actual Reward})/(\text{Just Reward})]. \qquad [5]$$

The logarithmic specification has several good properties, including these: First, it enables representation of J by the full real-number line, with zero representing the point of perfect justice, positive numbers representing degrees of unjust overreward, and negative numbers representing degrees of unjust underreward. Second, it quantifies the common human opinion that deficiency is felt more keenly than comparable excess.[6]

In the next sections the major aspects of the Justice Evaluation Function and of its aggregations and representations are systematically considered.

THE INSTANTANEOUS JUSTICE EVALUATION

Foundations: The Received Axiom of Comparison

The analysis begins with the received Axiom of Comparison, which formalizes the long-held view that a wide class of phenomena, including happiness, self-esteem, and the sense of distributive justice, may be understood as the product of a comparison process. For example, the first recorded social event in Judeo-Christian literature (postcreation) involves a comparison ("If you eat this, you will have as much knowledge as the gods"). After the fall, the next recorded social events are conjugal relations and a new comparison (Cain compares his reward to Abel's, and as a result kills him). Similarly incisive accounts may be found in the classical Greek and Roman authors (especially Epictetus and the Spanish Romans, Marcus Aurelius and Seneca), in the Patristic literature (especially Augustine), and in the Scholastic analyses of human behavior (especially Thomas Aquinas); other examples are found in the Renaissance and Enlightenment literatures, in fiction (where *Don Quixote* is perhaps the greatest example), in the work of the sixteenth-century religious reform in Spain (Ignatius Loyola and Francis Xavier, Teresa of

Avila and John of the Cross), and in the philosophical writings of Benjamin Franklin.

The first modern renderings of the Axiom of Comparison appear in Marx ([1849] 1968), Baldwin (1889-91), William James ([1891] 1952), and Durkheim ([1893] 1964, [1897] 1951). Their insights may be formalized as follows:

- *Axiom of Comparison:* There exists a class Z of human individual phenomena that are produced by the comparison of an *Actual Holding* (A) of a good to a *Comparison Holding* (C) of that good, such that Z is an increasing function of A and a decreasing function of C:

$$Z = Z(A, C), \quad \partial Z / \partial A > 0, \quad \partial Z / \partial C < 0. \qquad [6]$$

We do not hesitate to call this an axiom, for it would appear prima facie unexceptionable. The literatures of reference groups, comparison processes, relative deprivation, and distributive justice are built upon it. Cogent discussion of the axiom, of its founding literature, and of applications and extensions is found in Stouffer et al. (1949), Merton and Rossi (1950), Festinger (1954), Merton (1957, 1967), Runciman (1961), Hyman (1968), Lipset (1968), Sherif (1968), Zelditch (1968), Berger et al. (1972), Homans ([1961] 1974), Cook (1975), and Goode (1978). Other recent renderings of the ideas underlying the Axiom of Comparison include Wright (1963) and Sprague (1977).

Note that the literatures contain a large variety of words to denote members of the Z class of phenomena and to denote the two arguments. For example, a list of words used to label the quantities that play the part of Comparison Holding would include the following, inter alia: potentiality, pretension, expectation, want, desire, aspiration, investment, *suum cuique*.

Note also that the Axiom of Comparison, like the insights it formalizes, is silent on questions of measurement and of functional form. For example, the question whether the Actual Holding, the Comparison Holding, and the Z variable are to be represented by selected segments of the real-number line is not addressed. The axiom is compatible with many different functional forms, each constraining the domain and range of the function and specifying the quantitative nature of the effects of A and C on Z in a distinctive way.

As noted above, the comparison process may be generalized to encompass an observer's Z phenomenon about any subject's A and C.

The Arguments of the Justice Evaluation Function

In the distributive-justice context, the Actual Holding and Comparison Holding of the generic comparison process are usually called the Actual Reward and Just Reward, respectively. The theory thus describes the Justice Evaluation as arising from the comparison of the Actual Reward to the Just Reward. Two questions immediately arise, the first concerned with the measurement properties of the good and the second with the theorist's information, especially about the Just Reward.

Measurement properties of goods. It is obviously easy to measure the Actual Reward and the Just Reward when the good under consideration is a cardinal good — say, when the good is land, cattle, or wealth. But cardinal goods are not the only goods about which individuals experience the sense of distributive justice. Goods not susceptible to cardinal measurement (e.g., beauty, intelligence, athletic skill) also play important parts in the individual's justice life. Hence distributive-justice theory proposes a measurement rule (Jasso 1980), which states that additive, transferable goods are measured in their own units (the amount denoted by x), while nonadditive, nontransferable goods are measured by the individual's relative rank $[i/(N + 1)]$ within a specially selected comparison group, where i denotes the rank-order statistic in ascending order of magnitude and N denotes the size of the group or population. Following Norman Campbell (1921), the goods are respectively termed *quantity-goods* and *quality-goods*. The population counterpart of $[i/(N + 1)]$ is α, which appears in the ordinal forms of the Just Reward Function discussed above.[7]

Information about the Just Reward. From the theorist's perspective, the Justice Evaluation Function contains a rather large problem: While the Actual Reward is easily observed, the Just Reward is not. Accordingly, the Just Reward must be recast in a more accessible form, if a priori work is to proceed. This recasting has followed two directions. The first is to make additional assumptions concerning the Just Reward. The second is to represent the Just Reward in a more tractable yet equivalent way.

Further assumptions on the Just Reward. The Just Reward may be assumed to be either a constant or a variable quantity. If the Just Reward is assumed to be a constant, then the theorist may further assume its magnitude. For example, early versions of the Justice Evaluation Function fixed the Just Reward at equality (Jasso 1980). This procedure has the virtue of fidelity to many classical accounts (e.g., Plato, Cervantes, Simmel), but the obvious problem that counterexamples abound, or, put differently, that its scope is restricted and not yet well defined.[8]

If the Just Reward is assumed to be a variable, then the theorist has yet further interesting alternatives, including that of assigning it a probability distribution and that of assigning it a correlation with the Actual Reward. For example, if the Actual Reward and the Just Reward are dependent, then the Just Reward is potentially expressible as a function of the Actual Reward — hence rendering the Just Reward knowable.

Identity representation of the Just Reward. A useful device by which the theorist can partially overcome the problems arising from ignorance of the Just Reward is that of representing it by an equivalent quantity. To this end, Jasso (1986a) proposes an identity representation of the Just Reward. This new representation, based on the fact that any value in the domain of a good — and hence any Just Reward — can be expressed as a transformation of the good's arithmetic mean, expresses *JR* as the product of the mean and an individual-specific parameter ϕ, where ϕ captures everything that is unknown about an individual's *JR*. This representation of *JR* possesses the additional virtue that it enables theoretical prediction of the effects of the mean's constituent factors, which in the case of a quantity-good are the sum *S* of the good and the population size *N*. Assessment of the constraints imposed on theoretical prediction by ignorance of phi, under alternative characterizations of phi, becomes an integral component of distributive-justice analysis.

The Form of the Justice Evaluation Function

As noted above, specification of the Justice Evaluation Function by means of a logarithmic function has seemed natural and appealing, and has proved remarkably tractable, yielding large numbers of predictions. Yet it would be desirable to find a better rationale for the logarithmic function than its intuitive appeal.

To that end, a useful approach is as follows: Suppose that mild conditions are placed on the Justice Evaluation Function; we may then ask, How is its functional form constrained? Jasso (in press) addresses this question. Five conditions are reviewed, three of which appear to be unexceptionable. These three conditions are as follows: (1) the zero-point property — that *J* equals zero when the Actual Reward and the Just Reward equal each other; (2) additivity — that the effect of the Actual Reward on *J* be independent of the Just Reward and that the effect of the Just Reward be independent of the Actual Reward; and (3) scale-invariance — that *J* be invariant to the reward's measurement scale (e.g., to measurement of earnings in dollars or yen). In the case of ordinal goods, the third condition does not apply (ranks already being scale-invariant). The three conditions are expressed as a system of partial differential equations.

Solving separately the three-equation system for cardinal goods and the two-equation system for ordinal goods, Jasso finds that the logarithmic form uniquely satisfies the three-equation system (though the zero-point property is not required for the proof) and that, in the ordinal case, the first and second conditions constrain the admissible function to the form $[f(AR) - f(JR)]$, where f is a strictly increasing function. Moreover, the logarithmic form also satisfies the additional two conditions that were thought too stringent to impose a priori. Thus the stipulations on the Justice Evaluation Function, and, indeed, on all comparison functions of the *Z* class, yield the following statement:

$$Z = \begin{cases} \theta \left[\ln(A) - \ln(C)\right], & \text{quantity-good} \\ \theta \left[f(A) - f(C)\right], & \text{quality-good} \end{cases}$$

where θ denotes the constant of proportionality.

Accordingly, the logarithmic specification is put on a more secure footing — for the case of cardinal goods. As to ordinal goods, more theoretical work is required in order to reduce further the class of admissible functional forms. For example, one might argue that one or both of the two further conditions could reasonably be imposed, or that considerations of symmetry dictate a single functional form for both cardinal and ordinal goods.

Like the Just Reward, the parameter θ may vary by reward, rewardee, observer, time period, and society, giving rise to a family of Justice Evaluation Functions. Jasso (1980) proposes that θ be treated as the observer's signature constant, representing the observer's style of expression but not the actual experience of injustice. Future analysis of θ may yield especially interesting results. Consider, for example, that if J is a nonfundamental magnitude, then the parameter θ is visible only in behavioral propositions; but behavioral propositions, as will be seen below, may well have their own constant of proportionality, so that the two constants would be absorbed into a single parameter and not separately identifiable. In contrast, if J is someday found to be a fundamental magnitude, say, representing the length, area, or volume of a particular component in the brain at the instant of the experience of the Justice Evaluation, then θ may have concrete, identifiable meaning.

Combining the logarithmic functional form, attentiveness to the type of good (quantity-good versus quality-good), and the phi-including representation of the Just Reward, we may write the basic distributive-justice formulas in a number of alternative ways. These are summarized in Table 13.3. Where useful to avoid confusion, hereafter the Actual Reward will be denoted by A and the Just Reward by C (as in the more general Comparison Holding).

THE MULTIGOOD JUSTICE EVALUATION

Suppose that *at a single instant* an individual reflects on more than one good, say, on beauty and wealth or on athletic skill and land holdings. It appears reasonable to define the resultant Justice Evaluation as the average of the single-good J magnitudes. This notion is formulated as a postulate:

- *Postulate of Multigood Justice Evaluation:* The instantaneous J experienced about k goods is equal to the arithmetic mean of the corresponding single-good J scores:

$$J^* = (1/k) \Sigma J. \qquad [8]$$

The multigood Justice Evaluation J^* can be expressed in several equivalent ways, including statement as a weighted sum and, given the logarithmic form of J, a variety of statements highlighting geometric means of A, C, and of the ratio A/C. Some of these equivalent statements are displayed in Table 13.4. The advantage of a store of equivalent expressions is twofold: First, it permits use of the simplest possible expression

Table 13.3 Basic Distributive-Justice Formulas

A. **Basic General Formula**

$$J = \ln \frac{Actual\ Reward}{Just\ Reward}$$

$$J = \ln(Actual\ Reward) - \ln(Just\ Reward)$$

B. **Goods-Attentive General Formula**

$$J = \begin{cases} \ln \dfrac{x_A}{x_c}, & \text{quantity-good} \\ \ln \dfrac{i_A}{i_c}, & \text{quality-good} \end{cases}$$

C. **Formulas When the Just Reward Is Unknown**

$$J = \begin{cases} \ln \dfrac{x}{\phi\mu}, & \phi > 0, & \text{quantity-good} \\ \ln \dfrac{2i}{\phi(N+1)}, & 0 < \phi < 2, & \text{quality-good} \end{cases}$$

$$J = \begin{cases} \ln \dfrac{xN}{\phi S}, & \phi > 0, & \text{quantity-good} \\ \ln \dfrac{2i}{\phi(N+1)}, & 0 < \phi < 2, & \text{quality-good} \end{cases}$$

---

in particular theoretical or empirical contexts; second, it renders pertinent many mathematical theorems and results, thus enabling swift derivation of predictions.

THE INDIVIDUAL'S TIME SERIES OF JUSTICE EVALUATIONS: THE DISTRIBUTIVE-JUSTICE PROFILE

To this point we have conceptualized the Justice Evaluation J and its multigood counterpart J^* as instantaneous. Now we introduce time. We notice that some Justice Evaluations may be thought of as existing over time; they may be said to have a continuous duration, and this duration may greatly differ across Justice Evaluations. Moreover, some magnitudes of the Justice Evaluation may recur.

Attempting to capture this new complexity, we regard each individual as having a distinctive time series of Justice Evaluations — termed the *Distributive-Justice Profile*. Important parameters of this profile include, for any interval of time, the arithmetic mean, range, variance, jumps between contiguous J, gaps during which no J is experienced, means of the overrewarded and underrewarded truncates, and the like. These parameters are new theoretical terms produced by the framework.

Table 13.4 The Multigood Justice Evaluation

A. Definitional Formula

$$J^* = \frac{1}{M}\sum J$$

B. Alternative Equivalent Expressions

$$J^* = \sum\left(\frac{J}{M}\right)$$

$$J^* = \frac{1}{M}\sum \ln\frac{A}{C}$$

$$J^* = \sum \ln\left(\frac{A}{C}\right)^{\frac{1}{M}}$$

$$J^* = \sum \ln A^{\frac{1}{M}} - \sum \ln C^{\frac{1}{M}}$$

$$J^* = \ln \prod\left(\frac{A}{C}\right)^{\frac{1}{M}}$$

$$J^* = \ln \frac{\prod A^{\frac{1}{M}}}{\prod C^{\frac{1}{M}}}$$

$$J^* = \ln \sqrt[M]{\prod A} - \ln \sqrt[M]{\prod C}$$

Figure 13.1 depicts a day-unit Distributive-Justice Profile for a hypotheti-cal person.

Note that highly interesting new questions arise, for example: (1) the extent to which the Distributive-Justice Profile differs across persons; (2) the extent to which a given individual's Distributive-Justice Profiles for differing temporal units are replicates of each other; (3) whether, within temporal unit (such as the day), some periodicity may be detected; and (4) whether, holding constant the temporal unit, an individual's Distributive-Justice Profile changes systematically as age and experience increase. To illustrate, one may conjecture that a certain amount of attenuation sets in with age, so that, within person, the maxima diminish and the minima increase.

Note further that the concept of the *duration* of a Justice Evaluation, combined with the multigood Justice Evaluation, gives rise to a new measure of the importance of a good. When in ordinary language one observes that John cares more about wealth than about intelligence or that Mary cares more about intelligence than about beauty, the underlying notion of "caring more" can be given precise interpretation as the duration

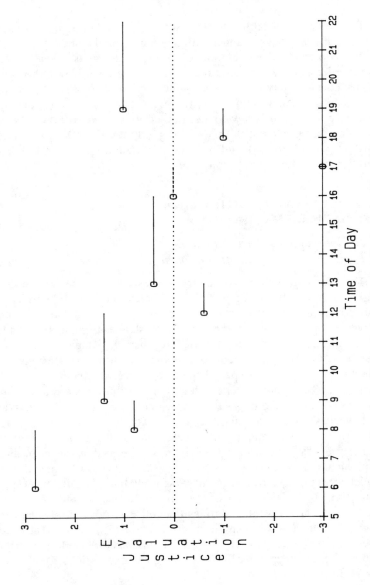

Figure 13.1. Distributive-Justice Profile: Hypothetical Time Series of Justice Evaluations, Day-Unit

that a good occupies the mind, weighted by the number of goods simultaneously occupying the mind. Formally,

$$\text{Importance of a Good} = \Sigma \; t^J/K^J \qquad [9]$$

To illustrate, if wealth is the sole subject of two hours' worth of Justice Evaluations and beauty and intelligence are jointly the subject of four hours' worth of Justice Evaluations, then all three goods — wealth, beauty, and intelligence — are equally important. In contrast, if wealth is always jointly considered with two other goods and the two other goods change on the hour, then wealth is far more important than any other good. Similarly, if wealth is always considered alone and all other goods are considered in groups of three with no good recurring, then wealth is the most important good if and only if its duration exceeds one-third the duration of all other good-groups.

THE SOCIETAL DISTRIBUTION
OF JUSTICE EVALUATIONS

The Instantaneous Distribution of
Justice Evaluations and Its Parameters

The theory of distributive justice suggests that the social life may be regarded as a meeting of justice sentiments. Thus a collectivity — any collectivity of any size, from a dyad to the population of a planet or universe — may, at any moment of its existence, be represented by the instantaneous distribution of reflexive Justice Evaluations among its members. Further, the parameters of the J distribution are regarded as potentially exercising a special hegemony over distinctive areas of the social life. These parameters include the distribution's arithmetic mean, inequality, lower and upper extreme values, proportions underrewarded and overrewarded, and other distinctive features.

In theoretical development to date, two of the parameters of the J distribution have been of special interest: the arithmetic mean and the Gini's mean difference. It has seemed useful to assert by postulate their social meaning. Accordingly, the Social Welfare Postulate defines the collectivity's Social Welfare as the arithmetic mean of the J distribution; the Cohesiveness Postulate defines the collectivity's cohesiveness as the negative of the Gini's mean difference of the J distribution. These postulates receive extended discussion in Jasso (1986a, 1988a, 1988b). Table 13.5 displays some of the equivalent expressions for the Social Welfare formula.

Thus two questions arise: First, what is the form of the distribution of Justice Evaluations? Second, what are the values of its major parameters? In theoretical work, attention is focused on the a priori versions of the two questions: First, what is the J distribution that arises from given combinations of the Actual Reward Distribution and the Just Reward Distribution?

Table 13.5 The Collectivity's Social Welfare

$$Social\ Welfare\ =\ E(J)$$

$$Social\ Welfare\ =\ E\left(\ln\frac{Actual\ Reward}{Just\ Reward}\right)$$

$$Social\ Welfare\ =\ \ln\frac{G(Actual\ Reward)}{G(Just\ Reward)}$$

$$Social\ Welfare\ =\ \begin{cases} \ln\delta\ -\ \ln G(\phi), & quantity\text{-}good \\ \ln\dfrac{2\sqrt[N]{N!}}{N+1}\ -\ \ln G(\phi), & quality\text{-}good \end{cases}$$

NOTE: The operator E denotes expected value. The operator G denotes the geometric mean. The symbol δ denotes the measure of inequality defined as the ratio of the geometric mean to the arithmetic mean.

Second, how do the parameters of the J distribution vary across the possible J distributions?

To explore the theoretical questions, it is necessary to consider the general relationships among the Actual Reward (A), the Just Reward (C), and the Justice Evaluation (J); and it is useful to assign to A and C specified distributional forms.

As noted above, it is obvious that J for a given individual in a given situation can be known only in two cases: first, when JR is known and, second, when JR is a function of AR and the function is known. On the other hand, even in informationally impoverished circumstances, much can be ascertained about the distribution of J in the collectivity.

The J distribution is uniquely determined by the joint distribution of the Actual Reward and the Just Reward. A large class of problems can be stated and solved using tools from the study of probability distributions. For example, the theorist may seek the bounds on the proportion under-rewarded in a society, varying the number of valued goods and the distributions of A and C.

The simplest case, of course, is the case where the Just Reward is assumed to be a specified constant. In this case, the J distribution is obtained by applying change-of-variable techniques to the Actual Reward. This case is investigated in Jasso (1980). Slightly more complicated cases arise when the Just Reward is an unknown constant (Jasso 1981).

Complexity can also be introduced via the multigood Justice Evaluation. In this case, the J^* distribution is a function of the distributions of the several goods. Jasso (1980, p. 30) reports generating an asymmetrical Laplace distribution of J^* for the case of two goods, one a quality-good and the other a Pareto-distributed quantity-good, and a gamma family of J^* distribution for the case of K quality-goods (in both cases setting the Just Reward at the mean of the Actual Reward Distribution).

Table 13.6 Prototypical Distributions of Material Goods

	Supremum	
Infimum > 0	Yes	No
Yes	Quadratic	Pareto
No	Power-Function	Lognormal

NOTE: In both the power-function and the quadratic distributions, the supremum is also the maximum. The lognormal and the power-function have an infimum at zero; the power-function of c > 1 also has a minimum at zero.

An even more interesting case arises when a society is viewed as a composite of two or more collectivities (in the justice sense), so that the J distribution for the entire society is a mixture of the several group-specific J distributions. Jasso (1981, pp. 357-58) describes the mixed J distribution arising in a two-group society, where both groups value a quantity-good and the two quantity-good distributions are different members of the Pareto family (again setting the Just Reward for each group at the group's own mean).

But there remains a large unexplored arena, namely, the case where the Just Reward is a variable, not a constant. Some of the many directions for future inquiry are indicated below. First, however, it may be useful to discuss desirable features in the distributions used to model the A and C distributions as well as the available graphical devices.

With respect to the modeling distributions, the collection should include, in addition to the rectangular distribution that represents the distribution of an ordinal good, a set of nonnegative distributions embodying combinations of important features of quantity-good distributions. At the present time, two dimensions appear important (the number may, of course, grow). These are whether the variate approaches zero from the right and whether the variate tends to positive infinity. Treating each dimension as a dichotomy, this approach leads to four possible combinations of interest: (1) a variate with nonzero infimum and a supremum, (2) a variate with nonzero infimum and no supremum; (3) a variate with zero infimum and a supremum, and (4) a variate with zero infimum and no supremum. To illustrate, the wealth distribution of a primitive society in good times may be modeled by the first type and in bad times (such as famine) by the third type; the wealth distributions of advanced societies near the end of a war may be modeled by the second type among the winners and by the fourth type among the losers. Table 13.6 shows the fourfold classification of distributions that results from this perspective, listing in each cell one tractable and, in most cases, well-known exemplar.

Table 13.7 Probability Density Function in Five Variate Families

Variate	Probability Density Function $f(x)$		
Lognormal	$\dfrac{1}{xc\sqrt{2\pi}}\exp\left\{-\dfrac{\left(\frac{c^2}{2}+\ln\frac{x}{\mu}\right)^2}{2c^2}\right\}$	$c > 0$	$x > 0$
Pareto	$\left[\dfrac{\mu(c-1)}{c}\right]^c cx^{-c-1}$	$c > 1$	$x \geq \dfrac{\mu(c-1)}{c}$
Power-Function	$\left[\dfrac{c}{\mu(c+1)}\right]^c cx^{c-1}$	$c > 0$	$0 < x \leq \dfrac{\mu(c+1)}{c}$
Quadratic	$\left(-\dfrac{6}{\mu^3 c^3}\right)x^2 + \left(\dfrac{12}{\mu^2 c^3}\right)x + \dfrac{3(c^2-4)}{2\mu c^3}$	$0 < c < 2$	$\dfrac{\mu(2-c)}{2} \leq x \leq \dfrac{\mu(2+c)}{2}$
Rectangular	1	---	$0 < x < 1$

NOTE: The lognormal, Pareto, power-function, and quadratic distributions are specified as two-parameter distributions, with a location parameter set equal to the mean μ and a shape parameter denoted c. For the rectangular, the unit form is specified.

The two distributional families used in Jasso's (1980) early work were the Pareto, which exemplifies the second type above, and the lognormal, which exemplifies the fourth type above. Subsequent work (reported in Jasso 1987 and more recent papers) uses a quadratic family (a generalization of one member of the beta family) to exemplify the first type and a power-function family to exemplify the third type. These are the four exemplars show in Table 13.6.

With respect to graphical representation, the function most familiar to social scientists is the probability density function (PDF). The PDFs for the five variates currently used to model the distributions of A and C appear in Table 13.7.[9] The top row of Figure 13.2 shows the graphs of the PDFs of J distributions arising from ordinal goods and from lognormal and Pareto quantity-goods, under the assumption that the Just Reward is constant at the good's mean.

Armed with these tools, we can now proceed to model the case where the Just Reward is a variable. Mathematically, the problem is to derive the distribution of J, where $J = \ln(A/C)$ and the distributions of A and C are given.

When A and C are independent, the distribution of J will be readily found. If, additionally, A and C are identically distributed, then results may already exist providing the distribution of J. The bottom row of Figure 13.2 shows the graphs of the PDFs of three J distributions in this new case where both A and C are allowed to vary. The leftmost curve represents the normal distribution of J that arises in the case where A and C are independent but different lognormals. The middle curve represents

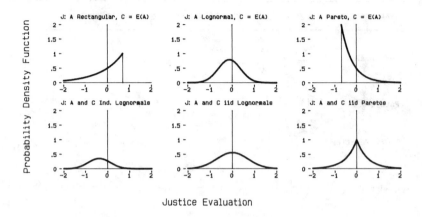

Figure 13.2. PDF of Justice-Evaluation Distributions

the normal that arises when A and C are independently and identically distributed lognormals. The third curve represents the double-exponential distribution of J that arises when A and C are independently and identically distributed Paretos. Notably, in the case where A and C are iid, the J distribution is symmetric about zero.

In the case where A and C are dependent, there are many possible subtypes, including the case where the function expressing the dependence is known, and hence the distribution of J may be derivable by change-of-variable techniques. Moreover, if the joint distribution of A and C is known, the J distribution may be derived by standard techniques.

The Intertemporal Distribution of Justice Evaluations

Like an individual's J, the societal distribution also may be characterized by its duration. Some societal distributions have longer life spans than others. Some recur, others do not. Many new theoretical avenues are possible, some a direct consequence of technological advances. For example, the population of viewers of a particular television program may be regarded as a collectivity; if, over the course of a half hour, a sequence of goods becomes salient, then information concerning the distributions of those goods in the viewing population may be used to derive the sequence of J distributions. The same viewing population is reconstituted regularly — say, daily, for a news program, or weekly, for a situation comedy. Accordingly, each parameter of interest of the J distribution in this population — the mean, inequality, proportion underrewarded, and so on — now has associated with it a time series. The time series, in turn, has its own distinctive parameters — duration, range, gaps — yielding new terms that may play distinctive parts in the social life. Moreover, a spatially bounded society may be represented by the collection of simultaneous *J* distributions among the separate viewing populations, for example, the mixed *J* distribution, where each component distribution refers to a television network.

The second set of questions may be summarized by one generalized equation, the goodwise-defined Justice Evaluation Function:

$$J_{grots} = \begin{cases} \theta_{grots} \ln(A/C_{grots}), \text{ quantity-good} \\ \theta_{grots} [f(A) - f(C_{grots})], \text{ quality-good} \end{cases} \quad [10]$$

The Justice Evaluation Function contains three unknowns: (1) the Just Reward, (2) the constant of proportionality θ, and (3) in the case of ordinal goods, the functional form. As in the generalized Just Reward Function, the subscripts *grots* denote, respectively, the reward, rewardee, observer, time period, and society.

The probability distribution of *J* can be solved for, using information or assumptions on the joint distribution of the Actual Reward and the Just Reward and, in the case of ordinal goods, on the functional form.

The Third Set of Questions:
Behavioral and Social Consequences
of the Sense of Distributive Justice

The first and second central questions in the study of distributive justice treat, respectively, the matter of what individuals and societies regard as just and the matter of the magnitude and distribution of the sense of injustice associated with given departures from perfect justice. Thus it may be said that to this point we have considered structures inside the minds and hearts of persons and the aggregations of these structures. That is, we have examined what persons think, believe, judge, and feel. The third central question moves to a new arena, namely, the behavioral and social consequences of the Justice Evaluation and its aggregations.

The goal is to accumulate predictions for a wide range of observable behavioral and social phenomena, including phenomena not yet observed.[10] In general, this enterprise requires two things. First, there must be a large and growing set of theoretical terms and a clear and growing understanding of the relations embodied in them. Second, there must be careful specification of the way in which one or more of the theoretical terms play a part in the determination of an observable phenomenon. With respect to the first requirement, the section of this chapter concerned with the Justice Evaluation Function discussed many of the terms currently contained in distributive-justice theory — *J*, multigood *J**, parameters of the Distributive-Justice Profile, parameters of the instantaneous distribution of *J*, parameters of the time series of the parameters of the instantaneous distributions of J. In this part of the chapter we consider (1) what is currently known about the relationships embodied in the theoretical terms and (2) some behavioral specifications of justice-dependent phenomena.

DISTRIBUTIVE-JUSTICE EFFECTS
AT THE INDIVIDUAL LEVEL

We may distinguish two classes of justice-dependent phenomena at the individual level, phenomena related to instantaneous J and phenomena related to the Distributive-Justice Profile and its parameters.

Phenomena Related to Instantaneous J

Relations embodied in the basic formulas. It is obvious from the formulas for J presented earlier that as a rewardee's Actual Reward increases, the associated Justice Evaluation increases in the direction of less underreward/more overreward, and that as a rewardee's Just Reward increases, J declines in the direction of less overreward/more underreward. The magnitudes of these rates of change, however, as well as the rates of change of J with respect to the arguments of the equivalent expressions, may be less obvious. Accordingly, Table 13.8 reports the first and second partial derivatives of J with respect to the x, i, S, N, and phi factors, in both the quantity-good and quality-good formulas shown in Table 13.3, together with the total differentials for both types of goods.

The derivatives make explicit some interesting relations. For example, the ceteris paribus effect on J of the collectivity's material resources operates only in the quantity-good case, and this effect is negative. The population size operates in both goods contexts, but has opposite effects — positive in the quantity-good case, negative in the quality-good case.

The derivatives and differentials can be used to derive many predictions. To illustrate, Table 13.8 immediately suggests that an individual's attitudes toward immigration and emigration (and their cognates, such as recruitment and deportation) depend critically on whether the individual principally values a quantity-good or a quality-good. More complicated predictions can be derived by employing more complicated forms of J (such as multigood J^*).

Two dimensions of individual behavior: four classes of behavior. The first step in the systematic derivation of predictions involving instantaneous J is to write down the equation stating the dependence of a given observable variable on J. Jasso (1986a) proposes a fourfold classification of such equations, corresponding to the four possible combinations of two binary considerations. The first consideration, following Coleman (1973), is whether the behavior under investigation is a responsive or a purposive behavior.[11] The second consideration is whether the behavior is a function of the *magnitude* of J or instead of the *absolute magnitude* of J, that is,

Table 13.8 Effects of Own Rank and Possessions, Societal Resources, Population Size, and the Phi Parameter on the Justice Evaluation

A. **Quantity-Good Case**

   1. **First and Second Partial Derivatives**

Amount of Quantity-Good	$\dfrac{\partial J}{\partial x} = \dfrac{1}{x}$	$\dfrac{\partial^2 J}{\partial x^2} = -\dfrac{1}{x^2}$
Collectivity's Resources	$\dfrac{\partial J}{\partial S} = -\dfrac{1}{S}$	$\dfrac{\partial^2 J}{\partial S^2} = \dfrac{1}{S^2}$
Population Size	$\dfrac{\partial J}{\partial N} = \dfrac{1}{N}$	$\dfrac{\partial^2 J}{\partial N^2} = -\dfrac{1}{N^2}$
ϕ	$\dfrac{\partial J}{\partial \phi} = -\dfrac{1}{\phi}$	$\dfrac{\partial^2 J}{\partial \phi^2} = \dfrac{1}{\phi^2}$

   2. **Total Differential**

$$dJ = \frac{dx}{x} + \frac{dN}{N} - \frac{dS}{S} - \frac{d\phi}{\phi}$$

B. **Quality-Good Case**

   1. **First and Second Partial Derivatives**

Own Raw Rank	$\dfrac{\partial J}{\partial i} = \dfrac{1}{i}$	$\dfrac{\partial^2 J}{\partial i^2} = -\dfrac{1}{i^2}$
Population Size	$\dfrac{\partial J}{\partial N} = -\dfrac{1}{N+1}$	$\dfrac{\partial^2 J}{\partial N^2} = \dfrac{1}{(N+1)^2}$
ϕ	$\dfrac{\partial J}{\partial \phi} = -\dfrac{1}{\phi}$	$\dfrac{\partial^2 J}{\partial \phi^2} = \dfrac{1}{\phi^2}$

   2. **Total Differential**

$$dJ = \frac{di}{i} - \frac{dN}{N+1} - \frac{d\phi}{\phi}$$

NOTE: All factors are assumed independent.

whether or not it notices the distinction between overreward and under-reward.

As discussed in Jasso (1986a), in the distributive-justice context, purposive behavior is behavior designed to achieve a new magnitude of J; responsive behavior, in contrast, does not alter the magnitude of J (whose outcome it is). From the perspective of the resultant equations, the essential difference between responsive and purposive phenomena is simple: A responsive phenomenon depends on an instantaneous magnitude of J. A purposive phenomenon, in contrast, depends on the *change* in J, that is, on J before and after the behavior. For example, the decision to steal may be modeled as a purposive phenomenon, dependent on the magnitude of J before theft, as well as the envisioned magnitude of J after the theft.[12]

With respect to the second binary consideration, we distinguish between phenomena that depend monotonically on J and phenomena that

Table 13.9 Equations of Phenomena Dependent on the
Instantaneous Justice Evaluation, by Type of Phenomenon and
Relevance of the Size of J

Type of Phenomenon	Relevance of the Sign of J	
	$Q = h(J)$	$Q = h(|J|)$
Responsive	$Y^R = Y^R(J, \Gamma, \epsilon)$	$Z^R = Z^R(|J|, \Gamma, \epsilon)$
Purposive	$Y^P = Y^P[(J_2 - J_1), \Gamma, \epsilon]$	$Z^P = Z^P[(|J_1| - |J_2|), \Gamma, \epsilon]$

depend monotonically on the absolute value of J. The first type includes all "happiness"-like phenomena. For example, the more underrewarded the individual, the lower the happiness (or the greater the unhappiness); the more overrewarded the individual, the greater the happiness (or the less the unhappiness). The second type, on the other hand, includes the classical grievance and redressing behaviors. The greater the absolute magnitude of J — regardless of its qualitative sign — the greater the propensity for this behavior type.

Table 13.9 displays the four kinds of equations resulting from the two binary dimensions. Each equation includes a term for other relevant variables (Γ) and a stochastic term (ϵ).

Deriving predictions. Once the effects of observable factors on J (or on its absolute value) are known (as in Table 13.8) and the equation of an observable dependent phenomenon is specified, the effects of the observable factors on the dependent phenomenon can be easily obtained (usually by applying the chain rule from calculus). At this early date, there are already hundreds of predictions derived in this way. For example, the initial predictions for theft-related behaviors (stealing, informing, being victimized, and the like), derived by considering the simplest possible case — that is, where there is a single good of value — and counting both first and second partial derivatives, already number 18 in the case where theft is from a fellow group member, 40 in the case where theft is from an outsider, and 5 for the choice between insider and outsider theft (Jasso 1986a, 1988a).

What is noteworthy is that the overwhelming majority of the predictions obtained to date have been obtained under the simplest possible conditions. The number of predictions grows greatly when complexity is introduced. For example, research currently under way introduces other goods into the theft problem, including the prospective thief's reputation.[13] For each new combination of number of goods and types of goods, another 63 primary predictions are obtained — plus new predictions expressing the difference between the one-good environment and the two-good environment, and so on.

Finally, note that a thorough understanding of the terms involving instantaneous *J* and the well-specified behavioral equations together make possible the rich set of predictions.

Phenomena Related to Parameters of the Distributive-Justice Profile

The second general class of justice-dependent individual-level behavioral phenomena consists of behaviors specified as functions of a *parameter of the individual's Distributive-Justice Profile*. That is, this set of phenomena respond to (one or more of) such profile parameters as, for any interval of time, the arithmetic mean, the range and the variance of the person's time series, the jumps between contiguous *J*, the gaps during which no *J* is experienced, and the means of the overrewarded and underrewarded truncates.

The general form of the equation for this class of phenomena is as follows:

$$Q = Q(P, \Gamma, \varepsilon),$$

where *Q* denotes the dependent phenomenon, *P* denotes the parameter(s) of the Distributive-Justice Profile, and, as before, Γ denotes a vector of other relevant variables and ε denotes the disturbance.

The Distributive-Justice Profile and its parameters are not yet understood. Much theoretical analysis is required before predictions can be derived.[14]

DISTRIBUTIVE-JUSTICE EFFECTS AT SOCIAL LEVELS

Many predictions for social phenomena can be derived from the individual-level theoretical terms. This is because most of the individual-level predictions lead naturally to social-level propositions. For example, the individual-level crime predictions lead to predictions concerning the growth of social norms and social sanctions; similarly, manipulation of the individual-level effects listed in Table 13.8 yields the prediction that affluent societies are more prone to deficit spending than less affluent societies. As a final illustration of deriving social-level predictions from the individual-level terms, consider the model constructed by Jasso (1987) in which societal choice of valued goods is predicted exclusively from individuals' magnitudes of *J* under alternative goods regimes.

Additionally, as we have seen, distributive-justice theory contains a large set of specifically social-level theoretical terms that potentially play parts in the determination of social phenomena; these include parameters of the instantaneous distribution of *J* as well as parameters of the time series of each of the parameters of the instantaneous J distribution. As with the parameters of the Distributive-Justice Profile, however, much more work has to be done before these parameters and their constituent terms are understood. For example, statement and proof of limiting theorems may illuminate the effects of idiosyncratic notions of what is just on the proportion of a society's members who feel underrewarded.

Currently, the best understood of the social-level theoretical terms is the arithmetic mean of the instantaneous J distribution. This is hardly surprising, given the availability of many pertinent statistical theorems and results. Accordingly, this section focuses on the term that by postulate is regarded as the Social Welfare. Note, however, that predictions for social phenomena have also been obtained from the Cohesiveness Postulate; Jasso (1988b) derives (and tests) a prediction for the effects of spouses' employment and earnings on their marital cohesiveness.

Relations Embodied in the
Basic Formulas for the Social Welfare

Look again at the formulas for the Social Welfare given in Table 13.5. The Social Welfare depends on (transformations of) three terms: (1) in all societies, on phi; (2) in quantity-good societies, on the inequality in the quantity-good's distribution; and (3) in quality-good societies, on the population size.

We examine first the universal effect of phi. The term involving phi is the natural logarithm of the geometric mean of phi. Thus whenever phi is constant (at whatever magnitude), its geometric mean equals that magnitude. The collectivity's Social Welfare decreases as the (constant) phi increases. When phi is a variable, on the other hand, its geometric mean, ceteris paribus, decreases with its dispersion. Hence the greater the variability in phi — the greater the variability in individuals' notions of what is just for themselves — the greater the collectivity's Social Welfare.

Next consider the effect of the quantity-good's inequality. The term is the natural logarithm of δ, the measure of inequality defined as the ratio of the geometric mean to the arithmetic mean. The measure δ, arising in Atkinson's (1970, 1975) family of inequality measures and described in detail in Jasso (1982), has bounds of zero and one and decreases as inequality increases. Thus as inequality in the distribution of the valued quantity-good increases, the collectivity's Social Welfare declines.

Finally, consider the effect of the population size in a quality-good regime. The term containing N is the natural logarithm of the ratio of the Nth root of N-factorial to the quantity $N + 1$. This ratio has an honorable history in higher mathematics. It can be shown to decrease as N increases, approaching the quantity $1/e$ as its limit. Thus as population size increases, the collectivity's Social Welfare decreases; however, at "large" population sizes the effect is negligible.

Deriving Predictions

Given the simplicity of the three basic relations in the formula for the Social Welfare, a remarkably large set of predictions has already been derived. This set begins with a straightforward application of the results above, leading to prediction of three basic social institutions, termed the *Social Welfare Institutions*. Briefly, the predictions are as follows: First, in all societies there arise devices that promote variability in individuals' notions of what is just for themselves; such devices include social differentiation, cultural pluralism, and the division of labor. Second, in societies that value at least one quantity-good there arise redistributive schemes designed to achieve inequality reductions; inequality-reducing redistributive schemes are the hallmark of quantity-good societies, being absent from exclusively quality-good societies, no matter how unequal their distribution of material resources. Third, in societies that value at least one quality-good, there arise devices for population control; such devices include policies on natural increase (natalism, family planning) and on migration (immigration, emigration).

Other predictions that have been derived from the Social Welfare Postulate include predictions for a guardian-focused variant of the process by which societies choose and discard goods they value (described in Jasso 1987) and a large cluster of predictions concerning monastic and mendicant orders.

Like the previous two central questions, the third may be represented by a single generalized equation, which we may call the *Justice Consequences Function* (JCF):

$$\Xi_{grots} = \xi_{grots}[T_{grots}(J), \Gamma_{grots,} \varepsilon_{grots}].\tag{12}$$

The unknowns in the Justice Consequences Function include the relevant theoretically derived transformation T of J (which may be absolute value, multigood, combination of several J's, and so on), the Γ vector of other relevant factors, and the functional form ξ. The equation is written with full subscripts for good, rewardee, observer, time period, and society. However, appropriate parametrization may differ across the behavioral and social consequences of interest; for example, the specification of a social consequence would not index over individuals.

Concluding Note

I have endeavored to describe the three central questions in the study of the distributive-justice force and to indicate as exactly as possible their mathematical statement and the contained unsolved problems. A wide range of "What if?" possibilities are seen to be encompassed in the general statement of the three basic questions, for example: What if individuals value several goods? What if individuals' notions of what is just for themselves and/or others fluctuate wildly? What if every neighborhood (or province, or caste) has distinctive distributions of Actual Rewards and Just Rewards?

As we have seen, each of the three central questions is expressible as a generalized equation. Repeating equations 3, 10, and 12, we may state the system of equations contained in the theory of the distributive-justice force:

$$\text{JRF: } JR_{grots} = h_{grots}(\mathbf{X}_{grots}; \mathbf{B}_{grots})$$

$$\text{JEF: } J_{grots} = \begin{cases} \theta_{grots} \ln(A/C_{grots}), \text{ quantity-good} \\ \theta_{grots} [f(A) - f(C_{grots})], \text{ quality-good} \end{cases}$$

$$\text{JCF: } \Xi_{grots} = \xi_{grots}[T_{grots}(J), \Gamma_{grots}; \varepsilon_{grots}]$$

Note that this three-equation system is not fully self-contained, as it includes, notably, the Actual Reward, which is fully producible by non-justice processes, and the vector of other relevant factors in the third equation.

The system of equations makes explicit the major unknowns in the theory of the distributive-justice force and as well signals the implicit unknowns, such as the distributional properties of the Just Reward, the Justice Evaluation, and other terms. The tasks ahead are clear.

But already there appear on the horizon new themes and ideas that may serve to generalize further the ideas presented in this chapter and to lead to a more general theory of the forces governing human behavior. This chapter ends with a brief look at some of these new currents.

First, the discussion of the Berger et al. Just Reward Function and of behavior processes whose goal is to change an Actual Reward Function into a replicate of a Just Reward Function suggests that both ARFs and JRFs may have a common form. Hence there is more than superficial unity in the study of, on the one hand, earnings, status, and stratification, and, on the other, the formation of expectations and Comparison Holdings. Indeed, future work might propose a new — and identical — structure for both the earnings function and the expectation function.

Second, building on an idea proposed by Anselm and developed by Duns Scotus, it may be possible to show that only a subset of the members of a society can choose between acting in their self-interest and acting for another's or the collectivity's good — for the remainder of society, the two alternatives being indistinguishable — and that the size of this critical subset depends on the society's resource endowment and technological level. Following this reasoning, if reducing income inequality is treated as enhancing the commonweal, then it will generally be the case that only a subset of the members of a society would become individually worse off under an inequality-reduction scheme; only this subset has a moral choice, and only in this subset can self-interested behavior be distinguished from altruistic behavior. Moreover, to the extent that the quality of a society's moral life reflects examination of and discourse about behavioral alternatives, the larger this subset, the richer the societal discourse. If the particular combination of endowments and technology constrains the size of this subset, then societies will have a history of richer and poorer moral reflections and of nobler and baser actions.

Third, one does not proceed very far in the quest to describe the operation of a basic force without confronting the question, What might be some of the other forces specifically affecting human behavior? We may begin a list of candidates for such basic forces, noting that each force may manifest itself through a set of cognates and anticognates. A starting list is as follows:

(1) *To know the causes of things:* This force may be said to give rise to the scientific impulse and to the market for information; its anticognates would include obscurantism.

(2) *To judge the goodness of things:* This force may produce norms, the utopian imagination, and love.

(3) *To be free:* This force may undergird both a theory of action and a theory of power (power being an anticognate).[15]

(4) *To be perfect:* This force may lead to the striving for excellence as well as to comparison processes; the distributive-justice force may be a special manifestation of this force.[16]

Because these, and other, forces may operate jointly to produce observed behavior, it may be useful to include among the attributes of forces the number of behavioral domains that a force governs and the strength of its operation.[17]

Notes

1. For discussion of the bipartite structure of theory, see Merton (1945, 1967) and Jasso (1988a, 1989a). Of course, when doing empirical work, it may be useful to think of a theory as possessing a tripartite structure: postulates, predictions, and *evidence*.

2. For a sampler of predictions, see Jasso (1988a); for exposition of derivations, see the other papers by Jasso listed in the References.

3. Exposition of the referential structure appears also in Anderson et al. (1969) and in Zelditch et al. (1970), both of which were written after Berger et al. (1972), which was circulated as a technical report in 1968.

4. On the ordinary-language connotations associated with the word *reward*, see Berger et al. (1972, p. 128, fn. 2); on the problem of making justice judgments about the natural goods, see Jasso (1980, p. 5, fn. 3).

5. Rossi's (1951, 1979) development of the factorial-survey method made possible the empirical estimation of the first-order Berger et al. Just Reward Function. The three nonconstant empirical functions were estimated on data generated by Rossi's method.

6. In point of fact, the logarithmic specification was suggested by empirical analyses of justice judgments obtained by Rossi's (1951, 1979) method (Jasso and Rossi 1977; Jasso 1978; Rossi and Anderson 1982). However, as will be seen below, for the case of cardinal goods, the logarithmic specification can be obtained via purely theoretical reasoning.

7. Further analysis of the properties of goods and of goods sets is found in Jasso (1987).

8. The proposition that "justice is equality" can be traced back at least as far as Plato's *Gorgias* (where it appears as words of Socrates). For further discussion of this proposition and of Simmel's ([1917] 1950) closely related sociability hypothesis, see Jasso (1980, 1988b).

9. Jasso (1980) relied exclusively on PDFs to represent the distributions of the valued goods and the corresponding *J* distributions. But, as shown in Jasso (1983b, 1983c, 1987), the quantile function (QF) may be a more useful and informative graphical device. Graphs of the QF depict the value of a variate as a function of its rank. Thus one picture communicates not only the distribution as a whole but also the magnitude and rank corresponding to each individual. Moreover, in some applications the quantile function is the tool of choice; some problems are more readily solved if it is used to represent the variate (Jasso 1986b, 1989b).

10. For lucid discussion of the requirement that a theory predict novel facts, see Lakatos (1970).

11. Coleman (1973) distinguishes between "causal" models and "purposive" models, noting that what he terms "causal" model appears in psychology under the rubric of "stimulus-response" model (and hence Jasso's 1986a use of the term "responsive") and that what he terms "purposive" model appears in psychology as "purposive action" model and in economics as "optimizing" model. Closely related to the distinction between responsive and purposive phenomena is the distinction arising in econometrics between the "behavioral equations" and the "technical equations" of a simultaneous-equation model; Judge et al. (1985) provide useful exposition. But note that the term *behavioral* is used here to encompass both responsive and purposive phenomena.

12. See Jasso (1986a, 1988a) for elaboration of this example.

13. This two-good case was suggested by Thomas J. Fararo.

14. Questions involving the Distributive-Justice Profile animate anew the ancient question of the part played by the memory, a question discussed by Augustine, Aquinas, and Shakespeare (Sonnet 30), and, of course, investigated by modern neurology, psychology, and psychiatry.

15. For insightful reasoning about the operation of what we may call a "freedom force," see Lawler (1988).

16. This starting list of possible basic forces reflects the analyses of Augustine, Anselm, Thomas Aquinas, and Duns Scotus. It also owes much to the careful theological and mystical reflections of Ignatius of Loyola, codified in his famous prayer: "Take into your hands my entire liberty, my memory, my understanding, and my will. All that I am and have you have given me, to be used according to your holy will. Give me your love and your grace; with these I am rich enough and desire nothing more."

17. This idea was suggested by Archibald O. Haller.

References

Alves, Wayne M. 1982. "Modeling Distributive Justice Judgments." Pp. 205-34 in *Measuring Social Judgments: The Factorial Survey Approach*, edited by P. H. Rossi and S. L. Nock. Beverly Hills, CA: Sage.

Alves, Wayne M. and Peter H. Rossi. 1978. "Who Should Get What? Fairness Judgments of the Distribution of Earnings." *American Journal of Sociology* 84:541-64.

Anderson, Bo, Joseph Berger, Morris Zelditch, Jr., and Bernard P. Cohen. 1969. "Reactions to Inequity." *Acta Sociologica* 12:1-12.

Aristotle. 1952. *The Works of Aristotle*, 2 vols., translated by W. D. Ross. Chicago: Britannica.

Atkinson, Anthony B. 1970. "On the Measurement of Inequality." *Journal of Economic Theory* 2:244-63.

— — —. 1975. *The Economics of Inequality*. London: Oxford.

Augustine, Saint. [c. 400] 1952. *The Confessions*, translated by Edward Bouverie Pusey. Chicago: Britannica.

Baldwin, James Mark. 1889-91. *Handbook of Psychology*, 2 vols. New York: Holt.

Berger, Joseph, Morris Zelditch, Jr., Bo Anderson, and Bernard P. Cohen. 1972. "Structural Aspects of Distributive Justice: A Status-Value Formulation." Pp. 119-246 in *Sociological Theories in Progress*, Vol. 2, edited by Joseph Berger, Morris Zelditch, Jr., and Bo Anderson. Boston: Houghton Mifflin.

Blau, Peter M. 1964. *Exchange and Power in Social Life*. New York: John Wiley.

Brickman, Philip, R. Folger, E. Goode, and Y. Schul. 1981. "Micro and Macro Justice." Pp. 173-202 in *The Justice Motive in Social Behavior*, edited by M. J. Lerner and S. C. Lerner. New York: Plenum.

Campbell, Norman R. 1921. *What Is Science?* New York: Dover.

Cervantes de Saavedra, Miguel. [1605, 1615] 1968. *Don Quijote de la Mancha*, edited and annotated by Martin de Riquer. Barcelona: Juventud.

Coleman, James S. 1973. *The Mathematics of Collective Action*. London: Heinemann.

Cook, Karen S. 1975. "Expectations, Evaluations, and Equity." *American Sociological Review* 40:372-388.

Durkheim, Émile. [1893] 1964. *The Division of Labor in Society*, translated by George Simpson. New York: Free Press.

— — —. [1897] 1951. *Suicide: A Study in Sociology*, translated by John A. Spaulding and George Simpson and edited by George Simpson. New York: Free Press.

Epictetus. 1983. *Handbook of Epictetus*, translated by Nicholas White. Indianapolis: Hackett.

Festinger, Leon. 1954. "A Theory of Social Comparison Processes." *Human Relations* 7:117-40.

Goode, William J. 1978. *The Celebration of Heroes: Prestige as a Control System*. Berkeley: University of California Press.

Homans, George Caspar. [1961] 1974. *Social Behavior: Its Elementary Forms*, rev. ed. New York: Harcourt Brace Jovanovich.

— — —. 1976. "Commentary." Pp. 231-44 in *Advances in Experimental Social Psychology*, Vol. 9, edited by L. Berkowitz and E. Walster. New York: Academic Press.

Hyman, Herbert H. 1968. "Reference Groups." Pp. 353-61 in *International Encyclopedia of the Social Sciences*, Vol. 13, edited by David L. Sills. New York: Macmillan.

Ignacio de Loyola, San. [1521-56] 1963. *Obras Completas*, edited by I. Iparraguirre and C. de Dalmases. Madrid: Espasa-Calpe.

James, William. [1891] 1952. *The Principles of Psychology*. Chicago: Britannica.

Jasso, Guillermina. 1978. "On the Justice of Earnings: A New Specification of the Justice Evaluation Function." *American Journal of Sociology* 83:1398-1419.

— — —. 1980. "A New Theory of Distributive Justice." *American Sociological Review* 45:3-32.

— — —. 1981. "Further Notes on the Theory of Distributive Justice (Reply to Soltan)." *American Sociological Review* 46:352-60.

— — —. 1982. "Measuring Inequality by the Ratio of the Geometric Mean to the Arithmetic Mean." *Sociological Methods and Research* 10:303-26.

— — —. 1983a. "Fairness of Individual Rewards and Fairness of the Reward Distribution: Specifying the Inconsistency Between the Micro and Macro Principles of Justice." *Social Psychology Quarterly* 46:185-99.

— — —. 1983b. "Social Consequences of the Sense of Distributive Justice: Small-Group Applications." Pp. 243-94 in *Equity Theory: Psychological and Sociological Perspectives*, edited by David M. Messick and Karen Cook. New York: Praeger.

— — —. 1983c. "Using the Inverse Distribution Function to Compare Income Distributions and Their Inequality." *Research in Social Stratification and Mobility* 2:271-306.

— — —. 1986a. "A New Representation of the Just Term in Distributive-Justice Theory: Its Properties and Operation in Theoretical Derivation and Empirical Estimation." *Journal of Mathematical Sociology* 12:251-74.

— — —. 1986b. "Distributive Justice and Social-Welfare Institutions." Paper presented at the International Conference on Social Justice in Human Relations, cosponsored by the Dutch Royal Academy of Sciences and Leiden University, Leiden, the Netherlands, July (revised).

— — —. 1987. "Choosing a Good: Models Based on the Theory of the Distributive-Justice Force." *Advances in Group Processes: Theory and Research* 4:67-108, 1987.

— — —. 1988a. "Principles of Theoretical Analysis." *Sociological Theory* 6:1-20.

— — —. 1988b. "Distributive-Justice Effects of Employment and Earnings on Marital Cohesiveness: An Empirical Test of Theoretical Predictions." Pp. 123-62 in *Status Generalization: New Theory and Research*, edited by Murray Webster and Martha Foschi. Palo Alto, CA: Stanford University Press.

— — —. 1989a. "Notes on the Advancement of Theoretical Sociology (Reply to Turner)." *Sociological Theory* 7.

— — —. 1989b. "Self-Interest, Distributive Justice, and the Income Distribution: A Theoretical Fragment Based on St. Anselm's Postulate." Paper presented at the annual meeting of the Midwest Sociological Society, St. Louis, MO.

— — —. in press. "Methods for the Theoretical and Empirical Analysis of Comparison Processes." In *Sociological Methodology 1990*, edited by Clifford C. Clogg. Washington, DC: American Sociological Association.

Jasso, Guillermina and Peter H. Rossi. 1977. "Distributive Justice and Earned Income." *American Sociological Review* 42:639-51.

Judge, George G., W. E. Griffiths, R. Carter Hill, Helmut Lutkepohl, and Tsoung-Chao Lee. 1985. *The Theory and Practice of Econometrics*, 2nd ed. New York: John Wiley.

Lakatos, Imre. 1970. "Falsification and the Methodology of Scientific Research Programmes." Pp. 91-195 in *Criticism and the Growth of Knowledge*, edited by Imre Lakatos and Alan Musgrave. Cambridge: Cambridge University Press.

Lawler, Edward J. 1988. "Choice, Emotion, and the Social Order." Paper presented at the annual meeting of the Public Choice Society, San Francisco.

Lerner, Melvin J. 1974. "The Justice Motive: 'Equity' and 'Parity' Among Children." *Journal of Personality and Social Psychology* 29:539-50.

Lipset, Seymour Martin. 1968. "Stratification, Social: Social Class." Pp. 296-316 in *International Encyclopedia of the Social Sciences*, Vol. 15, edited by David L. Sills. New York: Macmillan.

Markovsky, Barry. 1988. "Anchoring Justice." *Social Psychology Quarterly* 51:213-24.

Marx, Karl. [1849] 1968. "Wage Labour and Capital." Pp. 74-97 in *Karl Marx and Frederick Engels: Selected Works*. New York: International Publishers.

Merton, Robert K. 1945. "Sociological Theory." *American Journal of Sociology* 50:462-73.

— — —. 1957. "Continuities in the Theory of Reference Groups and Social Structure." Pp. 281-386 in *Social Theory and Social Structure*, 2nd ed. New York: Free Press.

— — —. 1967. *On Theoretical Sociology: Five Essays, Old and New*. New York: Free Press.

Merton, Robert K. and Alice S. Rossi. 1950. "Contributions to the Theory of Reference Group Behavior." Pp. 40-105 in *Continuities in Social Research: Studies in the Scope and Method of "The American Soldier,"* edited by R. K. Merton and P. Lazarsfeld. New York: Free Press.

Mirowsky, John. 1987. "The Psycho-Economics of Feeling Underpaid: Distributive Justice and the Earnings of Husbands and Wives." *American Journal of Sociology* 6:1404-34.

Rossi, Peter H. 1951. "The Application of Latent Structure Analysis to the Study of Social Stratification." Unpublished Ph.D. dissertation, Columbia University.

———. 1979. "Vignette Analysis: Uncovering the Normative Structure of Complex Judgments." Pp. 176-86 in *Qualitative and Quantitative Social Research: Papers in Honor of Paul F. Lazarsfeld,* edited by Robert K. Merton, James S. Coleman, and Peter H. Rossi. New York: Free Press.

Rossi, Peter H. and Andy B. Anderson. 1982. "The Factorial Survey Approach: An Introduction." Pp. 15-67 in *Measuring Social Judgments: The Factorial Survey Approach.* Beverly Hills, CA: Sage.

Runciman, William G. 1961. "Problems of Research on Relative Deprivation." *Archives Européennes de Sociologie* 2:315-323.

Shepelak, Norma J. and Duane F. Alwin. 1986. "Beliefs About Inequality and Perceptions of Distributive Justice." *American Sociological Review* 51:30-46.

Sherif, Muzafer. 1968. "Self Concept." Pp. 150-59 in *International Encyclopedia of the Social Sciences,* Vol. 14, edited by David L. Sills. New York: Macmillan.

Simmel, Georg. [1896-1917] 1950. *The Sociology of Georg Simmel,* translated and edited by Kurt H. Wolff. New York: Free Press.

Sprague, Hall T. 1977. "Happiness Is an Equation." *New York Times* (January 16):Section 10, pp. 1, 16.

Stouffer, Samuel A., et al. 1949. *The American Soldier.* Two volumes. Studies in Social Psychology in World War II. Princeton, NJ: Princeton University Press.

Teresa de Avila, Santa. [1546-82] 1982. *Obras Completas* (quatercentenary ed.), annotated by Luis Santullano (based on the text edited and annotated by P. Silverio). Madrid: Aguilar.

Thomas Aquinas, Saint. [1267-73] 1952. *Summa Theologica,* 2 vols., translated by Fathers of the English Dominican Province; revised by Daniel J. Sullivan. Chicago: Britannica.

Wright, Georg Henrik von. 1963. *The Varieties of Goodness.* London: Routledge & Kegan Paul.

Zelditch, Morris, Jr. 1968. "Status, Social." Pp. 250-57 in *International Encyclopedia of the Social Sciences,* Vol. 15, edited by David L. Sills. New York: Macmillan.

Zelditch, Morris, Jr., Joseph Berger, Bo Anderson, and Bernard P. Cohen. 1970. "Equitable Comparisons." *Pacific Sociological Review* 13:19-26.

14

Competitive and Institutional Processes in Organizational Ecology

MICHAEL T. HANNAN

In 1977 John Freeman and I asked: Why are there so many kinds of organizations? This seemingly simple question raised deep theoretical issues that had not been addressed squarely. We suggested that trying to answer it would clarify the relations between organizations and environments and the nature of processes of change in organizational populations. We also proposed a theoretical strategy for addressing the question, one that was inspired by theoretical developments in population ecology. Our proposed *population ecology of organizations* emphasized the role of competition for scarce material and social resources for building and sustaining organizations in shaping observable features of the world of organizations (Hannan and Freeman 1977).

In the same year, Meyer and Rowan (1977) offered a quite different answer to our question, proposing that many of the easily observable features of organizations serve as mythic or ceremonial arrangements and have little or nothing to do with production of outputs. According to this *institutional theory*, organizations face problems of maintaining legitimacy and adapt to these problems by creating structures that serve as signals of difficult-to-observe competencies. This perspective holds that the observable features of the world of organizations are shaped mainly by broad social norms and processes of ritual conformity to them.

Although these two perspectives are routinely treated as rival, it is not obvious that they disagree sharply. It is surely possible that organizations

Author's Note: The work reported here was supported by National Science Foundation grants SES-8510277 and SES-8809006. This chapter was originally prepared for this volume in 1986 and was circulated as a technical report (Hannan 1986) at that time. This version is the same as the earlier one, except that a now outdated report of a single empirical study has been replaced with an overview of a number of studies that have tested implications of the model developed in this chapter. I appreciate the suggestions and criticisms of Glenn Carroll, John Freeman, and Susan Olzak.

compete for legitimacy and that social norms serve to channel competition in certain directions. It may also be the case, as Scott (1981) has suggested, that competitive and institutional processes operate simultaneously but that competitive processes shape "core" features of organizations (those dealing with the organization of production) and institutional processes shape "peripheral" ones (those dealing with exchanges across the boundaries of the organization). Despite the seeming ease with which at least some aspects of competitive and institutional processes can be integrated, subsequent development of the two theoretical programs has tended to treat them as inconsistent.

Institutionalists have been particularly insistent on segregating the two kinds of processes. They have taken two tacks: partitioning by industry broadly defined and partitioning by stage in the life cycle of an organizational population or community. Meyer and Scott (1983) advance a proposal of the first kind, arguing that the world of organizations is partitioned into a "technical sector" composed mainly of organizations producing material products and an "institutional sector" composed of organizations producing services such as education and health care. They claim that efficiency considerations and competition for limited markets shape the distribution of organizational forms in the technical sector but that social norms shape the institutional sector. Thus there are two kinds of organizational worlds governed by different processes.

DiMaggio and Powell (1983) make a similar argument, but locate it in the life cycle of populations and communities of organizations. They argue that new populations of organizations are shaped by competitive interactions but that institutional processes strengthen over time and eventually dominate competitive processes. Thus young populations are shaped by competition; old populations are shaped by institutional conformity.

Freeman and I have argued against the tendency to treat competitive and institutional processes as inconsistent. For example, we have shown that strong institutional controls strengthen the boundaries between organizational populations and thereby intensify competitive processes in the neighborhood of the boundary (Hannan and Freeman 1986). This chapter continues this line of argument. It develops a model of growth and decline in the sizes of organizational populations that integrates competitive and institutional processes. It presents a formal model in which both the institutional standing of an organizational population and the strength of competitive interactions affect founding and disbanding rates and thus the expansion and contraction of organizational populations. The model holds that both institutional and competitive processes depend on the number of organizations in the population. Hence observable implications of the model can be derived that relate density to founding and disbanding rates. The model advanced here implies that founding rates and disbanding rates in organizational populations are nonmonotonic functions of density.

Classic Models of Density Dependence

In developing theories of change in organizational populations, ecologists have found useful precedents in population bioecology. The concept of niche, which plays a strategic role in this theory, provides a useful way to express how institutional environments and competition affect the growth rates of populations of *social* organizations. Modern niche theories began with Hutchinson's (1957) abstract geometric definition. He defined the niche as the set of environmental conditions within which a population can reproduce itself (in which its growth rate is nonnegative). Because growth rates usually respond to numerous environmental dimensions, the relevant environment consists of an N-dimensional space with each dimension telling the level of some relevant environmental condition, such as average rainfall or average diurnal temperature fluctuation. Each point in this space corresponds to a particular state of the N-dimensional environment. Hutchinson defined the *fundamental niche* of a population as the hypervolume formed by set of points for which the population's growth rate (fitness) is nonnegative. In other words, the fundamental niche consists of the set of all environmental outcomes in which the population can grow or at least sustain its numbers. It is called the fundamental niche because it refers to the physiological capacities of the members of the population.

The analogue for populations of organizations is straightforward. Classical sociological theorists, notably Marx and Weber, emphasized the social, economic, and political conditions required to sustain particular organizational forms, such as capitalist business enterprise and rational-legal bureaucracy. They suggested, for example, that the environmental dimensions that affect the growth of populations of rational-legal bureaucracies include the fraction of exchanges that are monetized, availability of literate employees, and stability in flows of resources to the state. Taking the various dimensions together defines an N-dimensional social environment. The niche of rational-legal bureaucracy (or of any other organizational form) consists of the set of social arrangements in which this population can grow or at least not decline. Usually the relevant social arrangements concern both the strength of competition from similar and dissimilar organizations and the set of institutional arrangements.

A fundamental niche characterizes growth rates of *isolated* populations. The next step in the development of niche theory considers *interacting* rather than isolated populations. Two (or more) populations interact, from an ecological perspective, if the presence of one affects the growth rate of the other. These effects may be positive, negative, or absent. Competition is a situation in which increases in the density of one population depress the growth rate of another. The term *competition* is often restricted to the case in which the negative effect is mutual, that is, to situations in which the presence of each population lowers the growth

rate of the other. The predator-prey (or host-parasite) case has one negative and one positive link. The case in which both links are positive is
called *commensalism* (or sometimes *symbiosis*).

When populations interact, the presence of one population changes the
niche of the others. If two populations compete, the presence of the
competitor reduces the set of environments in which a population can
sustain itself. Hutchinson called this restricted set of environments the
realized niche. Obviously, two populations compete if and only if their
fundamental niches intersect.

The development of competition theory in population bioecology was
influenced by Gause's (1934) experiments on coexistence of closely related species of beetles in controlled environments. He found that mixing
two populations invariably caused one population to disappear. Gause
summarized his findings by proposing a general ecological law. His
principle of competitive exclusion holds that two species that occupy
essentially the same niche cannot coexist in equilibrium.

Subsequent research has ruled out competitive exclusion as a general
principle. For example, it turns out to be simple to produce coexistence of
closely related species in the laboratory by making the environment more
complex (essentially creating subenvironments in which the inferior competitor can find refuge or may possess an adaptive advantage). Nonetheless, this "principle" has proven useful in directing attention to the crucial
role of *niche overlap* in competition processes. It has also stimulated the
application of general models of population dynamics to concrete ecological processes.

Alfred Lotka (1925) and Vito Volterra ([1927] 1978) independently
proposed models of population dynamics that incorporate effects of competition between populations. They began with models that imply that
population growth rates of isolated populations have S-shaped growth
paths. They assumed that the growth rate of an isolated population is given
by the product of a growth rate and the current size of the population:

$$\frac{dn}{dt} = \rho_n n, \qquad [1]$$

where n denotes the size of the population. The growth rate ρ_n is defined
as the difference between the birthrate and the death rate of the population:

$$\rho_n = \lambda_n - \mu_n. \qquad [2]$$

If the birthrate and death rate are constant (that is, if they do not vary with
the size of the population), this model implies exponential growth. But
exponential growth processes cannot be sustained in finite environments,
as Malthus pointed out. The growth model can be made more realistic by
assuming that birthrate and death rate vary with density (the size of the

population). Lotka and Volterra assumed that the birthrate falls (approximately) linearly with the size of the population:

$$\lambda_n = a_0 - a_1 n, \quad a_0 > 0, \, a_1 > 0 \qquad [3]$$

and that the death rate increases (approximately) linearly with population size (assuming that the resources available are finite):

$$\mu_n = b_0 + b_1 n, \quad b_0 > 0, \, b_1 < 0 \qquad [4]$$

Substituting equations 3 and 4 into the growth model (equation 2) gives:

$$\frac{dn}{dt} = (a_0 - b_0)n - (a_1 + b_1)n^2 \qquad [5]$$

This is the model of logistic population growth. It holds that the population grows essentially exponentially at low values of n, but that competition for fixed resources eventually drives the growth rate toward zero.

Note that the model of logistic growth implies a steady state for the population. Setting equation 5 equal to zero shows steady states at $n = 0$ and $n = (a_0 - b_0)/(a_1 + b_1)$. The nonzero steady state of the population is usually called the *carrying capacity* of the environment for the population in question. It has traditionally been denoted by K in population bioecology.

The logistic model of population growth can be expressed in terms of the carrying capacity:

$$\frac{dn}{dt} = r \left[K - \frac{n}{K} \right] n \qquad [6]$$

The *intrinsic growth rate*, $r = a_0 - b_0$, tells the speed with which the population grows in the absence of resource constraints. The carrying capacity, $K = r/(a_1 + b_1)$, indicates the limits on growth. According to this model, when the population size is small compared to the carrying capacity, the growth rate essentially equals r. When the population size equals the carrying capacity, the growth rate is zero. If population size exceeds the carrying capacity (perhaps because some shock has reduced the carrying capacity), the growth rate is negative. The parameterization in equation 6 provides a substantively appealing way to introduce competition. Two populations compete if the size of each population lowers the carrying capacity for the other.

The Lotka-Volterra (LV) model of competitive interactions, which plays a prominent role in most contemporary population bioecology theory, assumes that the effect of the density of the competitor on the "realized" carrying capacity is linear. In the case of two competing populations, the model is as follows:

$$\frac{dn_1}{dt} = r_1 \left[\frac{K_1 - \alpha_{12}n_2 - n_1}{K_1} \right] n_1; \qquad [7a]$$

$$\frac{dn_2}{dt} = r_2 \left[\frac{K_2 - \alpha_{21}n_1 - n_2}{K_2} \right] n_2. \qquad [7b]$$

Comparison of equations 7a and 7b shows that the presence of the competitor reduces the carrying capacity for the first population from K_1 to $K_1 - \alpha_{12}n_2$. The so-called *competition coefficients*, α_{12} and α_{21}, tell how the carrying capacity for each population declines with the density of the competitor. This model decomposes the growth rate for each population into effects of three components: (1) the intrinsic properties of the form that affect its speed of growth in the absence of resource limitations and competition, r_i; (2) limits on growth that reflect generalized conditions of resource availability, K_i; and (3) competition with specific populations, α_{ij}.

Sociological Models of Density Dependence

Does it make sense to assume that there are carrying capacity limits on the growth of populations of organizations? Discussion of the LV model above indicates that carrying capacities are simple functions of parameters expressing density dependence in birthrates and death rates. The existence of a finite carrying capacity depends on the assumption that the birthrate falls with density and that the death rate rises with density. Density serves as surrogate for the difficult-to-observe features of the material and social environment that affect the rates. Indeed, the models developed below are based on the premise that density in the organizational world activates both competitive and institutional processes.

INSTITUTIONAL PROCESSES

Recent institutional treatments of organization consider at least two distinct processes (which are not always clearly distinguished). One kind is purely structural: A social actor (using a specific organizational form) is institutionalized to the extent that other powerful actors in the system endorse its claims in disputes (Stinchcombe 1968). For instance, labor unions became institutionalized in this sense in the United States only after passage of the Wagner Act in 1935, which held that organizations using a specified "labor union" form had special standing in making certain claims. That is, the state became committed to intervening in certain ways to support claims of workers if they used this organizational form (but no other).

Institutionalization conveys powerful advantages. Because institution-alized actors can call upon other powerful actors for aid in resisting raids on their resources, institutionalization lowers mortality rates. Unless this tendency is offset by a founding process that blurs boundaries, such a process produces a world of organizations with clear discontinuities and defended boundaries. That is, selection in favor of institutionalized forms intensifies the boundaries around the forms that emerge from the selection process (Hannan and Freeman 1986).

A second institutional process pertains to the taken-for-granted charac-ter of certain forms (Meyer and Scott 1983). A form is institutionalized in this sense when no question arises in the minds of actors that a certain form is the "natural" way to effect some kind of collective action. In this sense, the labor union form became institutionalized long before the Wagner Act. This legislation occurred several decades after workers had stopped debating whether labor unions were the natural vehicles for collective action for improving conditions of work.

The capacity to mobilize members and other resources to begin unions, firms, and other kinds of organizations increases greatly when those who control resources take the question of organizational form for granted. Not having to defend choice of form saves time and other organizing re-sources. In consequence, attempts at creating copies of legitimated forms are more common, and the success rate of such attempts is relatively high.

Institutional processes imply a link between density and founding rates. If institutionalization means that certain forms attain a taken-for-granted character, then simple prevalence of a form gives it legitimacy. When numbers are small, those who attempt to create a form must fight for legitimacy. They must argue both for the special purposes of a proposed organization and for the design of the form. At low densities, the growth of populations of organizations is constrained by the novelty and rarity of the form. The fact that there are few organizations in the popula-tion presumably makes it difficult to convince key actors (such as banks and government agencies) to transfer material and symbolic resources to organizations in the population. It may likewise be difficult to convince talented people to join such organizations and to remain in them. Other things being equal, legitimation of a form increases the founding rate of populations using the form. If, as I argue here, legitimacy increases with prevalence of the form in society, then legitimation processes produce positive density and founding rates.

Each of these arguments has parallel implications for disbanding rates. Increasing density lowers disbanding rates by increasing the legitimacy of the populations using the form. Low density also hampers attempts at coordinated political action to protect and defend claims of the population or of some of its members. Increases in numbers alleviate these problems. Growth in numbers of organizations gives force to claims of institutional standing and also provides economies of scale in political and legal action. In other words, legitimation processes produce a negative relationship between density and disbanding rates.

COMPETITIVE PROCESSES

The main argument for negative density dependence involves competition within populations. The more abundant the competitors, the smaller the potential gains from founding an organization (and the bigger the cost to potential competitors) at a given level of demand for products and services. Fewer resources are available and markets are packed tightly in densely populated environments. For these reasons, collectives with the knowledge and skills to build organizations are less likely to make attempts in densely populated environments. Capital markets and other macrostructures often reinforce this effect. For example, investors may be reluctant to participate in new ventures in dense markets. Likewise, professional associations often try to restrict entry when density is high.

In general terms, high density implies strong competitive interactions within populations dependent on limited resources for organizing (when levels of such resources have been controlled). As density grows, supplies of potential organizers, members, patrons, and resources become exhausted. Moreover, existing organizations respond to increasing competitive pressures by opposing attempts at creating still more organizations. For both of these reasons, the founding rate declines as the number of organizations in the population increases. That is, competitive processes produce a negative relationship between density and founding rates.

Competitive processes stemming from density also affect disbanding rates. At high density, competitive interactions intensify. Growth in numbers increases the likelihood and intensity of both *direct competition* between pairs of organizations and *diffuse competition* among all (or many) of them. Individual organizations can easily avoid direct competition with others for members and other scarce resources when there are few organizations in the system. As the number of potential competitors grows, avoidance becomes more difficult.

For example, labor unions competed for the services of skilled organizers and dedicated staff, political support and influence, attention from the news media, and so forth. Sometimes such competition involved direct rivalry, as when two or more unions seeking to organize the same workers competed for support of and membership in a national federation such as the AFL and CIO. More often the competition was diffuse — it had more the character of congestion than of rivalry. As the number of unions grew large, more of the resources used to build and sustain unions were claimed by other unions that could defend themselves against raids. Such diffuse competition lowers the life chances of new unions and also affects the life chance of existing unions. That is, competitive processes produce a positive relationship between density and disbanding rates.

A Model of the Process

FOUNDING RATES

The arguments sketched above imply that the founding rate (λ) is proportional to the legitimacy (L) of the population and inversely proportional to the level of competition (C) within the population:

$$\lambda = a \cdot \frac{L}{C},$$
[8]

and that L and C are functions of density (n):

$$L = f(n) \quad \text{and} \quad C = g(n).$$

I assume that density increases legitimacy at a decreasing rate, that legitimacy is sensitive to variations in density in the lower range, but that there is something like a ceiling effect on the relationship, that is:

$$\frac{dL}{dn} > 0 \quad \text{and} \quad \frac{dL^2}{d^2n} < 0.$$

In the case of competition, I think that variations in the upper range have more impact on founding rates than variations in the lower range. In particular, increases in density increase competition at an increasing rate:

$$\frac{dC}{dn} > 0 \quad \text{and} \quad \frac{dC^2}{d^2n} > 0.$$

Moreover, I propose that the legitimacy process dominates when n is small but that the competition process dominates when n is large. That is, the effect of density on the founding rate is nonmonotonic.

The next step is to build a model based on particular functional forms of these relationships that agree with these qualitative restrictions. A simple model consistent with these assumptions and with the restriction that the rate be nonnegative is as follows:

$$L = f(n) = \alpha n^\beta, \quad \alpha > 0, \ 0 < \beta < 1$$
[9a]

and

$$C + \gamma e^{\delta n2}, \quad \gamma > 0, \ \delta > 0$$
[9b]

Inserting these equations into equation 8, the simplified model of the founding rate, yields the basic parametric model:

$$\lambda = \varphi n^\beta e^{-\delta n^2}$$
[10]

where $\phi = a\alpha/\gamma$.

This model was chosen because its qualitative behavior agrees with the theory. In particular, it implies that there is a *nonmonotonic* relationship between density and the rate. To see this, note that

$$\frac{d\lambda}{dn} = \phi n^{\beta-1} e^{-\delta n^2}(\beta - 2\delta n^2) \qquad [11]$$

There is a point of inflection (a minimum) at

$$n* = \sqrt{\frac{\beta}{2\delta}}$$

The rate declines with density until n reaches this level and then rises with increasing density.

In empirical testing the key issue is whether this nonmonotonic model improves over a simpler model with only monotone dependence of the rate on density. A secondary but still interesting issue is whether the point of inflection falls within the observed range of density. So in estimating models with this form, I check first to see that the estimated parameters have the predicted signs and second whether the implied behavior of the process over the range of density is nonmonotonic. If the founding rate rises initially and then falls with increasing density, the process implies the existence of a carrying capacity for the population. So it is important for evaluating this theoretical approach to learn whether founding rates vary with density and, if they do, whether the dependence is non-monotonic.

This model of density dependence in founding rates is more complicated than the corresponding assumption in the LV model. Whereas the LV model is built on the assumption that density dependence in this rate is linear, the model presented here implies that the density dependence is nonmonotonic. This added complexity in the model reflects the greater complexity of organizational ecology.

DISBANDING RATES

The arguments sketched in the previous section imply that the disbanding rate (μ) is proportional to the level of competition and inversely proportional to the legitimacy of the population:

$$\mu = b \cdot \frac{C}{L} \qquad [12]$$

As in the case of the founding rate, I assume that density increases competition at an increasing rate but increases legitimacy at a decreasing rate. There is no obvious reason not to use the same parametric assumptions regarding the dependence of legitimacy and competition on density as made above for the founding process. However, there is no reason to assume that the parameters of each part of the process are identical for the two rates. So I assume that

$$L = vn^{\kappa};$$

and

$$C = \zeta e^{\lambda n^2}.\qquad[13]$$

With these assumptions, the model for the disbanding rate is

$$\mu = \varphi n^{-\kappa} e^{\lambda n^2},\qquad[14]$$

where $\varphi = b\zeta/v$. What matters is the functional form and signs of parameters. Again, the crucial qualitative feature of the model is that the effect of density on disbanding rates is *nonmonotonic*. The model implies that *the disbanding rate falls with increasing density up to a point (the neighborhood of the carrying capacity) and then rises with increasing density.* (Note again the departure from the LV assumption of linear density dependence.)

Due to some early difficulties in obtaining convergent estimates of the model in equation 14 using the empirical data on one population, I also suggest an alternative specification, the parameters of which have essentially the same qualitative interpretation:

$$\mu = \exp(-\theta_1 n + \theta_2 n^2).\qquad[15]$$

Differentiating the rate with respect to density, we have

$$\frac{d\mu}{dn} = \mu(-\theta_1 + 2\theta_2 n).$$

Again the model implies a point of inflection (a minimum); this time the minimum is given by

$$n* = \frac{\theta_1}{2\theta_2}.$$

Below this level of density the rate declines with increasing density; above this level the rate increases with increasing density.

The last topic concerns the linkages between rates in one population of organizations and the density of other populations. The analysis here is restricted to the case of two populations that illustrate the general theoretical issues. Although there may be particular cases in which the legitimation of one population depends on the *size* of some other population, it seems unlikely that this is the case generally. However, whenever two populations seek to exploit the same limited resources, the density of each affects the strength of competitive interactions, as noted above in the discussion of the LV model. Therefore, in developing a multipopulation model, I specify only competitive effects between populations. It seems likely (as Lotka and Volterra assumed for the biotic case) that the strength of competitive interactions increases monotonically with density. So assume that the strength of competitive pressures on the first population has the form:

$$C_{12} = g(n_1, n_2),$$

with

$$\frac{dg}{dn_1} > 0, \ \frac{d^2g}{dn_1^2} > 0,$$

and

$$\frac{dg}{dn_2} > 0, \ \frac{d^2g}{dn_2^2} > 0, \ \frac{d^2g}{dn_1 n_2} > 0.$$

In other words, I assume that the effect of density of the competing population is monotonic.

A simple parametric model consistent with these assumptions (and with the constraint that rates be nonnegative) is as follows:

$$C_{12} = \exp(\beta n_1^2 + \psi n_2) \qquad [16]$$

This assumption, when combined with the assumption made above about legitimacy, implies the following form of density dependence:

$$\lambda = n_1^\alpha \exp(-\beta n_1^2 + \psi n_2) \qquad [17]$$

The cross-effect of density (ψ) captures the effect of *interpopulation competition*. Whenever the two populations use the same resources, the cross-effect is negative for both populations.

Empirical Status of the Theory

In the three years since the work in this chapter was first circulated (Hannan 1986), there have been numerous empirical tests. As these tests are evaluated elsewhere (Hannan and Freeman 1989; Carroll and Hannan 1989), I will summarize the patterns of findings only briefly.

Hannan and Freeman's (1987, 1988) analysis of national labor unions in the United States over the entire history of the population, 1836-1985, strongly supported the model of legitimation and competition. In analyses that controlled for differences among historical periods and for numerous environmental conditions, the nonmonotonic model improved significantly over monotonic models of density dependence for both founding rates and mortality rates. The point estimates agreed with the predictions of the model for both rates. Moreover, the estimates imply that the effect of density is nonmonotonic for both rates over the range of variation in density. The predicted founding rate rises and then falls over the range of density; the predicted mortality rate falls and then rises over the range.

Subsequently, researchers applied the model to other kinds of organizational populations. Most of the studies have yielded estimates of density dependence supporting the model of legitimation and competition. These include Hannan and Freeman's (1989) analysis of rates of exit from the population of American semiconductor manufacturers during 1945-1980, Barnett and Carroll's (1987) analysis of rates of founding and mortality of independent local telephone companies in several Iowa counties during 1900-1917, and Mitchell's (1987) study of rates of entry into the medical diagnostic imaging industry during 1959-1986. In addition, Carroll and Hannan (1989) tested the model using data on populations of newspapers in Argentina in the nineteenth century, Ireland in the nineteenth and twentieth centuries, and seven SMSAs in the United States in the nineteenth and twentieth centuries. In the case of founding rates, the expected pattern was found for all nine populations, although it was statistically significant in only seven. For mortality, the predictions hold in analyses of six of the nine populations, but the predicted nonmonotonic pattern is statistically significant only for the three largest populations: Argentina, Ireland, and San Francisco. Finally, Carroll and Swaminathan (1988) found strong support for the model in analyzing rates of founding and mortality of brewing firms in the United States from 1633 to 1988.

Tucker et al.'s (1988) analysis of foundings of voluntary social service organizations in Toronto from 1970 to 1982 provides limited support for the model. While Tucker et al. report that the predicted pattern of density dependence holds (Table 8-1, second equation), they conclude that this pattern holds only during increased public funding.

Several other studies have provided disconfirming evidence. Hannan and Freeman's (1988) analysis of rates of entry into the semiconductor manufacturing industry reveals that density had a monotonic positive effect on the rate. Delacroix et al.'s (1989) analysis of exits from the population of California wine producers from 1940 until 1985 shows at best weak support for the model. And Tucker et al. (1988) report that density dependence in rates of mortality is nonmonotonic but with signs opposite the predictions of the model.

Some of the differences in findings appear to reflect differences in research designs. As Carroll and Hannan (1989) point out, an important difference among these studies concerns time frames. The Hannan-Freeman union data cover the history of a population from its emergence to 1985, a period of almost 150 years. Carroll and Hannan's study of newspaper populations in three countries covers two centuries, and Carroll and Swaminathan's (1988) study of American brewing firms covers the complete history of the population over three centuries. The other studies cover periods of only 40 years (semiconductor manufacturers), 17 years (telephone companies), 45 years (wine producers), 27 years (diagnostic imaging manufacturers), and 13 years (voluntary social services). Moreover, only the studies of California wineries and Toronto social service agencies did not obtain information on the early history of the population. Excluding data on the initial period of low density is particularly problematic for testing the implications of the legitimacy process. Recall that the model holds that effects of density on legitimation (and indirectly on the vital rates) are particularly strong in this period. There is no reason to expect that these effects should be observable at late stages of a population's development, because the model predicts that competition dominates at this point. A similar argument applies to exclusion of the later phases of population evolution (whether by research design or by the censoring imposed by current time) as it pertains to the competition process. Those studies that have considered only the initial decades of a population's history, like Hannan and Freeman's study of American semiconductor manufacturers, are unlikely to provide good evidence on competition process.

It appears that the studies that have provided most complete coverage of the evolution of organizational populations have yielded estimates that agree with the implications of the model. The modeling approach taken here appears to point to an empirical regularity in the world of organizations — the nonmonotonic pattern of density dependence in vital rates — that had escaped notice previously.

References

Barnett, William P. and Glenn R. Carroll. 1987. "Competition and Mutualism Among Early Telephone Companies." *Administrative Science Quarterly* 32:400-21.

Carroll, Glenn R. 1984. "Organizational Ecology." *Annual Review of Sociology* 10:71-93.

Carroll, Glenn R. and Michael T. Hannan. 1989. "Density Dependence in the Evolution of Newspaper Populations." *American Sociological Review* 54:524-41.

Carroll, Glenn R. and Anand Swaminathan. 1988. "Density Dependence Among American Breweries with an Extension to Strategic Groups." Paper presented at the Conference on Strategic Management, University of Alberta, Edmonton, October.

Delacroix, Jacques, Anand Swaminathan, and Michael E. Solt. 1989. "Density Dependence Versus Population Dynamics: An Ecological Study of Failings in the California Wine Industry," *American Sociological Review* 54:245-62

DiMaggio, Paul and Walter W. Powell. 1983. "The Iron Cage Revisited." *American Sociological Review* 48:147-60.

Gause, G. F. 1934. *The Struggle for Existence*. Baltimore: Williams & Wilkens.

Hannan, Michael T. 1986. "Competitive and Institutional Processes in Organizational Ecology." Technical Report 86-13, Department of Sociology, Cornell University.

Hannan, Michael T. and John Freeman. 1977. "The Population Ecology of Organizations." *American Journal of Sociology* 82:929-64.

— — —. 1984. "Structural Inertia and Organizational Change." *American Sociological Review* 49:149-64.

— — —. 1986. "Where Do Organizational Forms Come From?" *Sociological Forum* 1:50-72.

— — —. 1987. "The Ecology of Organizational Founding: American Labor Unions, 1836-1985." *American Journal of Sociology* 92:910-43.

— — —. 1988. "The Ecology of Organizational Mortality: American Labor Unions, 1836-1985." *American Journal of Sociology* 94: 25-52.

— — —. 1989. *Organizational Ecology*. Cambridge, MA: Harvard University Press.

Hutchinson, G. Evelyn. 1957. "Concluding Remarks." *Cold Spring Harbor Symposium on Quantitative Biology* 22:415-27.

Lotka, Alfred. 1925. *Elements of Mathematical Biology*. New York: Dover.

Meyer, John W. and Brian Rowan. 1977. "Organizational Structure as Myth and Ceremony." *American Journal of Sociology* 83:340-63.

Meyer, John W. and W. Richard Scott. 1983. *Organizational Environments: Ritual and Rationality*. Beverly Hills, CA: Sage.

Mitchell, Will G. 1987. "Dynamic Tension: Theoretical and Empirical Analyses of Entry into Emerging Industries." Paper presented at the Stanford Asilomar Conference on Organizations, Asilomar, CA, May.

Scott, W. Richard. 1981. *Organizations: Rational, Natural, and Open Systems*. Englewood Cliffs, NJ: Prentice-Hall.

Stinchcombe, Arthur S. 1968. *Constructing Social Theories*. New York: Harcourt Brace Jovanovich.

Tucker, David J., Jitendra Singh, Agnes G. Meinhard, and Robert J. House. 1988. "Ecological and Institutional Sources of Change in Organizational Populations." Pp. 127-52 in *Ecological Models of Organizations*, edited by Glenn R. Carroll. Cambridge, MA: Ballinger.

Volterra, Vito. [1927] 1978. "Variations and Fluctuations in the Number of Coexisting Species." Pp. 65-236 in *The Golden Age of Theoretical Ecology: 1923-1940*, edited by F. M. Scudo and J. R. Ziegler. New York: Springer-Verlag.

Index

About the Editors

Joseph Berger is a Professor of Sociology and Chairman of the Department of Sociology at Stanford University. In addition, he is a Senior Research Fellow at the Hoover Institution. His research interests are in the areas of status processes and expectation states, reward expectations and distributive justice, and problems in the development of cumulative theory in sociology. Among his publications are *Expectation States Theory: A Theoretical Research Program* (with Thomas Connor and M. Hamit Fisek) and *Status Characteristics and Social Interaction* (with M. Hamit Fisek, Robert Z. Norman, and Morris Zelditch, Jr.). His most recent book, edited with Morris Zelditch, Jr., is *Status, Rewards, and Influence: How Expectations Organize Behavior.*

Morris Zelditch, Jr., is Professor of Sociology at Stanford University. He was Chair of the Department of Sociology at Stanford from 1964 to 1968 and editor of the *American Sociological Review* from 1975 to 1978. He is coauthor or coeditor of *Status, Rewards, and Influence: How Expectations Organize Behavior*; *Status Characteristics and Expectation States*; *Sociological Theories in Progress*, Volumes 1 and 2; and *Types of Formalization in Small Groups Research.* He is currently writing, with Henry A. Walker, a book on the politics of redistributive agendas.

Bo Anderson took his Fil. Kand degree in sociology and philosophy at Uppsala University, Sweden, in 1952, and his Fil. lic degree in 1955. He was Assistant Professor, Department of Sociology, at Stanford University from 1961, and has been Professor in the Department of Sociology, Michigan State University, since 1967. He has published a number of articles, in English and in Swedish, in professional journals and books. His major interests lie in the areas of theory and the sociology of politics. He has done research in Sweden, Mexico, and the United States, and has also lectured at the Universities of Helsinki, Finland, and Göteborg, Sweden.

About the Contributors

Bernard P. Cohen is Professor of Sociology at Stanford University. His principal interests are in social psychology and methodology. His most recent book, *Developing Sociological Knowledge*, deals with problem formulation, operationalization, and theory construction. He is completing a large-scale study of 224 research and development teams drawn from 30 large corporations that focuses on the effects of group structure on group interaction and group productivity. He is also engaged in a program of experimental research dealing with structural effects on group problem solving.

Dana P. Eyre is Assistant Professor of Sociology in the Department of Behavioral Sciences and Leadership, U.S. Military Academy, West Point, New York, and a Ph.D. candidate in sociology at the Department of Sociology, Stanford University. He teaches and researches in sociological theory and the sociology of organizations.

M. Hamit Fisek received his B.S. degree in electrical engineering from Robert College in Istanbul, Turkey, and his M.A. in sociology, M.S. in computer science, and Ph.D. in sociology from Stanford University. He has taught sociology and computer science at the Hacettepe and Middle Eastern Technical universities in Turkey, and has been a Visiting Professor at Rochester and Stanford universities in the United States. He is currently Professor of Psychology at Bogazici University in Turkey. His research interests are concentrated in mathematical models of behavior in small groups.

Margaret Foddy has a Ph.D. in sociology from the University of British Columbia and works as a Senior Lecturer in Psychology at La Trobe University, Melbourne, Australia. Her research interests include the social psychology of ability evaluation, bargaining, and the development of self-schemas in children.

Martha Foschi is currently Associate Professor of Sociology at the University of British Columbia, Canada. She received her Ph.D. in sociology from Stanford University in 1970. Her research interests include processes involving expectations, performances, and evaluations, as well as theoretical and methodological issues in cross-cultural social psychology. She has recently coedited (with Murray Webster, Jr.) a volume titled *Status Generalization: New Theory and Research* (Stanford University Press, 1988). Her current project is a series of experiments on double standards in the evaluation of men's and women's performance.

Thomas J. Fararo is Professor of Sociology at the University of Pittsburgh. He is author or coauthor of books and articles treating formal theoretical models and methods in sociology, including *A Study of a Biased Friendship Net* (with M. Sunshine) and *Mathematical Sociology*. He is the editor of *Mathematical Ideas and Sociological Theory*. His most recent work is a forthcoming monograph, *The Meaning of General Theoretical Sociology*.

Michael T. Hannan is Henry Scarborough Professor of Social Sciences at Cornell University. His main research interests are in the areas of organizational analysis, sociological ecology, and models and methods for the study of social dynamics. His most recent book, coauthored with John Freeman, is *Organizational Ecology* (Harvard Press, 1989). His previous books include *Social Dynamics: Models and Methods* (Academic Press, 1984), coauthored with Nancy Brandon Tuma.

Guillermina Jasso is Professor of Sociology and Director, Program in Theoretical Analysis, University of Iowa. Her recent papers include "Marital Coital Frequency and the Passage of Time: Estimating the Separate Effects of Spouses' Ages and Marital Duration, Birth and Marriage Cohorts, and Period Influences" (*American Sociological Review*, 1985); "A New Representation of the Just Term in Distributive-Justice Theory: Its Properties and Operation in Theoretical Derivation and Empirical Estimation" (*Journal of Mathematical Sociology*, 1986); "Using National Recording Systems for the Measurement and Analysis of Immigration to the United States" (with M. R. Rosenzweig, *International Migration Review*, 1987); "Whom Shall We Welcome? Elite Judgements of the Criteria for the Selection of Immigrants" (*American Sociological Review*, 1988); and "Principles of Theoretical Analysis" (*Sociological Theory*, 1988).

Barry Markovsky is Associate Professor of Sociology at the University of Iowa. He is working on theories, empirical tests, and computer simulations of a variety of social processes, including network exchange, distributive justice, status generalization, and group solidarity. He is coeditor of a series of annual volumes, *Advances in Group Processes* (with Edward J. Lawler, Cecilia Ridgeway, and Henry Walker). His recent articles in *American Sociological Review* include "Power Relations in Exchange Networks" (with David Willer and Travis Patton), "Toward a Multilevel Distributive Justice Theory," and "Do Status Interventions Persist?" (with LeRoy Smith and Joseph Berger). His other recent articles have appeared in *Social Forces, Social Psychology Quarterly, Sociological Theory, Social Justice Research,* and *Personality and Social Psychology Bulletin.*

Robert Z. Norman received his Ph.D. in mathematics from the University of Michigan in 1954, where he also served as a Research Assistant at the Research Center for Group Dynamics, applying graph theory to problems in social networks. Since 1956 he has been teaching at Dartmouth, where he is now Professor of Mathematics and Chairman of the Program in Mathematics and the Social Sciences. He is coauthor, with Frank Harary and Dorwin Cartwright, of *Structural Models: An Introduction to the Theory of Directed Graphs*, and coauthor, with Joseph Berger, Hamit Fisek, and Morris Zelditch, Jr., of *Status Characteristics and Social Interaction*. His research interests combine graph theory and combinatorial mathematics with the development of models in sociology and psychology.

Travis Patton is Visiting Instructor, University of Nebraska at Omaha. His current research concerns the application of formal models of power to contemporary and historical social structures. His recent work has appeared in the *American Sociological Review* and *Advances in Group Processes*, Vol. 4.

Cecilia L. Ridgeway is Professor of Sociology at the University of Iowa. She received her Ph.D. from Cornell University in 1972. Her research interests are in the area of group processes, with special attention to status and power processes and in the area of gender stratification. She is currently examining the role of micro status processes in the operation of macro-level stratification systems. She is author of *The Dynamics of Small Groups* as well as a number of articles, including "Dominance and Collective Hierarchy Formation in Male and Female Task Groups" (with D. Diekema, *American Sociological Review*, 1989) and "Nonverbal Behavior, Dominance, and the Basis of Status in Task Groups" (*American Sociological Review*, 1987).

Yitzhak Samuel is currently a Program Director in the Behavioral Sciences at RAFAEL Center for Military Analyses, and a Senior Teaching Fellow of Behavioral Sciences and Management at the Technion-Israel Institute of Technology. He holds degrees in sociology, political science, and management science from the Hebrew University, the Technion-Israel Institute of Technology, and the University of Michigan. For nearly two decades he has combined academics with applied professional work at a number of universities, in government, and in corporations in Israel. He has published articles in social science periodicals, and has a book forthcoming on organizations. His current professional interests include sociology of organizations, work and occupations, social change, and interpersonal relations.

Steven D. Silver is a Research Associate in social psychology at Stanford University. His interests are in information exchange and innovation in groups and organizations, organizational stratification, and consumer decision processes. His recent publications have appeared in *Advances in Group Processes* (1988) and the *Journal of Consumer Research* (1988).

John Skvoretz is Professor and Chairman of the Department of Sociology at the University of South Carolina. His principal research interest is in the construction of empirically testable theoretical models that provide structural explanations of phenomena in both large and small social systems. He has published recently on the structure of participation in small groups in *Social Psychological Quarterly*, on stratification and mobility in the *Journal of Mathematical Sociology*, and on networks and relations in the *American Journal of Sociology*.

Michael Smithson (Ph.D., University of Oregon) is a Senior Lecturer in Sociology at James Cook University, Townsville, Australia. His research interests include the study of ignorance and uncertainty, mathematical modeling, and prosocial behavior. He has recently published two books: *Fuzzy Set Analysis for Behavioral and Social Sciences* (Springer-Verlag, 1987) and *Ignorance and Uncertainty: Emerging Paradigms* (Springer-Verlag, 1989).

Aage B. Sørensen is Professor of Sociology and Chairman, Department of Sociology, Harvard University. His research interests are in the areas of social stratification, sociology of education, and mathematical sociology. He has published numerous articles on career patterns and processes of matching people to jobs or positions in social structure, on educational tracking and grouping, and on life-course processes. His current research focuses on the analysis of unemployment process.

Sheldon Stryker is Distinguished Professor of Sociology, Indiana University at Bloomington. He has served as Editor of *Sociometry* (now *Social Psychology Quarterly*), The Arnold and Carolyn Rose Monograph Series of the American Sociological Association, and the *American Sociological Review*. He has a long-standing interest in the development of and in research examining the validity of identity theory, a theory that emerges from a structural symbolic interactionist framework and that seeks to explain variation in behavioral choices as a function of variation in self-concepts and in the interactional patterns underlying those self-concepts. His works include *Deviance, Selves and Others* (with Michael Schwartz), *Symbolic Interactionism: A Social Structural Version,* "Symbolic Interactionism and Role Theory" (with Anne Statham), and "The Construction of Self and the Reconstruction of Social Relationships" (with Richard Serpe).

Jonathan H. Turner is Professor of Sociology at the University of California at Riverside. He is author of twenty books, editor of three additional books, and contributor to many professional journals and collected essays. His main interest is in the development of abstract and formal theory. The chapter in this volume is a first and very tentative statement of his ideas on macro social processes. The model presented in this chapter will form the core of a new book on social structure that is intended to be the macro-level complement to his micro-level analysis of social interaction in his *A Theory of Social Interaction*. Subsequent work will begin to explore the relationship between the macro and micro levels of social organization.

David Willer is Professor of Sociology and Director of the Laboratory for Social Research at the University of South Carolina. The focus of his research interest is the development, experimental testing, and historical application of a general theory of social structure. His previous research has focused on networks of exchange, conflict, and coercive relations. His research on exchange has uncovered two general conditions of power — exclusion and inclusion — which are opposed in their effect. Networks of other types of relations have analogous conditions. His major publications include *Scientific Sociology, Systematic Empiricism* (with Judith Willer), *Networks, Exchange and Coercion* (with Bo Anderson), and *Theory and the Experimental Investigation of Social Structures*.